The
Indian Arts and Crafts
Board

THE INDIAN ARTS & CRAFTS BOARD

An Aspect of
New Deal Indian Policy

Robert Fay Schrader

UNIVERSITY OF NEW MEXICO PRESS
Albuquerque

Library of Congress Cataloging in Publication Data

Schrader, Robert Fay, 1931–
  The Indian Arts and Crafts Board.

  Bibliography: p.
  Includes index.
  1. United States. Indian Arts and Crafts Board.
  2. Indians of North America—Government relations—
  1934–   . 3. Indians of North America—Art.
  4. Indians of North America—Industries. I. Title.
  E98.A7S37   1983   353.973005′4   83–5816
  ISBN 0–8263–0669–1

To my parents
LEONORE GERLACH SCHRADER
and
WILLIAM ALBERT SCHRADER

CONTENTS

ILLUSTRATIONS

PREFACE

FEW ADMINISTRATIONS CAN MATCH that of Franklin Delano
Roosevelt's in its energy and drive to do something positive for the nation. In Indian affairs this situation was particularly evident. Strong
personalities received a mandate to carry into action programs that had
been smothered for years by uninterested or inept administrators. The
Indian Office under Commissioner John Collier was an exciting and
innovative place to be, for the door was always open to new and promising ideas as cultural leaders from at home and abroad came to share
their experience and plans.

Indian administration under the direction of Commissioner Collier
seemed guided by what English artist William Blake wrote in 1804,
"He who would do good to another must do it in Minute Particulars. /
General Good is the plea of the scoundrel, hypocrite, and flatterer"
(Jerusalem). These words offer a rationale for New Deal Indian administration as Commissioner Collier directly involved himself and his programs in Indian life.

The Indian Arts and Crafts Board, an aspect of New Deal Indian
policy, was one vehicle by which the minute particulars of Indian life
could be improved. The multitudinous economic and cultural variations of the many Indian tribes demanded that any attempt to preserve
and to promote Indian culture be done with painstaking care. This important and delicate work was given to the Indian Arts and Crafts Board
by Congress in 1935. What followed certainly could not have been
predicted.

The attempt to promote Indian arts and crafts and thereby help the
Indians financially and preserve their culture is important because the
effort reflects an unselfish devotion to a new set of ideals on the part of
individuals working in and with the Indian Office between 1935 and

1945. Preservation rather than destruction of Indian life and values became the guiding principle behind official policy. This attitude was not conceived by the Roosevelt administration, but was the product of independent critical thought and experience developed over the preceding forty years. What was startlingly new was the energy and skill with which New Deal personnel implemented the policy. How Commissioner Collier, Indian Arts and Crafts Board General Manager René d'Harnoncourt, and their supporters addressed themselves to the important problem of preserving a future for Indian arts and crafts is the subject of this book. The study ends with 1945—the end of Franklin Roosevelt's administration and John Collier's commissionership—the conclusion of an imaginative period in the administration of Indian affairs.

Surprisingly, no previous scholarly studies have been made of this vital aspect of New Deal Indian policy, perhaps partly because the Indian Arts and Crafts Board only recently released its records for the New Deal period to the National Archives.

My interest in American Indian history was sharpened and nurtured by Fr. Francis Paul Prucha, S.J., of Marquette University, to whom many thanks are due. Other members of the history department at Marquette played an important role in this project. Assistance in the pursuit of this study came unhesitatingly from the staffs at the Marquette University Library; the University of Wisconsin, Oshkosh, library; the National Archives, particularly Robert M. Kvasnicka; the Library of Congress; the Princeton University library; the Yale University library; and the Institute for Government Research in Washington, D.C. My wife, Carol Ann, gave generous support at every stage of the work.

The
Indian Arts and Crafts
Board

1

HARBINGERS

In the second half of the nineteenth century, United States government interest in American Indian arts and crafts emerged, following and reflecting a surging public interest in age-old crafts. This sweeping popular force was itself the product of an increasing national intellectual concern over the effects of industrialization on the quality of everyday life. As a result, the commissioners of Indian affairs, through their superintendents in the field, began as early as 1863 to praise the Indians' ingenious craft skills. As the years passed, however, the Indian Office came to emphasize the development of Indian crafts into manufacturing industries. Contrary to the popular emphasis on arts and crafts as an antidote to the effects of industrialization, the motivation behind the federal govenment's early role in Indian arts and crafts was a desire to industrialize the Indians. [1]

The popular arts and crafts movement had begun in England, where Thomas Carlyle, John Ruskin, and William Morris warned of the dangers of industrialization to the human soul. Morris's influence spread to America and prospered under the promotional skill and writings of Gustav Stickley, an inventor, designer, and editor of *The Craftsman*.

Arts and crafts societies blossomed across America, and soon various missionary and Indian reform groups saw in the demand for Indian crafts an opportunity to industrialize the Indians, and, thereby, to assimilate them more quickly into white society. At the eighth annual meeting of the Lake Mohonk Conference of the Friends of the Indian in 1890, a member of the Board of Indian Commissioners, Philip C. Garrett of Philadelphia, called the members' attention to the basis that certain industries, already in operation among the Indians, afforded to educate the Indians and improve their lives. He called for converting "rude" decoration into classic art, building up crafts industries, and fitting them for larger and cheaper markets.[2]

Garrett pictured Yuma, Arizona, as "the hive of as busy an industry as Trenton [New Jersey], with a forest of smoking furnace stacks, and producing a style of pottery characteristic, unique, and meritorious." Here was the nucleus of an industry, this member of a respected government board proclaimed, and he called on fellow members to avail themselves of the opportunity and build upon it.[3]

At the same conference, Sybil Carter, a deaconess of the Protestant Episcopal Church and a special agent of the Episcopal Board of Missions, spoke of her efforts to industrialize the Indian women by promoting the white culture's craft of lace making.[4] Although basically humanitarian in concept, these efforts were designed to help the Indians to become white people, and exhibited no concern for the preservation of the crafts or the culture that produced them. No consideration was shown for the Indians' choice in the matter.

This early attempt to "put the Indian to work" actually promoted Indian arts and crafts and may have been directly responsible for the preservation of Indian culture in an industrial age. The Indian Industries League, founded in 1889 by the Lake Mohonk Conference Department of Libraries and Industries under Francis C. Sparhawk of Massachusetts and presided over by Lyman Abbott, Albert K. Smiley, and Herbert Welsh, all prominent, influential, and self-styled "Friends of the Indian," was organized to establish direct communication between the Indians on the reservations and interested people who wished to put young Indians to work. The league quickly seized on Indian arts and crafts as a means of carrying out its motto of "Helping the Indians to help themselves."[5]

The suggestions presented to the league for consideration reflected simply a basic economic concern for the Indians entering white society, but expressed no regard for the consequences assimilation would have on Indian culture. One such plan, submitted by an Indian Office field matron working among the Navajos to promote their advancement through the improvement of their home, educational, moral, sanitary, environmental, and social conditions, advised the league to install mechanized looms and knitting machines on the reservation. This plan also suggested the use of a broom-making machine, an invention which the matron felt the Navajo men would learn to use very easily. The Indian Industries League actually began to implement these suggestions, and in 1899 the league reported that it had begun instruction not only in traditional blanket-making methods but also in the use of machines for production. Two sewing machines and a knitting machine had been installed and the looms were to follow.[6] Though misguided in view of long-term Indian welfare, these plans pointed to an increasing awareness of Indian arts and crafts and the potential they represented for the Indians.

With growing public interest in arts and crafts encouraging missionary and Indian reform group work to promote Indian handcraft skills, government agencies sought to coordinate their own efforts with private Indian arts and crafts ventures. In 1900, for the first time, the government-supported Indian program at the Normal and Agricultural Institute in Hampton, Virginia, included training in the Indian arts of beadwork, basketry, and pottery. In the same year, William A. Jones became the first commissioner of Indian affairs to offer Indian Office support and cooperation in preserving Indian arts and crafts. While no organized government effort was considered, the Indian Office did instruct the field matrons to do what they could to stimulate the old industries, to prevent the Indian artists from using the commercially made German-town yarns and aniline dyes, and to keep their work up to the old artistic standards. At the same time, the superintendent of Indian schools, Estelle Reel, worked to introduce basketry instruction as part of the Indian students' curriculum.[7]

A new and deeper non-Indian understanding of Indian arts and crafts began to emerge along with the attempts at preservation through education. The platform of the 1901 Lake Mohonk Conference recognized the importance of Indian arts and crafts as a means of profitable occupation and natural expression for the Indians, as objects of a rare indigenous art—many examples artistically excellent, some unique indeed—and as a way of furnishing congenial and remunerative employment at home, fostering self-respect in the Indians and respect for them among white people. Candace Wheeler, the organizer of the Women's Exhibit at the 1893 Chicago World's Fair and a contemporary authority on Indian arts, told the 1901 Lake Mohonk Conference that "if more attention were paid to what the Indian had done and what he can do, the Indian would be very much better off today; and we as a people would be much richer, both in art and in revenue."[8] In art circles and among those interested in the quality of Indian life, Indian arts and crafts were beginning to be recognized as more than ethnological specimens to be displayed in museums. They were beginning to be appreciated in their own right and as representations of a great cultural advancement worthy of the non-Indian American's attention.

Support for Indian arts and crafts from private organizations like the Daughters of the American Revolution, the 100,000-member Sunshine Society, missionary groups, and women's clubs combined with government efforts through Indian schools to reflect this interest. Shops in the larger cities opened Indian arts and crafts departments as the demand for Indian wares increased. Articles on Indian arts and crafts multiplied in mass-circulation periodicals and newspapers. In New York, the American Museum of Natural History held a popular series of lectures on Indian basketry.[9]

Along with federal encouragement of Indian arts and crafts between 1897 and 1904, Commissioner Jones also sounded a warning about the dangers of the growing commercialization of Indian products. By promoting the instruction of Indian children in the handmade crafts of their own tribes, Jones was trying to maintain the integrity and commercial value of crafts that faced increasing competition from machine-made Indian articles. Jones was sensitive to the unpriceable value of Indian art that was the result of an Indian artist weaving "her soul, her religion, her woes, and her joys into every graceful curve and color of her handiwork." Without these beautiful, sentimental considerations, Jones warned, the idea that the native industry of the Indians could be developed into a successful one did not hold out much hope. "Increase and commercialize the native industry of the Indian," Jones concluded, "and its value readily falls by the inevitable law of supply and demand."[10] For the time being the demand for Indian arts and crafts was high.

Exact figures for the dollar amounts realized by the Indians from the sales of their products are impossible to estimate, because the sales were made through Indian traders with eastern dealers, and to a great extent, particularly in the Southwest, by individual Indians to tourists, dealers, and curio hunters, all of whom kept only personal records, if any at all. The president of the Santa Fe Railroad in 1904 indirectly told the Indian

Office that sales of Indian goods at stations along his lines had increased 1,000 percent in the previous ten years. Executives from the Southern Pacific Railroad echoed this estimate. Prices for individual Indian baskets of remarkable quality ran as high as $1,500 during this widespread revival of arts and crafts. [11]

Commissioner of Indian Affairs Francis E. Leupp in 1905 officially enunciated for the first time the concept of preserving the distinctive features of Indian life. "The Indian is a natural warrior, a natural logician, a natural artist," Leupp proclaimed. "We have room for all three in our highly organized social system. Let us not make the mistake, in the process of absorbing them, of washing out whatever is distinctly Indian." Citing the admirable contributions the Indians brought to the common experience, Leupp declared that the proper role of government with the Indians was one of improvement, not transformation. [12]

Despite the opposition that surrounded Commissioner Leupp within his own Indian Office, he was one of the earliest government figures to state publicly that Indian culture was of value in the modern age. "I like the Indian for what is Indian in him," Leupp proudly announced in the same report that carried remarks of the superintendent of the Pueblo Agency, who felt that the time spent by Navajo girls in manufacturing Navajo blankets would be devoted better "to acquiring a knowledge of dressmaking, housekeeping, and learning to cook rather than trying to promote and foster this ancient and crude Indian art of blanket weaving." [13] Yet except for public comments and support for the efforts of his like-minded superintendent of Indian schools, Estelle Reel, Commissioner Leupp took no specific steps to preserve the living native handcrafts of the Indians—although in 1906 he appointed Angel de Cora Dietz, a Winnebago Indian and professional artist, as a teacher of Indian art at the Carlisle Indian School. [14]

Other than the important early government efforts in the Indian schools to preserve Indian arts and crafts, and official support for the concept itself, the real influence on the Indians came from the traders. This was a logical development, because federal law prohibited government employees from trading with the Indians, required licenses to conduct business on an Indian reservation, and asked visitors to obtain permission from the agent for any activity beyond direct passage through

7

the area. By 1912, the Navajo blanket industry was bringing yearly to the reservation Indian artists approximately $675,000 for the native wool product and $36,000 for the Germantown wool product. This much-needed cash income helped to replace the ration system, the system which still prevailed on the Sioux and Apache reservations.[15]

Responding to an ever-increasing demand for Indian crafts, many traders tended to encourage production short-cuts. Their policy of paying the Indian weavers by the pound did not encourage quality work either. The result was large numbers of low-grade saddle blankets that the traders were finding difficult to sell. Some Indian Office superintendents and supervisors were concerned with this problem, because if the traders could not sell the blankets they already had in stock, they could not afford to buy more from the Indian artists, who then would be deprived of an extremely important source of income.[16]

The first government official to be concerned with the problem was Charles L. Davis, Indian Office supervisor of farming, who thought that the Navajo blanket industry was suffering from a lack of proper and efficient promotion and personally conducted an investigation of the various phases and conditions of the Navajo blanket industry. No sales problem existed in the market for quality goods, yet Davis discovered that buyers particularly wanted assurance that they were purchasing genuine Indian handwork. The Fred Harvey Company, holders of the exclusive right to sell Indian arts and crafts along the Santa Fe Railroad line, had satisfied a doubting public and increased its profits, Davis found, by attaching to each blanket a lead seal bearing the guarantee of the company that the blanket to which the seal was attached was a genuine Navajo product.[17] Davis's investigation produced the first viable plan for direct government involvement in the promotion of Indian arts and crafts.

Under the original Davis plan, each superintendent in the Southwest would be given a supply of linen tags upon which would be printed the name of the Indian agency, a line for the date, the words "This blanket is the product of Navajo Indians of this Reservation and made from native Navajo wool," and the name of the Indian superintendent. The superintendents would distribute these tags to the government's district farming representatives, principals of outlying boarding schools, and other employees, along with lead seals and presses. The Indian artists could bring the blankets to one of these employees for certification while the blankets were still in the Indians' possession.[18]

Davis did not suggest where or how to draw the line at what grade of blanket should receive the tag. When the plan finally went into effect on two reservations early in 1914, the tagging was done after the Indians had sold the blankets, and only if they had been paid eight dollars or more in cash or the equivalent for each blanket. The actual certification was done by the traders, the merchants, or the superintendents. The only safeguard against abuse by the traders or merchants was the threat to take away the abuser's use of the government certification system.[19]

Reactions from the traders to the tagging system were mixed. Many wished to have all genuine Navajo blankets tagged. Some supported the plan wholeheartedly; others were indifferent to it. The off-reservation traders were not interested nor were the wholesalers and jobbers, who feared that the purchasers might make their next purchases directly from the traders whose names appeared on the tags. The ambivalence of the Indian Office underscored Commissioner Cato Sells's lack of commitment to preserve Indian culture. Foremost in Commissioner Sells's mind was a vision of Indian industrial achievement that would "start the Indian along the road the purpose of which is self-support and independence." Indian Office efforts continued to be guided by the concept of racial progress.[20]

A combination of factors brought an end to the Davis plan. Although the system was extended to all Navajo jurisdictions in 1916 with the goal of gradually applying it to all Indian-made articles, Sells announced a year later that the plan had not proved to be as successful as hoped. He directly blamed the wholesalers to whom the traders sold the blankets for removing the government labels "apparently for commercial reasons."[21] No attempt was made, however, to obtain legislation to prevent the removal of the tags. Also contributing to the end of the label program was the high demand for Indian blankets, increased by the presence of United States soldiers and militia on the Mexican border, who completely bought out the traders and wholesale houses for the first time in the history of the Indian arts and crafts business.[22] Moreover, the shortage of blankets increased because the higher prices the Indians received for their clipped wool in 1916 made its direct sale preferable to taking the time to weave it into fabrics, and the piñon nut crop was so huge in

1917 that the Indians could earn three times as much gathering nuts as they could at the weaving loom.[23]

With the Southwest Indians' economic conditions so bright, Sells saw little need for government effort. Also, Indian Office attempts to open new markets in urban centers and to set up exhibits of Indian crafts at the Commercial Museum and the University Museum, both in Philadelphia, designed to direct the public to the retail sources for Indian arts and crafts, were abandoned when the demand exceeded the supply.[24] Thus, during 1917, then the second greatest year for Indian arts and crafts sales, the Indian Office confined its efforts simply to giving encouragement at "every opportunity" to the improvement of native industries and to directing the attention of the public to Indian arts and crafts "whenever possible." Nor were any aggressive campaigns pursued during the 1918 fiscal year to widen the market for Indian products, although Indian income from this important source fell better than 21 percent.[25]

Designed to encourage the quality of the native articles, the Davis plan competed with the commercializing efforts of the Indian Industries League. Beginning in 1903, the league had started to secure and to distribute aniline dyes to replace all of the colors used by the Indians which the league claimed were not mordanted properly and were seldom fast to light. At the same time, the league was busy buying Navajo wool, shipping it to Boston for scouring, spinning, and dying, returning it to New Mexico to be woven, and then shipping the finished product to the East once more for sale. Commissioner Sells and Assistant Commissioner Edgar B. Meritt encouraged these efforts to increase production, agreeing to tentative plans to locate wool processing plants near Shiprock, New Mexico, and Fort Defiance, Arizona.[26] A plan by Meritt to develop a homespun suiting material industry among the Navajos was labeled by one superintendent as another of the brilliant theories that result from a probable three-week stay in the Navajo country. The plan was abandoned finally as unfavorable for the time because it would require training the Indians and setting up a whole new marketing organization.[27]

Strictly motivated in Indian arts and crafts toward commercial success, yet unable to point to one successful venture for which his policy was responsible, Cato Sells and the Indian Office lost all interest in the subject and its possibilities in 1919 and 1920. Even so, the Indian income from arts and crafts climbed in 1920 to a record $1,869,907.[28]

" 'The Indian goes back to Nature for everything'—thus one Indian explained the native designs—and herein lies their vitality," declared Indian music expert Natalie Curtis. This statement and others by persons familiar with Indian life and history typified a growth in white attitude after World War I beyond purely economic concern for Indian welfare to a new emphasis on the Indians' great cultural attainments. "Much of value, spiritual and material, is now being lost to America through our ignorance of the suggestive stimulus in Indian arts and our neglect of our native craftsmen," Curtis stated.[29]

By 1919, new forces began gathering to add to the widely scattered protests heard over the years about those government policies believed by Indian reformists to be destroying the Indian culture. Ernest Blumenschein and Bert Phillips, founding members of the Taos Society of Artists, complained that the policy of assimilating Indians discouraged racial customs and eventually would destroy their wonderful art. Phillips labeled the Indians' contribution to art "invaluable." Both men stated that they had come to Taos to learn from the Indians and had found an apparently inexhaustable store of beauty and originality. The design, texture, and color of Indian rugs were as fine as those in any Persian rug, Phillips proclaimed. Furthermore, he predicted a great future for Indian art. After living with the Indians for years, Blumenschein felt qualified to label their art distinctive and absolutely original. "That is their contribution to the world," he declared in order to make quite clear the nature of the loss America would realize under current government policies.[30]

Natalie Curtis found the American disregard of Indian culture a "curious fact." In spite of their long contact with the strikingly interesting indigenous people of America, whites had never recognized the arts and crafts of the Indians as an asset to the nation's culture and a stimulus to its industries, she lamented. We echo Europe, she charged, while we might develop a truly American decorative art.[31]

Mary Austin of the Rockefeller-funded School of American Research in Santa Fe, and a popular author of Indian stories based on ancient Indian legends, wrote personally to Secretary of the Interior Franklin

11

K. Lane about "the great treasures of Indian art which, after all, were developed out of living on American soil." She warned that the source of these treasures was in great danger, and she indicted past federal Indian policy as one that tended to stamp out all original Indian arts. She said that the situation could be changed if the government would publicly recognize Indian art and spread this appreciation in schools and through the press. Then, specific steps must be taken to preserve the sources of native American art and to proceed to correlate these efforts. Finally, the government must establish "routes" over which this art could travel from the producer to the consumer.[32]

In the aftermath of world war, many Americans awakened to a new interest in Americana and found that the Indians were at the core of America's national experience. Their private convictions, publicly expressed by the more articulate leaders, now lacked the sense of racial superiority that previously had tainted attitudes toward Indian life. From these individual attitudes developed Indian reform activism and specific reform proposals.

Identifying the forces behind this growing interest in Indian culture expressed by educated, white Americans, Edgar L. Hewett, director of the School of American Research and the Santa Fe and San Diego Art Museums, acknowledged that America's increasing international contacts with other peoples of the world had compelled a reassessment of human values and a reconsideration of racial views. Society now had to admit, Hewett explained, that fitness to live and probability of survival did not depend solely on material efficiency and that the culture that rested on material power was probably the most unstable of all; that aesthetic and ethical values were persistent beyond all others; that the races previously referred to as inferior had qualities that were priceless to human society; and that in the discovery, recognition, and cultivation of the special abilities of the less powerful cultures rested our soundest insurance against spiritual decline and extinction by way of our own material violence.[33]

For Hewett, as for many Americans in 1921, European culture stood as an example of rapid cultural disintegration. In contrast, the American Indians had contemplated nature, had reflected on their relations to it, and had arrived at profound convictions which had been disturbed only slightly by contact with the Europeans. No race was doomed, de-

clared Hewett, so long as its culture lived; but when a culture was destroyed utterly, the soul of the people died, degradation through loss of
self-respect was inevitable, and the race was beyond hope. He was certain that the spirit of the Indian race was still alive and saw hope that
the growing intelligence of the dominant white race would at last bring
about an appreciation of and a vast pride in the survival and achievements of this splendid people whom he termed "one hundred percent
American" in ancestry and culture. Hewett optimistically predicted that
the Indians' greatest day still might be in the future, and his ideas and
influence were felt in many parts of the country, for he often traveled
to speak to gatherings and conventions about his archaeological and
Indian art projects in the Southwest.[34]

Acting both as a leader of and a direct participant in a changing non-
Indian conception of the indigenous American, the art world expressed
a reversal in social attitudes before most of society was conscious any
change existed. In 1922, art critic Edgar Holger Cahill saw a dramatic
and abrupt shift in the dominant conception of the American Indian
from "a strange, ferocious creature, good only when dead, and utterly
oblivious . . . to any need for economic activity" to a "comparatively
peaceful, industrious figure, a child of nature, close to the soil from
which he wins his living, cultivating the earth with a rough hoe, hunting wild creatures, and living with his tribe in a free democratic association." While attributing a great deal of this vivid change to the work
of scholars of Indian life, Cahill also recognized how much Indian civilization had added to the non-Indian world, a circumstance only now
becoming apparent to major segments of society. Cahill depicted a sense
of failure on the part of white culture when he pointed to the Indians'
joy in beauty as something totally lacking in American society. "We
great Machine People, who have carried ugliness well-nigh to apotheo-
sis in the fairest lands of earth," Cahill stated, "may forego the conqueror's
pride and learn wisdom from our humble brother of the pueblos, who
has made the desert bloom with beauty."[35]

More of non-Indian society began to awaken to Indian art. For three
successive years the Society of Independent Artists, influenced by the
Taos art colony, gave special recognition to Indian watercolorists in its
annual exhibition at the Waldorf-Astoria Hotel in New York City.
Smaller exhibits like that in 1922 at the Chautauqua Convention of

the Federation of Women's Clubs prominently featured Indian arts and crafts. In the same year Amelia Elizabeth White, a wealthy patron of Indian art, opened a permanent shop in New York City for the sale of Indian arts and crafts. Also in 1922, the Museum of New Mexico held its first annual exhibition of Indian artwork, designed to encourage the native arts and crafts, to revive the old Indian arts, and to keep the arts of each pueblo and tribe as distinct as possible. [36]

Unfortunately, not all of American society had reached the new stage of awareness and appreciation of Indian art and culture. From the President's cabinet, Congress, and the Indian Office itself came the traditional chorus of the forces of exploitation and total assimilation. Even though 1920 had been a record year for Indian arts and crafts income, Congressman Melville Clyde Kelly, Republican from Pennsylvania, used the Indian Office figures to illustrate what he considered to be the small per capita income most Indian artists received for their work. From the floor of the House of Representatives, Kelly attacked the Indian Office for failing to emphasize the need for the Indians to enter white industries. He demanded that Congress act to "free the Indians and serve America." Calling Indian arts and crafts "soft, nomad trades," Kelly reported that the Indians were encouraged to do this type of work which he believed rendered them unfit for a place in a real productive community and industry. In 1922, providing a clear example of economic exploitation of the Indians, Secretary of the Interior Albert Bacon Fall, sponsored the infamous Bursum bill, which would have opened the door to the transfer of disputed Pueblo land titles to white settlers. In 1924, Congressman Carl Trumbull Hayden, Democrat from Arizona, introduced what became known as the Indian Oil bill which would have equated executive-order reservations with public lands, deprived the Indians of clear title to this land, and resulted in the loss of the Indians' valuable resources. [37]

In the Indian Office, Commissioner Charles H. Burke, author of the Burke Act of 1906, which speeded up allotment of lands to individual Indians and furthered the loss of eighty-six million acres or 62 percent of the land in Indian ownership prior to 1887, could point only to an Indian arts and crafts booth at the exposition of the Travel Club of America in New York City as his sole attempt during his first two years in office to broaden the market for Indian wares and to stimulate interest in the perpetuation of the Indians' artwork. While on the one hand Burke praised the government's efforts in exhibiting Indian arts and crafts ·at Indian ceremonials, the ancient ritual expressions of the Indians' religion, on the other hand he labeled these same gatherings degrading and detrimental to the Indians' moral and economic welfare because the ceremonials interrupted the Indians' self-supporting duties.[38]

Aside from the miniscule venture to display Indian arts and crafts, the Indian Office had no positive policy and reported no attempts to promote Indian art or to preserve Indian culture. By 1924 Burke had eliminated most of the strictly Indian fairs that had been initiated years earlier by the Indian Office to stimulate Indian interest in agriculture and related industries including Indian arts and crafts, and he planned to abolish the rest so that the Indians would participate in county fairs just like their non-Indian neighbors.[39]

In response to a perceived crisis in American Indian affairs, in 1922 concerned private citizens formed the Eastern Association on Indian Affairs in New York City and the New Mexico Association on Indian Affairs in Santa Fe, and in 1923 similarly motivated individuals formed the American Indian Defense Association with offices in Chicago, New York, and Washington, D.C. These organizations, although established primarily in response to the crisis over Pueblo lands, prominently affirmed support for preserving and fostering Indian arts and crafts. For the Indian Defense Association, Indian arts and crafts represented an ancient economic wealth that still could become important in the Indians' material economy as well as in their social and moral economy. "Business intelligence applied to the subject would bring results valuable to the American public as well as to the Indians," the Indian Defense Association asserted in a presage of things to come.[40]

John Collier was one of the original fourteen directors of the Indian Defense Association. At thirty-eight years of age, Collier in 1922 had begun his association with Indian life as a research agent of the Indian Welfare Committee of the General Federation of Women's Clubs after twelve years as an editor and social worker among the immigrants of New York City and two years as an adult and college sociology and psychology instructor in California. Collier had the credentials to combat what he publicly labeled the "ancient and lamentable tradition" now practiced by Hubert Work, who had replaced Albert Fall as secretary of the interior, Indian Commissioner Burke, and Assistant Commissioner Meritt. That tradition, he charged, was designed "to attack and destroy, by direct and indirect means, by force and persuasion, the culture, the spiritual life, and civilization of the Indians." By using the methods of lobbying, grass-roots politics, editorials, exposé articles, and professionally written, specialized reports, the Indian Defense Association led by John Collier as executive secretary brought public attention to the increasingly deteriorating situation faced by the reservation Indians, which the Indian Defense Association believed was caused by an archaic and detrimental government attitude.[41]

Forced to respond in some manner to the public charges from influential citizens involved in the Indian reform movement, Secretary Work organized what he called the Advisory Council on Indian Affairs "for the purpose of discussion and recommendation on the government's Indian policy." Sixty-six appointees—including John Collier, Amelia White, and other charter members of the private associations concerned with Indian affairs—traveled to Washington at their own expense. After just two days in discussion and deliberation, they adopted fourteen resolutions for presentation to Secretary Work. Six months later Work published the resolutions accompanied by his comments and a report on the progress so far accomplished by the Indian Office.[42]

The resolutions expressed dissatisfaction with the ability of the government to make any progress on problems in existence for nearly fifty years. The committee unhesitatingly encouraged the production of the highest quality Indian basketry, pottery, and blanket weaving. Work's response hid behind the customary defense of traditional policy. He blamed the Indian situation on the failure of the Indians to assimilate because of racial inferiority, on the inability of the complicated administrative policies of the central government to advance Indian welfare, and on the need for the Indians to accept white standards and attitudes. Secretary Work further evaded responsibility by calling on Congress to provide adequate appropriations to increase Indian education and to encourage the administration of Indian affairs by the states. Unable to point to any specific steps taken by the Indian Office to promote Indian art and crafts, Work lamely cited the use of Indian schools for community meetings aimed at developing Indian organizations for promoting and fostering local native industries.[43]

To his credit, Work realized that the attitude of the majority of the American people toward the Indians was changing from hostility to sympathy and friendship. Still, he underestimated the growing spirit when he labeled this attitude "characteristically somnolent" and advised the critics of federal policy that "until the people as a whole are aroused to a purposeful instead of emotional interest, we can not hope to protect the Indian from himself nor the further encroachment of the minority who have no respect for his welfare and property."[44]

The Indian Office continued to ignore Indian arts and crafts and to labor under attitudes and policies no longer acceptable to the more vocal elements in society. During the annual House Appropriations Subcommittee hearings, Congressman Louis Convers Cramton, Republican from Michigan, accused Assistant Commissioner Meritt of publicly announcing the establishment of a position of Supervisor of Native Art to encourage the Indians in their arts and crafts and afterward never filling the post. Cramton queried whether the Indian Office was making any organized effort to advance the development of Indian industries and the marketing of their products. The best answer Meritt could give was that the Indian Office was encouraging the superintendents to take some action. Meritt mentioned that the Industrial Section of the Indian Office employed fifteen people under the direction of a twenty-five-year veteran of the Indian Office. When Cramton asked if the director ever had been in the field, Meritt replied that the director went out in the field a great deal although he had no experience in that capacity. Meritt weakly described how his office was encouraging more than ever before the development of arts and crafts in the schools and encouraging the superintendents to find markets for the products of Indians, both through local traders and outside correspondence.[45]

In response to growing attacks by John Collier and others upon the entire operation of the Indian Office, Secretary Work in 1927 requested an unbiased, professional investigation from the private Institute for Government Research of Washington, D.C. The survey was conducted by Lewis Meriam with a staff composed of specialists employed in their respective fields across the country. As the specialist in Indian arts and

17

crafts, Meriam selected Edward Everett Dale, chairman of the department of history at the University of Oklahoma. Since Dale's only Indian arts and crafts credentials were his great interest in Indians which had prompted him to collect examples of their arts and crafts and to write a book about their folklore for the University of Oklahoma, his selection appeared weaker than those for the areas of education, medicine, and agriculture, yet when the Meriam Report was submitted to Secretary Work on 21 February 1928, it stated that "the possibilities of Indian arts would make a book in themselves." Lamenting that no systematic effort had been made to encourage or to develop the Indian handcrafts on the reservations, the report assailed the past general policy of attempting to make a white person of the Indian rather than endeavoring to encourage things native. "The fostering and development of the native arts is a wholesome thing in inter-racial relations," the report asserted. With the depth of social understanding which had become increasingly prevalent in recent years, Meriam's staff declared that it was "good for both Indians and whites to realize that Indians have a distinctive contribution to make to the world."[46]

Most important, the staff advised the Indian Office to include in its program the development of Indian handcrafts, involving, on the one hand, the securing of marketable goods and, on the other, the organization of a market. The Meriam Report further stressed that the quality of products should be standardized and their genuineness guaranteed under this government plan. Meriam's staff perceptively warned that this work of government encouragement of Indian arts and crafts "would, of course, be slow, and spetacular results could not be expected." Emphasizing the deep implications Indian arts and crafts had for the future, the report cautioned that the development of handcrafts "should be a means to an end; namely, the improvement of the economic and social conditions of life. The success of the enterprise should be measured, therefore, not merely by financial results but more particularly by social consequences."[47]

According to Meriam's survey, the general tendency was for native arts to disappear and this already had occurred in various localities. With passing generations, the fine old artists died without having taught anyone their craft. When the staff investigated, they found that many of the young people considered the work of their elders to be old fashioned and that government employees blamed this attitude on the influence of the schools. More fundamental in the staff's eyes was the impact of modern life upon Indian society, which tended to decrease the hold of the ancient religious and ceremonial customs. Significantly, the survey team found that the old handcrafts flourished most where the native religious beliefs were still powerful and the Indian culture remained relatively intact.[48]

In every instance of government encouragement of Indian artists, the Meriam Report strongly emphasized the need for an Indian-centered approach. Specifically, the development of Indian arts and crafts should have a place in Indian community plans, such as in the use of community houses and school buildings to provide well-lighted, comfortable rooms and workshops for the use of individuals or clubs. Community resources should be used; for example, one day school sent its girls to the home of the best local potter for lessons in her art and employed a local weaver to teach in the school. The report particularly singled out the dangers of the imposition of an industrial system as a means to Indian arts and crafts education, a method that could not be defended because it left little or no leisure time for creativity, the essence of artistic endeavors.[49]

The report also warned against a program to develop Indian arts and crafts which aimed too directly at business success, a situation which might result in a system of "sweating," or long hours of work at low wages and under unfair or unhealthful conditions. Under too much pressure to produce, family life might suffer if the burden of support fell unduly upon the women. An even more sensitive concern was the potential damage should the government aim at an exclusive standard of art which would eliminate workers who could produce a good grade of work at a profit to themselves and to their customers.[50]

The independent Meriam staff found it difficult to see how some Indians ever would achieve a reasonably satisfactory standard of living in their present locations without the fostering and development of their native crafts. Viewing the possibilities in Indian arts and crafts to be very significant, the Meriam Report believed the national government well could afford for several years to retain at least one competent person, who with the assistance from temporary specialists could go into the matter thoroughly and could determine its possibilities. Organization

19

of a market would not be difficult, the report maintained, if the experience of private ventures was at all relevant. Such experience had determined the existence of a continuous demand for high quality products that went far beyond the available supply. The Meriam Report even outlined what the government should strive to maintain in Indian craftwork—products that were characteristically Indian, of good materials, of good quality of execution, of good color and design, usable unless intended merely for display, unique or original so far as compatible with other requisites, tagged with the government's guarantee of genuineness and quality, and priced fairly. In addition, this plan of action for a positive Indian arts and crafts policy included advice about the necessity for some supervision over the Indian artists in their homes in order to help them avoid mistakes that would make their articles unsalable and to help them secure the best materials available. The government also would have to stimulate originality of design, encourage regularity of production, and require as far as possible good working conditions in the homes.[51]

In conclusion, the Meriam Report noted, in what many Indians would have called gross understatement, that on most reservations Indians were isolated from industrial opportunities in regions unfavorable to agriculture, that economic prosperity depended upon family earning power, and that natural resources had to be utilized fully by all adult members of the family if life was ever to be more than bare existence. To give further substance to the Indians' economic plight, the report gave data for the total income of 188,363 Indians or approximately three-fifths of the Indian population of the United States, tribal and individual combined. These figures showed that almost one-fourth of the reservation Indians in the territory studied had a per capita income of less than $100 a year, and 71.4 percent had incomes of less than $200; only 2.2. percent had incomes of $500 or more. In short, while a majority of the Indians were engaged in agriculture, many of them were living on lands "from which a trained and experienced white man could scarcely wrest a reasonable living."[52]

With these desperate conditions, the only choices for the dominant white race were either to continue with the utter destruction of the ancient Indian culture or to move forward on the long road to white acceptance of an Indian culture within an ethnic democracy in which the Indians could maintain their dignity and could contribute their centuries of experience to the benefit of all peoples. Either direction threatened formidable obstacles since concerned and influential friends of the Indian no longer appeared to be willing to accept business as usual in the Indian Office, yet precedent for positive action was lacking and any attempted reform policies would have to compete with years of entrenched bureaucracy. In the struggle to find the most favorable course of action to follow in Indian affairs, the Meriam Report provided a publicly accepted, factual framework upon which to base Indian policy.

2

CONTROVERSY

THE MERIAM REPORT CLEARLY defined the distinction between current Indian policy based on white cultural dominance and a proposed, somewhat idealized Indian policy of active government support for Indian culture. Collier called the report "an indictment of the present, not the past." He was convinced that not since Helen Hunt Jackson's 1881 denunciation of government treatment of the Indians in *A Century of Dishonor* had a document appeared that was as important, and "none as challenging, humiliating, and horrifying." At the same time, he perceived the report's major weakness to be the assumption that a will toward improvement existed or might arise in the Indian Office to redeem the situation. The Meriam Report only hinted at the wide economic and political forces surrounding the Indian Office. According to Collier, these forces always extinguished the will toward improvement and their dominance in 1928 was greater than at any previous time. Confident that the report had pointed out the proper direction for government policy makers, Collier challenged his opponents, "Let others, whose proper freedom of action is greater, provide the rest."[1]

Soon after the publication of the Meriam Report, Secretary of the Interior Hubert Work resigned and on 20 July 1928 was replaced by the seemingly more sympathetic Roy O. West. For the first time since 1920, the annual report of the secretary of the interior contained figures representing the yearly income from Indian arts and crafts for the 355,901 reservation Indians. The report admitted the existence of "wide interest among our people in these [arts and crafts] activities of the Indians; for the preservation and encouragement of Indian arts and crafts; and in the purchase of the articles they make." Sales totaled $1,267,816 from twenty-two states, 74 percent or $944,863 of which was earned by the Indians of Arizona, Minnesota, and New Mexico. Admitting the

22

significance now attributed to Indian arts and crafts, Secretary West referred to his visits to Indian reservations and schools in Arizona, New Mexico, and other states, during which he had given "special attention to their handiwork." He suggested that "perhaps the governemnt could recognize these products in some official manner and thereby render a real service to those Indians now engaged in such crafts and to those who might be encouraged to interest themselves in them," and he referred to a proposal to adopt a trademark design which could be registered with the United States Patent Office. This plan renewed the Davis plan except that the projected tag or label could be attached to the various craft articles not just to blankets or rugs. [2]

Once more a top government administrator used the current popularity of Indian arts and crafts to create a public image of interest and concern and then failed to carry his announced plans to completion. As Secretary West's administrative assistant, Ebert K. Burlew on 10 October 1928 requested the Commission of Fine Arts to design "at the earliest possible date" a label to be used on all Indian arts and crafts which would authenticate them as genuine Indian handwork. The Commission of Fine Arts consulted sculptor and designer James E. Frazer, who had designed the Indian head on the five-cent piece and who now suggested a war bonnet as the Indian trademark because, in his opinion, that article was the North American Indians' most distinctive product. On 28 February 1929, five days before he left office, Secretary West issued a press release stating that he had approved Frazer's design for an Indian trademark for Indian-made goods as a guarantee that they were genuine. He further announced that the idea was an outgrowth of his trip to the Indian Southwest the previous autumn where he had "conceived of the possibility of protecting their products by means of a trademark." Four months later another artist, Arthur J. Elder, and not Frazer, received the "reasonable sum" of one-hundred dollars since he actually had designed the trademark. [3]

After Secretary West resigned with the advent of the new administration in 1929, Burlew attempted unsuccessfully to complete a patent application for the Indian arts and crafts trademark. The Patent Office informed Burlew that neither the Indian Office nor the Interior Department could qualify under the requirements of the statutes as owner of a trademark. The Patent Office questioned whether the Indian Office had carried on or contemplated carrying on any commercial business under the trademark.[4] The trademark never was patented, although an informal agreement was reached by which the Patent Office kept photographs of the Indian trademark design on record in order to deny registration to any applicant submitting a conflicting trademark.[5]

President Herbert Clark Hoover appointed Ray Lyman Wilbur, president of Stanford University, to be secretary of the interior; Charles J. Rhoads, a Philadelphia banker and past-president of the Indian Rights Association, to be Indian commissioner; and J. Henry Scattergood, a Quaker businessman and fund-raiser for the Indian Rights Association, to be assistant commissioner. Hoover thereby temporarily placated those critics who had brought on earlier investigations of the Indian Office.

Hoover's appointments reflected the philosophy of government that he had worked to implement from 1921 to 1928 as secretary of commerce. Neither his commissioner nor his assistant commissioner had had any administrative experience either in government or in Indian affairs. Secretary Wilbur also lacked such experience although he made no secret of his belief in a refined manifestation of rapid assimilation. Being acceptable to both friends and critics seemed to be more important than experience. Their apparent assignment was to carry out the Hoover plan of encouraging and coordinating private interest activity.

Herbert Hoover believed the role of government was to assist the people to deal effectively with modern conditions by means of temporary committees, conferences, and commissions. His plan called for experts to gather, sift, and weigh the facts, and then, instead of the government taking action, the experts would give this data to the people who would judge the best course. Hoover stressed the need for the government to inspire individuals to work together in voluntary organizations whereby through their own action they could remedy abuse and initiate progress. The role of bureaucracy was to foster individual, community, and private efforts to deal in the interests of American society. Hoover disliked any measure that would directly involve the federal government in a business enterprise.[6]

A reflection of Hoover's associative policy was the movement to establish a private organization of traders to protect genuine Indian arts and crafts from imitations offered by unscruplous dealers. When William Atherton Du Puy, author, journalist, efficiency expert, and executive assistant to the secretary of the interior, visited the Navajo area late in the spring of 1929, he was the agent for Hoover's policy. Du Puy openly carried on discussions with the Indian traders concerning the advantages that might accrue from an organization of traders, namely a marking of authentication for Indian handcrafts.[7]

Within weeks after his mission to the Indian traders of the Southwest, Du Puy met with Collier and began the chain of events and years of work that would culminate in the Indian Arts and Crafts Board Act of 1935. Du Puy's suggestive skills brought an immediate response from Collier, who contacted Commissioner Rhoads the same evening concerning an arts and crafts marketing plan.

The initial conversation between Du Puy and Collier had involved a suggestion to enlist in the plan a wealthy Chicago advertising executive with the J. Walter Thompson Company and member of the Indian Defense Association board of directors, James W. Young. Collier told Du Puy the following morning that if they really wanted to enlist Young, they should wait until Commissioner Rhoads went to New Mexico, where Young had his winter home. Collier suggested that he also be in New Mexico at the same time in order to arrange a conference between Young, Herbert J. Hagerman, a former territorial governor and now the government's special commissioner to the Navajos, Chester E. Faris, who was the Indian Office supervisor of Indian industries, and others. "In any event," Collier concluded, "won't you please let me know what is decided and how I can give what little help may be in my power, whether with reference to Mr. Young, or in any other way?" Clearly, the first initiative for an organized approach to Indian arts and crafts came from the Hoover administration through Du Puy, but Collier immediately took over the development of an Indian arts and crafts marketing plan as his own personal mission just as Du Puy doubtlessly had hoped he would. Scribbling excitedly in pencil just before boarding a train for Montana the next day, Collier wrote Commissioner Rhoads that he already had talked with Henry T. Stanton, head of the J. Walter Thompson operations west of Cleveland, who encouraged Collier to enlist Young for the task. Stanton further suggested that Collier could find out all about Young's record and general availability through Harold G. Moulton of the Brookings Institution, also a close friend of Young's.[8]

Collier himself had had limited business and personal contacts with

Young several times over the previous three years although Indian arts and crafts never were involved directly.[9] Young had been the promoter behind a 1928 scheme in which the Indian Defense Association through Collier and the association's lawyers attempted to make arrangements with Fred Harvey Tours for a payment to the Pueblos for each tourist brought to a pueblo. The plan supposedly was to protect the Pueblos and to have the Pueblos reciprocate so that the Harvey Tours would be more educative and satisfying than they were.[10] Negotiations between the Harvey organization and the various pueblos never blossomed fully primarily because of the heavy legal expenses involved, and the promotional plan was dropped.

Young was enlisted in the cause of Indian arts and crafts, and he personally handed a concrete plan of action to Commissioner Rhoads at the Santo Domingo Pueblo on 1 September 1929. Young's presentation showed a depth of understanding and reflective thought attributable more to a group effort than to that of one person whose business had not involved a single Indian. Still, his professional mark was on much of the document, particularly in the repeated emphasis on "paid advertising" as the best method for expanding the market and ensuring the success of a trademark system, both goals which in turn would help to develop production. He called for a business organization with a practical monopoly over the sources of production and with broad trading powers.[11]

From four possible sources of ownership and control of such a business organization, Young settled on ownership by the Indians themselves "under the guardian's control and guidance." He dismissed the concept of the government in business and saw a lack of monopoly rights keeping an individual or group of individuals from risking capital or accepting the promotional expenses involved. More difficult for him to assess was cooperative ownership of the business by the factors in Indian trade: the licensed traders, both wholesale and retail, who took the Indians' wares for the sake of insuring the Indians' purchases of other merchandise and the retailers who bought from the traders and sold to the public. Young rejected ownership and control by the traders because their interest in crafts was primarily as the means to sell other products rather than to promote the crafts themselves. Because of the retailers' apparent lack of sufficient motivation to expand their outlets,

Young eliminated that group from further consideration. Even an association of producers was discounted because, in Young's view, the problem was mainly one of promotion and not one of production. For Young, the only remaining practical possibility was corporate ownership by all of the Indians.[12]

The alternative Young submitted was that the Indian Office provide a trademark system, encourage Indian arts and crafts in the schools and in adult groups, establish a trade promotion and publicity group similar to the Department of Commerce specialists for individual industries, and pay for publicity with a federal appropriation.[13]

When Young heard nothing from Rhoads, he worried that perhaps the commissioner was misinterpreting the memorandum as suggesting a mass-production enterprise. On 30 September he wrote to Rhoads to stress what he believed to be the importance of increasing the quantity of quality goods. He dismissed any interpretation of his memorandum as a mass-production project which, he emphasized, ultimately would destroy Indian handcrafts.[14]

When Rhoads finally responded on 10 October, he called Young's plan "a great contribution to the subject," yet he labeled it "so large as to require care in making even our first steps." Although he wondered whether it might be better to develop the plans at first in one locality, such as among the Navajos and Pueblos only, he suggested keeping the framework flexible enought to be able to extend it to other parts of the country in the future. He concluded by advising Young to develop his plan on the vital point of increasing the quality of Indian goods as he increased the quantity. Rhoads asked Young "to let us have the benefit of your views from time to time," so "we can gradually build up a method of handling this important asset of the Indians."[15]

Rhoads responded to whatever wind was strongest, yet he managed to concentrate on the Hoover principle of allowing the people to determine their own course of action. He discussed Young's plan with traders at the 1929 Gallup Intertribal Ceremonial and apparently received encouragement from them. Even so, he turned around and told those same traders that the Indian Office must "depend upon them to do whatever is to be done in this direction," with such help as the Indian Office could offer by way of advice and counsel. "We want the Indians to do business, without fear or favor, and on a basis of common community interest," Rhoads explained, "just as in a community of non-Indian people." Then on the same day he turned around again and wrote Young to come to Washington "in the near future so that we can develop your plans."[16]

Two weeks later, in his annual report Secretary Wilbur exhibited a similar vacillation and lack of direction. Reiterating his aim to merge the Indians with the rest of the nation, he revealed that he planned to revise the Indian educational program along "practical lines" and to perfect plans for absorption of the Indians into the industrial and agricultural life of the nation. Although he called for greater appropriations to achieve this goal, he announced his intention to decentralize the Indian Office as rapidly as possible and to turn over responsibility for Indian health and education to the various states. Wilbur characterized this "new" policy as a "new deal for the young Indian" and a "square deal for the old Indian." The objectives were to place the Indians and their property upon a "normal basis" and to eliminate the Indian Office within a period of twenty-five years. Yet Wilbur qualified his policy by stating that in some instances it might not be desirable to bring about a complete merger between the whites and the Indians since the Indian culture had the "means of subsistence and the vigor to survive" as in some areas of the Southwest.[17]

Meanwhile, plans were developing for legislation to protect and to promote Indian arts and crafts. After discussions in the Navajo Tribal Council and a conference of Indian superintendents in Phoenix on 15 November 1929, both dealing with the matter of protection for Indian arts and crafts through legislation and the use of trademarks, Rhoads repeated his invitation to a hesitating Young to come to Washington at his earliest convenience to study the form of legislation needed. Rhoads also suggested that Young then take a draft of this proposed legislation to New Mexico and "sound out the important traders in that vicinity, as it is essential that we secure their cooperation." The situation in the Southwest had reached the point at which certain Indian traders and dealers in Indian arts and crafts had decided to introduce a bill in the Arizona state legislature in the next session to protect Indian arts and crafts work and were actively enlisting the assistance of the Navajo Indian superintendents in framing or approving such a bill. When informed of this plan, Rhoads penciled a notation in the letter's margin that the Arizona state legislature was not scheduled to meet until 1931, and, in the meantime, the Young plan would "probably materialize."[18]

John Collier, for his part, sensed this atmosphere of urgency and immediately brought in on a voluntary basis Rufus J. Pearson, a lawyer the Indian Defense Association was considering for the very purpose of drafting legislation. Young arrived in Washington on the morning of 4 December 1929 and went right to work with Pearson. Later in the day, Collier, Young, Pearson, and Lewis Meriam spent two hours with Rhoads before presenting the plan to Secretary Wilbur. Wilbur then expressed his absolute accord in the effort, and Young and Pearson set to work on the complicated legal problems involved, a step that Collier believed would take at least two weeks. Before the second day, the voluntary legal services of Pearson had ended and another attorney, Benjamin V. Cohen of New York, was secured for the task, this time as a legal advisor to the Institute for Government Research. While that was going on, Collier hoped to draw many members of Congress into consultation and thereby to commit them to the plan.[19]

In a bulletin titled "The Immediate Tasks of the American Indian Defense Association," Collier listed the goals of an Indian arts and crafts marketing corporation. He called the plan a totally new mechanism of Indian Office operation designed to open new markets for Indian craft output, to safeguard the Indian crafts by the employment of a government trademark, and to carry back to the reservations, to the schools and the homes, a new industrial motive and a purpose toward higher craft standards. Young was praised in the bulletin for contributing his time to this enterprise without a salary.[20]

Although Young appeared to have dismissed the concept of the government in business, the first draft of the proposed Indian Cooperative Marketing Board bill seemed to create that very situation. The bill authorized and directed the secretary of the interior to create a suitable trademark and to grant the exclusive right to use that trademark to a corporation. Under the plan, the president would appoint a three-member Indian Cooperative Marketing Board which would form a corporation with $500,000 of nonvoting, preferred stock and 3,000 shares of no-par, nonparticipating yet voting stock. This corporation could buy, sell, deal in, own, and promote Indian arts and crafts with all the standard corporate powers. All profits would go to the United States Treasury to be distributed to the various tribal funds. The bill also provided an unspecified penalty for misuse of the government trademark and authorized a $5,000 appropriation for organizational expenses.[21]

Young, who usually spent part of each winter at his second home near Peña Blanca, New Mexico, used this time to carry his plan to the Indian traders in the area and to enlist the aid of the administration's special commissioner to the Navajos, Herbert Hagerman. In his discussions with Hagerman, Young explained that he represented the government and that his main interest was not in any way a personal one. His only desire, he said, was to bring about legislation which would secure a government guarantee of the genuineness of Indian products, provide a channel for a better market for these products, and raise sufficient funds to exploit and to advertise them properly. With the assistance of Chester Faris, recently appointed district superintendent, Young talked to thirteen of the largest and most influential traders and dealers in the Navajo country. Although the traders received Young cordially, some of them questioned his purely altruistic motives. The president of the Ilfeld Trading Company in Albuquerque believed such a corporation had to be strictly a business proposition. Herman Schweitzer of the Fred Harvey organization privately questioned Young's disinterestedness. He accused Young of planning to create a monopoly in Navajo rugs for his own benefit with a government guarantee behind it.[22]

The timing was excellent for Young's visit to the Navajo area. Crowded warehouses and a dull market had discouraged rug production and had placed the Navajos in difficult financial straits. Without an outlet, the reservation traders did little to encourage rug production and thus effectively shut off from one-fifth to one-fourth of the Navajos' income, a serious circumstance since rug production was an important factor in Navajo tribal subsistence during the winter season. Added to this situation was a 25 to 50 percent drop in the price for wool and lambs. Other sources of subsistence for the Indians of the Southwest were difficult if not impossible to find.[23]

Attempting to cover every avenue of support possible for the Young plan, Collier's Indian Defense Association used the January issue of *American Indian Life*, its regularly published newsletter, to plead for "citizen cooperation in every city and town in the United States" in this undertaking. Years of effort by the Indian Defense Association had culminated in this plan, Collier told the readers.[24]

Enthusiastic and excited, on 31 January 1930, Collier invited Young to Washington to help pave the way for the smooth acceptance of the Indian Cooperative Marketing Board bill. The situation for an Indian arts and crafts bill was "perfect," he told Young while at the same time admitting that "other situations" relating to the Indian Office chiefs were "decidedly bad." Perhaps with a kind of premonition, Collier also asked Young to bring "plenty of Taos Lightning."[25]

On 5 February Collier proudly announced in a confidential Indian Defense Association bulletin that the Indian arts and crafts plan was ready for introduction in Congress. Meriam, Rhoads, Hagerman, and Burlew had accompanied Collier when he interviewed Secretary Wilbur and received "complete endorsement." The Rockefellers had indicated that if the government refused to do the financing they would help to capitalize the project, a step that Wilbur considered more desirable than the use of public money for the undertaking. By this time any plan to use tribal funds was no longer under consideration. Congressman Scott Leavitt, Republican from Montana, promised to introduce the bill in the House and to expedite the legislation by every possible means, and Senator Lynn Joseph Frazier, Republican from North Dakota, was prevailed upon to do the same in the Senate.[26]

Thus, on 10 February in the House and the next day in the Senate, identical bills were introduced to promote the production and sale of Indian products and to create a board and a corporation to assist in that effort. Basically the same as the preliminary draft, the bill now contained specific criminal penalties for misrepresentation of Indian handcrafts of a maximum $5,000 fine or imprisonment not exceeding six months or both. The specification for the federal money needed to organize the corporation had been doubled to $10,000.[27]

Controversy besieged the Indian Arts and Crafts Cooperative Marketing Board bill from the beginning. Opposition surfaced quickly from a member of the board of directors of the Indian Rights Association, Ulric J. Mengert, a lawyer from Philadelphia. Mengert considered the legislation "unwise." While in sympathy with the goals of the bill, he believed that tribal funds would build up in the United States Treasury and would increase the dependency of the Indians on the United States government. Mengert further believed that the government was embarking upon a business enterprise conducted partly for private profit and partly for profit of one particular group in the community, neither of which he considered to be constitutional functions of the government.[28]

Collier responded to this criticism immediately. Private profit, he asserted, would not be possible under the plan except through the gains to the Indians from an increased market and the increased prices or the 7 percent payment on the preferred stock. Collier considered the preferred stock to be simply a loan. As for the buildup of tribal funds, Collier pointed out that to cease those operations would be revolutionary and a violation of treaty. Such a buildup was occurring all of the time with each court of claims adjustment, sale of tribal timber and tribal oil, and every lease of a power site on tribal grazing area. To show why the government provided numerous services for the Indians that it did not for any other group in the population, Collier cited the special status of Indians as wards of the government under its plenary jurisdiction. Finally, Collier sidestepped the constitutional issue by pointing to the range of activities carried on by the government in a direct way for and with the Indians.[29]

The "other situations" in Washington to which Collier had referred in his telegram to Young had contributed to the creation of an unreceptive atmosphere for the Indian Defense Association's Indian arts and crafts bill. First, Commissioners Rhoads and Scattergood failed to counter the opposition from Congressman Louis Cramton to the Hoover-supported $1.1 million emergency food and clothing appropriation for Indian school children. Then, the commissioners refused to support the Klamath Indians in legislation before the Senate Committee on Indian Affairs to incorporate their tribe. This inaction produced an irreparable conflict between the Indian Defense Association and the commissioners. Soon afterward, the relationship was further exacerbated by Collier's testimony in the Senate hearings on the development of the Flathead Indian power site in Montana.[30]

On 11 February 1930 in another of his confidential bulletins, Collier lashed out at Rhoads and Scattergood, Congressman Cramton, the influence of the Burke-Meritt old guard, which he believed was still inside the Indian Office, and unidentified influences in the Interior Department for overruling the advice of the Indian Defense Association in the Klamath matter. Collier reported that Haven Emerson, president of the American Indian Defense Association, had been present at these hearings and had concluded that Cramton was using his vital influence as chairman of the House Subcommittee on Appropriations for the Interior Department virtually to blackmail the whole department. Even more damaging in Collier's view was the fact that Rhoads and Scattergood served no useful purpose to the Indian effort. Collier charged that days of discussion with the commissioners produced only momentary agreement and then the next day they once more sank back into inactivity as in the case of Rhoads, or into "childlike optimism" as in the case of Scattergood. Rhoads's timidity and susceptibility, Collier believed, were being exploited by the still-active supporters of the Burke-Meritt Indian policy. Secretary Wilbur listened to the complaints voiced by the representatives of the Indian Defense Association, yet he took no action.[31]

Affairs rapidly had reached the state where Collier admitted that neither he nor Meriam were in a position to persuade Rhoads and Scattergood to support the Indian Cooperative Marketing Board bill. Collier thought that the whole Indian Office was in a "gummed-up state." On 14 February he urged Young to return immediately to Washington because time was vital and the Indian Office was "going onto the rocks as fast as it knows how to travel."[32]

Collier was so concerned over the apparent confusion in the Indian Office that he took it upon himself to prepare an Interior Department report on the Frazier-Leavitt bill for Secretary Wilbur. He planned to have Judson King, executive secretary of the Popular Government League in Washington, issue a similarly strong endorsement through the Senate press gallery. In his statement Collier emphasized how the native crafts were perishing rapidly over most of the Indian country, except for the Navajo Reservation and a few of the pueblos, because all connection between production and market was missing. Even in these areas of the Southwest, he pointed out, the lack of an organized retail market and the presence of public uncertainty about the genuineness of the products had created a state of overproduction in blankets and had encouraged the mass production of ruinous imitations in silverwork. The pottery and basketry markets among the various tribes were sharply restricted by a similar lack of effective marketing.[33]

At the same time, open opposition to the Frazier-Leavitt bill developed. Percy Jackson, acting president and treasurer of the Eastern Association on Indian Affairs, sent an unsolicited opinion to Senator Frazier in which he proclaimed his sympathy for the objectives of the bill yet stated that the government did not have the ability to pass judgment on what was or was not a product meriting a government trademark. Basically, Jackson seemed to feel this responsibility belonged only to authorities in the field of Indian arts and crafts. Collier immediately forwarded Jackson's letter to Benjamin Cohen in New York. Cohen ably refuted Jackson's objections and argued that the power for doing good given to the board far outweighed any potential harm that might come from this power. He pointed out that the bill did not give a monopoly to the corporation to determine the genuineness, description, and quality of Indian products; instead, it gave an authority to act, an authority which had to be given to someone if trademarks were to be used at all. From Collier's viewpoint, Jackson's "obstructionist" criticism was "mostly irrelevant."[34]

More formidable opposition came from Mary Austin, who, just one day after Jackson had written to Frazier, launched her personal campaign against the Cooperative Marketing Board bill. She considered Collier's efforts in this area an affront to herself and other members of the Indian Arts Fund, a private organization formed in Santa Fe in 1925 as an outgrowth of the School of American Research in an effort to save the fine old examples of Indian art from dissipation into the growing tourist market. Founding members included Hagerman, Austin, Amelia White, Mabel Dodge Luhan of Taos, writer Elizabeth Shepley Sargeant, archaeologist Alfred V. Kidder, and Frederick Webb Hodge of the Museum of the American Indian, Heye Foundation, New York. "Why do you not, before rushing ahead with these things, consult with the Indian Arts Foundation [Fund]?" she demanded. Its years of experience, a museum of its own, and Rockefeller support, established it as the natural reference in this matter, Austin maintained. She argued that everything accomplished so far would be destroyed if the bill went through without an amendment that would take Indian artistry into account. She advised Collier to put his plan before the Indian Arts Fund at once, something that Young had done indirectly by giving a copy of his proposal to Kenneth M. Chapman, a director of the Indian Arts Fund.[35]

34

While Collier did not approach the Indian Arts Fund as Austin had suggested, he did see the immediate need to publicize the bill more fully. With that end in view, he forwarded one hundred copies of the bill to the J. Walter Thompson Company in New York for them to disperse to the leading newspaper editorial writers in the country. Superintendent G. A. Trotter of the Zuni Agency in New Mexico was one of the interested people who subsequently read about the bill. Trotter rejected the bill because the independent activities of the proposed board did not provide for any participation by the Indian traders or the government employees. Their years of experience should be utilized to secure the greatest results, he advised, although he went on to praise the movement to protect the Indians and their crafts.[36]

No one at any level questioned the fact that the Indian arts and crafts situation needed prompt and skillful attention. The desperate condition of reservation Indian life spoke through the pages of the Meriam Report, and individual Indian artists gave testimony that affirmed their need for a wider market.[37] Something had to be done. A sense of impending disaster filled the air. The Indians clearly could not help themselves alone. Yet who should come to their aid, a new, all-powerful, government-sponsored corporation, or a relatively small, privately funded group of well-entrenched, interested citizens?

Before Congress could decide, the Indian arts and crafts bill had to be submitted to the Bureau of the Budget to determine whether the proposal would be in conflict with President Hoover's financial program. In this manner, Hoover was asked to determine how much he would insist on his ideology in the face of the threat to the economic and cultural survival of the American Indians. Hoover's answer two weeks later was a clear-cut decision in favor of the associative function of government. Citing the government's liability in the sale of stock, Budget Bureau Director J. Clawson Roop specifically demanded the elimination of the government-controlled corporation to make the legislation fit the financial program. Roop suggested that the Indian Cooperative Marketing Board make contracts with private corporations to carry out the overall purposes of the legislation.[38]

Believing the issue to be settled, Wilbur, Rhoads, and Scattergood did nothing. Collier, on the other hand, refused to give up and wanted to adapt the bill to meet the Budget Bureau director's criticism.[39] After conferences with Meriam and Nathan R. Margold, a New York attorney newly recommended by Harvard law professor Felix Frankfurter because of Benjamin Cohen's illness, and retained, like Cohen, by the Institute for Government Research, Collier was convinced that the bill was "easy enough to fix up." He believed that the real obstacles were Congressman Cramton, Budget Director Roop, and the Eastern Association on Indian Affairs, and that the only way to break them down was to get to President Hoover. He considered criticism of the Indian arts and crafts bill to be merely an excuse for delay, and he wired Young to come once more to Washington to try to get a showdown involving "action through the President."[40]

The opposition in the Southwest refused to give any support. One observer described the Santa Fe group as largely interested in crafts that really could not have an extensive market and therefore opposed to a bill which it felt was designed to industrialize them. Moreover, when James Young had met earlier in Santa Fe with traders and members of the Indian Arts Fund, he apparently had offended many with his high-handedness and had failed to gain support for the bill.[41]

Mary Austin claimed that not a dissenting voice was heard at the meeting to the verdict that the bill was "the worst possible thing for the arts of the Indian." In her opinion, the "very obvious and appalling fact" was that the bill had been drawn by someone who knew nothing of Indian arts or Indian life. She told Collier that she could not understand his support since he was well aware of the need to begin with the artists themselves. The bill was merely "another modern mechanism clamped down on the Indian[s] without their cooperation or understanding."[42]

Amelia White, secretary of the Eastern Association on Indian Affairs, sent Rhoads and Leavitt copies of several letters from traders who had attended the meeting with Young. The traders sought to give the association support in the fight against the Frazier-Leavitt bill in Congress and generally supported Austin's contentions. One letter explained that many traders around Gallup originally had approved the measure without so much as reading it simply because they had hoped it possibly might help them to dispose of an overstock of rugs and blankets.[43]

Fighting to hold his position, Collier used the influential arm of Charles deYoung Elkus, a San Francisco attorney and a member of

36

the Indian Defense Association, in an attempt to stir up some administrative support of Indian arts and crafts legislation. So far Rhoads had issued only one memorandum recommending the enactment of the bill with a few minor changes in legal phraseology and calling for the preservation of the native arts and crafts "as an artistic heritage to future generations." In Collier's opinion, the Indian Office seemed paralyzed. Elkus contacted Rhoads personally and accused him of not giving any active support through his office. Mere approval was not sufficient, Elkus warned. Totally unenthusiastic, Rhoads replied that he and Wilbur had gone about as far as they could, believing that personal lobbying would be a mistake. He suggested that the responsibility to support the Indian arts and crafts bill lay with the general public.[44]

For his part, Collier defended the bill in correspondence with Mary Austin. He claimed he had not worked out the plan, although he would be quite proud if he had. Contrary to what she had been charging, he contended, the bill was vitally concerned with the artistic well-being of the individual craftsmen. Just as the development of the Indian artists was important, so was a concern for a market. The history of crafts revealed that the need for a market occurred when an ethnic group no longer was economically self-sufficient and when the demand within the group for beautiful crafts—created with no commercial motive—had disappeared. At this point, Collier explained, craft production could not be expected to take place by "subliminal uprushes" or as a fine art pursued with no end beyond itself. For examples of efforts to organize a quality handcraft market, Collier cited the craft guilds of India and the organization of the Hungarian and Irish cottage crafts. In this manner Collier considered the Young plan inseparable from the pursuit of an expanded quality market. The opposition of the Eastern Association on Indian Affairs and its connected groups would not be decisive, he advised Austin, although it was "kind of disheartening in another way."[45]

Austin, meanwhile, was dealing directly with Secretary Wilbur and informed him that the trustees of the Indian Arts Fund had agreed to prepare their own Indian arts program and to submit it to him. She said that their program would embody "our ideas of the most practicable method of instructing Indians, . . . primarily Indian school teachers, in those arts and crafts which our experience shows us can be made profitable to Indians." She also promised "some ideas of how to deal with cases of special talent among young Indians and with methods of creating a market for Indian art products through the education of the American public." Essentially, however, Austin saw the core of the Indian arts and crafts problem to be educating the Indians to sustain high quality production. "It would be a mistake to clamp down on the Indians any untried legislation," she warned. "I think with the proper cooperation of Washington, we shall be able to manage these things in a completely satisfactory manner."[46]

Austin boldly asked Wilbur to refer all activities relating to Indian arts to the Indian Arts Fund in Santa Fe. A week later Austin wrote Rhoads that all of the members of the fund were busy working out various plans to solve specific problems in Indian art. "I question whether very much legislation will be necessary," she said. The whole Indian Arts Fund organization had been worked out "without government support, without creating any government antagonism, and without legislation," she reminded Rhoads.[47] Despite her claims, no plan ever reached the Indian Office.

When Austin specified to Collier her objections to the Frazier-Leavitt bill over and above her chagrin at not having been consulted, she revealed her dedicated yet limited vision. Cognizant of the continuous need to preserve the Indians' artistic integrity yet insensitive to the urgency of the overall Indian arts and crafts situation, Austin's one-sided concern could not see the current need for a market. A more important concern from her viewpoint was to find "a method of persuading Indians to produce art." This attitude reflected the approach of those whites who felt a need to instruct the subservient Indians in the continuing production of their age-old crafts. Despite her sincerity, an attitude of superiority was even more obvious when she accused Collier of "the incredible folly of . . . compelling these people to a quantity production on something that they don't know how to make." Austin repeatedly refused to recognize the economic plight of the Indians and charged that the Frazier-Leavitt bill was drawn up "to meet a situation which does not exist, by people who know nothing whatever of the conditions to be met." She concluded by imperiously advising Collier to become a member of the Indian Arts Fund.[48]

Austin's opposition provided an excuse for inactivity on the part of the Indian Office, yet this inactivity was in reality immediately dictated both by the simple refusal of the budget director to approve the legislation and by the refusal of the secretary of the interior to report on the measure for the Congressional Committees on Indian Affairs.

Besides Chairman Frazier, one other member of the Senate Indian Affairs Committee appeared to be eager to alleviate the Indians' economic plight. On 2 May, John William Elmer Thomas, Democrat from Oklahoma, introduced a joint resolution directing the secretary of the interior to investigate and to report on the business and industrial affairs of the various Indian tribes in order to determine the most effective methods of conducting those affairs in the best interests of the Indians and the advisability of establishing facilities on the reservations "for the purpose of encouraging and assisting the Indians in the manufacture and sale of articles of commercial value." The resolution specifically directed the secretary to list the articles of commercial value which the Indians could manufacture and to recommend the most effective method of stamping or marking such articles to prevent fraud and to encourage their sale. Thomas's resolution never emerged from the Senate Indian Affairs Committee and Wilbur ignored it.[49]

Budget Director Roop continued to oppose the Indian Arts and Crafts Cooperative Marketing Board bill. The initial appropriation of $10,000 was not the obstacle considering the huge 13 to 18 percent increases in appropriations granted annually to the Indian Office between 1929 and 1932.[50] Nor was the $500,000 preferred stock at issue, for private sources were available to participate in such a venture, particularly since Secretary Wilbur was a director of the Rockefeller Foundation. Instead, Roop's request for substitute legislation to eliminate the government-controlled corporation and to limit the power of the Indian Cooperative Marketing Board to initiating contracts or agreements with private corporations represented the perfect mechanism for Hoover's ideal of a superior socioeconomic order wherein the people would regulate themselves without government interference.

Unable to discern this motivating force and driven by an overwhelming desire to achieve the needed legislation, Collier, Young, and Margold pondered their course of action. Collier narrowed the choices to two: either to attempt passage with the original bill slightly altered to have the government provide all of the financing and thereby eliminate the liability; or to have philanthropic interests organize a corporation and then try to pass legislation giving that corporation exclusive control of the government trademark. Collier and his friends believed that both methods would eliminate the Budget Bureau's objection to financial partnership between the government and private interests, yet they hesitated to follow the first course because they believed it would involve a lengthy battle in Congress. As for the second, they realized that Congress would be very slow to give control of a government mark of certification to a private corporation or foundation. Both approaches would demand effort and patience.[51]

Collier believed that the threat to any course of action requiring a congressional appropriation came not only from the Bureau of the Budget but also from Congressman Cramton, who long had been an advocate of strict economy in the federal government. Cramton's zeal in this area had led him to embrace the policy of rapid assimilation and proposals damaging to Indian welfare in the name of practical economy and a balanced budget. He and Collier had clashed openly in the past, and Collier considered Cramton's influence a threat even after the congressman was defeated for renomination in 1930. Still, Cramton never entered directly into any developments surrounding the legislation, primarily because the Budget Bureau, Wilbur, and Rhoads successfully eliminated any need for overt action on his part. Since his role in Indian affairs as chairman of the House Interior Department appropriations subcommittee was pivotal, Cramton became the easy scapegoat in Collier's eyes for the difficulties faced by the Indian arts and crafts bill because of their personal confrontations. If, indeed, Cramton alone was destroying the Frazier-Leavitt bill as Collier often charged, then the head of Cramton's political party, President Hoover, could have stepped in. No such action took place. In fact, Cramton was rewarded with further federal employment after leaving Congress.

The American Indian Defense Association and Collier were perplexed over what direction to take, and Young now began to exhibit discouragement about ever succeeding in the effort to involve the government in the promotion and protection of Indian arts and crafts. No effort had been made to change the bill to meet administration objections.

40

The fact that Scattergood and Rhoads informed Young personally that they had made a deliberate choice in favor of working with rather than opposing Cramton on Indian legislative matters may have all but crushed the Indian Defense Association's earlier optimism. Young believed that the commissioners had been forced to this decision by the direction of Secretary Wilbur who, in turn, only was carrying out policy from a higher source. While admitting the plausibility of Young's assessment, Collier expressed the opposite view that Rhoads and Scattergood were not able to push any legislation or program and would go on "surrendering to any and every reactionary influence." In short, they were, for Collier, "exhaustively inadequate."[52]

Dissatisfaction in the Collier group reached the boiling point in May 1930 when after more than a year the Indian Office had failed to put into effect a single constructive plan to deal with even elementary projects. The Indian Defense Association curtly asked Secretary Wilbur, "What is going to be done to reorganize the Indian Bureau and to make your program real?" All cordiality ended when Wilbur indicted the officers of the Indian Defense Association for their "widespread, intemperate, and illy digested emotional attacks." In response, the Indian Defense Association asked only that Indian Office actions and results match promises and requested a statement of the results of Wilbur's Indian program.[53] No reply came from Secretary Wilbur.

No progress was made on the Frazier-Leavitt bill. Rhoads informed Collier that he had had another conference with the Budget Bureau and Roop had told him "they all like the bill and want it and that President Hoover does, too," yet the economic program was clamping down on all appropriations, and the preferred stock or loans plan carried an "undesirable government responsibility."[54] Nothing positive happened, and the Indian Defense Association now began to call the Frazier-Leavitt bill "emergency legislation." The collapse of wool and lamb prices, the depreciation of Navajo blankets, and the flooding of the market with imitation Indian jewelry had brought on a crisis. The Indian Defense Association predicted that the Navajos would suffer acutely during the winter ahead and that even the reservation traders, who were indispensable to the Navajo economy, would face extreme difficulties.[55]

Whatever James Young's motives may have been in regard to Indian arts and crafts, he refused to be thwarted personally. When the Frazier-Leavitt bill appeared to have been blocked successfully in Congress, Young planned to join Fred Leighton, the proprietor of a retail Indian arts and crafts business known as The Indian Trading Post with branches in Chicago and New York, in a private plan to establish a chain of high-class retail shops in major American cities and possibly in Europe to handle Indian arts and crafts. For two years, at his Michigan Avenue store in Chicago, Leighton had been holding a series of teatime gatherings featuring Indian entertainment and lectures by authorities on the American Indian. In his prospectus for the new company, Leighton listed the following aims: "To present the American Indian heritage of art and handicrafts, till now neglected, to the people of the United States on its true basis—that of Art," and "To ensure thereby a steady demand for high grade Indian and Latin American art and handicrafts which will help solve the sociological and psychological problems of people of American Indian blood." Leighton justified his belief in the venture on his success in Chicago and on the general awakening of interest in Indian and Mexican arts. He emphasized the publicity and the interest in Mexican Indian art aroused by a recently opened exhibition at the Metropolitan Museum of Art in New York and a similarly large exhibit of American Indian art to open in November 1931 at the Grand Central Galleries in New York, both of which would tour the chief cities of the country.[56]

In September both he and Young met in Santa Fe with Amelia and Martha White and Mary C. Wheelwright from Boston, wealthy philanthropists and proprietors of their own arts and crafts shops, each of whom agreed to subscribe $10,000 to the $140,000 capitalized project. At the same time, other prominent figures, including Mary Austin, provided tentative subscriptions. Leighton claimed to have the support of Hagerman, Faris, Jesse Nusbaum of the Laboratory of Anthropology in Santa Fe, and Berton I. Staples, Indian trader and promoter of Indian arts and crafts. Young agreed to serve on the board of directors. When Leighton asked Rhoads for his approval and support, Rhoads told him he thought the plan contained "great possibilities for the Indians," yet he officially could not endorse private enterprise.[57]

Despite Young's enthusiasm and Leighton's experience in the field, the private corporation scheme never took hold. Leighton proceeded to open his third store in Los Angeles in 1930 and completed the legal papers for incorporation. He was unable to find sufficient capital, however, and the expansion of the business halted. Perhaps a contributing factor was what Young called the public financial temper of "extreme caution and even gloom." By 1933, Leighton was forced to close the Los Angeles store and also his original Chicago establishment, and to concentrate his efforts in New York City.[58]

In December 1930, Rhoads finally ended all remaining hopes for the Frazier-Leavitt bill by refusing to report the bill favorably to either the Senate or the House Indian Affairs Committees. He also seemed to close the door to the several similar plans that had been suggested in the meantime or would be suggested in the immediate future.[59] Margaret McKittrick of the Eastern Association on Indian Affairs helped to develop the plan that the organization submitted. Amelia White and Oliver LaFarge, an ethnologist, the author of the 1929 Pulitzer Prize-winning *Laughing Boy*, a novel of life among the Navajo Indians, and a director of the Eastern Association on Indian Affairs, submitted their own personal plans for Indian arts and crafts, none of which ever received serious attention.[60] Traders, superintendents, and public-spirited citizens contributed their ideas only to receive the usual unenthusiastic reply from Wilbur, Rhoads, or Scattergood. Lip service was all the Hoover administration contributed to Indian arts and crafts. Secretary Wilbur in his annual report proclaimed "we should not destroy what is best of his [the Indian's] own traditions, arts, crafts, and associations, but encourage their development and survival." Wilbur, Rhoads and Scattergood offered no plans of their own. Instead, they pleaded for assistance that they subsequently ignored.[61]

3

ESSAYS

THE ECONOMIC CONDITION OF the Indians worsened with the depression, and income from the sale of crafts assumed increasing importance. Among the Navajos particularly—the largest tribal group living on the largest reservation—arts and crafts were essential for existence. Estimates of the total Navajo income derived from arts and crafts were between 12 and 25 percent.[1]

Very few Indians had the opportunity to reveal the direct circumstances surrounding their lives. A fear of retribution and a resignation to their lot kept many from testifying even when given the opportunity. In April 1931, Ignatio Pinto, a Navajo, through an interpreter told a Senate subcommittee of the Committee on Indian Affairs investigating Indian conditions around Crownpoint, New Mexico, that his total income in 1930 had been $280. He had been paid fifteen cents a pound for wool for a total of a little over thirty dollars and his wife had woven blankets which he had sold for one dollar a pound or a total of about one hundred dollars. While he did not specify the source of the remaining money, the sale of livestock and day-wage work presumably made up the rest. With this sum they had supported themselves and six children. Since no rain at all had fallen on the reservation in 1930, what corn he had been able to plant had gone to waste.[2]

The average income for the southern section of the Navajo Reservation was not much different. Despite any tendency on the part of Superintendent John G. Hunter not to make his administration appear ineffective and the fact that exact records were impossible to maintain in any case, a clear picture of the relative importance of arts and crafts in the economic life of the Navajos emerged. Hunter submitted income data for 1930 for the approximately 16,000 Navajos living in the five-million acre southern section. On the basis of five persons to a family, the Navajos' total income showed an average of only $460 per family for the year. Arts and crafts income was 25 percent of this. No wonder Superintendent Hunter stressed to the Senate subcommittee the urgency to enact legislation which would afford adequate protection to the arts and crafts of the Navajos.[3]

Among the neighboring Pueblos, farming remained the core of Indian life, yet limited agricultural areas and limited water supply had increased the importance of arts and crafts as an economic necessity. In 1930, the total arts and crafts income of the northern pueblos of Taos, Picuris, San Juan, Santa Clara, San Ildefonso, Nambe, and Tesuque was 16 percent of their total income, while farming and stock raising was 39 percent and miscellaneous income such as cutting and delivering firewood in the winter and day-wage work was a huge 45 percent.[4] When crops were poor or employment scarce, the Pueblos like the Navajos were forced to rely on their unique arts and crafts to see them through their difficult times.

When the Navajos could sell their blankets and rugs in 1931, they were getting less than the already low prices paid a year earlier. One Navajo testified that his wife had been making two four- by seven-foot rugs a month, each weighing about nine pounds. The previous year she had received only a dollar a pound or nine dollars for two weeks work and now she was receiving even less. In response, Indian trader Lloyd Ambrose testified that when times were good he could take a truckload of blankets to the wholesalers, and he had no trouble selling all of the blankets. Now the wholesalers would not buy any.[5]

Concern over the methods of marketing Indian arts and crafts beyond the traders' transactions also surfaced. Ambrose pointed out that Marshall Field, John Wanamaker, Parker Brothers, and several other large department stores had tried to sell Navajo rugs. They had purchased them from a wholesaler who himself had taken a 10 to 25 percent markup. Then the department stores turned the merchandise over to their oriental rug department or linoleum department sales personnel, who "didn't know a Navajo rug from an Apache robe." With a markup of 100 to 300 percent, the department stores did not sell many rugs, and by 1931 nearly all had discontinued handling the Navajos' work.[6]

The Navajos left no doubt that they sought every bit of help in the protection and in the marketing of their arts and crafts. When Senator

Thomas told one Navajo that he was hopeful "that the government may interest itself in trying to help you market your merchandise," the dignified and reserved Navajo artist simply and directly replied, "It would be appreciated very much if you would." Meanwhile, the Indians' economic situation deteriorated further. In some areas the Navajos once more had to call for rations.[7]

With aroused interest the Senate Indian Affairs Committee affirmed its willingness to push an Indian arts and crafts bill in the next Congress. Collier began to gather his forces once more although he could not help wondering what the President would do to such a plan when he had control of it and created the board. A few months later, Herbert Hagerman told a traders' meeting in Gallup that the old Frazier-Leavitt bill was the only definite plan before the Indian Office, and if nothing else was presented by the time Congress convened, the Indian Office probably would take this bill up and push for its passage. Harold L. Ickes, a Chicago lawyer and a member of the American Indian Defense Association, attended the Gallup meeting and reported that Hagerman had in his possession the entire Indian Office file on the subject, including Young's original memorandum, a situation which created the general impression in the mind of everyone present that the Indian Office had given him the job of getting something going.[8]

A second Indian arts and crafts bill was introduced in the Senate by Lynn Frazier on 4 February 1932. Like the original bill, its immediate purpose involved the creation and development of a larger market and better marketing facilities for the Indians' products and also a plan to guarantee the genuineness of Indian handcrafts, yet the bill contained a number of changes. These had been worked out by Charles Elkus and the Indian traders during the Gallup traders' meeting the previous summer, and the fact that these changes were included reflected a new respect for the traders' influence. The new bill increased from three to five the number of commissioners on the board, apparently to achieve a greater diversity of representation, which now would include traders. Indian traders could be elected directors of the corporation, affix the government mark to Indian products, and serve on the corporation's advisory committees. Most significant of all the changes was the specific power given to the board to define and to prescribe standards, grades, and quality, a power added only because the traders themselves were unable to agree on anything other than a definition of the word "standards." By default, the traders had turned this controlling power over to the proposed government board. Elsewhere, the new bill placed no limitation on the preferred stock dividend, and it made no reference to the promotion of cooperative enterprises to help to develop Indian arts and crafts, another concession to the influence of the traders, who were fighting to maintain their monopolistic advantage. Finally, the person authorized to apply the government mark no longer had to supervise the actual application of the mark. Young fully approved of these changes. Probably because of his experience with private financing when the Fred Leighton plan failed to find adequate capitalization, Young now suggested that the source of capital be reconsidered to allow for the government to provide it all.[9] This suggested change was not included, no doubt because it might have given the administration an excuse to block the measure.

In a three-page memorandum to Secretary Wilbur, Rhoads indentified what he considered to be the opposition to the legislation, namely those who believed the government would be thrown into private enterprise, those who felt that in a short time a monopoly would develop in Indian arts and crafts, and some traders who opposed the measure on the ground that they would be deprived of a portion of their business. He reminded Wilbur of the Budget Bureau's opposition in 1930 and its suggestions for acceptable legislation in order to eliminate the government's liability. Then, in one final sentence he effectively killed the measure: "While the purpose contemplated by S.3511 has good features, we are not yet in a position to give the measure our full support, and therefore, recommend that action thereon be deferred for the present."[10]

Frazier had requested the usual report or statement of support from the Interior Department concerning the second arts and crafts bill before the Senate Indian Affairs Committee began hearings on the measure, and the acting secretary, Joseph M. Dixon, replied. Apparently overlooking the fact that in 1931 the Southwest traders already had formed the United Indian Traders Association, Dixon commented on the advantages to be gained by the federal government in the formation of such an association. The federal government actually would not engage in business, and the Indian Office or the Interior Department simply would grant a revocable license to the traders' association authorizing the attachment of the certificates of genuineness to be issued under rules and regulations formulated by the traders' association and approved by the Indian Office. Dixon concluded that despite the vast amount of consideration and discussion which this subject had had, the Interior Department did not feel it was "yet in a position to recommend the enactment of the legislation, or to propose a substitute therefor."[11]

Public interest in Indian arts and crafts continued to grow in spite of the Hoover administration. For its part, the Indian Office was satisfied to write letters supporting Indian art and to have its name used publicly whenever private efforts were involved in the philanthropic promotion of Indian arts and crafts, so long as the commissioners did not have to do anything specific or to provide funds for anything. In the fall of 1930, for example, Scattergood answered an advertisement in the September issue of *House and Garden* magazine for participants in that magazine's first annual exposition in the spring of 1931. Citing in his letter the need for the Indian Office to develop Indian arts and crafts and the importance of attention to the matter of marketing, Scattergood expressed his belief that the *House and Garden* Exposition in New York City would afford "an opportunity for showing the wonderful adaptability of Indian handicraft to decorative purposes." When the Indian Office was informed of the potential cost, Rhoads contacted Amelia White. He explained that "as happens so often, we find ourselves without funds to finance any official participation in the show," and unless someone could be enlisted as a financial angel, "it is not at all likely that Indian handicrafts will be represented." White accepted the private-party role in associative government, complied fully, and agreed to present the show in the name of the Indian Office at no expense to the government.[12]

Before anything positive materialized, the exposition was canceled for 1931 and the whole arrangement shifted to the International Antiques Exposition at the Grand Central Palace. Rhoads failed to see any conflict between promoting Indian arts and crafts for popular decorative usage in a contemporary design exhibit and attempting to achieve the same goal in an antiques exhibit, so he told White to go ahead since "the antique exposition will serve the same purpose so far as the exploitation of Indian arts and crafts is concerned."[13] A ten- by twenty-foot mezzanine booth was designed by a New York architect in an Early

48

American-cum-Victorian style complete with fireplace, mantel, twenty-four-pane glass windows, and bookcases. Across the top of the booth was a full-length sign reading "Bureau of Indian Affairs, Department of the Interior, Washington, D.C." The official guidebook for the exhibit told of textiles, baskets, beadwork, and pottery that were arranged as interior decoration in the display booth. "I think we shall start a new fashion yet," White told Rhoads when she formally invited him to come to New York to attend the exposition.[14]

After the exposition, White suggested to Rhoads that an exhibit of similar character be taken to other large centers of population to stimulate the sale of Indian arts and crafts. Rhoads responded in characteristic fashion, first by citing the advantages to be gained by such a step and what it would do for the Indians, and then by pleading that he had no funds for this purpose. Even the following year, when the director of the International Antiques Exposition offered the Indian Office space at the 1932 exposition at no charge whatsoever, Rhoads backed out. White could not be reached in the West, so Rhoads again cited the lack of funds "to defray the expenses necessarily incident to the assembling, shipping, and care of the materials."[15]

Perhaps recognizing by now the specious attitude of the Indian Office toward Indian arts and crafts, White ignored the Indian Office completely as she and John Sloan, a New York artist who had promoted Indian artwork since the early years following World War I, used a privately funded organization called the Exposition of Indian Tribal Arts to put on a large exhibition at the Grand Central Art Galleries in New York. Sponsored by the College Art Association, the exhibition took place from 30 November to 24 December 1931. After New York, the College Art Association planned to circulate the exhibit around the principal cities in the United States for two years. The purpose of the exposition was to emphasize Indian crafts as art and to foster for them a greater and more selective demand, so that Indian artists would be able to conserve the finest traditions of their art and, incidentally, to better their economic condition.[16]

Officially supporting the Exposition of Indian Tribal Arts, the offices of the secretary of the interior and the commissioner of Indian affairs were listed in the exhibit catalogue as sponsors. Although Wilbur only wrote a few bland sentences of praise, the government's assigned role as a promoter of private effort was thereby fulfilled. Reference to the Indian Office in the catalogue was limited to one short sentence which applauded it for "encouraging the Indians to continue to create and to develop their own arts."[17]

Critical response to the 1931 Exposition of Indian Tribal Arts was enthusiastic and reflected the advance Indian arts and crafts had made in the minds of many culturally alert Americans. Walter Pach, art critic of the *New York Times*, typified this advance when he called the art of the Indians simply "American art, and of the most important kind." He gave credit for this realization to "the new insight we have." Pach also cited America's waste of her natural resources, oil, forests, water-power, and soil, and warned that Americans must not permit further waste of this last asset, Indian art, "the greatest we have."[18]

Accounts, articles, and essays about Exposition of Indian Tribal Arts repeatedly emphasized pride in the Indians as part of the American heritage. Ralph Flint, an art critic for *Art News*, considered the exhibit to be an inauguration of a national campaign on behalf of the American Indian as an artist worthy of serious consideration and not merely as a purveyor of souvenirs and trophies for a traveling public. He saluted "our fellow American" and welcomed him into the American brotherhood of the arts.[19]

The Exposition of Indian Tribal Arts was also very popular during its tour of major European cities. While at the International Art Show in Venice, the exhibit received a request to come next to Budapest, and John Sloan asked Rhoads if the Indian Office would pay the costs for transportation and insurance for an extension of the exhibit's European tour. Rhoads pleaded that he had no funds available, and he made no effort to locate the money.[20]

Despite the critical acclaim accorded Indian arts and crafts, the economic status of Indian arts, as well as Indians in general, worsened. In Washington State, traders refused to buy Indian baskets because their stores were overstocked and the baskets could not be sold. Tourist agencies and national parks refused to purchase the Indians' baskets for the same reasons. Navajo rugs were piled high in the trading stores on the Navajo Reservation and no market existed. The Navajos were getting only five cents a pound for their wool and were forced to sell it all to meet their needs. Nothing was left to pawn. Hunger and want existed in every home. When Senator Carl Hayden, Democrat from Arizona, had to call Rhoads's attention to this desperate situation among the Navajo artists, Rhoads did not answer. After Hayden wrote again more than two weeks later, Scattergood responded with the usual plea of a lack of funds to do anything to help to alleviate the conditions for the Navajo artists.[21]

Senator Hayden was deeply concerned, and he brought about one of the few specific actions to help Indian arts and crafts during the Hoover era. On 4 May 1932, he introduced an amendment which ultimately was adopted as part of the Revenue Act of 1932. The amendment exempted from taxation "any article of native Indian handicraft manufactured or produced by Indians on Indian reservations, or in Indian schools, or by Indians under the jursidiction of the United States Government in Alaska."[22]

By November 1932, the commissioner of Indian affairs reported that practically every division of the Indian Office having to do with the Indian as a person was called upon for relief of some sort.[23]

Pressure on the Rhoads administration from Indian superintendents and legitimate Indian arts and crafts traders and retailers had mounted over the manufacture and sale of spurious Indian products, yet little or nothing concrete was done at the government level during the Hoover presidency. The superintendent of the Grand Canyon National Park, M. R. Tillotson, had written to the director of the National Park Service suggesting a regulation banning the sale of fraudulently made or labeled Indian arts and crafts within the national park system. Tillotson feared that unless something was done the Navajo silversmiths would be driven out of business altogether and their handcraft might become one of the lost arts. When Congressman Godfrey Gummer Goodwin, Republican from Minnesota, received a complaint about the sale of imitation Indian handwork from one of his constituents, he immediately wrote to Commissioner Rhoads. Rhoads's reply to Goodwin was another example of the seemingly calculated inaction so characteristic of his commissionership. "The question of how to handle this matter has been under consideration for some time," Rhoads commented matter-of-factly. He closed off further inquiry into the problem by telling Congressman Goodwin that "we find it exceedingly difficult to formulate a Federal law which will remedy the evil."[24]

One law, the Federal Trade Commission Act (1914), long had been in effect, and Rhoads might have made use of it had he been concerned and interested enough to pursue the matter. Apparently without Rhoads's knowledge, the Federal Trade Commission began hearings in just such a case only one week after Rhoads had told Goodwin how difficult it was to formulate federal law to protect Indian arts and crafts. The Jeffrey Jewelry Company of Chicago was found to have shipped in interstate commerce jewelry made in mills or factories that was labeled as Indian handcraft. When the case was concluded on 21 September 1932, the firm agreed to a cease and desist order prohibiting them from using the words *Indian* or *Navajo* or any other words, markings, or labels that implied its jewelry was made by hand by American Indians. Similarly, the Federal Trade Commission issued a cease and desist order on 28 June 1932 to the Beacon Manufacturing Company of Massachusetts, which had advertised its blankets as woven or made by Indians.[25]

Since preliminary investigation and filing of these cases began long before Rhoads's letter to Congressman Goodwin, the commissioner was clearly out of touch with one of the most serious problems facing Indian welfare. Reliance on the private sector to deal with issues of deep social impact had led to an abandonment of official responsibility. Had the problem been handled in 1929 under Rhoads's leadership, the growth and spread of misrepresentation might have been inhibited, if not fully halted, before it began to take the serious economic and cultural toll which individual Indian artists subsequently experienced.

Pressure from members of Congress whose constituents were complaining seemed to be the only stimulus to which Rhoads responded. When Senator Sam Gilbert Bratton, Democrat from New Mexico, told Rhoads that a well-informed constituent had complained in writing about the sale in the national parks and national monument areas of imitation Indian products in preference to the genuine article, Rhoads adroitly sidestepped the issue at first by pointing to the existence of the new traders' association in the Southwest and the work of the Federal Trade Commission in reducing the sale of imitation Indian goods. This time, though, Rhoads said he would ask the National Park Service if it could control the sale of imitation goods by its concessionaires. Rhoads did exactly that and no more. The reply from the acting director of the National Park Service was a further indictment of government inactivity. The National Park Service told Rhoads that the question of the sale of imitation Indian handcrafts had been "before this Service for some time and we have no doubt but what the Secretary [Wilbur] has authority to control this matter." It asked that Senator Bratton obtain the names of the companies and the national parks involved so that a definite recommendation could be made to the secretary. As far as the Wilbur-Rhoads administration was concerned, the matter was ended. Nothing more was done until almost a year later when the United Indian Traders Association and the Indian superintendents formed their own committee to investigate the sale of imitation Indian arts and crafts in the national parks.[26]

Without Indian Office instigation or support, the Federal Trade Commission was attempting to help the Indian artists. In May 1932 it had instituted proceedings in the United States Court of Appeals for the Tenth Circuit against the privately owned Maisel Trading Post Company of Albuquerque, New Mexico. Acting in the public interest, the Federal Trade Commission charged that Maisel had been and was continuing to use "unfair methods of competition in interstate commerce," in violation of the provisions of section 5 of the Federal Trade Commission Act of 1914.[27] Specifically, the complaint charged that the Maisel Company sold and distributed "Indian" jewelry produced by Indian workers "by means of modern equipment and machinery, including rollers, modern dies, punching machines, acetylene torches, and lathes and stamping machinery." Maisel's Indian laborers were supervised by whites, and the complaint charged that the products of the Indians' labor were not those of handcraft or artistry. Rather, their products were machine-made at lower cost and with less beauty than the actual Indian hand-made products. These same products, the Federal Trade Commission had ascertained, were uniform within their respective types instead of being individual articles differing from any similar articles produced. Maisel had represented these products as "Indian-made" and as "made by the Navajos." In certain of its advertisements, Maisel had suggested that its products were made by Indians through the time-consuming, basic methods of hand production.[28]

53

The government complaint concluded that the Maisel Company had misled and deceived the public, and had diverted, and was continuing to divert, trade from its competitors and otherwise injuring them. These actions operated as a restraint upon and a "detriment to the fair and legitimate competition afforded by handmade Indian jewelry in interstate trade." Under these circumstances, the Federal Trade Commission charged the Maisel Trading Post Company with false, misleading, and deceptive acts, practices, and methods considered to be unlawful and to constitute unfair methods of competition under federal law. [29]

In response to the 1932 Federal Trade Commission charges, Maurice M. Maisel, president of the company, at first denied each and every allegation. He maintained that his chief place of business in Albuquerque was a "workshop," not a "factory," where he employed only full-blooded Indians, and that these Indians produced all of the jewelry the company made and sold. The Indians used hand and power machinery to cut out blanks from coin silver furnished to them in sheet form. After the blanks were cut, the pieces were turned over to other Indian workers, who fashioned, cut, stamped, decorated, and ornamented them with "symbols" and designs by means of hand tools, such as hammers, anvils, saws, files, and other instruments, which Maisel charged were in common and everyday use among all Indian silversmiths in the Southwest. Maisel specifically denied that his products were machine-made or that they were uniform within respective types, yet in subsequent personal testimony he admitted that his six-year-old operation was substantially as the federal government had charged, including the use of stamping and die-cutting machines. [30]

The extensive and well-attended hearings held in Gallup, Santa Fe, and Albuquerque in the Maisel case were concluded in November 1932 and the commission's findings were announced on 21 August 1933. The hearings had shown that machinery was not in general use by Indian silversmiths in the Southwest except where a very few Indians, under the stress of competition from producers of jewelry largely made by machinery such as Maisel's, had resorted to machine rollers to replace hand-hammering. Maisel was found to employ as many as sixty Indians who were supervised by a white overseer. The officers and the sales force of the firm were white people. More than eight different machines were used by the company to make silver jewelry. The hearings found that the production costs of Maisel's products were far less than that of Indian handmade jewelry made in like designs and weights of material.[31] In short, Maisel had seen the gradual increase in public demand for Indian handmade jewelry and had attempted to capitalize on this demand by deceptively applying modern technology to an old arts and crafts process.

The Federal Trade Commission recognized that the Indians had valuable goodwill in the terms *Indian* or *Indian-made* as generally coupled with the word *jewelry* or other terms descriptive of Indian arts and crafts articles when those words were applied to products hand-fashioned exclusively by hand tools and processes. This goodwill was greatly enhanced by a widespread and still growing sentiment in favor of the Indians and their arts and crafts products. The commission further ruled that the desire to purchase and to retain an article of Indian jewelry was almost entirely destroyed if the ultimate buyer believed or learned that the Indian maker of the article employed machinery in the rolling or fashioning of the silver as a partial or entire substitute for hand hammering and hand ornamentation.[32]

Along with the damage to public goodwill, the commission determined that Maisel's method had contributed to an increased depression in the Indian jewelry market beyond the effects of the general economic depression. Lower manufacturing costs and misleading trade terms allowed Maisel to undersell his competitors who made and marketed exclusively handmade jewelry and tended to eliminate the true, handmade product from trade outlets to the detriment of the manufacturers and traders of that product. In this manner, Maisel indirectly had brought great hardship to Indian silversmiths throughout the Southwest. Testimony had developed that one-tenth, or approximately 4,500 Indians, of the large Navajo tribe were dependent for their livelihood on the silver jewelry craft. Among the other tribes affected in a like manner, the smaller Zuni tribe had one-fifth of its people dependent on this craft. By 1933, the commission found, great numbers of Indian silversmiths who employed exclusively hand methods of production could not dispose of the products of their skill.[33]

Alternative terminology was available to Maisel and was currently in use by his competing manufacturers. The commission was careful to point out that Maisel's competitors, who manufactured and sold jewelry made in the styles of Indian handmade jewelry and who designated their products as *Indian design* jewelry, also were injured by Maisel's use of the specified trade terms. By the use of the term *Indian design*, the commission suggested, Maisel's competitors at least were giving some notice that their products were not made necessarily exclusively by hand tools and processes.[34]

The Maisel Trading Post Company was ordered to cease and to desist from using the terms *Indian* or *Indian-made* unless it clearly specified that the products were the result of machine processing except in the situation where the machines used were buffing wheels for the polishing of fully hand-fashioned pieces of jewelry.[35]

"With the Maisel decision as a precedent, we intend to cleanse the market of the imitators and chislers of Indian craft," the new secretary of the interior, Harold Ickes, told Berton Staples, now president of the United Indian Traders Association. Ickes promised prosecution of every case in which Indian handmade craft products were receiving unfair competition through the use of machines and unfair advertising practices or methods. "We will not tolerate any misrepresentation which will injure our Indian craftsmen," Ickes warned.[36]

The Maisel Trading Post Company was not intimidated, either by Secretary Ickes or by the Federal Trade Commission. Thus, Maisel refused to comply with the terms of the order, and, in accordance with the appropriate statutory provision, the commission applied to the United States Court of Appeals for the Tenth Circuit for a decree enforcing its order. The court of appeals rendered an opinion on 1 May 1935. The court affirmed the order of the commission with certain modifications. The commission disagreed with these modifications and filed for a rehearing and modification of the court's order. A rehearing was granted and on 28 August 1935 the court modified in certain aspects its previous order. The second order directed Maisel to desist from describing its jewelry as *Indian* or *Indian-made* when machinery other than hand tools, non-mechanical equipment, or buffing wheels was substituted for hand hammering, shaping, or ornamenting unless the label, stamp, catalogue, or advertising clearly stated the method of manufacture in immediate context with the descriptive terms. On 30 September and 1 November, Maurice Maisel reported to the commission on the steps he had taken to comply with the order of the court. The commission rejected Maisel's reports and requested that he take additional steps to comply with the court's order. A supplemental report was submitted by Maisel in November 1935 which also was rejected by the commission. Then, on 6 December Maisel informed the commission that the company would not meet the requirements which the commission sought to impose. Basically, the commission wanted Maisel to use language that the public could understand and contended that the phrase "press cut and domed blanks" used by Maisel was an inadequate indication to the public that a machine press was used.[37]

Finally, on 14 January 1936, the Federal Trade Commission filed in the United States Court of Appeals for the Tenth Circuit a motion for an interpretation of the final order of the court. A hearing was held on 13 April, and on 21 July the court of appeals handed down an opinion denying the interpretation of its first order which the commission had sought and holding that the steps taken by Maisel were sufficient to meet the requirements imposed by the court's order. The commission's request to the Attorney General's Office that the case be reviewed by the United States Supreme Court came to naught when Hugh B. Cox, special assistant to the attorney general, determined that the case presented no procedural question calling for review by the highest court.[38]

The commissioners of Indian affairs, 1929–33. *Left*, Charles J. Rhoads, commissioner, and *right*, J. Henry Scattergood, assistant commissioner, both of whom came under bitter attack by reformers for their failure to act decisively in the Indians' behalf. (National Archives)

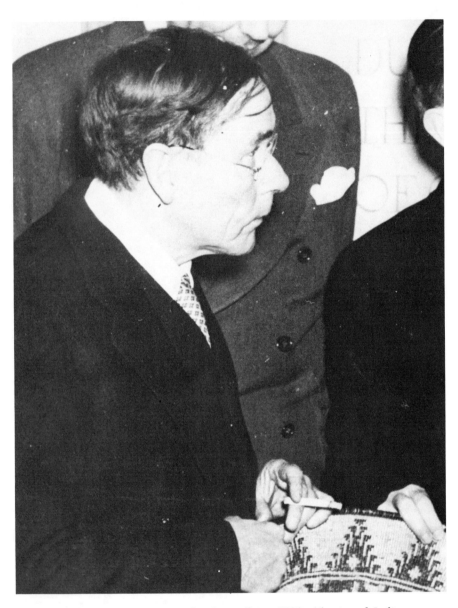

John Collier, commissioner of Indian affairs, 1933–45, viewed Indian arts and crafts as a basic element in his long struggle for Indian cultural survival. He is shown here in 1940 accepting Indian baskets donated to the Department of the Interior museum. (National Archives)

René d'Harnoncourt, general manager of the Indian Arts and Crafts Board, 1936–44, planned individualized tribal arts and crafts programs to fit local needs and often traveled to the area concerned personally assessing the situation. He is shown here in Navajo country in 1938. (Museum of Modern Art)

Indian Exhibition Building at the San Francisco Golden Gate International Exposition, 1939. This is a view of the northwest corner of the court with the Totem Pole Tower in the back. (National Archives)

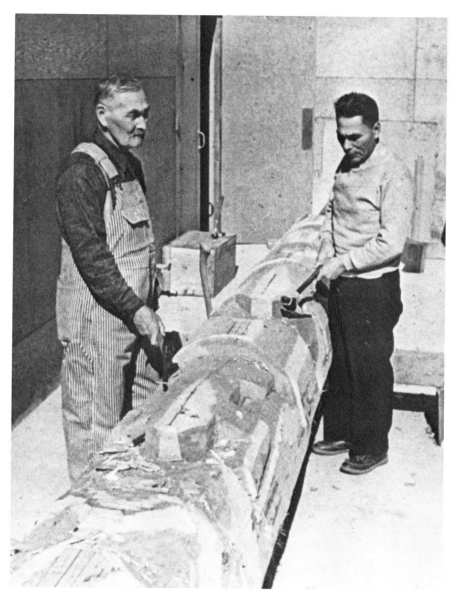

John Wallace and his son are working on one of the totem poles that were erected in the courtyard during the exposition. The Wallaces are Haidas from Hydaburg, Alaska. (National Archives)

View from the entrance to the Indian exhibit. The first displays seen on entering the Gallery of Indian History from the court were the two maps that showed
the areas of Indian cultures in the United States and in Alaska and established
the geographic scope of the San Francisco exhibit. (National Archives)

San Francisco Exposition posters. Indian-designed posters produced by the
Federal Arts Project emphasized the variety of cultures in Indian America and
were distributed across the country. (National Archives)

The totem pole display was an awesome sight seen from the Gallery of the Fishermen of the Northwest Coast. (National Archives)

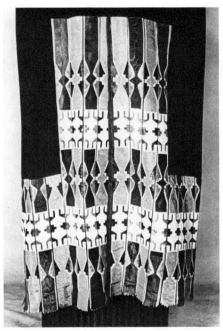

Above, left: parfleche. To transport their food and clothing, the Plains Indians folded rawhide into large envelopes. The artists usually painted the pouches with geometric designs. (National Archives) Above, right: ribbonwork cape. A fine example of modern Osage work showing the type of design that developed out of the earlier porcupine quill embroidery. (National Archives) Left: a Haida interior house post, about fifteen feet tall, loaned to the exhibition by John Wallace, shows the totems of the Frog and Bear Clans. (National Archives)

Tepee and mural. Calvin Larvie, a young Sioux artist, combined cutout figures wearing authentic headdresses and saddlebags in the foreground with painted figures in the background. His mural represents the traditional Plains style of conventionalization. (National Archives)

Demonstrator at the exposition. Mrs. Berrychild of the Blackfoot tribe is showing the technique of buckskin work and bead decoration. (National Archives)

Vincente Mirabel, from Taos Pueblo, working on one of his watercolors later to be added to the Gallery of Temporary Exhibits' display of work completed during the time of the exposition. (National Archives)

Charles Loloma, Hopi, *left*, at work on his Kachina mural. Two other Pueblo artists, Ignacio Moquino and Joseph Duran, provide assistance. (National Archives)

Spring: Hopi Kachina Dance mural by Charles Loloma shows the Pueblos'
centuries-old skill in their native forms of representation. Although willing to
adapt to the paints and other art equipment of non-Indians, the Pueblos show
little outside influence in their idea of design. (National Archives)

Summer: the Santo Domingo Corn Dance by Joseph Duran and Ignacio
Moquino. Pueblo dances were not performed at random, but followed a definite schedule which was keyed to the rotation of the seasons. A late summer
harvest dance is shown here. (National Archives)

Fall: the Tsia Crow Dance by Ignacio Moquino. The dancers imitate crows raiding the cornfields. (National Archives)

Winter: the Tesuque Deer Dance by Joseph Duran. In their winter dances, the Pueblos impersonate animals with the idea of magically influencing the game to come within reach of the hunters. (National Archives)

Mabel Burnside shows the carding of wool. Demonstrators of the processes in Navajo blanket making performed on platforms installed in the Gallery of the Navajo Weavers. (National Archives)

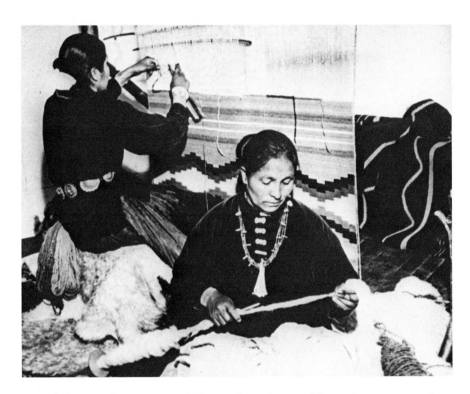

Mabel Burnside weaving and Zonnie Lee spinning. The various raw materials used by these Navajo artists in blanket weaving were on display in this gallery. (National Archives)

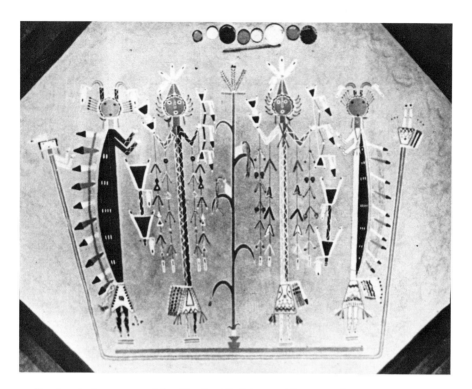

Sand painting executed by Hastine Todokozie, Navajo. This is a completed painting; above are the baskets containing different colored sands and the stick used to smooth the sand. Four goddesses and a rainbow are represented. (National Archives)

4

NEW DEAL, NEW EFFORT

JOHN COLLIER'S APPOINTMENT on 21 April 1933 as commissioner of Indian affairs in the new Franklin D. Roosevelt administration brought a zestful sense of urgency, a need to struggle and act before it was too late. In a press release announcing the appointment, Secretary of the Interior Harold Ickes assured the public that Collier would safeguard the property rights of the Indians, help them to help themselves toward a fuller and happier life, respect their customs, encourage them in their arts, and assist them to maintain their rich and unique culture. In addition, Ickes promised that Collier would try to interpret the Indians sympathetically to their non-Indian fellow Americans. Ickes then presaged what Collier and the Indian Office hoped to accomplish in Indian arts and crafts when he pointed out that "our American Indians possess possibilities in which white people may share, if those possibilities are realized and cultivated."[1]

In his new position as commissioner, Collier pledged at his swearing-in ceremony that he would "try to be useful to them [the Indians]." The responsibility of the United States as guardian of the Indians ought to be continued. Within this continuing guardianship, he considered the establishment of a framework of Indian rights and responsibilities, including Indian self-help, to be entirely possible by means of administrative reorganization and new legislation. He saw the realization of constitutional guarantees with all they implied becoming a reality for the Indians without any curtailment of the federal responsibility for Indian welfare. "Indirect administration," which previously had succeeded with the Cherokees and with the Pueblos and currently was succeeding among dependent peoples as widely distributed as Asia, Africa, Canada, and Mexico, Collier asserted, could be made effective in the government's

Indian work. Collier saw his role as supportive rather than dominative. "The race to be run is their race," he proclaimed.[2]

Appropriations for the Indian Office had reached record levels during the Hoover administration. While Commissioners Rhoads and Scattergood repeatedly pleaded a lack of funds, their appropriation for fiscal year 1931 was $21,984,868 and for fiscal year 1932 was a new high of $27,030,047. This figure fell dramatically to $22,140,098 for fiscal 1933, but it was still the second highest in Indian Office history. During the 1932 election campaign, both political parties had called for sharp reductions in government expenditures. A "general economy movement" was initiated in 1933, which once more cut the Indian Office appropriation, this time over three million dollars, to a total of $18,966,546 for fiscal 1934.[3] Collier had his work cut out for him, yet unlike Rhoads and Scattergood, he did not have to work under a restrictive philosophy which basically called for the decentralization of government to permit the free expansion of private enterprise and the eventual elimination of the Indian Office. Roosevelt's avowed program of economic nationalism and social reconstruction comported with Collier's personal concept of the function of the Indian Office.

Still, the task was not to be easy. The prevailing economic conditions among the bulk of the Indian population remained unfavorable during 1933. In common with current direction throughout the country, Indian relief had increased manyfold during the past few years. Generally unfavorable economic conditions in the farming and livestock industries, from which most of the Indians' normal income was directly or indirectly derived, and the difficulty, if not impossibility, of securing outside employment had seriously disadvantaged the Indians. In the vicinity of the reservations, work for able-bodied and willing Indians was not to be had. The market for Indian arts and crafts had dwindled and the traders were overstocked with handcraft articles. As a result, traders greatly curtailed the volume of credit to the Indians.[4]

The new administration took immediate steps to combat these conditions. One such step, publicizing Indian arts and crafts at the Century of Progress Exposition in Chicago, held high promise in the beginning yet ended in disappointment. Despite the world-wide depression, the city of Chicago wished to show the world just how greatly it had prospered and advanced, and to this end it determined on a world's fair.

Before Collier was confirmed as commissioner, Secretary Ickes had telephoned Rufus Dawes, president of the Century of Progress, to explain that the Department of the Interior wanted to conduct a large Indian exhibit during the course of the fair in 1933 and 1934. On the day that Collier was confirmed as commissioner, Ickes contacted John D. Rockefeller, Jr., in the hope of obtaining the release of Jesse Nusbaum from the Laboratory of Anthropology for the period of the exposition and also in the hope of obtaining "a little under-writing." The scope of Ickes's hopes could be measured by his assurances to Charles Elkus that the government would put on an Indian exhibition that would meet even his aesthetic tastes.[5]

The Chicago World's Fair authorities had different ideas about progress than those of the new administration, and a "regular knock-down-drag-out" battle occurred, according to Collier, when the fair authorities granted a monopolistic commercial concession to an experienced carnival exploiter of Indians. Faced with a choice between cooperating with this promoter in the establishment of an Indian village with an accompanying Indian trading post or withdrawing his participation, Ickes chose the latter. Ickes's decision was more than just aesthetically and culturally correct, for the fair's American Indian village exhibit was a fiasco.[6] The Interior Department confined its efforts to a small exhibit of contemporary Indian art set up on the ground floor of the Federal Building by the supervisor of home economics of the Indian Office.

Another small Indian art exhibit was held successfully in Collier's hometown, Atlanta, Georgia, in October 1934. Like the Chicago display, the government's effort was designed to increase sales for the Indians and also to educate the public concerning Indian arts and crafts. In addition, a permanent exhibition of Indian art became possible at the Indian Office because Amelia White donated many arts and crafts articles from recent expositions in Paris and Seville. At this same time, the departmental employees' Welfare and Recreation Association in the Department of Commerce obtained Ickes's approval to open an exhibit and salesroom for Indian arts and crafts.[7]

A government Indian arts and crafts effort was made under the Public Works of Art Project, which had been initiated on 8 December 1933 through a grant from the Civil Works Administration to the Treasury Department. Under the grant regional committees were established to give unemployed artists work decorating public buildings and making a record of the American scene. The project employed forty-five Indian painters and craftsmen from the Albuquerque and Santa Fe Indian schools to paint wall murals and to make rugs, pottery, and other objects for new Indian schools, hospitals, and community centers, which were being constructed across the country under a separate Public Works Administration program. Under this project for example, Munroe Tsa-to-ke and several other Indian artists worked in Oklahoma City at the Historical Society Building while Acee Blue Eagle was at work on murals at the Edmund State Teachers College and Stephen Mopope and James Auchiah painted murals at the Tahlequah State Teachers College.[8]

With the cooperation of both Jesse Nusbaum, serving as regional director of the Indian branch of the Public Works of Art Project in the New Mexico and Arizona area, and Chester Faris, superintendent of the Santa Fe Indian School, Santa Fe became the art center of the government's emerging Indian employment enterprise. This situation was good in its limited way, although many Indian artists were kept out of the program because they could not leave their homes and because most Indian artists were not dependent solely on their artwork for subsistence and, therefore, were not eligible for employment under the project.[9]

The Public Works of Art Project had been able to employ only a very small percentage of available Indian artists. When this limited effort was terminated at the end of March 1934, Nina Perera Collier, the energetic wife of Commissioner Collier's son Charles, who had served as the liaison officer between the Indian Office and the Public Works of Art Project, devised a plan specifically to provide relief employment for greater numbers of Indian artists. In a memorandum for Harry L. Hopkins, director of the Federal Emergency Relief Administration, Nina Collier proposed an extended Public Works of Art Project to employ a qualified group of Indian artists. Their job would be to produce rugs, baskets, watercolor paintings, murals, pottery and tiles, carved doors, curtains, carved furniture and balustrades, and other decorative features for the approximately two hundred public schools, community centers, auditoriums, and hospitals being constructed by the Indian Office. The plan also would include the preservation and restoration of monuments important in tribal history and the gathering of photographic, aural, and manuscript records for permanent preservation. Nina Collier planned to develop this project in cooperation and conjunction with the Indian Office. A separate director, assistant director, and necessary staff would handle the project. To facilitate their efforts, Nina Collier compiled a seventy-page directory of Indian artists obtained from superintendents, Indian traders, and other informed persons in direct contact with the Indians. Commissioner Collier gave his full support to his daughter-in-law's efforts. Hopkins, on the other hand, failed to respond to the memorandum, and the matter was ignored until March 1936 when Nina Collier once more attempted to establish a federal Indian art project.[10]

Now employed by the Federal Emergency Relief Administration division on relief of unemployed professionals, Nina Collier suggested a meeting on 7 March at the Indian Office between Indian Office representatives, Holger Cahill, director of the Federal Art Project which was initiated formally with his appointment on 1 August 1935, and herself to discuss how the Indian Office might cooperate with the Federal Art Project in developing purely Indian arts and crafts projects. No definite conclusions were reached other than the unanimous agreement that such cooperation was highly desirable, but at the request of the conference Nina Collier drew up a plan for an Indian project. Her program was extensive and included stress on mural painting, easel painting, furniture making, silverwork, leatherwork, illustration graphics, compilation of an index of Indian design, education of children and apprentices in Indian arts and crafts, and the establishment of strategic craft units to develop and to teach techniques.[11]

Collier submitted her plan to Secretary Ickes, who outlined the proposal in a letter to Hopkins, now director of the Works Progress Administration and responsible for examining the various projects proposed by federal agencies, coordinating their execution, and inspecting their progress. Ickes stressed that since the Federal Art Project had the complete machinery to deal with field work in art matters, it had the most convenient setup to handle an Indian art program. Although he professed great intrest in the project, Hopkins would not commit Works Progress Administration funds until its appropriation cleared Congress.[12] No further steps were taken, for the difficulty over funding blocked the establishment of a separate federal Indian art project similar in structure to the Indian branch of the Civilian Conservation Corps. Never having a separate organization, a small number of Indians applied for and received employment under the Federal Art Project during the depression years.

Unsure whether federal legislation to protect and to promote Indian arts and crafts would ever become a reality, the Collier administraton, often through the seemingly Herculean individual efforts of Nina Collier, continued to search for a successful approach to the very real Indian arts and crafts problem. While in New York City in June 1934, Nina Collier had begun one of her efforts by contacting an old friend, Ralph Straus, vice-president of the R. H. Macy and Company department store. She suggested to Straus that Macy's put on a fall exhibition and sale of good, modern, Southwest Indian products complete with a promotional campaign. Straus was interested and after consultation with the manager of the home furnishings department decided to go ahead with the plan. All goods were to be on consignment, and Macy's agreed to take care of the advertising and to provide adequate display areas. The store's markup would be as much as 100 percent. Armed with a written agreement, Nina Collier considered herself authorized to make arrangements for such a sale. Her first step was to contact James Young to be sure that her plans met with his approval.[13]

Young considered Nina Collier's plan for a large Indian arts and crafts sale in New York City to be a "real experiment." He believed the situation would be a test of the popular middle-class market. Nina Collier's role, in his view, was that of a private individual representing several Southwest traders. By keeping careful, detailed records of the results, Young hoped to learn something of value about large-scale marketing. With an estimated $40,000 worth of merchandise, the Macy venture was to be the largest public marketing effort to date.[14]

No one disputed the nature of the experiment as it was set forth or the Indian artists' need which the Macy sale was intended to serve. Nina Collier described one of the difficulties of the current Indian arts and crafts marketing situation to be the hit-or-miss merchandising methods employed. Sales outlets often indiscriminately mingled fine products with tourist souvenir articles and made little attempt to select and to grade merchandise carefully. Instead of being offered as household furnishing objects which could fit into the non-Indian home, either modern or early American in character, Indian products were sold in the curio and department stores as mementos with no thought given to their decorative or utilitarian value.

The Macy sale would be the result of careful selecting and grading of Navajo and Hopi rugs, Hopi and Pueblo pottery, and a small amount of Navajo silver jewelry. Two sales were planned, a smaller one for December stressing an assortment of objects suitable for gifts, and a larger one in the spring emphasizing the home-furnishing aspect. Nina Collier's plan called for the deliberate grouping of rugs into various price ranges and clearly describing for the buyers the nature of the product: a vegetable-dyed rug, a natural-colored wool product, or a so-called modern Navajo rug. The prices were to be based on a combination of the weight of the wool, the size of the rug, the quality of the weaving, and the excellence of the color and design. This experiment was highly important, Nina Collier stressed, because in its first stage it would show whether development of the product to meet the demand could take place. Finally, with her typical directness and candor, she explained that the Indian traders who would supply Macy's had agreed to turn over 10 percent of the amounts paid to them to the American Indian Defense Association "to be used to further and promote additional experimentation in the marketing of Indian arts and crafts," according to a program to be drawn up in the near future. Commissioner Collier told Charles Elkus that if the Macy experiment worked out, the plan would grow considerably to "the benefit of the Indian arts and crafts situation and to the Association as well." Collier discussed the plan fully with Charles Fahy, the assistant solicitor of the Interior Department, and Fahy considered the plan wholly desirable so long as the fund was kept separate and not used for political purposes. [16]

Had the Macy effort kept the purely altruistic image it originally displayed, no problems would have developed. But the announcement that money would be paid to Collier's old employer, the American Indian Defense Association, was enough for those who opposed Collier's policies to stir up trouble. The first attack on the Macy plan came in February 1935 when Jacob C. Morgan, a Navajo and a member of the anti-Collier American Indian Federation, told a House subcommittee investigating Indian conditions and affairs that Collier's family was engaged in trading with the Indians. Collier easily disposed of this facile accusation by asserting that his daughter-in-law was currently employed by the Federal Emergency Relief Administration and had acted as an intermediary and a volunteer without compensation and with full coverage by formal Interior Department releases. Collier noted, moreover, that anybody could buy anything from the Navajos or any other Indians that the Indians wanted to sell, and he read into the record a telegram from Thomas H. Dodge, chairman of the Navajo Tribal Council, which repudiated Morgan and described him as a "tool and associate of unscrupulous white parasites and [a] small group of non-Navajo Indian victims of such parasites."[17]

Morgan had suspicions about the relationship between the leadership of the American Indian Defense Association and the traders. Earlier in the House hearings he had charged that Collier and Ickes had been instrumental in establishing the United Indian Traders Association and that Ickes as an attorney specifically had helped to draw up the bylaws of that association. Morgan's view was hardly new and was not disputed by Collier. Morgan attempted to show that the alleged close link between Collier and Ickes and the traders' association was stronger than ever. He quoted a 6 January 1935 article in a Gallup, New Mexico, newspaper which reported that William Zeh, a white Indian Office employee acting as temporary head of the reorganized Navajo Reservation administration, had told a United States Traders Association meeting that the traders' past efforts had only scratched the surface. "The part we expect traders can play offers opportunities for increased personal gain as well as greater service to the Government and Indians," Zeh had assured the group in response to trader opposition to the liberal credit and cooperative trade features for Indians established in the Indian Reorganization Act (1934). After a roundabout attack on the business methods practiced by Indian traders, Morgan continued his testimony by pointing to Nina Collier's article on the Macy sale in *Indians at Work*, the official New Deal Indian Office newsletter. He asked the House subcommittee to look into this situation where the Navajos were getting such small pay for their products yet Macy's could afford to pay a 10 percent commission to the American Indian Defense Association. Morgan incorrectly referred to Macy's as the source of the commissions in question rather than to the traders whom Nina Collier had identified in her article.[18]

Joseph Bruner, a Creek from Sapulpa, Oklahoma, successful businessman, assimilationist, and president of the American Indian Federation, picked up on Morgan's statements six weeks later at the same subcommittee hearings. He singled out Collier's own statement that Navajo rugs brought the Indians a top figure in 1929 of $1,200,000 and charged that even at the currently low return of $300,000 the annual income for the Indian Defense Association easily would be around $10,000 "for no indicated service whatever." These charges were totally in character with other statements made by Bruner to the House subcommittee such as charging that Collier was "wholly unfit by temperament and honest principles" to be the commissioner of Indian affairs.[19]

Congressman Usher L. Burdick, Republican from North Dakota, was present as a member of the House subcommittee when Morgan asked for an investigation of the Macy sale, and Burdick took it upon himself to make a report on the affair. An advance copy was sent to Collier to review. In it Burdick determined that the commissioner should not be criticized for this enterprise although suspicious circumstances existed which "perhaps the Commissioner should have avoided." Burdick pointed out that the traders were licensed to do business through the recommendations of the Indian Office, that Collier was for many years executive secretary of the American Indian Defense Association and, no doubt, was interested in seeing his own work carried forward, that his own relative was the contact person, and that the American Indian Defense Association would make money on the transactions. Burdick's personal feeling was that the effort to build markets for the Indians where they could sell their goods and receive the greatest possible price was a worthy object. He concluded that the plan, in the commissioner's mind, may have been conceived as eventually leading to direct marketing by the Indians or serving to increase the prices which the traders currently paid to the Indians.[20]

Collier vigorously dissented from Burdick's report and told Assistant Commissioner William Zimmerman, Jr., that the statement could not be left unchallenged. Collier believed that the "suspicious circumstances" were nonexistent because all of the facts were made public and his daughter-in-law had given voluntary service only. He also asserted that all contracts to sell Indian goods helped the Indians and the 10 percent commission to the American Indian Defense Association was segregated for use solely in Indian arts and crafts promotion. Collier again stated what he was sure had been made fully clear to the subcommittee, namely, that the Indian arts and crafts situation was troubled by two conditions: first, that existing merchandising outlets placed little, if any, premium on the better work as compared to the poorer work so that the standards constantly were being dragged down instead of being elevated; and, second, the total market was negligible as a result of a lack of organized outlets in the metropolitan centers and the lack of advertising facilities. Both of these conditions could be met now, Collier concluded, through the application of modern merchandising techniques and capital without having to wait for the time when the Navajo artists become organized into guilds or cooperatives to market their own goods. In short, Indian arts and crafts were obtainable in quantity nowhere else except from the traders unless the Macy Company or somebody else went out and organized the Indians into cooperative groups to merchandise their own crafts. Collier also stressed that Morgan, Bruner, and Alice Lee Jemison, Bruner's assistant, had exploited the Macy topic through innuendo and now Burdick's proposed statement would do the same thing although in a less extreme fashion. Despite its qualifying phrases, Collier declared Burdick's proposed statement to be "invidious."[21]

Collier did not respond directly to Congressman Burdick. Instead, Assistant Commissioner Zimmerman returned Burdick's statement with a somewhat watered-down summary of Collier's memorandum. Zimmerman tactfully suggested to Burdick that, before making his report public, he should consider the use that inevitably would be made of it by those whose interests were purely partisan.[22] Burdick quietly took this advice and withheld his report.

The Macy sale, in the meantime, had been sufficiently successful to warrant the continuation of an Indian department in the New York store as a "permanent institution." Nina Collier considered the experiment to be proof that the sale of the finer Indian products could be based on sound business principles and be a successful business venture. She predicted that the time might come when the Indians would use a cooperative marketing system to conduct their own marketing operations.[23]

Three days after receiving an independent report of a committee of traders and superintendents investigating the national parks' sale of imitation Indian arts and crafts, Secretary Ickes notified Collier that he had issued an order that after 1 July 1933 no Indian arts and crafts were to be sold in any of the national parks unless they were authentic Indian products, and, in the ten-day interval, no imitations were to be sold unless they were so represented.[24]

Not until May 1935 was Ickes's national parks ruling specifically challenged. A representative of the Southwest Arts and Crafts Company, owned and operated by Julius Gans of Santa Fe, came to Washington seeking permission from Secretary Ickes to sell its products in the national parks. Collier quickly telegrammed the principal of the government Indian school in Santa Fe and Oliver LaFarge, currently in Santa Fe, to investigate immediately for Secretary Ickes. At the same time, Ickes also had his investigations department dispatch a special agent to investigate the Southwest Arts and Crafts Company. Their reports were completed and on Ickes's desk within three days. On the basis of these reports, Ickes promptly banned the Southwest Company from the national parks' concessions.[25]

H. Reed Newport, the Southwest Company representative, complained to the Indian Office that he was unable to get any information as to what were the actual standards of genuineness his company had to meet. Newport charged that if Secretary Ickes's action stating that Southwest's products were not genuinely Indian handmade was made public, the company would be forced out of the silver business. Three days later, Congressman John Joseph Dempsey, Democrat from New Mexico, asked Ickes to suggest changes Southwest might make in its "manufacturing" in order to comply with his requirements. Ickes had to explain that as yet no standards or requirements had been formulated.[26]

Despite this lack of standards of genuineness, the acting director of the National Park Service issued a final ban on the Southwest Company's jewelry in a memorandum to all park superintendents on 4 June 1935. Four days later, Ickes required that all concessionaires in all national parks and monuments state in writing whether they handled Indian-made silverware, and, if so, from whom they bought their supplies. Ickes directed their attention once more to the fact that they were not to sell anything except genuine handmade silverware bought from accredited dealers. All national park superintendents and custodians were required to acknowledge in writing the receipt of the memorandum banning the products of the Southwest Company.[27]

A special agent's report on 22 June 1935 indicted the Bell Trading Post, owned and operated by John Michaelson of Albuquerque, for the use of sheet silver and for not labeling or advertising the product as such. This use of the lighter and thinner sheet silver (instead of slug silver that required more working) was also the major issue in the banning of the Southwest Company, so the possible question of favoritism apparently was not a factor in Ickes's rulings and never became an issue. When confronted over his national parks stand, Ickes carefully referred the questioner to the Federal Trade Commission's Maisel case.[28]

After the second decision by the court of appeals in the Maisel case, Julius Gans protested to Collier that his company was well within that decision; namely, Southwest did not use any machinery except for buffing, which had been excepted in the decision. Gans now claimed that although his company used sheet silver, it acknowledged that in its advertising. Gans expressed his belief that the government should listen both to the United Indian Traders Association and to those Indians and producers using sheet silver. Gans called for public hearings on the definition of genuine Indian handmade silver so that Indians and dealers could state their views and the government could serve the majority, not a minority.[29]

When Gans continued to protest through lawyer friends in Santa Fe, Assistant Secretary of the Interior Charles West flatly replied that since no official standards had been set up as to what constituted genuine Indian silverware, the Interior Department had accepted the standards of the United Indian Traders Association in determining the character of Indian jewelry which could be sold in the national parks and monuments. West promised that when the products of the Southwest Company conformed to the standards of the traders' association, the Interior Department would authorize their sale. Gans again contacted Senator Dempsey, who in turn got in touch with Collier. Aware that the traders' association had not formulated any silver standards, and apparently tired of having to be part of a seemingly endless controversy over something that as yet had not been established, Collier abruptly informed Senator Dempsey that "the action affecting the Gans output, as related to National Park sales, had not been cleared through the Indian Office and was not within our jurisdiction."[30]

Action on the application to Indian hand industry of Code 175, "Medium and Low-Priced Jewelry," under the National Recovery Administration Codes of Fair Competition also awaited the establishment of standards. The jewelry codes had been established in 1933 upon a petition by the Council of Jewelry and Allied Industries and the advice of the Labor Advisory Board. These regulating codes were permitted under the National Industrial Recovery Act (1933), which attempted to revive industrial and business activity. Code 175 regulated the maximum number of hours workers were permitted to work each week and the minimum wage they were to be paid. Based on the principle of industrial self-regulation operating under government supervision, the codes legalized the fair trade codes many industrial and trade associations had used after World War I. Now, associations set up their codes, the President approved them, and the law upheld them. Anti-trust laws did not apply to actions under the codes, and the President could prescribe codes for industries and make agreements with the individual associations.[31]

Under pressure from the United Indian Traders Association, a conference was held on 26 April 1935 between Indian Office personnel, National Recovery Administration officials, and other interested persons including Nina Collier, Berton Staples, Thomas Dodge, and Margaret McKittrick Burge, a field representative for the New Mexico Association on Indian Affairs.[32] Manufacturers, however, did not attend. Three questions were considered at this meeting. First, should the Gans-Maisel type of manufacturer of "Indian design" goods be required to comply with Code 175? The conference agreed unanimously to do so. Second, should these same provisions apply to Indian traders on the reservations? The consensus was that the Indian traders were not conducting their businesses in such a way as to be affected by the codes. In short, they were not manufacturers paying wages. Third, the conference addressed the question of whether any attempt should be made at this time to work out a special code for Indian arts and crafts. Unanimously, the group concluded that in view of the extreme difficulty of evolving a code of this kind and the possibility of the passage of an Indian arts and crafts bill which would offer "all in the way of protection that could possibly result from a special code," no attempt should then be made to formulate such a code. If such a bill failed to pass, however, the conference decided something of this nature might be attempted.[33] No further action was needed since on 27 May 1935 the United States Supreme Court declared the National Industrial Recovery Act unconstitutional.

5

THE COMMITTEE ON
INDIAN ARTS AND CRAFTS

THE NEED TO LAUNCH a new effort to promote the distribution of Indian arts and crafts was more imperative than ever. Charles Elkus, the San Francisco attorney, wrote Secretary Ickes on 17 July 1933, less than three months after Collier took office as commissioner, to report that he had talked personally about a renewed effort with James Young, who was now a member of the faculty of the department of commerce at the University of Chicago. While Young had not committed himself to the cause, Elkus believed him to be receptive to heading an effort. Unlike Rhoads's response under similar circumstances, Collier's was almost instantaneous. Upon learning from Ickes about Elkus's letter, Collier immediately took it upon himself to contact Young.[1]

Collier requested that Young "take up the responsibility which you would have been willing to take up three years ago," namely, "making a plan or plans respecting the whole arts and crafts situation, in general all of the things that were aimed at in the arts and crafts marketing corporation bill." Collier offered Young an official position in the Indian Office or the Interior Department "with whatever title that might be best" on a dollar-a-year basis. Such an arrangement, Collier pointed out, would enable Young to meet his travel costs, something that Young previously had contributed on his own. Collier assured him that Ickes, unlike Wilbur, believed in the Indian arts and crafts marketing plan. The urgency of the overall Navajo situation seemed foremost in Collier's mind when he told Young that the deterioration of nearly the whole Navajo range as a result of erosion was appalling. He stressed to Young that one of the ways to meet this situation had to be a rapid diversification of Navajo industry.[2]

Collier repeated this same theme in *Indians at Work* when he stressed the need for the development of crafts and secondary industries for a

90

successful Indian economic policy, which he believed, in turn, would lead to cultural preservation. Economic conditions had become the primary concern in 1933, this worst-of-all depression years, and for the time being seemed to overshadow the cultural aspects involved in preserving Indian arts and crafts. Collier kept his humanitarian perspective, nevertheless, and saw New Deal Indian policy as part of a larger aim in the national effort to assert the "direct well-being of human folk." For Collier, economic success in climbing out of the depression was necessary to achieve this larger aim. In a direct challenge to the American concept of rugged individualism, Collier lashed out at the old policies of "planless individualism," which had brought his country "to the verge of wreckage." His years as a social worker in New York City now found their fullest expression. Planned community living and community development and planned cooperative use of the land and its resources, according to Collier, were for the Indians more absolutely needed than for most of the non-Indian population of the country. Yet he believed that what would be done to meet the distress and genuine crisis of Indian life unquestionably would blaze the way for the larger New Deal experiment and readjustment now being started. For Collier, the New Deal was intended to bring about "a rebirth of the American people—a rebirth in spirit, even more than a rebirth of a more fairly distributed prosperity." The Indian lands and the Indians would become "laboratories and pioneers . . . in this supreme new American adventure now being tried under the leadership of the President."[3]

President Roosevelt echoed Collier's convictions. On 19 April 1935, members of the Navajo Tribal Council Executive Committee met with the President to tell him of their task of "planning the physical and social development of a whole people and of a great region of land, and of executing the plan through much sacrifice, over a term of years." In reply, Roosevelt told the Navajos that their situation was that of the whole country. "Such planning is ahead for all our people," he revealed to the Navajos. Then, despite all of the power and expertise at his command, Roosevelt humbly acknowledged that "you, the Navajos, if you can successfully plan, will mark the way for all of us."[4]

The specter of the extinction of the Indians seemed to drive Collier in his every effort as commissioner. He considered this battle for the ethnic survival of the American Indians to be in its last gloomy stages

91

after centuries of struggle. He thrived on the still glimmering possibility of successful Indian cultural salvation. Idealistic yet still practical, Collier realized that the government could only remove obstacles and extend material aid to the utmost. The rest depended upon the Indians. The view that "no people which must depend on a government to save it can be saved at all" tempered Collier's vision of white responsibility toward the Indians. Almost as if he saw himself as an emancipator, Collier now called upon the Indians in their tribal groupings to "vigorously—clear mindedly and experimentally" attack the problem of their own political, civil, cultural, and industrial organization. "They are now free to attack this problem," Collier proclaimed. Although the official arm would try to help them, he declared, the issue lay with the Indians "first, last, and here and now."[5]

While Collier was brimming with enthusiasm to carry out his plans as commissioner, Young seemed less enthusiastic, probably hesitating to commit himself to what experience had taught him was a personally expensive, time-consuming, and potentially unsuccessful task. The previous year Young had cited financial problems when he had turned down Collier's personal solicitation for funds for the financially faltering American Indian Defense Association. The small government per diem and the troublesome paperwork and delays involved under the dollar-a-year status probably held little attraction for Young. By November 1933, Collier had fathomed Young's problem and had found a solution. He telegrammed Young that the Indian Office could meet an Indian arts and crafts study committee's travel expenses up to one thousand dollars or somewhat more if the need arose.[6] The contrast in style and resourcefulness between Rhoads and Collier as commissioners was beginning to take on a night versus day quality.

Young failed to respond immediately, so Ickes was enlisted to invite Young to serve as "chairman of a consultant group which would deal with the subject of Indian arts and crafts." Ickes asked Young, if he accepted, to send a list of persons who might be asked to serve as members of such a group. This time Young accepted and nominated the following Indian arts and crafts committee: Kenneth Chapman; Thomas Dodge; Oliver LaFarge; Berton Staples; Deschne Clah Chischillige, a former chairman of the Navajo Tribal Council from Shiprock, New Mexico; either Maria Martinez, a celebrated potter from San Ildefonso

Pueblo, or Martin Vigil, a political leader of Tesuque Pueblo; and Leslie Denman, a San Francisco socialite, patron of Indian arts, and member of the Indian Defense Association of Northern California.[7]

In response, Collier questioned the choice of Leslie Denman, who Collier believed was generally not disposed to serve as a member of a committee. From the point of view of an administrator, Collier also told Young that Maria Martinez might be aligned in the current factional fight at San Ildefonso and her appointment might create political problems. He also pointed out the affront that would be created by the appointment of an ex-chairman rather than the present chairman of the Navajo Tribal Council. On the positive side, Collier suggested Charles Elkus, although Collier was not sure Elkus would serve even if asked.[8]

In the end, Secretary Ickes made the final choices for the Committee on Indian Arts and Crafts. His choices provided the careful balance needed for the task at hand. Besides Young, Chapman, Denman, Staples, Dodge, and LaFarge, Ickes added the following: Charles Elkus; Lorenzo Hubbell, Jr., a prominent member of the United Indian Traders Association and long-time friend of the Ickes and Collier families; and at Young's discretion, either Diego Abeita, a craftsman of the Isleta Pueblo, or Martin Vigil, with Ickes's preference for Abeita.[9] Young subsequently acceded to Ickes's preference for Abeita.

When Secretary Ickes publicly announced the Young committee on 11 January 1934, he defined the group's purpose to be "to study and make recommendations concerning the whole problem of Indian arts and crafts, in their relation to the economic and cultural welfare of the American Indian." The members of the committee would serve without pay. After studying the status of Indian arts and crafts among the various tribes, they were to recommend practical procedures for organizing marketing methods, for improving and reviving the arts themselves, and for training the newer generation of Indians in their production.[10]

The eyes of all concerned with the future of Indian arts and crafts now centered on James Young. Mary Austin made her last appeal concerning Indian arts and crafts before her death at sixty-six years of age in August 1934. In a characteristically sincere yet egocentric note to Young, she identified herself as having been associated with Indian arts and crafts for thirty-five years and as "the first person to have dealt with the subject in the United States." Once more she expressed her deep concern "to find the subject of Indian arts and crafts entrusted . . . to people who have no experience and know nothing whatever about it." Austin offered to put her knowledge and experience at Young's disposal and expressed the feeling that she had a right to know what Young's plans were and how he was going to go about them. Clearly, Austin felt left out at this stage. She concluded that "it would relieve my mind greatly to know what you are doing." Young apparently did not wish to stir up trouble for his committee, for he never answered Austin's letter. Instead, he sent a copy of the letter to Collier for Collier's "amusement." Collier had more understanding. In a personally signed editorial in *Indians at Work* published the day after Austin died, Collier paid tribute to her contributions to the Indians' cause. Bitter differences of opinion had not clouded Collier's awareness of the wider scope his efforts and the similar work of others were serving.[11]

Another concerned person was Allan G. Harper, who had left his position as secretary of the Pennsylvania Civil Liberties Committee in 1933 to take Collier's place as executive secretary of the American Indian Defense Association. He, like Collier, saw his task to be that of monitoring every move at the Indian Office. Two weeks after the official announcement of the Young committee, Harper wrote Collier that it seemed that Young was dragging his feet. Harper encouraged Collier to push Young to move more rapidly so that the committee's report would be available during the current congressional session. The Indian Defense Association listed the promotion and protection of Indian arts and crafts as one of twelve legislative items considered to be the very minimum that the Indian Defense Association must "guarantee."[12]

Collier diplomatically asked Young whether the Indian Arts and Crafts Marketing Corporation bill should be presented at the current session of Congress. In answer Young expressed his belief that such a course would be a mistake before his committee had had a chance to reconsider the bill. Acknowledging Collier's anxiety over getting something going, Young explained that the delay in appointing the committee had created a difficulty which he yet had not been able to solve. He told Collier that he personally was tied down in Chicago, although he was hoping to organize his affairs so that he could get away for about a week. Finally, Young scheduled a meeting of the Committee on Indian Arts and Crafts for 15 March 1934 at the Museum of Anthropology in Santa Fe. He advised the committee members that they would receive four dollars and fifty cents per diem plus railway and Pullman fares. He hoped they would plan to give two days to the committee's work since the meeting would be open to all interested persons, some of whom would be desirous of being heard on the subject.[13]

In a general memorandum sent to committee members, Young outlined his thoughts about how the committee should approach its problem. He reminded the committee that they were invited to participate for the purpose of advising Secretary Ickes and Commissioner Collier as to what, if anything, should be done by the government to preserve and to develop the Indian arts and crafts in their cultural, artistic, and economic aspects. The committee was composed almost entirely of people connected with or personally familiar with the arts and crafts of the Southwestern Indian groups, and Young justified this situation because of the higher proportionate volume of Indian arts and crafts production in the Southwest. Citing how, even in the Southwest, the problems posed appeared in a wide variety of forms because each product and each tribe and locality created variations, Young suggested that, if the committee was not to get lost in the detail of these specialized problems, it would have to seek some simplified approach to the establishment of general principles and policies. To this end, Young proposed that the committee confine itself exclusively in the beginning to Navajo weaving in order to establish a pattern which would somewhat ease the solution to the individual problems of the other crafts and tribes.[14]

Navajo weaving presented many problems for the committee to consider. The first was to assess the present production and marketing conditions. On the basis of these conditions, the committee had to decide what should be the government's objectives and to consider the implications of those objectives. Finally, decisions had to be made regarding the necessary organizational approach to be taken with consideration given to existing laws.[15]

Because of the short advance notice for the meeting on 15 March and the reported conflicts in the various committee members' schedules, the first meeting of the Young committee was limited to an inconclusive discussion among the few who were able to attend, yet Young's personal plan for Indian arts and crafts was sufficient to provoke a great deal of argument, primarily among Elkus, LaFarge, and Young. This dialogue continued through the mail long after the March meeting. Direct Indian contribution came at this time from Diego Abeita, who submitted a plan for developing a guild and a permanent exhibition of Indian arts and crafts in the Southwest.[16]

Another meeting of the committee was difficult to arrange until Secretary Ickes stepped in almost five months later. He pressured Collier, who in turn telegrammed Young to hold the second meeting the last week in August during the 1934 Gallup Intertribal Ceremonial. Young's enthusiasm seemed to be less than before Collier took office, perhaps the result of dashed hopes of becoming Indian commissioner himself. Collier personally did not urge Young to get on with the work of his committee probably because his attention was riveted on efforts to achieve congressional passage of the all-important Wheeler-Howard bill, which he had designed as one of his vehicles for social achievement among the Indians.[17]

The Committee on Indian Arts and Crafts held a successful three-day meeting in Gallup immediately following the ceremonial. Once more Young's plan, now somewhat revised from the first meeting in March, was submitted to the committee. Elkus and LaFarge used this plan to develop their own views, which they presented in a second report. From this difference of opinion, a final report was worked out in a conference of an appointed subcommittee made up of Elkus, LaFarge, and Young. Their mutually satisfactory plan then was presented on the third day to the whole committee, of which all members still were present except Dodge, whose signature had been promised and was obtained later. Elkus predicted that if the report was followed, something substantial would come out of it, "depending upon the effectiveness, naturally, of the executive and his understanding of the Indians and their problems." To that end, Elkus suggested to both Ickes and Collier that James Young would be the most effective person to be the chairman.[18]

The "Report of the Committee on Indian Arts and Crafts" provided the most realistic appraisal of the Indian arts and crafts situation to date. Sensitive to both the economic and cultural needs of the Indians, the report addressed itself directly to the problem basic to all bicultural proposals: on what premises and to what extent, if any, can a dominant group enter into the cultural affairs of a weaker one without ultimately causing irreparable loss to both? The report's concrete recommendations provided an intelligent and responsible approach if not a direct answer to this question.

The committee's report sidestepped no major issues nor was its language anything less than direct. It realistically warned against the dangers of any program for promoting Indian arts and crafts. Elkus and LaFarge were concerned that the existing market might be damaged from any one of three sources. The first danger was that the art values in the products might be damaged by extensive commercial exploitation. Second, both men worried that successful exploitation could make the market more attractive to machine imitators, who seriously would invade the Indian craft market. Their third concern was that the mere process of formalizing the marketing and thereby subjecting it to white society's influence might tend to destroy the indigenous, individualistic, noncommercial connotations which currently were behind so much of the arts and crafts business resulting from tourism, and which were also the source of interest for the limited yet high purchasing power group.[19]

From the standpoint of the Young committee the needs of the current market for Indian arts and crafts were quite different from the heavy emphasis on the all-out promotion of these crafts advocated in the earlier Indian Cooperative Marketing Board bills. Now the thinking had had an opportunity to develop more fully, and the committee's conclusions reflected the considerations produced by a greater range of experience directly involved in all aspects of Indian arts and crafts. Surprisingly, the committee flatly stated that no evidence existed that the present major market, the tourist market, was in any need of better organization of its marketing channels. Perhaps the influence of the traders produced this stand. Although Hubbell was not credited for pushing the view that private enterprise, both Indian and non-Indian, was thoroughly developing the tourist market possibilities, that conclusion was reached by the committee and seemed to suggest leaving the future marketing process to the traders. The committee further commented that while the present marketing methods might appear on the surface to be unorganized, irregular, incidental, and even inefficient, they were the result of thousands of experiments in finding out what paid and what did not pay. In essence, the committee defended the current methods as the practical outgrowth of a production system which was itself unorganized, irregular, incidental, and even inefficient. On the other hand, the committee saw more than anything else a definite need to improve the production of the present types of goods. In an acknowledgement of the work of the Indian Arts Fund and the National Association on Indian Affairs, formerly called the Eastern Association on Indian Affairs, the committee referred to their efforts as demonstrating that, within the current market, greater salability was achieved with a better return to the craftsmen when the art and technical standards of the Indians' products were raised. Such improvements, the committee advised, involved no conflict with traditional Indian ways of working; rather, they implied an adherence to tradition, the best in that tradition even when applied to new forms. This work involved education of the craftsmen in both the art standards and the technical processes of their crafts. Larger related problems affecting the quality of production were involved, also, such as that found in changing the breeds of Navajo sheep. Even the dissemination of information to overcome preconceived ideas of Indian crafts was needed. The prevailing idea that Navajo rugs were always harsh in color and bold in design now had to be supplanted by public awareness of a class of rugs of harmonious colors and designs suitable for general use. Indian traders, in turn, would have to be kept aware of the evolving demand.

The Young committee devoted only one brief paragraph to the presentation of the very real threat of imitation Indian arts and crafts products. Citing the need, particularly with regard to silverwork and jewelry, the committee advocated protecting both the buying public and the Indian artists by the establishment of a distinguishing mark of identification. In their final recommendations, the committee called for a government Indian arts and crafts agency with the power to create government marks of genuineness and quality, to establish standards and regulations for the use of such marks, to license corporations or individuals to use them, and to charge a fee for their use. This important responsibility now was seen as a government charge and no longer within the realm of private activity.

The Young committee was united in the view that what was vital and essential in Indian art was distinguished by the following: first, what the Indian had within himself—"his feeling for form, color, and design";

and, second, "certain characteristics in his products" which could only be retained by true handcraft methods of production. Unanimously, the committee agreed on the need to prohibit the use of any more efficient aids to production that might alter the aesthetic character of the products. On the other hand, the committee also agreed to encourage the use of such technical processes as better firing methods, which it believed would not alter the essential character of the products yet would improve the products or lower the labor cost in producing them. In this manner, the committee was convinced that the Indians would retain their essential characteristics as artists and would make, as they had in the past, new adaptations to a changing world simply by employing new materials, tools, and facilities.

Fully aware of the risks to Indian art and ways of life involved in the implementation of the report, the Young committee again was unanimous in advising caution. Specifically, it agreed that unless its program was guided by "people acutely conscious of these risks and prepared and equipped to feel their way slowly and experimentally, in cooperation with the Indians, it would be unwise to enter upon any such program." The problem was such, however, that if the extreme traditionalist point of view was maintained, whereby the Indians were prohibited or discouraged from making improvements in the technical processes of their arts or deprived of the assistance of persons qualified to help them develop these processes, then the Indians probably never would achieve any materially wider market. The key to a wider market and an increased income from Indian arts and crafts was to be found, the Young committee declared, "in an improved production—through improved production processes, through better products, and through better adaptation of products to American usage."

The influence of Oliver LaFarge over the Young Committee on Indian Arts and Crafts should not be underestimated. His sensitivity to Indian life kept the group from the hasty, one-sided decisions that seemed to be so prevalent when cultural minority questions were under discussion by a culturally dominant group. While the first Indian arts and crafts bills probably were sincere efforts to help the Indians, they failed to reflect the depth of concern and intelligent analysis that the Young committee now provided. The varied experiences and attitudes represented on the committee plus a common awareness of a state of emergency had given an element of convincing force to the report. Both as a novelist and as the president of the National Association on Indian Affairs, LaFarge contributed his great store of knowledge to the question of Indian arts and crafts development. In fact, LaFarge insisted upon and wrote the "controlling views" section of the Young committee report.

On the basis of their deliberations, the Committee on Indian Arts and Crafts recommended the formation of a government agency. Such an agency, they decided, might be called the Indian Arts Development Board. It would be composed of five members appointed by the President for terms of six years at a compensation of one dollar a year plus expenses. The committee agreed that of the five members two should be businessmen, of whom one should be a dealer in Indian products, one should be an Indian, one a nominee of the Laboratory of Anthropology of Santa Fe, and one, Leslie Denman insisted, an authority in the field of art who had given evidence of an interest in Indian art. Denman defined the purpose of this board to be the promotion of Indian arts and crafts within the guidelines established by the Young committee.

The committee steered a wide path around any implication that the board would be, in itself, a business organization. Its functions and operations, the committee stated, should be more nearly comparable to those of a management corporation in the business field than to those of an operating corporation. Such functions and operations would include research, planning, recommendations for financing, and management supervision of other operating groups, either Indian or white. Under the influence of the Indian traders, some of whom previously had opposed Indian arts and crafts legislation on the grounds that it would interfere with their established businesses, the committee designated in detail the scope of the board's activities.[20]

This uniquely specialized organization should have powers, the committee concluded, permitting it to undertake market research to determine the best opportunity for various products; to engage in technical research and give technical advice and assistance; to engage in experimentation, directly or through selected agencies; to correlate and to encourage the activities of various private and governmental agencies in the field; to assist in the management of operating groups to further specific projects; to make recommendations to the secretary of the interior for loans (something Staples insisted upon, perhaps remembering that the Rhoads Indian Office administration refused even the smallest requests for funds); to enter into management contracts with operating groups to supply management personnel and supervision at cost; and to employ a full-time general manager and any necessary permanent or temporary staff. Then, in simple, direct language, the committee emphasized that the board should be prohibited from borrowing or lending and from becoming a dealer in Indian goods. Finally, the committee recommended an annual expense budget of not less than $50,000 and the right to retain any income it might derive from management fees or trademark licensing, to be used in the advancement of its purposes.

The "Report of the Committee on Indian Arts and Crafts" under Chairman Young was a milestone in the growing white awareness of the cultural attainments of the American Indians. As an expression of an unselfish depth of interest and a belief in the future of a minority group by an officially appointed government body, the report had few, if any, equals.

Although Commissioner Collier initially labeled the Indian arts and crafts committee report "very good, I think,"[21] his subsequent reactions seem confused. He had difficulty understanding why the 1930 and 1932 Indian Cooperative Marketing Board bills had been disregarded completely. Confessing his inability to express a final opinion on the report and its recommendations, Collier told Ickes that the report represented a compromise between those who strongly had favored the original marketing corporation project and those who had gone on record just as strongly opposed.[22]

Many decisions Collier made stemmed from a deep sense of unwavering conviction, and an unfaltering belief in his own infallibility often rendered him a poor bargainer. He had made up his mind in favor of the Indian Arts and Crafts Cooperative Marketing Board bill, and he now found the aura of compromise which he believed characterized the Young committee's report difficult to accept. He told Ickes that he did not believe that the present administration ought to be limited by a compromise between those who had taken opposite positions at an earlier time. As a result, over a month passed before LaFarge and the other committee members had any response to their report from either Ickes or Collier. Young tried to smooth the ruffled feathers of the impatient committee members by explaining that Secretary Ickes had received the report on 8 October 1934 and then had referred it to Collier, after which time both men had been out of Washington. According to Young, when Collier had returned, he had said he was waiting to talk it over with Ickes. Young was hopeful that the committee would hear something definite in the near future. He expressed his disappointment that Secretary Ickes had not sent some sort of acknowledgement to all of the members of the committee, adding that not much time was available for amenities in the New Deal. "It seems to be a game played with aces and knaves, according to your prejudices," Young commented, "at any rate, the deuces are wild."[23]

In an attempt to ease the impact of the report on Collier, Elkus explained to him that the committee had given practically no attention to the marketing corporation bill, as such, and that it had not come under discussion. The committee had started anew, Elkus said, in an effort "to frame a plan on which immediate action could be had and practical steps taken at once." All of the members of the committee wanted to see something real accomplished, he continued, and all felt that now was both a particularly "happy time" and a necessary one during which to go forward. Elkus even detailed how differences of opinion in the committee meeting had been worked out by the subcommittee made up of Young, LaFarge, and himself. He fully supported the report's recommendations and stressed to Collier that the board should be started fully staffed and equipped or not at all. The board would be "under suspicion," he admitted, and, as such, should be given a fair opportunity to succeed. If the personnel were efficient, and if Young could be obtained to guide it from the start, the board would produce some very real accomplishments, Elkus assured Collier, for "surely the need for this is immediate."[24]

Not until 27 December did Collier accept the Young committee's proposal and then he qualified his decision. Only then did he make his first attempt to involve Young in the implementation of the committee's report. Even so, when he contacted Young, Collier was thinking only of a kind of trial run without any legislative action, to see whether the recommended arrangement really would function. He simply could not assent, as a matter of permanent policy, to the proposition that the government itself never should go into trading in Indian arts and crafts in a direct way. Almost grudgingly, he told Young that the setup the Indian arts and crafts committee had proposed was promising and that the future would grow out of it. Collier claimed to have won Budget Bureau approval for $15,000 for arts and crafts research, experimentation, and promotion, yet he had no actual congressional appropriation to work with when he asked Young to set up an Indian arts and crafts organization. He assured Young of the adequacy of this amount by explaining that the Indian Office simply would transfer other personnel into "this arts and crafts job." He added that the loan fund under the Indian Reorganization Act could be used in part for this purpose. Whatever his motives may have been, Collier, in truth, was doing just what the Young committee had recommended, proceeding with caution. Although he specifically had told Young that the Budget Bureau had refused to authorize more than $15,000, Collier actually had sought only that amount, which he considered to be sufficient at this stage.[25]

Secretary Ickes finally acknowledged receipt of the "Report of the Committee on Indian Arts and Crafts" on 18 January 1935, more than three months after it was submitted to him. Without any explanation for the delay, he called the report "an extraordinarily thorough and persuasive discussion of the problem and opportunity." Ickes seemed to be trying to avoid becoming a party to any further conflict over the course of action best suited for the future of Indian arts and crafts and merely echoed Collier when referring to the work of the Young committee. Ickes told LaFarge that the report brought together the several points of view on Indian arts and crafts, and in both his and Commissioner Collier's judgment, it laid "the foundation for action from this time forth."[26]

Collier alone seemd to be holding up this action, for Young was ready and anxious to move ahead. On 24 January he told LaFarge he was hoping for a conference in Washington with Collier in the near future to see what further steps could be taken to secure action. Within the Indian Office among Collier's close associates, the pressure to do something for Indian arts and crafts continued to grow. Walter V. Woehlke, the former editor of *Sunset Magazine* and now an Indian Office field representative, reported the urgency of the Indian situation. He predicted that economic and racial pressures would compel the majority of the Indians to continue to make their living on the reservations for many years to come, yet the reservations could offer almost no opportunities for employment. The development and expansion of Indian arts and crafts was an immediate and pressing necessity in order to supplement the bare living derived from subsistence farming. The development of Indian handcraft was the Indians' one chance at self-employment.[27]

The final nudge toward full approval by Collier for the Young committee's recommendations came from Assistant Solicitor William H. Hastie of the Department of the Interior. Hastie advised Collier that a corporate organization such as had been favored by Collier in the 1930 and 1932 cooperative marketing board bills would not facilitate the research, experimental, and advisory functions as they were designed to take place within the plan submitted by the Young committee. A day earlier Hastie had agreed with Collier's view that a "corporate organization would tend to aid the enterprise." He explained to Collier that at that time he had not understood that the proposed organization would not engage in the actual marketing of the products of Indian craftwork.[28] Within three weeks Hastie drafted a proposed Indian arts and crafts bill, and the controversial effort moved into the legislative sphere once more.

6

THE INDIAN
ARTS AND CRAFTS BOARD

COMMISSIONER COLLIER SENT A COPY of the proposed Indian arts and crafts bill to James Young and requested that Young send his views to him via air mail. In his reply, Young advised Collier to give the matter "some serious thought personally before we are committed." He pointed out how everything under this bill depended upon administration. The Indian Office could assign the entire board from permanent employees and achieve little or no difference in the operations compared to what might be carried out under the Indian Office itself without such a board. Young suggested that the risks in this plan were so great that it raised afresh the whole question of whether the possibilities of harm were not greater than the possibilities of good. Young wondered once more whether the situation would work itself out better through private trade and philanthropic organizations rather than under a very risky, uncontrolled government operation.[1]

Despite Young's obvious qualms and general uneasiness over the proposed bill, Collier's sudden enthusiasm somehow led him to construe Young's letter to mean that the draft was all right with him. At the same time Collier pointed to what he considered to be "an active—rather an eager—interest" in the subject of Indian arts and crafts being displayed by the House Committee on Indian Affairs, and he advised Ickes that they ought to get the bill into Congress. Collier perhaps based his precipitous judgment upon changes in the leadership of both the Senate and the House Committees on Indian Affairs with the seating of the Seventy-fourth Congress. In the Senate, Elmer Thomas succeeded Burton K. Wheeler, Democrat from Montana, who became chairman of the Senate Interstate Commerce Committee. In the House, Will Rogers, Democrat from Oklahoma, succeeded Edgar Howard, Democrat from Nebraska, who was not returned to office. Still wishing to avoid further controversy, Secretary Ickes somewhat naively told Collier to go ahead with the bill without waiting for him to read it. Ickes explained that he was willing to accept Collier's judgment, "backed as it is by Mr. Young" and the Solicitor's Office.[2]

Accordingly, on 6 March 1935, Congressman Will Rogers, by departmental request, introduced House Bill 6468, "To promote the development of Indian arts and crafts and to create a board to assist therein, and for other purposes." Two days later, Senator Thomas, also by departmental request, introduced Senate Bill 2203, a duplicate of the House measure. Both Houses then referred the bills to their respective Committees on Indian Affairs where their initial fate would be determined.[3]

The 1935 Indian arts and crafts bill varied only slightly from the recommendations of the Young committee. An "Indian Arts and Crafts Board," was to be created in the Department of the Interior. The terms of office for the five board members appointed by the President were shortened from the suggested six years to four years. Career categories for the board were dropped, and both public officers and private citizens were eligible for membership. The board would elect one of its members as chairman. The board's specific function and duty was "to promote the economic welfare of the Indian tribes and the Indian wards of the government through the development of Indian arts and crafts and the expansion of the market for the products of Indian art and craftsmanship." The powers given the board to execute this function were the same as those presented in the Young committee report. Although the board was empowered to prescribe rules and regulations for the conduct of its business and the execution and administration of the powers granted to it, the board was directed to "advise and consult" with the General Accounting Office on any disbursement of money. Also, all rules and regulations which the board proposed had to be submitted to the secretary of the interior for approval in order for them to become effective. Misrepresentation of Indian products and the production of counterfeit or imitation government trademarks were now to be criminal offenses punishable in the federal courts by a fine not exceeding two thousand dollars, or imprisonment not exceeding six months, or both.

The bill differed most significantly from the committee's recommendations in failing to specify an exact sum under which the board would operate. While the Young committee had made abundantly clear that not less than a $50,000 annual appropriation would be needed, the 1935 bill only authorized "such sums as may be necessary to defray the expenses of the board and carry out the purposes and provisions of this act." This timidity over appropriations would cloud government promotion of Indian arts and crafts for years.

When the acting director of the Bureau of the Budget reported the Indian arts and crafts bill on 11 May 1935, the future of this important legislation was placed in jeopardy. While sympathizing with the general purposes of the proposed legislation, the acting director believed the project should be commercially self-supporting rather than one that required annual appropriations from the general fund of the Treasury. The Budget Bureau said that the bill would be in accord with the President's financial program if it were modified to eliminate appropriations from the Treasury and if disbursement of the special fund from management and trademark licensing fees were placed under the control of the Treasury rather than left in the hands of the board.[4]

Instead of meekly accepting the dictum of the Budget Bureau as had Ray Lyman Wilbur, Secretary Ickes cleverly sidestepped the Budget Bureau's recommendation. Responding to requests of the Senate and House committees for a report on the Indian arts and crafts bill, Ickes all but ignored the report by the Budget Bureau. Although he proposed that eventually the Indian arts and crafts board should be self-supporting, he told the committees that, until firmly established, the board would need to have sums appropriated for traveling expenses and for other incidental expenses. Ickes opposed control of the disbursement of management and trademark funds by the Treasury, but agreed to an insignificant change in wording which only eliminated the board's right to make expenditures from the fund not its right to authorize the dispensing of the funds. By refusing to place any significance on the Budget Bureau's report and by seeming willing to conciliate differences, Ickes successfully defused a potentially disastrous turn of events. Three days after Ickes sent his letters, the House Indian Affairs Committee issued its report in which it totally ignored the opinions of the Budget Bureau and recommended that the Indian arts and crafts bill pass with only one minor change in wording.[5]

Ickes had suggested nine changes in the Indian arts and crafts bill, seven of which were wording changes for clarity. In addition, Ickes suggested that the secretary of the interior rather than the President appoint the five commissioners since they would serve under the secretary's supervision anyway. He also recommended clarification of the federal criminal law segment to cover situations where goods were offered or displayed for sale, not where misrepresentation took place in ordinary conversation where no sale was contemplated. The House Report failed to support these recommendations.[6]

The next step was to obtain approval for the Indian arts and crafts bill from the Senate Committee on Indian Affairs, and that procedure proved to be more precarious. Although the Senate committee reported the Indian arts and crafts bill, Senator Carl Atwood Hatch, Democrat from New Mexico, under appeal from the Maisel Trading Post Company, objected to the bill on the Senate floor and succeeded in having it recommitted to the Senate committee. In a regular committee meeting on 27 May 1935 with Collier present, Senator Hatch suggested amendments to Section 2(g), authorizing the board to create government marks of genuineness and quality for Indian products, to establish standards and regulations for the use of such marks, to license corporations, associations, or individuals to use them, and to charge a user fee. No agreement was reached; instead, the committee urged Collier and Hatch to confer further on the matter. Apparently anything that was agreeable to both of them would be accepted by the committee. Allan Harper attended this committee meeting and reported that Hatch appeared to be very sympathetic to the general purpose of the bill. Hatch even assured those present that he had no intention of preventing the bill's passage.[7]

The campaign to achieve passage of the Indian arts and crafts bill began in earnest that same day. The Interior Department issued an afternoon press release supporting the bill under what was termed the "bold and comprehensive" New Deal program. This New Deal policy called for the preservation and expansion of salable arts and crafts, which had supplied and could supply an important supplemental income to the American Indians. In a letter to Senator Hatch, Collier pleaded the cause. He apprised Hatch of his satisfaction with the whole bill and that, in his view, opposition could arise only from a belief that the board could be deliberately unfair. Such an anticipation was wholly unjustified. If one started trying to set down the exact technical conditions that would entitle a person to receive the government trademark, Collier asserted, "he would produce an inoperable act and one which would be entirely objectionable to the Maisel and similar enterprises." In an effort to shift the burden of proof to his opponent, Collier told Senator Hatch that Maisel need not fear this bill if he believed that his product was genuine Indian work.[8]

The next day Oliver LaFarge initiated a personal letter-writing campaign that probably produced greater results at this crucial time than any other effort. LaFarge appealed to others to join in supporting the bill. He pointed out that both he and the National Association on Indian Affairs with all of their years of Indian arts and crafts experience were backing the proposed legislation. LaFarge urged the traders' association to communicate with Senator Hatch to urge a favorable report on the bill. Reminding the traders that the bill followed almost exactly the specifications set down in the Committee on Indian Arts and Crafts report, which had been worked out in accord with Staples and Hubbell to keep in mind the needs of the traders, LaFarge emphasized how the traders stood to gain from the bill. When the Young committee had discussed what type of marketing and advertising assistance an organization like the traders' association would need, the committee had drawn up a provision, now incorporated in the bill, that made it possible for the board to assist just such an organization to obtain financing and to give it advice and guidance. At the same time, provision had been made to prohibit the board from operating in competition with the traders. On that basis and with the standards of genuineness, LaFarge told the traders' association that it had a "swell setup."[9] LaFarge felt this approach was necessary because he feared some of the individual traders had misunderstood the bill, and the traders' association was having difficulty holding them in line. In LaFarge's eyes, this difficulty stemmed mainly from the Maisel group's political power within New Mexico,[10] although the structure of this political power was weakened after the death of Herbert Hagerman, the former territorial governor of New Mexico, on 29 January 1935.

Pleading for support for the bill from Senator Thomas, LaFarge charged that the fringe of the Indian country in the Southwest was full of non-Indians who were making improper use of public goodwill toward Indian products to market articles not correctly described, and, in that manner, were forcing out of operation many true Indian artists. The situation was such, LaFarge concluded, that on many reservations, crafts capable of tipping the balance for the Indians from penury to a reasonable margin of comfort were now stagnant or dying out for lack of just such services as this bill would make possible. To Senator Hatch, LaFarge briefly reviewed these same points and implored the Senator to express himself in favor of the bill.[11]

New problems arose in the House of Representatives on 15 June when the clerk of the House called up the Indian arts and crafts bill, and Congressman Charles Vilas Truax, Democrat from Ohio, requested that the bill be passed over without consideration. When Congressman Rogers, the bill's sponsor, asked Truax why he objected to the bill, the congressman from Ohio exploded, "It is an extension of bureaucracy. It proposes to set up another bureau of executive officers. It is creating more jobs and additional burdens on the taxpayers. I have been fighting all my life against this extension of bureaucracy."[12]

Truax was far from finished. He was not against Indian arts and crafts; instead, he was attacking the actions of the Democratic party. "The Democratic platform promised to cut the bureaucracy and reduce its expenses 25 percent. Yet we have bills brought in here everyday and every session . . . extending and expanding bureaucracy with more governmental jobs, more burdens upon the taxpayers," Truax raged. "It is time to call a halt to further expansion of bureaucracy." Congressman William Doddridge McFarlane, Democrat from Texas, agreed, and the House Indian arts and crafts bill was tabled and removed from further consideration.[13]

In spite of this setback, the future of the Indian arts and crafts bill in the Senate looked brighter when Senator Hatch withdrew his opposition and the Senate Committee on Indian Affairs on 18 June once more favorably reported the bill. Secretary Ickes credited Hatch's decision to the numerous telegrams Hatch received from members of the United Indian Traders Association. The Senate began discussing the Indian arts and crafts bill on 28 June. At that time Senator William Henry King, Democrat from Utah, although he admitted frankly that he was inclined to favor the bill, announced that he had some objections to the measure and asked that it be passed over until the next call of the calendar. Senator Frazier, sponsor of the first two Senate Indian arts and crafts bills in 1930 and 1932, attempted to persuade King to withdraw his objection by reminding him that the bill was an administration measure and one for which the authorities have been working for a long time. As a member of the Senate Committee on Indian Affairs, Frazier reported that his committee was "very strongly in favor of it." Nevertheless, King explained that a number of Indians had spoken to him about the bill, and, since he was profoundly interested in the Indians and their welfare, he again asked that the bill go over until the next consent calendar day. The presiding officer agreed and the bill was passed over.[14] King never did reveal which Indians had opposed the bill or why they opposed it.

Not until 29 July was the Indian arts and crafts bill once more announced on the Senate floor. No objection was made. The Senate agreed to each of the Indian Affairs Committee's suggested amendments, which were the amendments Ickes had proposed in his report, and then passed the bill.[15]

Collier was ecstatic. In what he considered to be a "field day," he joyfully reported to Ickes that the Senate had passed the Indian arts and crafts bill plus the bill authorizing a capital fund for the Chippewa Cooperative Marketing Association, the Indian Claims Commission bill, the Indian Pension bill, and the California Indian Jurisdictional bill.[16]

After the sudden death of Congressman Truax on 9 August, the way seemed clear for House action on the Indian arts and crafts bill. In a clever piece of strategy, on 21 August Congressman Rogers asked permission of the Speaker to call up S. 2203, the bill which the Senate had passed on 2 August. Rogers asked for and received unanimous consent that the bill be considered by the House acting as a committee of the whole. With no further questions, the House passed the bill. On 23 August the bill was presented to the President of the United States, yet for no apparent reason Roosevelt waited until 27 August, the day after the first session of the Seventy-fourth Congress had adjourned, to sign the bill. This action precluded any appropriation until Congress resumed in January 1936 and immeasurably delayed the establishment of the Indian Arts and Crafts Board.[17]

Collier took great satisfaction in the fact that the long-sought Indian arts and crafts bill had passed Congress at a time when other major Indian legislation was stymied. The Oklahoma General Welfare bill passed the Senate, yet was never reported out of committee in the House. The Indian Claims Commission bill and the Navajo Boundary bill also were blocked in the House of Representatives.[18]

Collier was particularly pleased that enactment of the bill had taken place at such an opportune time since he considered the 28 August decision of the court of appeals to have so modified the Federal Trade Commission order in the Maisel case as to render further action against producers of spurious Indian products "all but useless."[19]

Charles Elkus had definite ideas about the type of leadership needed to implement the Indian Arts and Crafts Board Act. Already he was asking what this legislation would accomplish. In his view, the answer would be determined mainly by who headed the new organization, who was the major influence in determining policies, and who became the salaried general manager to carry out the dictates of the board. He still was convinced that James Young was the best person to head the board. Should Young be unwilling, Elkus suggested that Young could be made to feel that taking the position was his obligation. As the person largely responsible for the Committee on Indian Arts and Crafts report Young had displayed, in Elkus's estimation, "a peculiar ability for this particular job." He responded to the art of the Indians, was quite familiar with the handcrafts of the Southwest, and was familiar with merchandising and marketing nationally and internationally, having just returned from an assignment in England for the J. Walter Thompson Company. He had an understanding of the Indians' viewpoint and the need for a just discrimination between the commercial, artistic, and cultural factors.[20]

Elkus's views had their intended effect. Secretary Ickes talked with Commissioner Collier, and Collier contacted Young. "We are strongly agreed that you are the man for chairman if you can give the time necessary," Collier openly told Young. Young indicated his willingness to accept the position because he felt an obligation "to see things through" although he frankly told Ickes that he did not want the job. Within days he was in Washington discussing the composition of the board.[21]

The difficult process of selecting and obtaining the board members now began. Ickes and Collier had agreed that the makeup of the board was to be delayed until Young could be consulted. Even so, Collier could not refrain from suggesting Mary-Russell Colton of the Museum of Northern Arizona and Amelia White, executive secretary of the National Association on Indian Affairs, for consideration by Young as possible board members. Instead, Young had his own ideas. He saw a definite need for one person of high standing in the field of general merchandising, and for this person he suggested William Warner, president of the McCall Company and chairman of the board of the American Woolen Company. Warner formerly had headed the Hudson Store in Detroit and had been in publication and pattern businesses. Young called Warner "ideal if he could be secured." Next, Young wanted someone representing the scientific field, and here he chose Kenneth Chapman of the Laboratory of Anthropology. For representation directly from the field of art, Young selected Robert B. Harshe, the director of the Art Institute of Chicago. The choice of one person to represent the Indians was left up to Collier because of the difficulties expected over the language barrier and in assessing the degree of experience of any Indian candidate.[22] On paper Young's candidates seemed ideal and beyond reproach.

In the next two months, political considerations at the highest level began to play a determining role in the future development of the Indian Arts and Crafts Board. Two weeks after Young had made his choices for the board, Collier wrote Young stressing the importance that Young come to Washington once more for talks with both himself and Ickes. Young dragged his feet. Finally, on 14 December a distressed Collier wired Young that appropriations hearings were to begin in three days, and he needed immediate information from Young on the status of the organization of the board. Young's reply was a shock. Because his choice of William Warner had been rejected by President Roosevelt, who had no such authority under the Indian Arts and Crafts Board Act, Young no longer wished to be a part of the Indian arts and crafts program. "After careful consideration of [the] reasons given . . . for Warner's rejection," Young wired, "I am forced to conclude [that the] implication of this is that no one who might publicly oppose [the] administration is eligible." Young announced that if this was Roosevelt's policy then he himself also would have to be eliminated.[23]

Suddenly, Young was uncertain whether he would have any time available, and he regretfully suggested that Collier proceed without him. Collier wired back that the White House decision concerning Warner did not indicate general policy at all. "Ickes and I must have you for chairman," Collier pleaded. In a more detailed letter sent the same day, Collier tried to impress Young with Ickes's belief that the President's "reaction" connected with Warner was not indicative of any "future reactions." Ickes had instructed Collier to tell Young "for goodness sake not to be influenced by this particular incident but to go and be chairman *pronto.*" Collier emphatically echoed Ickes's judgment. "When can we proceed in this matter?" Collier asked Young. But Collier made the mistake of suggesting to Young that Young's appointment of Kenneth Chapman would contribute little to the actual work of the board, since Chapman could and would contribute just as well as an unofficial advisor to the board.[24] With that, Young disengaged himself from further direct Indian Arts and Crafts Board activity for years.

Whether he wanted to or not, Collier now had to begin what turned out to be a seemingly interminable search for board members. Collier was aware that the effort to find an adequate chairman would be a troublesome pursuit.[25] When he was absolutely sure that Young would not serve, Collier sought advice about how to organize the board from staff members at the University of Denver, Cornell University, and from numerous other sources.[26] Finally, by 18 January 1936 he had compiled a list of prospective members, only one of whom had been consulted as to willingness to serve. For chairman, Collier suggested Morris De Camp Crawford, the research editor of Fairchild Publications. Crawford had written *The History of Cotton*, a textbook on textiles, and was a well-known merchandising expert. He had introduced Peruvian and African motifs into products for the Bonwit Teller and Bloomingdale department stores in New York. Once a research associate with the American Museum of Natural History, Crawford more recently had been a research associate in textiles for the Museum of Science and Industry in Chicago. Significantly, Collier had been informed that Crawford was a Democrat. Collier offered no alternatives for the position of chairman of the board.[27]

From a list of seven choices, Collier hoped to find the remaining four commissioners. First on the list was Alfred V. Kidder of the Carnegie Institution and the National Research Council, both in Washington, D.C. As a recognized authority on the archaeology of the Southwest, Kidder would add "prestige and equipment" to the board, Collier believed. Robert Harshe, one of Young's first choices, was next, followed by Willard W. Beatty, the director of Indian education, who would represent the Indian Office and the Department of the Interior. Collier suggested to Ickes that Lorenzo Hubbell would contribute the experience of the Indian trader living close to the Indian. Collier still was considering Mary-Russell Colton along with two other candidates, Hardie Phillip, an architect profoundly interested in Indian arts and crafts, and Ruth Reeves, considered by many to be the foremost textile designer in the United States. Because Elkus lived in California, so far away from Washington, Collier decided not to recommend him to Ickes, and Elkus agreed with this view. No Indians were under consideration after Young earlier had left that decision up to Collier.[28]

Ickes did not object to Morris Crawford as chairman, so Collier immediately concentrated his efforts on obtaining Crawford's services. His first step was to send Nina Collier to New York to interview the candidate. After the visit, Crawford took it upon himself to send a three-page letter to Nina Collier expressing his view on the problem of craftwork among the Indians. Crawford was offered the job on 5 February, and although he hesitated because of other commitments, two weeks later he accepted the position. Then, on 9 March, he abruptly turned around and declined the chairmanship for personal and financial reasons. The next day Collier called Crawford's decision "another case of money-making needs in competition with unpaid public service." Collier now had to ask Ickes for more time to run down other possibilities.[29]

At the same time that Ickes had formally invited Crawford to serve as chairman, Ickes also had invited Hubbell, Harshe, Beatty, and Kidder to serve on the board. Beatty, Hubbell, and Kidder readily agreed, but two board members, including the chairman, still had to be found. On 24 March, Ickes, apparently at Roosevelt's urging, offered Samuel W. Rayburn, an Arkansas lawyer, banker, and businessman, the post of board chairman. Rayburn had retail merchandising experience as a director of numerous large department stores, such as Lord and Taylor of New York. Ickes informed Rayburn that Oscar Jacobson, chairman of the department of art at the University of Oklahoma, would be offered the fourth position on the board unless Rayburn accepted the chairmanship and wished to suggest some other name for board membership. Rayburn failed to respond immediately, and the situation became increasingly difficult when Collier pointedly reminded Ickes that both of them had preferred Delos Walker, vice-president of the R. H. Macy and Company department store in New York, over Rayburn even though President Roosevelt wanted Rayburn. After agonizing for six weeks, Collier wired Rayburn that he was "awaiting most anxiously" word from him. By return wire the same day Rayburn finally and definitely turned down the position.[30]

Collier was frustrated. Instead of turning to academe once more for advice, he now sought help from the business segment of society. "I am in a state of bafflement," Collier told Edward A. Filene of William Filene's and Sons, Boston merchants. Collier explained how both he and Ickes were convinced that the board needed a chairman who knew merchandising and who had wide contacts in the field. After months of negotiating with first one and then another individual who seemed to have the qualifications, Collier still was without a board chairman. Until the right person was found, Collier stressed, the board should not be organized, yet until the board organized, no operations were possible under the Indian Arts and Crafts Board Act. Collier revealed to Filene that one by one the candidates had told him either that the job looked too big or that the responsibility was too complicated or indefinite. He now believed the chairman was going to be someone identified with the department store, mail order, or advertising fields, and who had an interest in the development of the cooperative movement among the Indians, an effort to organize the Indians to help themselves.[31]

Fully aware that the position of Indian Arts and Crafts Board chairman ultimately would be decided by President Roosevelt, Collier offered the job to Delos Walker and even pressed him to accept, feeling confident in the knowledge that Roosevelt and Walker were "pretty good friends." In fact, Collier directly told Walker that if he were willing to consider the matter, then it would be "laid before the President."[32] Even Nina Collier tried to persuade Walker to join the board, yet Walker cited business demands and declined. Consideration then turned to others including P. G. Winnett, president of Bullock's department store in Los Angeles; Lessing Rosenwald, chairman of the board of Sears, Roebuck, and Company; Ira A. Hirschman, vice-president and manager of Saks Fifth Avenue in New York; and John Hartford, president of the Great Atlantic and Pacific Tea Company, all to no avail.[33]

Time was running out to organize the board in order to receive the appropriation for the 1937 fiscal year beginning 1 July 1936. Over ten months had passed since the Indian Arts and Crafts Board Act had become law and Collier's efforts to get things moving had produced only three of the needed five board members.

Collier wanted to get the board funded and activated, and he went to great effort to explain and thus sell his policy to a hesitating, querulous House appropriations subcommittee when he appeared before it in December 1935. He condemned previous Indian policy for seeking to wipe out Indian ways of life and Indian modes of thought "utterly regardless of their significance, beauty, or adaptation to the intellectual and spiritual needs of the Indians." The old policy was primarily "static and nihilistic, successively abstracting from Indian life its human values and activities." He warned that only sheer fanaticism could continue the further destruction of Indian languages, crafts, poetry, music, ritual, philosophy, and religion. These significant and beautiful cultural possessions were the result of patient growth "through endless generations of a people immersed in the life of nature, filled with the imaginative and ethical insight into the core of being," and their destruction would be no different than destroying the rich cultural heritage of the Aryan people. Collier described New Deal Indian policy as "dynamic and functional, seeking to release the Indians into the normal activities of human life" by striving for three goals: economic rehabilitation of the Indians, organization of the Indian tribes for managing their own affairs, and civic and cultural freedom and opportunity for the Indians. This policy was based on the simple principle of treating Indians as normal human beings capable of working out an adjustment to, and a satisfying life within, the framework of American civilization, yet maintaining the best of their own cultural and racial idiosyncracies.[34]

Fitting firmly within this policy was the work Collier perceived for the Indian Arts and Crafts Board. "Its work can reach as intimately to the heart of Indian life," he proclaimed, "as the workings of the [Indian] Reorganization Act can do." He considered Indian arts and crafts as all-embracing and all-important to Indian culture. They were of the home, of the old as well as the young, for play as well as economic well-being, and of the community as well as the individual.[35] Through the Indian Arts and Crafts Board Act, the government now was setting out "to preserve, enrich, and protect from factory-made imitations the rapidly disappearing and unique Indian crafts."[36]

The task of the Indian Arts and Crafts Board would not be easy. Before the same House appropriations subcommittee two days later, Collier specifically described the job of general manager of the Indian Arts and Crafts Board as one requiring a very capable businessman working full time. Collier explained that the general manager would run a management corporation, organize production and merchandising, and yet not at any time engage in buying or selling. Collier went on to warn that the talented merchandising specialist he sought to carry out New Deal Indian policy as the executive officer for the board would face chaotic conditions in the Indian crafts market. The market was dying as a result of this chaos. The situation, as Collier expressed it, was that the Indians were receiving very low prices, the middlemen were taking enormous profits, and the cost of getting the product to the ultimate consumer was excessive. Most of the larger department stores in the cities did not want to have anything to do with Indian crafts because the system was unorganized and unreliable. Collier's views were much the same as those expressed in the Indian Arts and Crafts Committee report.[37]

The money needed for the Indian arts and crafts program, like the personnel, was agonizingly slow in coming. Collier had to plead with congressmen for the money to carry out legislation which Congress already had approved. Collier told both Secretary Ickes and James Young that up to $7,500 could be obtained by the Indian Office for the expenses of the organization and the employment of a specialist or executive until appropriations could be obtained around January or February 1936, yet Collier never produced this money, and the new appropriation was not approved until 1 July 1936, more than ten months after the Indian arts and crafts bill became law. Hampered by a lack of congressional interest, by an inability to recruit the people he wanted for the board, and by his continuing personal, time-consuming concentration on the implementation of the Wheeler-Howard Act, Collier was forced to move slowly in his approach to the Indian arts and crafts problem. In the meantime, he had to deal with impatient supporters of the Indian arts and crafts movement. Leslie Denman wrote in March from San Francisco about "the importance of the Arts and Crafts Board functioning *now*," and she asked, "When will it come to life?"[38]

So determined was Collier to obtain the right person to administer the Indian arts and crafts program that he asked Congress in the first appropriation request to authorize a salary for the general manager which exceeded that of the commissioner himself. Congressman Jed Johnson, Democrat from Oklahoma, called the salary of $10,000 for one person "entirely out of line." Collier had to explain again that the board would serve as a management corporation. He tirelessly repeated that the job required advertising and specialty merchandising skills and could not be done "except by that type of man, and those men, if they are any good, get salaries far above $10,000 in the competitive field." Collier pleaded for the funds to get the project going. It would pay its own way after it was started, he claimed, by charging for services to beneficiaries. The pump had only to be primed to have a self-sustained proposition.[39]

Reflecting the American philanthropic experience produced by massive industrial growth, Committee Chairman Edward T. Taylor, Democrat from Colorado, asked Collier whether he thought he could get "some public-spirited person" to make a donation to get the board started. Collier commented that at one time the money might have come from the Rockefellers although after further consideration that approach had not looked good. Congressman Marion A. Zioncheck, Democrat from Washington, asked why a dollar-a-year man could not be obtained, referring to the World War I war effort organizers. Collier patiently explained that the five board commissioners were, in fact, to be paid only for the actual expenses they incurred, but that the executive officer had to be a merchandising specialist and such talent could not be hired for $5,000 or $6,000 a year. Moreover, he continued, it was the opinion of the Young committee that it was necessary to pay a good salary for a capable general manager or it would be impossible to enlist the required board members.[40]

The first appropriation request for the Indian Arts and Crafts Board called for $60,000 less $15,000 for lapses and delays or a tentative total of $45,000. This amount was to be made available immediately rather than waiting six months until the start of the 1937 fiscal year on 1 July 1936. Section 4 of the Indian Arts and Crafts Board Act specifically authorized "to be appropriated, out of any sums in the Treasury not otherwise appropriated, such sums as may be necessary to defray the expenses of the Board and carry out the purposes and provisions of this Act." Samuel M. Dodd, Indian Office finance officer, called the first appropriation figures tentative because a comprehensive and satisfactory budget could not be submitted until the members of the board and the general manager entered on duty, since existing Indian Office personnel had little or no experience in this type of undertaking. The figures for this first budget, Dodd pointed out, were derived from the report of the Young committee in 1934 and "through consultation with several unnamed individuals." Dodd also noted that the final figures for 1937 took into account possible savings that might accrue because of delays in getting the full program under way. He estimated that from $60,000 to $70,000 would be required annually for the board's work when it was once organized.[41] Obviously ignorant of the past congressional difficulties Indian arts and crafts efforts had faced over financial needs, Dodd innocently opened a Pandora's box.

When committee member Zioncheck asked how many years the Indian Arts and Crafts Board would run, Collier failed to stress the plan of the Young committee that in the future the board eventually would become self-sufficient. Instead, he responded, "undoubtedly, as long as Indian arts and crafts last." Collier added that it was not a five-year plan and no reason existed why Indian arts and crafts should not go on for a hundred years and grow ten times in volume.[42]

Congressman Johnson attempted to cut the appropriation request and wanted to allow the board one salesman and to eliminate the rest of the appropriation by having the present Indian Office personnel take care of arts and crafts duties. Collier was adamant. "There is no present personnel. The Indian Office has no person who knows about these things in any real way. We have no merchandising person, and we have no arts and crafts expert." Collier added that "we have not even got an arts and crafts supervisor for our schools."[43] The hearings dragged on in this vein well into 1936, and no interim funds were made available by Congress. The final appropriation was $42,500 with the proviso that no one person's salary should exceed $7,500.

Thus began Collier's official difficulties with congressional appropriations committees over Indian Arts and Crafts Board matters. These difficulties were repeated and compounded over the next eight years. Considering the sums legislated earlier in the New Deal for depression relief and rehabilitation, such as the $500 million under the Federal Emergency Relief Administration, the Indian Arts and Crafts Board request in relation to the anticipated results was not out of line. It was special legislation for an American minority, however, despite the fact that that minority was still officially considered a ward of the government.

Still unable to find a chairman, Ickes and Collier agreed that until a permanent chairman could be found Collier himself would hold the position.[44] For the still-vacant board position, they agreed on the temporary appointment of Ebert Burlew, Ickes's administrative assistant. These "dummy directors" would be replaced, Collier promised, as soon as adequate merchandising specialists could be found.[45]

On the day after the board's appropriation was available and the same day he assumed the chairmanship of the board, Collier approved the appointment of Louis C. West, an investment banker and former financial director for the city of Cleveland, as the board's general manager. This surprise move was prompted both by the impossibility of finding a more qualified candidate at that time and by the need for immediate action to carry out the mandate Congress grudgingly granted. As if admitting the weakness of his choice, Collier at first privately labeled West the "acting secretary of the Board."[46] Although temporarily halted by the 1936 election campaign which precluded the necessary contact with the President, the search for permanent board members resumed in January 1937 with no success.[47]

While the formal work of the Indian Arts and Crafts Board was slow in getting under way, Collier, the Indian Office, and the Interior Department took advantage of every opportunity to publicize Indian arts and crafts. On a personal level, for example, Collier contacted Leslie Denman. "Does it occur to you," Collier asked, "that a modest sum of money—say $1,000 or $2,000 or $3,000—could be well used to help out the arts and crafts work at Anadarko [Oklahoma] among the Kiowas?" He admitted that he might be able to find the money somewhere in the Indian rehabilitation grant, but that the Indian Office as yet did not have that money. This letter expressed a sincere concern for the future of Indian arts and crafts.[48]

The Indian Office director of Indian education, Willard Beatty, announced increased emphasis on instruction in the older Indian crafts and a move toward a revival of Indian art within the Indian schools. Recognition of the individual ethnic value possessed by the Indians in their art became a primary tenet of New Deal Indian education policy. "It is now being generally accepted," said Beatty, "that the Indian in his distinctive racial characteristics is possessed of certain assets which may form the basis of his resources. One of the first resources of our present-day Indian is the fact that he is an Indian—that racially he is the direct heir to an art, a culture, a way of life that made its own unique contribution to the conquest of a continent in the centuries before the white man came."[49] Most important of all, Beatty felt, was to make Indian children feel that they were "a superior race, able to achieve the same scholastic accomplishments as anyone else."[50]

With approximately 86,000 Indian children of school age subject to Beatty's philosophy of education, the significance of his influence was readily apparent. Beatty was currently the president of the nationally organized Progressive Education Association. He came to the Indian Office on 4 February 1936 from the superintendency of the Bronxville, New York, public schools where he maintained the policy of no grades, no monthly marks, and each pupil progressing according to his ability.[51]

Collier's unhesitating choice of Beatty as one of the original commissioners for the Indian Arts and Crafts Board reflected the general patience and consummate skill which he displayed in organizing the New Deal Indian program. In general, the time consumed in the search for the right people to further Indian arts and crafts paid rich dividends later in furthering New Deal Indian policy.

Beatty directly reflected Collier's view of the importance of Indian arts and crafts to the well-being of the Indians and their culture. In a 1936 article titled "Planning Indian Education in Terms of Pupil and Community Needs," Beatty called previous Indian education policy in error for minimizing the cultural contribution of the Indian racial heritage. "The encouragement of Indian young people in the development of handicrafts may," Beatty predicted, "through activities of the new Indian Arts and Crafts Board, bring results in the form of a definite contribution to the cash income of many families."[52]

Secretary Ickes also was working to publicize Indian arts and crafts; in February 1936, he established the Department of the Interior Office of Exhibits with a supervisor directly under the control of the secretary's office. Ickes had made an apparently purely political selection when he appointed George C. Dickens, a Chicago-based, government-employed, general agent for the Alaskan Railroad, as supervisor. In 1936, Dickens organized the Interior Department's Indian exhibits at the California Pacific International Exposition, the Texas Centennial Exposition, and the Great Lakes Exposition. Later in the year this new office began to make preliminary and tentative plans relating to the forthcoming San Francisco and New York expositions.[53]

Others shared Collier's views concerning the importance of Indian arts and crafts. In 1936 another in a series of small but significant exhibits of paintings from the Santa Fe Indian School was scheduled at the Gallery for Living Artists in the Brooklyn Museum, Brooklyn, New York, from 20 March to 12 April.[54] While chairman of the board of the Laboratory of Anthropology, Alfred Kidder had called for a study leading to the technical improvement of Pueblo pottery. In January 1936, after the project had been under way for one year with the financial assistance of the Carnegie Corporation, H. Warren Shepard of the Laboratory of Anthropology called the revival of Indian crafts an important movement in Indian welfare. "The value of crafts to the Indian cannot be measured in economic terms alone," Shepard stated, "no less important is their psychological effect. In a period of general cultural disintegration, it is most important that a people preserve their self-respect and their sense of racial worth. The successful exercise of an art and a skill serve this function."[55]

The New Mexico Association on Indian Affairs also urged the American public to cease regarding the Indians as curios and to accept them as intelligent beings "still creating a native American art of the highest order which should not be allowed to die out for lack of appreciation." Its policy, like that of other organizations of friends of the Indian, called for encouraging the Indians to continue their crafts according to their own development.[56]

RENÉ D'HARNONCOURT AND
THE FIRST YEARS OF THE BOARD

COLLIER'S PROBLEMS WITH getting the Indian Arts and Crafts Board into successful operation were solved by the appearance on the scene of René d'Harnoncourt, the man he picked to be the future general manager of the board and whose name became as synonymous with the promotion of Indian art as John Collier's with New Deal Indian policy.

D'Harnoncourt was no stranger to art. His personal background was well-suited for the person destined to accomplish what Collier sought for Indian arts and crafts—public recognition of Indian arts and crafts as a manifestation of American culture. Born in Vienna, Austria, in 1901, into a titled family of Franco-Belgian origin, d'Harnoncourt spent his early years in Graz, the site of the Jenneum, one of the earliest folk art museums in Europe. A relative of d'Harnoncourt's long had been associated with the museum, a fact which doubtlessly provided an influence on his future artistic development. As a teenager in Graz, he enjoyed collecting Dürer prints and along with three friends also put on an exhibit of Picasso and Matisse prints. Art was still considered an avocation by d'Harnoncourt when he studied philosophy and chemistry at the state university in Graz from 1918 to 1921. Then for two more years he continued his studies in chemistry at the Technische Hochschule in Vienna, but he had to withdraw for financial reasons. His support had been derived from part of his great-grandfather's estate, and, with the dissolution of the Austro-Hungarian Empire, Czechoslovakia had expropriated the property. D'Harnoncourt spent a brief time in Paris before proceeding almost penniless to Mexico City early in 1926. Without a speaking knowledge of Spanish or English and no prospect of employment as a chemist, he supported himself as a free-lance commercial artist painting postcards of bullfights for tourists, touching up advertising photographs for a newspaper, and decorating shop windows for department stores.[1]

D'Harnoncourt's struggle for a livelihood in Mexico City can be credited for developing his patience, understanding, and skill in handling personal relationships that were so evident in his later career in the United States. The personal qualities of the man fit the needs required at the moment for the success of Collier's Indian Arts and Crafts Board. At six feet six inches and 230 pounds, d'Harnoncourt was an imposing figure. Through his artwork he soon came in contact with important Mexican artists and dealers. One such contact with the American art dealer Frederick Davis proved to be a major stepping stone. D'Harnoncourt helped Davis to include pre-Columbian and folk art in his contemporary gallery, and in 1927 he arranged a major showing of the Mexican artists Diego Rivera, José Clemente Orozco, and Rufino Tamayo. Davis was one of the first to recognize d'Harnoncourt's organizational and artistic talents and offered to provide him with rent-free quarters at the gallery.

The Mexican Minister of Education was also a part of the Mexico City art scene and helped d'Harnoncourt to coordinate his efforts in promoting contemporary Mexican folk art at the Davis gallery. United States Ambassador Dwight W. Morrow and his wife Elizabeth Cutter Morrow had come to know d'Harnoncourt through the Ministry of Education and commissioned him to complete a fresco on the garden wall of their Cuernavaca home. D'Harnoncourt also became an advisor in the development of Elizabeth Morrow's art collection and illustrated two children's books written by her: *Painted Pig* (1930) and *Bird, Beast, and Fish* (1933). As an author and artist in his own right, d'Harnoncourt completed *Mexicana: A Book of Pictures* in 1931, in which he showed in his drawings a sensitivity to his surroundings beyond the visual, projecting a keen knowledge of the essence of things.[2]

D'Harnoncourt displayed his promotional abilities when helping to revive some of the Mexican village crafts. In Olinalá, for example, he and Roberto Montenegro, a versatile Mexican revolutionary, muralist, and promoter and collector of Mexican folk art, encouraged the production of the rich, resilient lacquer work that had been introduced from China over the Orient-to-Mexico-to-Spain trade route of the sixteenth century. To do this, they first located a few old Olinalá pieces in

125

Mexico City and then they took them to the village to remind the elderly artists what Olinalá work at its best was like. With money supplied by Frederick Davis, d'Harnoncourt and Montenegro purchased the necessary raw materials for the use of the old artists who had not yet forgotten this skill. With an offer to buy all the good pieces, d'Harnoncourt stirred up the Indians' enthusiasm. They started to practice their craft once more and began to teach willing young people. Income for the village mounted as Olinalá chests, caskets, and other objects were once more prized objects with a market. Thus a combination of forces led the Mexican government to ask d'Harnoncourt to help the Ministry of Education to preserve the folk art of the country and to make it economically fruitful. The ministry had become increasingly aware of the decadence being forced on the artists by the growing tourist trade. [3]

Ambassador Morrow's effort to improve relations between the United States and Mexico by changing the popular image of Mexico among Americans led to his suggestion to the Mexican government that it organize an exhibition of Mexican art for circulation in the United States. In New York, Morrow contacted Robert de Forest, president of the Metropolitan Museum, and the two went to see Frederick Keppel of the Carnegie Corporation, who agreed to finance the Mexican exhibition for one year through the American Federation of Arts. Homer St. Gaudens, director of the Art Institute of Pittsburgh, was dispatched to Mexico to pick out the director of the exhibition. He decided on Dr. Atl, an important Mexican landscape artist, revolutionary, writer, and organizer, and d'Harnoncourt as codirectors, but Dr. Atl was occupied with another project and the full burden fell to d'Harnoncourt. The Mexican exhibition brought d'Harnoncourt to the United States and ultimately launched his career. [4]

D'Harnoncourt spent the year 1930 collecting over 1,200 specimens for the arts and crafts exhibition, which then opened in Mexico City at the Ministry of Education. The combined pressure of Keppel, de Forest, and Morrow convinced the director of the Metropolitan Museum in New York to agree to an exhibition of this kind. Mexican folk art, the director believed, was something highly deplorable. His suspicions were confirmed, he thought, when the Metropolitan took an unauthorized preview of the first Mexican shipment and found a replica of Mexico City made by rush mat workers, which d'Harnoncourt termed "the least

dignified of everything we had." Hasty conferences were held and letters circulated, but the exhibit was not abandoned. The Metropolitan
refused to help d'Harnoncourt set up the show or to accept any involvement in its presentation. Native arts and crafts as yet had not reached
the full acceptance in the art world that they would have some ten years
later as a result of d'Harnoncourt's work.[5]

Despite the Metropolitan Museum's misgivings, the Mexican arts
and crafts exhibition was one of its greatest successes of the year. Keppel was so enthusiastic that upon request he immediately agreed to expand the itinerary from seven to fourteen cities and to provide the money
for a second year. In the process Keppel proved to be more than just an
employer for d'Harnoncourt. During the second year of the tour,
d'Harnoncourt had become engaged to Sarah Carr, an advertising copy
editor for Marshall Field and Company in Chicago, and because he
was not in the immigration quota, he asked Keppel's help to return to
the United States after the conclusion of the Mexican exhibition. Keppel quickly agreed to provide testimony and the promise of employment for d'Harnoncourt, who had to return to Austria to obtain an
immigration visa. Thanks to the Keppel testimonials, d'Harnoncourt
had his visa after only six months of waiting in Austria. Upon his return to New York in March 1933, he immediately called on Keppel to
thank his "godfather," who then lived up to his word and provided the
much-needed employment that was so scarce in a depression year. In
July, d'Harnoncourt began as director of the first nationwide broadcast
on the subject of art in America over the National Broadcasting Company radio network. In a complete change around, the Metropolitan
Museum now was happy to help d'Harnoncourt organize the first year
of broadcasts covering American art up to 1900. The five-year-old Museum of Modern Art provided assistance for the period following 1900.
The job kept d'Harnoncourt so busy, he said, that he waited to apply
for his United States citizenship until 1934. By 1939 he had become a
naturalized American citizen.[6]

While d'Harnoncourt held the radio broadcast job, Keppel sent him
to Washington to see if he could help out at the headquarters of the
American Federation of Arts, an organization in which Keppel had invested over half a million dollars of Carnegie money. It was Keppel's
belief that, since America was without a ministry of fine arts or an offi-

127

cial department of fine arts, the American Federation of Arts could perform those functions often carried out in other countries by an agency of their government. The Carnegie Corporation provided the president of the federation, a former director of the Cleveland Museum, with a chauffeured limousine to enhance the prestige of the federation as a great national agency on art. Among other duties, d'Harnoncourt was made assistant to the president of the American Federation of Arts and reported back to Keppel about the problems of the organization. Along with this work Keppel also used d'Harnoncourt to investigate applications for Carnegie art grants from across the country.[7]

As d'Harnoncourt's broadcasting job neared an end, Keppel worked discreetly behind the scene to bring d'Harnoncourt to the attention of the Faculty Central Committee at Sarah Lawrence College in Bronxville, New York. After the appropriate interviews, d'Harnoncourt in 1935 accepted a part-time position teaching introductory art history. In 1936 with Keppel's encouragement, he took the position on a full-time basis. For d'Harnoncourt his teaching was "a terribly interesting thing. God knows what the girls learned, but I learned an awful lot."[8] Regardless of these promising and successful circumstances, d'Harnoncourt responded with enthusiasm to Collier's offer to join the Indian Arts and Crafts Board.

According to d'Harnoncourt, his first meeting with Collier took place in Mexico in 1936 during one of d'Harnoncourt's annual summer trips to serve on the Mexican Committee on Cultural Relations with Latin America. These summer conferences were financed and sponsored by the Mexican government in an effort to get intellectuals from the United States to form a different picture of Mexico. Such Mexican artists as Rivera and Orozco mixed with American authors like Stuart Chase and Elmer Rice as participants in seminars and conferences on the two cultures. Collier was invited to participate in the 1936 conference along with Moises Saenz of the Indian Office Education Division. Collier wanted to know what Mexico was doing about Indian arts and crafts, and, at Saenz's urging, Collier had several conversations with d'Harnoncourt. From these meetings came the offer to d'Harnoncourt to join the Indian Arts and Crafts Board as assistant manager.[9]

The potential of the Indian Arts and Crafts Board grew in d'Harnoncourt's mind, and his appointment to the board as assistant to the general manager took place on 11 September 1936. Collier was so confident that he had found the right person to carry out the functions and the duties of the board that he had obtained a part-time release for d'Harnoncourt from his teaching contract at Sarah Lawrence College. At Collier's request, the college had agreed to reschedule d'Harnoncourt to teach art history only three days a week in order to complete the experimental program in which he was involved and which was financed by the General Education Board of the Rockefeller Foundation.[10] By necessity, d'Harnoncourt's first year of work for the Indian Arts and Crafts Board was limited and confined primarily to the New York area.

From experience, d'Harnoncourt believed that the only method possible in dealing with Indian arts and crafts was to work with each tribe and also with each local group or tribal subdivision as a separate entity. This made sense, he felt, since the work of the board was spread over such an immense and diversified area and one in which more than two hundred tribes existed. Any attempt, he maintained, to establish and practice a generalized method of procedure would be defeated at the outset. The key to the success of the Indian Arts and Crafts Board, according to d'Harnoncourt, "involved background research; careful consideration of the past history and present condition of each tribe; and, most important of all, close contact and cooperation with local Indian leaders and local Indian Service administrators."[11]

He had adhered carefully to this approach during his experience in Mexico and continued it during his service with the Indian Arts and Crafts Board. While Collier personally followed essentially the same approach in dealing with other aspects of Indian life, the magnitude of his total undertaking occasionally may have compelled him under pressure of time to follow a more generalized approach. This he undoubtedly recognized and attempted to rectify by surrounding himself with technically qualified administrators, such as d'Harnoncourt, whose responsibilities were more limited and who could develop more carefully an investigative and professionally knowledgeable plan of action. Collier's approach was representative of a growing acceptance of the use of technical and scientific experts in government administration, an approach which grew out of America's mobilization experience for the First World War.[12]

Collier enthusiastically responded to the addition of d'Harnoncourt to the staff of the Indian Arts and Crafts Board when he traced for the benefit of the House subcommittee on appropriations d'Harnoncourt's activities in Indian art in Mexico. D'Harnoncourt had put Mexican lacquer work on the world market, and it was sold everywhere. "Their income was quadrupled in a few years," Collier asserted, "and he succeeded in salvaging the craft. Now that is exactly the kind of thing that we must do, and we are using that same man, d'Harnoncourt, now." Collier labeled d'Harnoncourt "probably the leading technical authority in the world on the subject of Indian arts and crafts." He told the congressmen they would be intensely interested in talking with d'Harnoncourt, but the only response forthcoming was that of Congressman James M. Fitzpatrick, Democrat from New York, who revealed his real concern when he asked whether d'Harnoncourt had the same power here that the congressman thought d'Harnoncourt had had in Mexico. Fitzpatrick was exhibiting the deep concern of many congressmen over the power they had allowed the Roosevelt administration to garner in its battle with economic depression. Collier reassured him that d'Harnoncourt was simply "our employee." The congressman persisted and asked if d'Harnoncourt had the same privileges or authority as in Mexico. Diplomatically, Collier answered that in Mexico d'Harnoncourt had had the backing of the Mexican government. In the United States, he continued, "we do not spend much money on it [Indian arts and crafts]."[13]

Lacking funds until July 1936 and then operating from July to September with only one paid employee, Louis West, the Indian Arts and Crafts Board produced no tangible accomplishments in its assigned tasks and duties until d'Harnoncourt and three new employees were added. The three additions to the staff in September were Julia Lukas, a marketing specialist, Maria Chabot, a production advisor, and Ethel Petty, an administrative clerk. Collier was concerned over this delay and the lack of a sense of common purpose which he had observed at a 24 October board meeting. The minutes of this meeting showed consensus only on the decision to conduct a survey of the teaching of arts and crafts in the Indian schools and to hire a person to carry out this survey. Collier felt that this meeting "made it clear that there must be numerous and quite intensive meetings in order to develop common thinking and stable policy."[14] Such impatience to turn around the conditions surrounding Indian life could be seen throughout Collier's tenure as commissioner of Indian affairs.

For his first step as general manager, West wanted to determine just what kind and how much craftwork was being done at each Indian agency. Immediately after his appointment, he undertook an extensive field trip canvassing the Indian reservations to determine what problems existed in arts and crafts and to develop plans to handle them. The task for one person was overwhelming, and by October West devised a more efficient method of gathering the needed information. He sent out a form letter and questionnaire to all Indian agencies under the Indian Office telling them of the work of the Indian Arts and Crafts Board and requesting information regarding the arts and crafts produced in the area under their individual jurisdiction. Replies ranged from a complete negative from the Quapaw Agency in Oklahoma, where no arts and crafts were being produced and the whole topic was characterized by the superintendent as a "dead issue," to a lengthy and complete analysis with photographs and statistical data from the Sells Agency in Arizona.[15]

The most obvious and urgent of the board's tasks, that of establishing standards for the government mark for Navajo, Pueblo, and Hopi silver products, got under way at a meeting set up by the board on 5 October in Albuquerque. Invited to the meeting were representative dealers, traders, so-called "manufacturers," museum heads, and others who were interested in the preservation of the distinctive Indian silver crafts. Surprisingly, this meeting did not include any Indian artists. One of the discussion topics was the question whether or not to permit the use of sheet silver. Viewpoints differed greatly on this point and consensus was impossible. Another question was whether Indian jewelry, to be considered genuine, should be the work of a single artist from the raw material to the finished product. Only the problem of the use of apprentices prevented a unanimous agreement in favor of this requirement. A third question was whether to permit any but hand-cut and hand-polished stones. Sharp disagreements developed on this suggested requirement, but most of those present seemed to favor the use of machine-cut stones.[16]

As a result of this meeting, Collier predicted that no attempt would

131

be made to establish a single minimum standard such as only requiring that the silverwork be of good design and made by Indians. Instead, he believed that a set of maximum standards would be adopted because of the many variables in the craft process. The board again discussed the whole question at the meeting on 24 October and attempted a tentative statement of maximum standards for Indian jewelry and silverwork. At an open meeting in New Mexico of Indian traders and others, the board presented its inconclusive position for debate. From this meeting, held in Albuquerque on 19, 20, and 21 February, the Indian Arts and Crafts Board produced a unanimous final declaration of standards for the Navajo, Pueblo, and Hopi silver and turquoise products. In publicly announcing the standards on 9 March 1937, the board called Navajo, Pueblo, and Hopi silverwork an art and a product with a quality market, yet one that had been overwhelmed by machine production. "The Indian craftsman," the report continued, "struggling to compete in price with the machine-made and factory-made imitations, had in turn been forced to adopt a machine technique, while at the same time his wages or earnings have been depressed to the 'sweatshop' level." Quality had been sacrificed, the board maintained, to that extreme where Indian jewelry had become little more than a curio or a souvenir.[17]

The Indian Arts and Crafts Board still held out hope, for some Indian silver and turquoise work as fine as ever created in the past continued to be produced although in a relatively small quantity. The board claimed that many Indian artists existed who would "capably produce work as good as the best of earlier times" if a quality market could be restored. They could not produce it, the board maintained, in price competition with factory output, machine output, and bench work semimachine output. After studying the situation thoroughly, the board concluded "that the Government mark should be applied only to the finest quality of wholly genuine, truly hand-fashioned, and authentic Indian silver and turquoise products." The Indian Arts and Crafts Board statement, signed by John Collier, the chairman, nevertheless noted the limits to the government standards:

Use of the Government mark is not obligatory on any Indian, any factory, or any merchant. The Board has no power or purpose to forbid such production by time-saving methods and with machine stereotyped and stinted materials as now supplies the curio market. But for that production which is worthy of a fine Indian tradition, the Board will make available the Government certificate of genuineness and of quality; and the Board will seek to widen the existing "quality" market and to find new markets for such output as deserves the Government mark. In the measure of its success, the Board will help to bring about a larger reward for a greater number of Indian craftsmen, and to save from destruction a noble, historic art, which under right conditions can have a long future.[18]

The board's standards were purist to the core. The government stamp could be affixed only to work individually produced and to work entirely handmade. No objects produced under conditions resembling a bench work system and no objects in whose manufacture any power-driven machinery had been used were eligible for the use of the government stamp.

Specifications that had to be met by Indian silver objects in order to merit the government stamp were as follows:

1. *Material.* Silver slugs of one ounce weight or other silver objects may be used, provided their fineness is at least 900; and provided further, that no silver sheet shall be used. Unless cast, the slug or other object is to be hand-hammered to thickness and shape desired. The only exceptions here are pins on brooches or similar objects; ear screws for earrings; backs for tie clasps and chain, which may be of silver of different fineness and mechanically made.

2. *Dies.* Dies used are to be entirely hand-made, with no tool more mechanical than hand tools and vice. Dies shall contain only a single element of the design.

3. *Application of dies.* Dies are to be applied to the object with the aid of nothing except hand tools.

4. *Applique elements in design.* All such parts of the ornament are to be hand-made. If wire is used, it is to be hand-made with no tool other than a hand-made draw plate. These requirements apply to the boxes for stone used in the design.

5. *Stone for ornamentation.* In addition to turquoise, the use of other local stones is permitted. Turquoise, if used, must be genuine stone, uncolored by an artificial means.

6. *Cutting of stone.* All stone used, including turquoise, is to be hand-cut and polished. This permits the use of hand- or foot-driven wheels.

7. *Finish.* All silver is to be hand-polished. For the present the Arts and Crafts Board reserves to itself the sole right to determine what silver, complying with the official standards shall be stamped with the Government mark.[19]

One month later, on 2 April 1937, Secretary Ickes approved the regulations governing the use of government trademarks of genuineness and quality. This power had been conferred on the Indian Arts and Crafts Board by the Indian Arts and Crafts Board Act. Federal enforcement of these regulations was based on criminal prosecution under Section 5 of the same law.

Under the new regulations for silver products, the Indian Arts and Crafts Board provided and owned all dies used to mark silver. Also, for the present, only an agent of the Indian Arts and Crafts Board could mark the silver; who or when was not specified. Even though the silverwork complied with the Indian Arts and Crafts Board standards, the government mark could not be added unless the weight and design were in accord with Indian usage and custom and the work displayed good handcraft techniques. A different stamp would be used for each tribe, the name of which would be on the die. The numbering of each die identified the dealer or wholesaler for whom the silver was marked, and the dealer or wholesaler alone would be responsible for misrepresentations of quality and methods of production. The dealer was authorized to attach to the silver a label or ticket advertising the government mark and to display in a prominent place a placard provided by the Indian Arts and Crafts Board listing these regulations.[20]

The standards for application of the government stamp and the regulations for its use presented an excellent example of New Deal activity and New Deal Indian policy, government movement into the public sphere toward goals that the previous administration had left for associations, foundations, and corporate bureaucracies to achieve. Collier involved these same organizations in carrying out his New Deal Indian programs. His work was a realization of the concept of the national government offering a helping hand by promoting individual economic and cultural endeavors. New Deal Indian policy was a government attempt to resurrect and to preserve not only the individual identity of the oldest culture in America but also its very existence. The Indian Arts and Crafts Board was one of the vehicles adopted by the New Deal administration to carry out that policy.

The next step was the completion of the long-awaited Navajo wool regulations. These regulations for the use of a government certificate of genuineness for Navajo all-wool woven fabrics were established by the Indian Arts and Crafts Board on 15 June 1937 and approved by the secretary of the interior on 20 October 1937. Under these provisions any person might obtain a license to use the government certificate after applying to the board and signing a contract with it based on conformity with the regulations. An indemnity bond of $500 was required. Under the regulations, no fabric could carry the government certificate of genuineness unless the following conditions were met:

1. The fabric is made entirely of local wool that is locally hand-spun and is entirely woven on a native Navajo loom;

2. The fabric is made by a member of the Navajo Tribe working under conditions not resembling a workshop or factory system;

3. The size and weight of the fabric are indicated in the certificate;

4. The licensee dates and signs the certificate.[21]

As under the silver regulations, criminal penalties provided by Section 5 of the Indian Arts and Crafts Board Act served to give force to the Navajo wool regulations. After the licensee paid an initial registration fee of two dollars and a license fee of one dollar for each forty certificates ordered, he was furnished one hand seal press and the requested number of certificates, which all remained the property of the board. In case of public complaint to the board against the licensee, the board retained the right to suspend the rights of the licensee for thirty days, in which time an investigation of the charges was to be made. Violation of any regulation meant permanent revocation of the license and possible fine or imprisonment.[22]

The certificate was documentary proof of the genuineness of the product. Only the licensee could fasten the certificate to the woven fabric. The ultimate retailer, if he was not the person who originally attached the certificate and if he was licensed under the Indian Arts and Crafts Board regulations, could also date and sign in designated spaces at the top of the certificate and detach the original date and signature from the bottom. Only those products in the ownership or possession of the licensee could receive the certificate. The certificates were consecutively numbered, and the Indian Arts and Crafts Board kept a record of their allocation. The licensee was responsible for the proper use of the certificates and the government hand seal.[23]

135

The government certificate of genuineness for Navajo all-wool woven fabrics and the regulations for its use realized one of the major goals behind the establishment of the Indian Arts and Crafts Board. For years agitation for governmental assistance to preserve Indian arts and crafts had centered around the example of the Navajo weavers and their problems. The concept of a government certificate was not original with Collier or the Indian Arts and Crafts Board, but Collier and the board succeeded in bringing the idea to reality. A sympathetic New Deal administration based on a general public recognition of the tragic circumstances of economic depression provided the basis for the cooperation that produced the Navajo weaving regulations. Previous attempts had failed primarily because cooperation had been lacking with the individual traders and agency superintendents. This attitude resulted either from their experience under previous government policies toward Indian culture or their own inertia.

Lingering vestiges of that uncooperative attitude surfaced during the first year after the inauguration of the government certificates of genuineness for Navajo all-wool woven fabrics. Simple complaints were made that the tag was awkward and too large and that no need existed for the information as to date and weight. The certificate's size and the date designation seemed minor and somewhat trivial complaints that easily could be remedied.[24]

Elimination of the fabric weight designation was more difficult to accomplish. While the purpose of the certificate was to ensure quality, the required weight designation brought in another element for the purchaser to consider. Confusion existed in some minds over the relative importance of weight, a measurement which had been used by many traders for years to determine what they would pay the individual Navajo weaver for her work. Design and weaving skill were often less important in earlier years than the amount of wool used in the product. Now, most traders viewed the weight designation as an unnecessary distraction in the sale of a Navajo fabric. After he became a full-time employee, d'Harnoncourt investigated these complaints and found unanimity among the traders against the weight labeling. Attempting to amend the regulations, he obtained the full approval of everyone concerned except Louis West. Not in touch with the realities of quality craftwork, West remained adamant in his belief that a weight designation was a measure of quality and protected the consumer.[25]

The response of the Indian Arts and Crafts Board to the certificate problem seemed inordinately slow. Fully two years passed after the initial regulations were published before they were amended. The board was aware after the first year that the certificates were not being used. The only trader who reordered certificates and renewed his license for the second year was Lorenzo Hubbell, a member of the Indian Arts and Crafts Board. The Fred Harvey Company returned all but one of the certificates ordered a year earlier and also its hand-press seal. Harvey called the certificates impractical and said he could see no object in renewing the license. Like most volume traders, he supported the concept if not the reality. "We understand that something else more suitable is intended to be worked out," said Harvey, "and, whenever this is accomplished, we will, of course, be glad to go along with the proposition." The reorganized and expanding United Indian Traders Association also expressed its cooperation and interest and asked when the new wool certificate was coming. In a business estimated by Collier to sell $750,000 worth of merchandise a year, the government certificate of genuineness promised to be of incalculable benefit to the Indians, yet in practice the plan was not achieving that potential. [26]

In addition to establishing standards for silver and woven products, improving the marketing of all Indian arts and crafts was a primary target for the board. One of the first steps in that direction by Indian Arts and Crafts Board general manager Louis West was his successful effort in May 1936 to persuade the Great Northern Railway to reconsider its policy of excluding from its stores the handcraft products of the Dakota and Montana tribes. [27] In another attempt to organize marketing efforts, on 29 April West sent a four-page list of Indian crafts to each agency superintendent and requested the superintendent to circle those crafts produced on his reservation. The responses were to be used in the publication of a directory of currently produced Indian goods "to use in discussing with interested persons the possibility of expanding markets outside the area where any particular item is made." Even this simplified approach produced responses which illustrated the lack of knowledge of and experience with Indian arts and crafts on the part of many agency superintendents. Inertia produced by years of discrediting Indian culture seeped through the lines of many of the comments that accompanied the circled items. Where Indian craftwork had remained an important source of income, the superintendent was either knowledgeable or could find a subordinate or a trader who could provide the requested information. Elsewhere the questionnaire was viewed as another time-consuming, thankless task foisted upon an already overburdened staff and one they felt would only be filed and forgotten.[28]

Meanwhile, d'Harnoncourt spent his spring vacation from Sarah Lawrence College examining the craft possibilities in every part of Oklahoma and arranged for a modest flow of craft output from that state. The difficulty he found was not in marketing but rather in good craft production.[29] He did not recommend government standards just as he had played no part in the development and establishment of the silver standards or the Navajo woven products standards. Although he never spoke directly against government standards, he never encouraged their use or expressed any belief that they would become a major factor in the promotion of Indian arts and crafts.

The difference between West's and d'Harnoncourt's approach to Indian arts and crafts could be seen most readily at this point. West lacked direct contact with the crafts and artists and preferred to operate as a corporate executive logically would through business meetings and correspondence. On the other hand, d'Harnoncourt, experienced in artistic evaluation and promotion, saw his Indian Arts and Crafts Board role as one of direct contact with the art and artists to enable him to speak from firsthand knowledge. In a situation filled with innumerable skills, customs, and details, West's approach was not what Collier wanted for the future of the Indian Arts and Crafts Board. West apparently became aware of the difficulty and offered to step down as general manager in return for a position as an arts and crafts specialist with the Division of Education and appointment as a board member. With his characteristic combination of diplomatic and political skills, Collier took the opportunity to make the change.

On 15 June Collier informed West that the Indian Arts and Crafts Board had taken the following actions "in conformity with your suggestion": first, Beatty had requested to be relieved from duty on the board and the board had recommended to the secretary of the interior that West take his place; then, the board had accepted West's resignation, effective upon the date of his appointment as arts and crafts specialist in the Division of Education; and finally, the board had voted that d'Harnoncourt would take over the duties of general manager upon the completion of West's appointment. In addition, Collier emphasized that in releasing Beatty from membership the board did not feel it would be losing any of his attention or energy. With a personal note of encouragement, Collier told West that his relationship to the arts and crafts enterprise would become more comprehensive as a result of the adjustments.[30] Collier's dreams for Indian arts and crafts now could move forward under the experienced leadership he long had sought.

More problems arose, however, because the infrequency of board meetings contributed to delays in policy decisions. By 1938 West had moved to Cleveland, Ohio, Alfred Kidder continued his residence in Cambridge, Massachusetts, and Hubbell never left Oraibi, Arizona. Only Ebert Burlew, promoted in December 1937 to first assistant secretary of the interior, and Collier resided in Washington. In June 1938, d'Harnoncourt found it necessary to remind Collier, the board chairman, that the bylaws adopted at the first meeting of the board, 7 July 1936, contained the provision that meetings of the board "shall be held not less frequently than twice during each fiscal year." Hubbell had been in ill health for several years, a situation which had prevented him from attending any Washington meetings. As an old friend of the Hubbell family, Collier earlier had refused Hubbell's offer to resign. Aware now that the effectiveness of d'Harnoncourt's work depended on action by the board, Collier considered not reappointing Hubbell when his term expired in July, yet no action was taken when Hubbell announced suddenly that he was now able to give more time to the board and to attend its meetings. No doubt Hubbell was influenced in his decision when travel expenses finally were approved for board members on official duty. Collier's assurances in his representations to prospective board members regarding reimbursement for travel expenses to board meetings had not been upheld by the Department of the Interior finance officers, who could find no statutory justification that applied. A special authorization by Ickes was necessary to charge board member travel expenses to the Indian Arts and Crafts Board appropriation.[31]

Despite the various setbacks, 1938 proved to be the board's single most active and successful one to date. Now d'Harnoncourt was moving ahead in his own right after delays due to the change in management and difficulties in obtaining staff personnel for carrying out the board's work. He added three exceptionally well-qualified field representatives and an assistant manager to the board.[32] Their surveys and d'Harnoncourt's covered practically all areas of the United States and southern Alaska and provided the basis for planning future board activities since each reservation and tribe required an individual approach. The work at a small experimental laboratory set up a year earlier by the Indian Arts and Crafts Board at Tesuque, New Mexico, for tanners, weavers, and silversmiths was just beginning to be productive. The work of other governmental agencies began to dovetail with the Indian Arts and Crafts Board's efforts as in the case of the Southwestern Range and Sheepbreeding Laboratory established in 1936 on the Navajo Reservation at Fort Wingate, New Mexico, under the supervision of specialists in the Department of Agriculture. Encouragement of Indian self-help and organization continued as cooperatives and marketing groups began to appear under the guidance of the Indian Arts and Crafts Board. When plans for participation in the 1939 San Francisco Golden Gate International Exposition began to take concrete form, d'Harnoncourt found the assistance Collier had deemed so necessary at the time of his appointment as Indian Arts and Crafts Board general manager.

D'Harnoncourt's selection of employees reflected his primary concern for experience in the field. Early in 1938 he requested the appointment of Kenneth B. Disher, an employee in the Museum Division of the National Park Service, as assistant manager at a salary of $3,800 per year. Preparation for the promotion of Indian arts and crafts not only at the San Francisco Exposition but also wherever the public could be influenced was reflected in the appointment of Henry Klumb, an expert on interior design and display, at a salary of $3,600 per year. Klumb's general assignment was to create displays stressing the adaptability of Indian arts and crafts to modern rooms. Among the temporary specialists needed by d'Harnoncourt for the expanding promotional push was a professional photographer. New York photographer Konrad Cramer was secured to assist with Indian Arts and Crafts Board publications for three months in 1938.[33]

The organization of Indian Arts and Crafts Board efforts in the field became possible early in 1937 when board members approved the appointment of several regional field workers designated as arts and crafts investigators and later as specialists in Indian arts and crafts. Budgetary planning and exhaustive searching delayed the filling of these posts, however, until the end of fiscal year 1938. The first specialist, Gladys

Tantaquidgeon from Mohegan Hill, Norwich, Connecticut, was assigned to the Sioux area in North and South Dakota. She first had been employed by the Indian Office in 1934 to inform the surviving New England Indians of their new privileges under the Wheeler-Howard Act. Tantaquidgeon was almost literally "the last of the Mohicans." She was a direct descendent of one of the aides to Uncas, who was made famous in the James Fenimore Cooper novel, and of Sansom Occum, a self-educated Indian who had become a missionary and minister prominent in early Connecticut history. Tantaquidgeon was an artist and worked in anthropology at the University of Pennsylvania.[34]

Soon after Tantaquidgeon received her assignment, Alice Marriott of Oklahoma City became specialist among the Oklahoma tribes with primary attention to the Kiowas. Educated in anthropology and a writer on ethnographic subjects, Marriott had experience in museum work and in the native arts and crafts of Oklahoma tribes. Her specific duties included reviving old Indian craft groups as bases for setting up practical Indian cooperatives, collecting raw materials, researching old techniques of beadwork, and preserving techniques of leatherwork and pottery making.[35]

In July 1938, Gwyneth B. Harrington from Boston was transferred from the Soil Conservation Service to the Indian Arts and Crafts Board as a specialist. Her previous work as a soil conservationist involved making socioeconomic surveys on Indian reservations. D'Harnoncourt assigned her to the Papago Indian country and southern Arizona in general with the express purpose of reviving basketry. He considered this extremely urgent work because the Papago basketmakers were in danger of being ruined by unwise commercial exploitation. Harrington had been employed in that geographical area for some time and was familiar with local conditions and the arts and crafts situation.[36]

The life of a specialist in Indian arts and crafts was demanding and rugged by any measurement. The full-time position as an Indian Arts and Crafts Board field representative paid $2,100 per year in 1938. The job description seemed deceptively simple as a general assignment. First, the specialist had to cooperate with the Indians in local areas by discussing with them the production and improvement of their native arts. Second, the specialist had to serve as an intermediary between the Indian Arts and Crafts Board and all local groups, cooperatives, or individuals who were interested in planning, producing, or selling arts and

141

crafts products. Third, the specialist was required to criticize Indian handcrafts from the standpoint of both technique and design. Fourth, the specialist had the important task of encouraging the production of only such arts and crafts as would find a ready market. Finally, the specialist was required to establish contacts with existing retail outlets and to discover new ones.[37]

Personal working conditions of the Indian Arts and Crafts Board specialist were clearly not for the weak in body or spirit. On a typical day on the 45,000-square-mile Papago Reservation in Arizona, Gwyneth Harrington left Sells at eight-thirty in the morning and drove from village to village, never returning before eight o'clock in the evening. Then the work of entering purchases on ledgers, plus making out all of the receipts and tags required not only for the Indian Arts and Crafts Board but also for Papago tribal records and for the reservation's administrative office, kept her busy until ten-thirty or eleven o'clock at night. Somewhere in this schedule, she did her own housekeeping in "a very dirty little shack where the wind blows through," did the cooking, and kept the stove going in the cold weather. As a transplanted Bostonian, Harrington successfully adjusted to life in the Southwest, and she married a Papago chieftain's son in 1942 while still employed by the Indian Arts and Crafts Board.[38]

Prior to acquiring the services of the three new specialists, the board had completed intensive surveys for possible board activity in North Carolina, Oklahoma, New Mexico, Arizona, Southern California, North and South Dakota, Montana, Washington, Oregon, Wyoming, and New York.[39] The personal contact work of the board was now to be extended to and concentrated on the three areas assigned to the new specialists: the Southwest, Oklahoma, and North and South Dakota.

D'Harnoncourt left the disagreeable and often discouraging political situation in Washington for Collier and others to handle and concentrated on the task of cultural and economic promotion of Indian arts and crafts, a task in which he was to prove successful within a few short years.

D'Harnoncourt's philosophy about Indian arts and crafts was both realistic and optimistic. He was aware that the place of handcrafts in the twentieth century had not been defined. Mass production had provided cheaper and frequently more useful articles than previously had been made by hand, forcing the abandonment of many types of handcrafts. Yet, d'Harnoncourt discerned a glimmer of hope. Increasingly in the last few years, evidence showed that the factory-made articles did not satisfy the needs of that part of the buying public demanding individual design and individual craft skills. Numerous efforts to establish new studios and shops devoted solely to the sale and production of handmade objects had been made everywhere, particularly in the larger cities where industrialism was centered. D'Harnoncourt called this time a period of transition which eventually would lead to a new position for handcrafts in the world market where they would not attempt to compete with machine products, but would supplement them. Because their future functions could be a matter of conjecture only, d'Harnoncourt based his plan of action on an assessment of their present status relative to the existing four areas of market demand.[40]

D'Harnoncourt believed that the market within the producer's group was far greater and more important than was generally believed. While the local market for Indian handcrafts that was based solely on economic considerations was decreasing steadily with increased means of transportation and the gradual reduction in the price of machine products, the market that was based on the preference for Indian form and design for traditional usage was declining only in places where tradition itself was on the decline. D'Harnoncourt was encouraged by what he believed was a new attitude displayed in recent years toward tradition among some tribal groups who recognized tradition simply as an expression of tribal identity rather than as an inflexible pattern opposed to progress.

The small but extremely important collector's market posed both existing and potential benefits for Indian arts and crafts. D'Harnoncourt attributed the limited number of collectors to the widespread belief that the contemporary production was inferior to the work of earlier days, and also to the fact that Indian art in itself was still relatively unknown. The collector's market for Indian art never had been developed systematically, and d'Harnoncourt believed intensive promotional work could increase its demands. He warned, nevertheless, against overestimating the financial benefits of such development. The prices paid for individual pieces on this market were significantly higher, but the direct benefits would always go to only a comparatively small number of artists. The indirect benefits of an increased collector's market were of extreme importance in d'Harnoncourt's view. Although certainly not measurable, the promotional value of fine private and public collections would stimulate wider demands among the general public, and the existence of a discriminating and exacting group of buyers would be an invaluable aid in maintaining high standards of craft skill.

The market with the deepest and most immediate implications for the Indian artists was the souvenir market. Despite its extent and turnover, no stable future existed because the business involved articles that were considered useful objects of value by their makers but merely trinkets by their purchasers. D'Harnoncourt saw no way to reconcile the exigencies of traditional production with those of the souvenir market in a long-range program designed to take full advantage of the potentialities of Indian arts and crafts. Economic problems created by this conflict, however, compelled d'Harnoncourt to entertain two possible solutions. The first involved educating the buying public to an appreciation of the intrinsic values of Indian handcrafts, a step that actually would have removed the customers from the class of souvenir buyers. This was already a part of Indian Arts and Crafts Board work. The second solution involved the stimulation of a distinct souvenir industry based on speed and volume of production, a step that would have led to the loss of individuality in design and craft skills characteristic of traditional craftwork. Obviously, the latter step was objectionable to d'Harnoncourt because it did not fall within the scope of arts and crafts work proper. As a mark of his deep concern and commitment not just to Indian arts and crafts but also to the overall welfare of the individual Indians, he realistically recognized the necessity of considering this plan in certain regions as a matter of economic expediency.

The best opportunities for a sound development of Indian crafts, d'Harnoncourt asserted, were found in the market for useful quality products. This market included not only all types of practical household and clothing accessories such as furniture, sporting goods, fabrics, and jewelry but also items purchased exclusively for the sake of their decorative function in the buyers' homes. The group included the table centerpiece and the wall hanging that were purchased to fill an aesthetic need and excluded the collector's item that was acquired simply for its ethnological or technical interest and the souvenir acquired solely on the strength of its associations. The products for such a market appeared to d'Harnoncourt to be unlimited and their prices were based on the real values of usefulness and quality of execution rather than on the intangibles of association or rarity. The customers were assured of their money's worth in any price range. D'Harnoncourt truly believed that the market for useful quality items offered the artists and the buyers both immediate and long-range advantages not to be found in the other three markets. He stressed this point continuously over his years with the Indian Arts and Crafts Board and this belief became one of the board's foundation stones.

D'Harnoncourt, unlike the so-called purists, was not afraid to encourage adaptations of Indian crafts to enable the Indians to take advantage of this market. He was aware that such adaptations had taken place in the course of the production history of all crafts and were part of the normal development of any living art form.

The market for useful quality Indian products had been neglected almost completely in many places. D'Harnoncourt was amazed that most of the people interested in the production and sale of Indian arts and crafts had given so little encouragement to well-made, useful products. He was deeply disturbed about the false emphasis in the commercial presentation of Indian art and labeled it the reason rather than the result of a lack of a widespread appreciative public. Potential buyers for Indian products of good quality lost their initial interest when their concern for real value was met with fanciful pretentions. This approach at its worst involved brochures purporting to give a picturesque background to the articles or folders claiming to explain the meaning of all symbols of all tribes with every ten-cent purchase. D'Harnoncourt considered this "quite a bargain considering the fact that a medicine man usually needs a lifetime to understand [the] true significance of all the symbols used by his own immediate group." That sound merchandising and promotion practices in Indian arts and crafts had been given so little thought or effort seemed incomprehensible to the manager of the Indian Arts and Crafts Board. He called most present practices "just a continuation of the first fumbling efforts to meet the casual demands of early tourists in Indian country." Unlike all other types of merchandising, no intensive studies of adequate display and sales methods ever had been made for Indian crafts. Up to that time such simple devices to gain public confidence as the separation of quality work from poor work and imitations were used only in very outstanding sales outlets. D'Harnoncourt advocated extensive research work to provide the knowledge to advise on production and merchandising. In time, d'Harnoncourt became completely involved in a personal crusade to improve all aspects of the Indian arts and crafts situation in the United States.

Indian participation by artist-representatives of the various tribal groups was one of the most important factors contributing to the success of the San Francisco exhibition. Mr. and Mrs. Spanish of the Blackfoot tribe are greeting Eleanor Roosevelt. George Creel, United States commissioner for the Golden Gate Exposition, stands next to Mrs. Roosevelt. René d'Harnoncourt is at the far right. (National Archives)

Mabel Burnside, a Navajo weaver, worked as a demonstrator at the exposition during the time of the commencement exercises at Wingate Vocational High School. Commissioner Creel is presenting the artist with her diploma, sent to San Francisco by the school. (National Archives)

Dinner at the Indian lounge on Yerba Buena Island. To make the Indian participants comfortable and to avoid the Buffalo Bill atmosphere often connected with Indian camps at fairgrounds, the demonstrators and tribal representatives lived at a nearby United States Navy base. (National Archives)

The Maharajah of Kapurthala is greeted at the exhibit by Hastine Todokozie, a medicine man, who for two months directed Navajo sand painting at the exhibit. Commissioner Creel observes from the steps. (National Archives)

René d'Harnoncourt pauses in 1938 during one of his trips to the Southwest to carry out the activities of the Indian Arts and Crafts Board. (National Archives)

Indian life. An unidentified Southwest Indian family on a wagon trip in the winter of 1938–39. (National Archives)

René d'Harnoncourt in New Mexico in 1938. Although educated in Europe, he understood the problems Indian artists faced. (National Archives)

Proud artists and their work. Chilkat blanket-capes like this masterpiece of the weaver's art are made from the wool of mountain goats left natural white in many design areas and dyed black, yellow, or green for others. The blankets are worn at ceremonies. (National Archives)

Tlinkit ceremonial garb consisting of a blanket decorated with mother-of-pearl buttons and a carved wooden headdress inlaid with abalone shell and draped with animal pelts. (National Archives)

Totem pole seen by d'Harnoncourt in Saxman, south of Ketchikan, during his Alaskan trip in May 1938. The beaver at the top of the wooden memorial honors the lineage of the woman, Eagle Sitting on a Nest, to whose memory the marble monument in the rear is dedicated. (National Archives)

156

A collection of totem poles is the main attraction of this Alaskan community park. The importance of quality work along traditional lines was evident to d'Harnoncourt in every place he visited in Alaska where art was practiced for local consumption. (National Archives)

A huge house pillar illustrates the size of the traditional Northwest Coast community building. Even more apparent is the spiritual power that cannot escape the beholder of this art. (National Archives)

A grave totem in one of the deserted villages near Hydaburg. D'Harnoncourt found that the people from these villages, who now lived in Hydaburg, still talked of the abandoned carvings as their personal possessions and wanted to carry on the traditional art work. (National Archives)

Grave fences surround this totem grave marker made from stone in a style similar to European cultural practices. D'Harnoncourt noted that almost everyone he spoke to emphasized the importance of doing work the "right" way and that a fear existed that the old arts might deteriorate or disappear. (National Archives)

159

Sister Providencia, affectionately known to the Northwest Indians as "Sister Buckskin," is showing Eleanor Roosevelt an exhibit of Indian handcrafts. At this 1941 display in the House Indian Affairs Committee Room, Sister Providencia credited d'Harnoncourt and the San Francisco Exposition for the Indian craft revival. (National Archives)

A Florida Indian dugout canoe carver is shown here talking with d'Harnoncourt about 1953. His desire for direct contact with the Indian artists was a life-long need which contributed greatly to the success of the Indian Arts and Crafts Board. (Museum of Modern Art)

Apprehension. World War II and a few politicians disrupted and almost de-
molished the Indian Arts and Crafts Board at a time when the need for its
existence was even greater than during the depression. Photographed here at
about the time of his resignation as general manager, d'Harnoncourt shows the
concern he deeply felt for the future of Indian art. (Museum of Modern Art)

8

PLANNING, PROMOTING, AND FINANCING THE SAN FRANCISCO EXHIBIT

THE INDIAN ARTS AND CRAFTS BOARD'S efforts at the Golden Gate International Exposition at San Francisco in 1939 were designed to open new vistas for the future of Indian arts and crafts by means of public education about and exposure to those arts. The exhibition was not to be an end in itself but rather a means of gaining the public's attention and creating a better understanding of the Indians' talents.[1] While exhibitions of Indian arts and crafts had been increasing in number, particularly in the Southwest, none had had the total involvement of the board or the size and the influence of the San Francisco Exposition.

Some earlier exhibits had provided experimental forums for the San Francisco effort and had proved to be powerful instruments of public education in the beauty and usefulness of Indian arts and crafts products. In August 1938, the Indian Arts and Crafts Board in cooperation with the United Pueblo Agency and the Pueblo area traders presented a unified exhibit at the Gallup Intertribal Ceremonial. Under d'Harnoncourt's influence, the exhibit emphasized for the first time the importance of the methods of displaying Indian goods. The theme throughout the presentation was the usefulness of Pueblo arts and crafts in the modern home.[2] The display also showed the use of Indian products as accessories to modern clothing. During the ceremonial, Indian products valued at $10,000 were sold. Another display similar to that at the Gallup Intertribal Ceremonial was presented at the American Indian Exposition at Tulsa, Oklahoma, in October 1938. In cooperation with the Indian Office and the executive committee of the exposition, the Indian Arts and Crafts Board used objects made exclusively by Indians in Oklahoma. More stress was placed on clothing accessories and on show-window displays in an effort to interest the merchants of Oklahoma in

163

carrying quality Indian goods in their shops. The increased demand for Indian products in these areas following the exhibits convinced the board of the effectiveness of its method of displaying Indian objects in modern settings.[3]

Originally the concept of a large Indian arts and crafts exhibit at the San Francisco Exposition belonged to a small group of San Francisco social figures, most active of whom was Leslie Denman, the long-time supporter of Indian art. Even before the Indian Arts and Crafts Board Act was passed, Denman was in touch with Washington officials and others about such an exhibit. Collier reported having had "a little talk with the President," during which Eleanor Roosevelt brought up the idea of an Indian exhibit at the San Francisco Exposition. "There can be no doubt of the interested attitude of both the President and Mrs. Roosevelt toward it," the commissioner reported. As soon as Collier named Louis West general manager of the Indian Arts and Crafts Board, Denman began to involve him in her efforts. Subsequently, she was asked by Leland W. Cutler, newly named president of the Golden Gate International Exposition, to initiate official contacts with government officers and the most prominent and influential Indians regarding the proposed Indian exhibit and to determine their reactions and what help and cooperation might be expected from them.[4]

In an article for the *Women's City Club Magazine* for July 1936, Denman explained what she considered to be the driving forces in the revival of Indian arts and crafts. She understood that archaeology and anthropology were news at the time. She saw that Indian arts and crafts had cultural significance as well as future economic value. "Man is curious about himself," Denman declared. She defined the purposes of an exposition as attempts "to increase the sum of human knowledge, to lay the foundations for increased economic good, to create more understanding social relations, and to present opportunities for a development of trade."[5]

This drive to promote Indian arts and crafts at the San Francisco Exposition drew a coterie of influential enthusiasts. Their private efforts and public contributions produced a momentum that grew with each stage of development, drawing others into their spirit of enthusiasm. The San Francisco Exposition became the light on the horizon not only for the Indian Arts and Crafts Board but also for the many Indians planning directly or indirectly to participate. The board realized that careful planning was necessary to achieve the desired public awareness and acceptance of Indian arts and crafts as a contribution to modern society. In the view of the board and its supporters such an achievement would benefit immeasurably both Indian and non-Indian cultural life. Collier dramatically expressed this view in 1936 at the outset of the preparations for San Francisco. This goal "would be realized in terms of [Indian] numbers increasing, not dwindling; of [Indian] property-holdings increasing, not continuing to melt away; of [Indian] cultural values preserved, intensified, and appreciated and sought for by the whole world." No longer, Collier hoped, would the Indians be treated as being significant only in terms of an outlived or crushed world.[6]

The 1939 San Francisco Exposition Indian exhibit was a concrete result of the work of the Indian Arts and Crafts Board although the board's efforts would have been curtailed drastically without the influence and cooperation of the small group of Indian art enthusiasts clustered in San Francisco. D'Harnoncourt revealed the significance of the group headed by Leslie Denman when he was questioned by the House Subcommittee on Interior Department Appropriations in 1938. "Why not [exhibit] in New York?" asked Congressman Emmet O'Neal, Democrat from New York, referring to the 1939 New York Exposition. "You certainly would have a greater market there." "First of all," d'Harnoncourt replied, "we found that we were backed in San Francisco by a committee of local residents interested in Indian affairs, who cooperated with us in a most energetic and efficient way." D'Harnoncourt also stated that "in San Francisco, we can become one of the largest, if not the most outstanding feature in the fair and get national recognition, which could not possibly happen in New York." The ever-diplomatic Collier attempted to smooth things over by adding the statement that a sufficient supply of high-grade products could not be obtained to take care of the market in both places. "We can, no doubt, sell all that we can produce in San Francisco," he added.[7]

D'Harnoncourt gave great credit to Denman for her role in the Indian exhibit. In his estimation, she was "an incredible woman, a marvelous woman, terribly excited by the Indians." Denman knew the Franklin Roosevelts and many members of Congress. A story was popularly circulated and later related by d'Harnoncourt, although no evidence existed for its substantiation, that Denman "persuaded Congress just to make a special sentence which would say that the government pavilion would represent the various government agencies in a proportionate manner, which was more or less by budget, except in cases where the subject was of particular local interest." Local interest, d'Harnoncourt explained, was interpreted to mean that Indians were more interesting to the West than anything else. "As a result we got over one-third of the whole place [United States government pavilion area], where normally we would have got one-half of one percent, . . . This was an enormous thing."[8]

Before any government plans were developed, Denman submitted her own thirteen-page preliminary plan for an extensive Indian exhibit. Requiring eight to twelve acres and involving twenty-two or more agencies, organizations, institutions, and museums, the Denman plan was presented to Collier on 27 October 1936 as "Notes and Suggestions for a Plan for an Indian Presentation at the San Francisco Bay Bridge Exposition of 1939." Contagious enthusiasm permeated every line of her plan, which was also exceptionally creative in concept. A memory existed, Denman believed, in the minds of people the world over of the San Francisco Panama-Pacific Exposition of 1915, and a parallel was apparent between these two expositions that gave a sense of urgency to the moment. "The world came to us then as the great war in Europe closed the gates to the European countries. It is a curious turn of events," Denman observed, "that the situation seems on the verge of repeating itself." In this manner the Indian exhibit and, indeed, the whole San Francisco Exposition took on an even greater significance by providing an assurance of unity in the face of impending danger.[9]

As a preliminary approach, the Denman plan provided the important basic concept and direction from which others could proceed to develop the necessary specifics. Louis West, still general manager of the Indian Arts and Crafts Board in 1936, stressed only the board's role of demonstrating the adaptability of modern Indian products in modern homes. He wanted this point "sold to the public," but he showed his lack of sensitivity to the whole situation when he commented that he also realized "such an exhibit must be surrounded with something that will attract attention."[10]

West's work on the board's exposition plans was limited. Collier had spotted his representative in d'Harnoncourt and used him as his emissary to San Francisco late in 1936. The choice of d'Harnoncourt was rewarded when Charles Elkus wrote Collier to suggest d'Harnoncourt for the directorship of the San Francisco Exposition Indian arts and crafts project. "He made a very favorable impression upon us all," Elkus explained, meaning himself, his wife Ruth, Leslie Denman, Alfred L. Kroeber, an anthropologist from the University of California at Berkeley, and Timothy L. Pflueger, a San Francisco architect who had been appointed the architect of the United States Commission for the Golden Gate International Exposition. At the same time, d'Harnoncourt also reported to Collier that he thought "things went quite well in San Francisco." Leland Cutler and other exposition officials had helped with and approved of the Indian arts and crafts exhibit plans. Cutler was delighted with the possibilities presented in d'Harnoncourt's proposed outline for an Indian arts and crafts exhibition. "Coupled with our many conversations on the subject while you were here," Cutler told d'Harnoncourt, "I feel that your approach is a dramatic one and at the same time a natural and sound one."[11]

D'Harnoncourt's approach had struck a responsive chord in San Francisco. In an outline of some of the specific opportunities for educational work offered by the exposition, d'Harnoncourt suggested a study of Indian arts and crafts as a result of physical and cultural environments, a comparative study of the development of the same branches of Indian arts and crafts under different conditions, a study of the fundamental principles of industrial design demonstrated under primitive conditions that did not demand a knowledge of complicated mechanical processes and that were understandable to anyone, and a study of raw materials and production methods that were practically unknown to most everyone. These thoughts were compatible with the atmosphere the San Francisco group wished to develop. Elkus had warned Collier that "there will be no Indian concession, that is, there shall be no Indian show at all other than that contemplated in the plan." Elkus was emphatic that the concessionaires in the entertainment division "should not be permitted to show a so-called 'Indian village' or any other kind of Indian exhibit or performance."[12]

One of the early versions of what finally became known as the Denman plan had talked vaguely of an Indian village, but the memories of some in the San Francisco planning group about how other displays of this type had turned out to be degrading sideshows prevailed. Undoubtedly, d'Harnoncourt's influence played a part in many such decisions involving taste. When he returned from San Francisco in January 1937 to resume his teaching duties at Sarah Lawrence College, he brought along a complete plan for the Indian exhibit. Conferences were held with the Interior Department's supervisor of exhibits, George Dickens, and agreement was reached quickly on the specific needs to be incorporated in the design of the Federal Building. D'Harnoncourt, West, Collier, Dickens, Pflueger, Denman, and George Creel, the United States commissioner for the San Francisco Exposition, met in Washington for final agreement on budget requirements to be submitted to Congress for approval.[13]

With so many strong individualists participating in the San Francisco Exposition project, Collier soon saw the need to give one person the overall responsibility for the Indian exhibit. D'Harnoncourt was Collier's obvious choice for the position. While d'Harnoncourt saw the project as a "chance to do a really fine piece of creative work," and naturally wanted to have a part in it, he could not visualize himself as a "practical executive," supervising the collecting, installing, and correlating of exhibits, simply a "following through with the main idea." D'Harnoncourt's artistic nature could not accept such a limited role. He wanted to work between the architect and the executive, a position he called working with the field people on the ground floor. Chiefly, he told Collier, he saw himself working with the architect as "co-designer and supervisor of decorative elements of the building as related to the exhibits and handling the dramatic arrangement of exhibits to get their greatest possible visual value—in all a sort of glorified decorator's job." D'Harnoncourt concluded that "without too much interference and with some assurance of proper authority, I could work as an artist and be of most possible value to the undertaking." Always sensitive to those around him, d'Harnoncourt expressed his concern as to whether Pflueger would welcome him as a co-worker. The decision was left to Collier.[14]

On 1 February 1937 two alternate forms for the Indian Arts and Crafts Board section of the San Francisco Golden Gate Exposition bill had been prepared and delivered by special messenger to George Creel. The drafts were identical except that one earmarked a specific appropriation and the other did not.[15] No designated appropriation for the Indian exhibit appeared in the final draft of Senate Joint Resolution 88 of 29 June 1937, which provided for the participation of the United States in the world's fair at San Francisco in 1939. A lump sum of $1,500,000 was authorized for the purposes of the joint resolution. The joint resolution defined the exposition as:

> a world's fair and celebration commemorating the completion of the San Francisco-Oakland Bridge and the Golden Gate Bridge, and designed to gather, arrange, and exhibit the varied cultures of the countries tributary to the Pacific Ocean and the origins, progress, and accomplishments in science, the arts, education, industry, business, and transportation of the Pacific area of the United States, and the nations of the world.[16]

Section 7 of the joint resolution was tailored to fit the projected needs of the Indian arts and crafts exhibit. Collier had expressed satisfaction with the wording of this section and had called the language used "necessary" if the Interior Department was to play the role which had been discussed. Specifically, Section 7 authorized the commissioner to pay for the construction of buildings and the employment of personnel out of the appropriation. More importantly, contributions from any source could be accepted for these same purposes including contributions of material and services or the borrowing of material or exhibits to aid in the general purpose of the exposition. Except for the all-important amount to be allotted for the Indian arts and crafts exhibit, Collier had provided for whatever authority might be needed to put on the complete presentation the San Francisco group had proposed.[17]

In the meantime, d'Harnoncourt's skills had not gone unnoticed in other quarters. Both Cutler and Creel entertained thoughts of adding him directly to their staff, and they asked Collier for permission to make him an offer. Collier told them that d'Harnoncourt, who was still only the part-time general manager, had no obligation to the Indian Arts and Crafts Board or to the Department of the Interior. At the same time, Collier assured Cutler and Creel they would be supplied whatever services they needed without d'Harnoncourt's release from government service. In a letter to d'Harnoncourt in New York, Collier expressed the belief that Cutler and Creel probably would make a proposition financially more attractive than the board could hope to match. But Collier added a postscript: "I also told them that if the [Indian] Arts and Crafts Board is to get anywhere, your continued work for it is imperative—indispensable."[18] D'Harnoncourt remained with the board.

Public expressions of enthusiasm for the world's fair contributed to the momentum being generated by the planners. San Francisco attorney John Francis Neylan, speaking at a promotional dinner in the Fairmont Hotel, called the united civic planning for the 1939 exposition "a safety valve relief from the depressing problems of economics and political life." Neylan suggested that those present give thanks that they had finally discovered an occasion for a gathering which had "a constructive objective, in the attainment of which all of our distracted people may join with enthusiasm and good will." Attention to cultural enrichment seemed to provide the vehicle by which this unity could be reached.[19]

Planning the specific details of this cultural project was the next step. At the same time these important plans were to be made, Collier, as commissioner, also would have to contend with all the normal procedures of the Indian Office and any unexpected distractions which often developed. "For three weeks," he wrote Denman, "I have been continuously engaged in hearings, appropriations, and Red-baiting, with mighty little time for other work." Even though Collier was chairman of the Indian Arts and Crafts Board, he certainly could not have been expected to take a definite part in the San Francisco Expositions's planning stages, and although d'Harnoncourt's prominent role in the Indian arts and crafts exhibit at the exposition was assumed, no definite appointment of a director had been announced. In June 1937, Denman telegrammed d'Harnoncourt in New York in an effort to obtain some sort of commitment. She related how the board of management of the exposition had appointed a committee to study a comprehensive and unified presentation of the ancient and modern cultures and civilizations bordering on the Pacific Ocean. This committee, Denman explained, was to suggest the plan and to name the director. The committee members included Alfred Kroeber, Ray Lyman Wilbur, former secretary of the interior and now president of Stanford University, Robert Gordon Sproul, president of the University of California, and other well-known figures.

"Will d'Harnoncourt be available for director of this wider plan as well as that of the Indian presentation?" Denman asked.[20] D'Harnoncourt was in no position to answer for he had made his decision regarding the Indian Arts and Crafts Board and was bound by its directives.

At the meeting of the Indian Arts and Crafts Board in June 1937 that named d'Harnoncourt to replace Louis West as general manager, board member Alfred Kidder recommended his friend Charles Amsden, an authority on Indian weaving who was associated with the Southwest Museum in Los Angeles, for the position of director of the Indian exhibition at San Francisco. Within a week, d'Harnoncourt had met with Amsden in Gallup and reported to Denman that he was very much in favor of Amsden's appointment. The San Francisco group opposed the appointment of anyone, however, except d'Harnoncourt for the job. As far as the Department of the Interior was concerned, the choice for chairman of its figurehead Committee on the Indian Presentation at the Golden Gate Exposition also was d'Harnoncourt. Named to the committee along with d'Harnoncourt was Willard Beatty, George Dickens, Howard M. Gillman, Jr., from the Public Works Administration, and Paul Fickinger, the associate director of the Indian Office Education Division. Still, someone was needed to be on the scene in San Francisco through whom the actual planners could speak, and Amsden appeared to be the logical choice. Not a dedicated crusader fired by the vision projected for the 1939 exposition, Amsden never became a real contributor to the project and bowed out early in January 1938.[21]

Undaunted, d'Harnoncourt continued to move forward on the necessary arrangements for the exposition. Form letters detailing the nature of the Indian exhibition and the need for the participation of others were sent out to twenty major museums in the United States. D'Harnoncourt's name was prominently included so that his connection would be known when he wrote personal follow-up letters.[22]

D'Harnoncourt had little need to worry that his name and connection with the San Francisco Exposition would be unknown. On 29 January 1938, he accepted an invitation to lunch with the President and Mrs. Roosevelt the following day. The surprise invitation for Sunday, 30 January, had been arranged by Leslie Denman. "Aside from the fact that I had a perfectly grand time, I also do believe that it helped the cause a great deal," d'Harnoncourt commented afterward. "After hearing a description of our general plans," d'Harnoncourt related, "Mrs. Roosevelt showed so much interest that I asked her to come to the office in about two weeks when I shall be able to show her in sketches and models what the exhibits will look like." Appreciation from Eleanor Roosevelt boosted d'Harnoncourt's enthusiasm to even greater heights. "We are now redoubling our efforts to get things ready and in good shape for her," he exclaimed. She had asked d'Harnoncourt to keep her informed on the progress of the tentative plans and promised to come to see them as soon as given the opportunity. She commented on the occasion in her next "My Day" newspaper column when she referred to the exclusive nature of the luncheon that had only two guests present and how she was particularly interested in talking with René d'Harnoncourt. The whole idea of the Indian exhibit at San Francisco sounded to her to be "most original and interesting." Three weeks later after viewing the Indian exhibit model in d'Harnoncourt's office, she reflected more fully. "I think the exhibition of this Indian work is going to open the eyes of many of us to what they are capable of doing as artists and craftsmen," she reported in her newspaper column.[23]

At the ground-breaking ceremonies for the $500,000, seven-acre Federal Building in San Francisco, Eleanor Roosevelt gave a speech confined to the Indian exhibit. D'Harnoncourt remarked afterward that her emphasis on the Indian display was so strong that "it gave the impression that there would be nothing else to see, which did not please most of the people. For us, however, it was the best send off possible."[24]

D'Harnoncourt used the widespread interest in the San Francisco Exposition to publicize Indian arts and crafts. News releases appearing in community newspapers across the nation described the nature of Indian arts and crafts and their function in modern society. "Aside from the fact that the gathering [of the artifacts] of these various tribes together for the first time will give the American public a better idea of them as a whole," a widely used article commented, "it is expected that it will help the Indians in bringing about a rebirth of their arts and crafts and popularize Indian designs so that the Indians themselves may become more self-supporting." Some publicity articles contained local additions to the basic themes and educational articles attempted to stir public interest in the crafts themselves. A newspaper article in California asserted that "Indian baskets, which vary in quality from a 'slightly organized brush heap' to a symmetrical beauty that actually is watertight, demonstrate as aptly as any single product the ability of the American Indian as an artisan and craftsman." The same baskets, the article continued, also demonstrated "the wide range of civilizations which were forced upon the Indian by foods, raw materials, and climates that surrounded him in various parts of the country." As an example, the article cited the buffalo-hunting Plains Indians who found baskets ill-adapted to life on horseback and developed them only slightly.[25]

This adaptability theme based on the relationship between the Indians and their environment would be displayed prominently at the Indian exhibit. The baskets, pottery, and other arts and crafts provided an example of artistic perfection achieved and maintained under the most adverse conditions possible. How the Indians' culture had managed to survive at all in their situation could not help but be a source of wonderment even to the casual observer. A subtheme at the San Francisco Indian exhibit was whether the Indian culture possessed something that other Americans lacked in their own cultural existence. By 1939 the question had become pertinent to the lives of all Americans, and d'Harnoncourt's exhibit plan consciously and subconsciously addressed itself to this interest. People were, in Denman's words, curious about themselves.

In a further effort to satisfy this curiosity, d'Harnoncourt retained the services of Frederic H. Douglas, curator of Indian art at the Denver Art Museum, as director of educational activities at the Indian exhibit. His duties were primarily to lead scheduled discussions on Indian art as an expression of its cultural background, the raw material and technology in Indian art, and the aim and method in exhibitions of Indian art. Having assessed the extensive contemporary Indian arts and crafts interest, d'Harnoncourt realized early in 1937 that the exhibit at San Francisco would create a demand for illustrated, informative material. Both he and Collier called for a book which would show Indian crafts in color and black and white photographs with accompanying descriptive texts. Collier commented on the "curious fact that we have such authoritative texts as to arts and crafts in New Guinea and in Africa, but nothing of the sort about the arts and crafts of the American Indians."[26]

Unsuccessful in obtaining funds from the American Council of

Learned Societies, to whom he first applied, d'Harnoncourt took the plan to David H. Stevens of the Rockefeller Foundation and asked for a preliminary grant of $2,000 from the foundation's General Education Board. Within five days a grant of $2,000 to the American Museum of Natural History was approved for "a national survey of materials on Indian arts and crafts useful for publication projects and for exhibitions." The Indian Arts and Crafts Board was "allied" with the project. George C. Vaillant, associate curator of Mexican archaeology at the American Museum of Natural History in New York, was to do the field work and assembly of data. The Rockefeller grant stipulated that upon completion of Vaillant's initial work, the project would be submitted to the American Council of Learned Societies for further funding. Since the Indian Arts and Crafts Board already had conducted numerous field surveys on the state of Indian arts and crafts, Vaillant's actual task was to assemble photographs and exact descriptions of typical Indian arts and crafts.[27]

Six months later, the work on the book was considered by the Rockefeller Foundation to have advanced rapidly although difficulties began creeping in to plague the effort to have the book ready for the San Francisco Exposition. The American Council of Learned Societies no longer was considered as a source for further funding of the project. A proposed budget of $6,500 was thought to be adequate to finish the publication of the book, and in February 1938 d'Harnoncourt applied again to Stevens at the Rockefeller Foundation for the additional funds. Vaillant and Philippa Whiting, also of the American Museum of Natural History, had prepared an outline of the text as well as a dummy containing sample illustrations and samples of the index. The book was to give a representative pictorial record of American Indian art. The effort was justified, d'Harnoncourt believed, because no effort had been made to date to present this material in a manner that would make aesthetic judgment of North American Indian art, as a whole, possible. All previous publications had treated the subject merely as illustrations for ethnological studies.[28]

Although the Rockefeller Foundation supplied the requested $6,500 on 1 April 1938, the Indian arts and crafts book project was still short of funds. The second grant was also to the American Museum of Natural History; $6,000 was designated for salaries and $500 for photographic materials. Even so, the photographer, Konrad Cramer, who was hired just for the book project, was not able to go to the Southwest to complete the collection of photographic plates without an additional $1,500. Unable to accept an imperfect product and under the pressure of time to have the book ready for the opening of the San Francisco Exposition, d'Harnoncourt generously decided to contribute the needed $1,500 out of his own pocket in monthly payments of $250 starting 1 July. Vaillant was ecstatic. "We are all deeply grateful for the pains which you have taken in the midst of the myriad harried details of your present career," he exclaimed. The final step in the process came late in 1939 when the American Council of Learned Societies contributed half of the publication costs.[29] Sadly for everyone and particularly for d'Harnoncourt in view of all his efforts, the book came on the market only after the 1939 San Francisco Exposition had closed.

Indian Arts in North America crystalized the findings of the surveys conducted up to 1939 by the Indian Arts and Crafts Board. In fifty-two pages of text and with ninety-six full-page plates, the book surveyed North American Indian art from pre-Columbian times to contemporary achievements and concisely described what was known of Indian origins and cultural differences. In all, 983 specimens were photographed, 111 color plates were taken, and enlargements were made of 372 photographs. Duplicate prints of the representative objects of Indian art were given to the Indian Arts and Crafts Board and became a reservoir for its future publicity needs. One reviewer called the effort "the most comprehensive study of the subject."[30]

D'Harnoncourt used an Indian poster and design contest to give early public exposure to the quality of Indian art to be displayed at San Francisco. He arranged for the exposition commission to sponsor the contest and to provide a jury. Denman, Kroeber, Pflueger, Ruth Elkus, and Grace McCann Morley of the San Francisco Museum of Art served as the judges. The first prize went to Vincente Mirabel of Taos, a young Pueblo artist attached to the Santa Fe Indian School, for his depiction of the Turtle Dance with the dwellings of the Taos Pueblo in the background. The second prize was won by Narcisco Abeyta, a Navajo, for "At Sa Teaches His Son to Hunt," a design in black on white paper that was considered very bold and decorative. Otis Polelonema, a Hopi, was the third-prize winner for a design derived from Indian motifs that were highly stylized and boldly handled in color. A scene of Sioux camp life in a balanced overall pattern by Andrew Standing Soldier, a Sioux, took the fourth prize in the contest. All the entries in the competition were displayed in an exhibition of Indian posters and designs at the San Francisco Museum of Art in October 1938 as part of the publicity buildup for the Indian exhibit. Better known Indian artists who submitted posters and designs were Fred Kabotie, Marina Luhan, Ma Pe Wi, Stephen Mopope, Alan Hauser, and Acee Blue Eagle.[31]

Through the poster and design contest, the Indian Arts and Crafts Board was encouraging the Indians to help themselves. Ideas presented in the competition were used to make up a highly prized and sought after set of posters distributed across the nation to promote the exposition. The posters were reproduced by the silk screen process under the auspices of the Federal Art Project.[32] The coordination of the work of government agencies toward a common goal was another accomplishment by d'Harnoncourt and the Indian Arts and Crafts Board.

In the general plan and budget for the Indian presentation that the Department of the Interior supervisor of exhibits, George Dickens, submitted to Collier on 22 December 1936, sponsorship would be provided by the government from 18 February to 2 December 1939. When Congress made the general government appropriation, the funds for the Indian exhibit were to be transferred to the Interior Department. The Interior Department's plan for the Indian exhibit required a direct allocation of $250,000 from the 1939 United States Golden Gate International Exposition Commission.[33]

In all, three separate and different Indian exhibit budgets were circulated: one was made up by Dickens for the Interior Department, another was d'Harnoncourt's work, and a third was proposed by the California group. Dickens's $250,000 budget included thirteen administrative people, an average employment of one hundred Indians at one dollar per day for ten months, transportation of Indians to San Francisco and back to their reservations, Indian living costs and quarters for ten months, $50,000 for the Indian arts and crafts building, and $25,000 for the purchase of Indian arts and crafts through revolving funds. D'Harnoncourt's budget estimate was set at $263,940, a deceptive figure because he did not include the exhibit building, housing of the one hundred and fifty Indian staff members for ten months, physical maintenance of the buildings and grounds, or insurance. While d'Harnoncourt's estimate was not a precise figure, his budget was dwarfed by the $669,295 proposed by the California group. Among the larger items were $185,970 for the exposition building, $78,350 for equipment and furnishings, and $220,000 for transportation, salaries, and maintenance of an Indian staff of two hundred and fifty persons. Just as with the Interior Department budget, the California group budget was drafted to function under a possible reduced allocation. All of the details had been worked out on paper so that a base figure of operation would be known in the event of such a reduction.[34]

Since Congress had appropriated the sum of $1,500,000 for the participation of all government agencies at the 1939 San Francisco Exposition and had left the allocation of this sum up to the government exposition commission, the Indian Arts and Crafts Board had to wait to find out what amount it would receive. As of August 1937, Exposition Commissioner Creel had provided the Indian Arts and Crafts Board with only the promise of all of the space and all of the money the board needed. The matter was not under Creel's full control, for he had to submit a budget in September to the commission in Washington where the general appropriation would then be divided up among the different government exhibits. Under Senate Joint Resolution 88 (1937), the commission making the allocations was composed of the secretary of the interior, the secretary of agriculture, the secretary of commerce, the secretary of labor, three members of the House appointed by the Speaker of the House, and three members of the Senate appointed by the president of the Senate. Creel was appointed by the President and received a salary of $10,000 per year.[35]

No one could have been prepared for the shock created when Creel announced that the Indian exhibit would receive only $50,000 of the government funds. Even though the Indian Arts and Crafts Board rapidly revised its budget estimates and pared the cost, the planned Indian exhibit still would need a bare $190,500. Creel tried to explain how he had estimated that the commission had only $700,000 for the entire federal exhibit after the Federal Building was constructed and all salaries were paid. He lamely sought understanding for what he considered might have been his absurd position in putting the Indian exhibit budget before the commission. Creel suggested that the other departments of government probably would have felt a sense of outrage.[36] For these reasons, Creel had never presented the proposed Indian exhibit budgets to the commission for its consideration. Instead, he had submitted an arbitrary figure that was totally unrelated to the plans that had been developed.

D'Harnoncourt was not defeated, and within a week he wrote to Leslie Denman that he had just spent two days in New York where he had made "contacts that may prove valuable for the exhibition." D'Harnoncourt was hopeful that they could obtain outside help and was convinced that they would be able "to count on contributions of various sorts from groups interested in the educational value of this exhibit." Taking encouragement from d'Harnoncourt's approach to the problem, others began the search for financial contributions. Denman contacted the Santa Fe Railroad in the hope of obtaining concessions on transportation costs. Feeling some responsibility for the Indian Arts and Crafts Board's plight, Creel also took up the cause with the Santa Fe Railroad.[37]

Creel's efforts with the railroads seemed anticlimatic after he had placed the whole Indian exhibit in jeopardy. Showing that he was aware of the consequences of his action, he announced that "some means must be found to provide at least $100,000 from an outside source," otherwise the plans would have to be scrapped. At the same time, he claimed he was taking over "the very difficult job of persuading the railroads to give free transportation" to the Indians, and "the task of inducing the WPA [Works Progress Administration] to put up barracks" for Indian housing. Unless funds were forthcoming from other sources including the Department of the Interior, Creel threatened, he would "give up the Indian exhibit" or "cut it down to a point where it would be a mere shadow of what we had hoped."[38] Creel had placed himself in an untenable position and was searching frantically for a way out. He could not blame the commission for the failure to provide necessary funding for the long-anticipated and influentially supported Indian arts and crafts exhibit.

Creel's subsequent actions only aggravated the situation. When Elkus suggested to Creel that he find additional funds under the Indian Reorganization Act, Creel turned around and recommended to d'Harnoncourt that he take this very step, a procedure of which d'Harnoncourt already

178

was aware. Creel presumptuously asked d'Harnoncourt to make a survey of the whole question and report to Elkus and Denman. Creel's experience in Democratic politics should have prepared him more fully for the political demands of his present position. In the matter of free railroad transportation for the Indians at the exposition, Creel went directly to the Interstate Commerce Commission and asked for a formal opinion. The Interstate Commerce Commission responded negatively, and Collier felt that Creel had brought about a situation making it unfeasible for the railroads to give free transportation. "There are ways and ways that the free transportation can be arranged," Collier exclaimed, "but the one way is not to ask the ICC whether it is legal." Creel's direct threat to the Department of the Interior to force it to come up with funds for the Indian exhibit also brought a negative legal opinion. Nathan Margold, now a Department of the Interior solicitor, expressed the view that the appropriation of $1,500,000 made by the Joint Resolution was "specific and exclusive." The payment of items of expense in connection with the proposed exhibit "from funds appropriated for the Department of the Interior would be unauthorized."[39]

In the midst of Creel's negative efforts, d'Harnoncourt quietly worked behind the scene. He asked the superintendents of the various reservations to suggest to their tribal councils the designation of some of their funds for the purchase of arts and crafts to be used at the exposition. Chester Faris, the long-time Indian Office employee now serving as Collier's field representative, was enlisted to follow up on the matter and visit the Plains tribes to help the superintendents in presenting the case to the tribes. Within weeks practically all of the tribes had agreed to finance their own purchases of goods for the exposition. This effort meant approximately another $50,000 for the exposition budget.[40] By the middle of February d'Harnoncourt had raised contributions in terms of personnel and material amounting to $97,000. In the face of such an effort, Creel was forced by d'Harnoncourt to release the $50,000 allocated for the Indian exhibit. The nature of the understanding reached between the two men remained unclear. D'Harnoncourt reported that Creel had agreed to raise more money from the State of California and other sources. Creel, on his part, claimed that he released the $50,000 after d'Harnoncourt had promised "to uncover methods for raising the rest." In addition, Creel grandly claimed to have allocated the whole north side of the Federal Building to the Indian arts and crafts exhibit "at a pretty heavy building expense."[41]

The lines of communication between Creel and d'Harnoncourt never flowed very freely, possibly because the support and publicity the Indian exhibit generated at all levels seemed to overshadow Creel's role. Politically, Creel could not ignore d'Harnoncourt's efforts. "Through the use of tribal funds, the loan of personal services, and by contributions from museums," Creel admitted, "Mr. d'Harnoncourt seems to be in reach of his goal." Creel had little choice in the matter. "I know of your deep interest in the Indian exhibit," he told Ickes, "an interest, I may say, that is shared by the President and Mrs. Roosevelt."[42]

The full burden of funding and organizing the 1939 Indian arts and crafts exhibition now rested on d'Harnoncourt's shoulders. Confident that he had sufficient contributions from philanthropic foundations and museums to complete the exhibits and the arts and crafts market and to guarantee the necessary space at the exposition, d'Harnoncourt embarked on what he called the "second phase of this venture." He busily began to expand the dramatic aspects of the program. The search for funds never stopped. "Every $10,000 will add additional glamour to the project," d'Harnoncourt enthusiastically told Denman.[43]

The difficulties with Creel were forgotten as he faded from the board's final preparations. Persistence and a diplomatic approach brought a much sought contribution. In September, almost a year after the Interstate Commerce Commission had rebuffed Creel, the Santa Fe Railroad quietly sent word to d'Harnoncourt that it as well as the Union Pacific and Southern Pacific Railroads would transport the Indians free of charge to and from the exposition. D'Harnoncourt also obtained $25,000 from the California State Commission for the San Francisco Exposition, after which Collier reported to Ickes that the prospects for the Indian exhibit were "more exciting all the time." Then in November, d'Harnoncourt's friend, Frederick Keppel, president of the Carnegie Corporation of New York, approved a grant of $13,800 for personnel and publications for the Indian exhibit.[44] The grant had been promised tentatively the previous spring when the prospects for an Indian exhibit were bleak. Even though the grant was not unexpected, d'Harnoncourt was relieved when the final approval came through. He was now free to employ Frederic Douglas as well as the necessary assistants and secretarial help for the duration of the fair without touching any Indian Arts and Crafts Board funds. The Carnegie grant assured d'Harnoncourt that the exhibit would have constant and efficient guide and lecture services as well as a very fine series of pamphlet publications. The grant also covered all personnel needs during the period of installation.[45] In all, the Carnegie money was to be used for a "well-defined educational program," which d'Harnoncourt further designated as "a valuable experiment in visual education."[46]

D'Harnoncourt became totally immersed in the San Francisco project. In June he had made a tentative request for Rockefeller Foundation aid for the Indian arts and crafts exhibit. He told Stevens that he wanted to start "studies on special tribes to give academic reports on arts and crafts." Stevens had to reply that "this sounds too vague for us to bring it up." In a personal reply, d'Harnoncourt explained that his failure to make an adequate, in-depth presentation was due to overwork; he had just had thirteen meetings in twenty-four hours. Along with his regular Indian Arts and Crafts Board duties and the demands of the San Francisco Exposition, d'Harnoncourt also was acting as an advisor and go-between for Sarah Lawrence College in its efforts to obtain foundation support for its general endowment. Collier revealed the extent of the burden that d'Harnoncourt had assumed when he told members of the House Subcommittee on Interior Department Appropriations that "a very small part of the Board's time and money had gone into the San Francisco Fair, if you leave out Mr. d'Harnoncourt."[47]

At the San Francisco Indian exhibit, the Indian arts and crafts bought for the anticipated market were financed individually by the forty-eight tribes represented. Tribal funds and monies borrowed from the revolving loan fund were used for this purpose. Approval from the commissioner's office came on 13 January 1939 for the use of the Indian Monies Proceeds of Labor funds by tribal organizations to purchase the arts and crafts from individual Indian artisans. The fund officially was considered a trust fund to be used by the agency for the benefit of the Indians. Articles purchased by the superintendent with such funds were considered Indian-owned to the same extent as articles purchased by the tribal governments through the use of tribal, rehabilitation, or credit funds. Since the Indian Arts and Crafts Board Act specifically forbade the board from engaging in buying or selling Indian arts and crafts, the

181

board could not participate legally in the proposed arts and crafts market at the San Francisco Exposition. To get around this apparent barrier, the Indian Arts and Crafts Board determined on a contract with the Covelo or Round Valley Indian Community of California, which was legally equipped to assume the risks and obligations of a corporation. After negotiating with the Indian Arts and Crafts Board, the community offered to act as the agent for all Indians desiring to sell goods at the exposition. A contract was drawn up by Elkus on 4 January 1939 between d'Harnoncourt, as the agent for the Indian Arts and Crafts Board, and the Covelo Indian Community of the Round Valley Reservation, an agreement which established the organization known specifically as the Indian Market of the Covelo Indian Community to conduct Indian arts and crafts sales. The board assumed no financial obligation whatsoever. In the contract, the board agreed to furnish supervision, management, and personnel as authorized under the Indian Arts and Crafts Board Act, the complete cost of which was to be borne by the Covelo Indian Market.[48]

The funds the Covelo Market would use came from several sources. Sidney Ehrman, a contributor who wished to remain anonymous, donated $5,000 out of personal friendship "to some of his friends" in San Francisco interested in the Indian exhibit. Ehrman attached no strings to the money and left its use solely up to d'Harnoncourt.[49] Up to $3,000 of the Carnegie money also could be used for the Covelo Market. The Indian Defense Association turned over $500 in an unforeseen contribution to be used as a revolving fund for the market and then returned later.[50] In d'Harnoncourt's words, the Covelo contract was, in essence, "simply a safeguard to give us [the Indian Arts and Crafts Board] the control of this money without ever owning it."[51]

Collier defined the Covelo Market contract as an arrangement in which the management of the Indian arts and crafts market would be completely under the Indians, and an agreement in which the relationship of the Indian Arts and Crafts Board was that of a management agency. Section 7 of the Covelo contract modified and enlarged this potential government role. In an effort to determine how the monies would be disbursed after the close of the market, the contract stated that after paying for all merchandise and meeting all charges and expenses of any kind, a payment would be made to the Covelo Community of 10 percent of the remaining money as compensation for services rendered. This compensation was not to exceed $1,000 and was to be used by the community for the development of its arts and crafts. All sums remaining were to be "turned over to John Collier, Charles de Young Elkus, and René d'Harnoncourt, as trustees, to be used by them in whatever manner they deem proper for the development of the arts and crafts of the Indians of the United States and Alaska." A month after the Covelo contract was signed, Collier told the House Subcommittee on Interior Department Appropriations that the tribes would manage the Indian Market "with the Board acting as a sort of executive agency in behalf of the tribes." At the end of the market, the earnings would go back to the contributing tribes; "nothing will come into the possession of the government," Collier assured the subcommittee members.[52]

The actual monetary returns from the Covelo Market were not very large. A little under $17,000 was taken in after a slow start followed by experimentation with merchandising methods which helped to sell the higher-priced, quality items.[53] Sales averaged only $100 per week for the first six weeks and then began to improve steadily when the board's experimentation showed that the proper display of goods could turn a very slow-moving article into an excellent sales item. The best examples of individual crafts that prospered under the improved marketing technique were gloves and moccasins.

Encouraged by the increase in sales after such a slow start, d'Harnoncourt confidently assured Eleanor Roosevelt that the Indian Market was constantly improving. He was particularly pleased that the finer type of product was finding more public appreciation as a result of a new emphasis on quality. The new sales approach involved transferring certain goods that did not move in the trading post market area, where sales consisted mainly of lower priced merchandise, to the quality merchandise display area and asking a higher price, partially to compensate for an increased overhead and partially to create a sense of exclusiveness. The board felt it had found the answer to the market limitation from which Indian goods suffered.[54]

9

THE 1939 SAN FRANCISCO
EXPOSITION

THE INDIAN ARTS AND CRAFTS EXHIBIT at the 1939 San Francisco Golden Gate International Exposition was the crowning achievement of two and one-half years of work by the Indian Arts and Crafts Board. For the first time in history, the United States government gave the Indians a place of honor at an important international exposition.[1] The presentation demonstrated the Indian Arts and Crafts Board's contribution to the long-sought economic independence of the Indians. From all parts of the United States and Alaska, representative products of original, genuine, and useful Indian arts and crafts were assembled. Thousands of visitors acquired an appreciation of the dignity, beauty, and utility of Indian handcrafts, an understanding that probably contributed to increased sales. In 1938, the year before, Indian arts and crafts activities supervised by the board had showed a money and non-money income of $863,267. In the year of the exposition, that figure jumped to $1,007,422. These figures did not include the Indian arts and crafts money and nonmoney income from Alaskan activities totaling $90,000 to $100,000 per year.[2]

In determining whether the Indian Office should participate in the San Francisco Exposition, those involved at the government level were convinced that "the people of the United States had little, if any, knowledge of the beauty and utility of the things Indians made, to say nothing of having any idea of his cultural heritage." An exhibit would emphasize not only Indian achievement in the arts, but also what could be done "toward restoring the Indian to that freedom and security which are no less significant elements of his heritage than the skill of his craftsmanship." Collier was convinced that the San Francisco Exposition would bring a renaissance to native American art.[3]

From d'Harnoncourt's point of view, the exhibit aimed to give the public a representative picture of the Indian civilizations of the United States and Alaska, showing both past and present achievements of these cultures and attempting to open new vistas for their future. The organizers of the exhibit believed that in the past the American Indians had shown an admirable ability to cope with their physical surroundings, to build a well-ordered society, and to develop a highly specialized culture even in the most unfavorable environments. If these valuable achievements were generally known, they would earn the Indians the cultural and artistic recognition of their fellow citizens. D'Harnoncourt saw the display of Indian art not as an end in itself, but as a means of gaining the public's attention and thereby creating a better understanding of the Indians' problems and talents.[4]

In contrast to previous Indian policies, New Deal Indian policy fully realized that the Indians' own culture was a source of strength to them and that its values were essential to the conservation of their self-esteem. This policy did not aim to encourage the Indians' cultural isolation. It simply demonstrated that the government believed that a race, aware and proud of its own tradition, had a better chance to survive than one that disclaimed its inheritance. Along with these ideological reasons, d'Harnoncourt expressed the practical aims of the Indian exhibit at the San Francisco Exposition. The exhibit attempted to show that Indian arts and crafts were indeed still alive and of a quality that merited artistic recognition—both in respect and hard cash.[5]

D'Harnoncourt's concrete aims naturally called for carefully planned presentations. "The exhibit must do more than show the beauty or the skillful methods of production of individual Indian works of art," he pointed out. "It must endeavor to link these objects together in a way that gives the visitor a unified picture of the people who produced them, and some conception of the future possibilities of these people."[6]

Fifteen galleries and a court were developed to present eight general areas of Indian culture: the Eskimo hunters, the Northwest fishers, the seed gatherers of the Far West, the hunters of the Plains, the woods dwellers of the Eastern forests, the Pueblo farmers, the Navajo shepherds, and the desert dwellers of the Southwest. This variety of cultures in Indian America, which made the European nations seem almost uniform by comparison, was emphasized by the architecture of each room. Color scheme, lighting, and type of display had been chosen to suit the individual culture. The Plains room, for example, was very high and wide, flooded with bright but diffused light. The exhibits and display were kept low and the walls were constructed to give the illusion of unlimited space. In contrast, the room of the Eastern woodlands had been designed to give the visitors a feeling of being enclosed, surrounded by a rich variety of forms.[7]

Within each room d'Harnoncourt gave consideration to the relationship between descriptive and exhibit materials. The captions in each room had a definite sequence, indicated by their size and location, leading from the most important general statement to the most subtle details.[8] Visitors' attention was caught first by the large sign identifying the room. Beneath "The Hunters of the Plains" was a large mural of a buffalo hunt subtitled "Over the treeless plains on swift horses, the Plains tribes hunted the buffalo that gave them food, clothing, and shelter." From this mural which provided the dominant recurring theme of the room, their eyes were led to a pictorial chart showing the tribes' annual wanderings on their great hunts, and to the exhibits that illustrated how nomadic life made the Plains people create a movable architecture, the tepee, and folding furniture. Every piece shown in this room was connected with the basic element of Plains culture, the concept of motion through space. Some pieces showed this influence by choice of material, others by their form and design.[9] Such organization of labels and exhibit materials actually turned each exhibit hall into a chapter of a book, d'Harnoncourt explained; the captions represented the text, and the exhibits the illustrations.[10]

The galleries were situated in a crescent around the large court that served to separate the Indian exhibit from the other half of the Federal Building to the south. The architectural form of this court developed only after the size and shape of the individual galleries, as well as their sequence, had been formulated completely. The court was kept very simple and was to be used for Indian festivals and dances. The walls were of stark, unpainted wood, and two totem poles, carved by a Haida Indian during the course of the exposition, were its only decoration. The entrance to the galleries on the southwest corner of the court was decorated with a large Haida design cut from plywood and attached to the wall of the building.[11]

The first gallery was devoted to a general introduction to the various

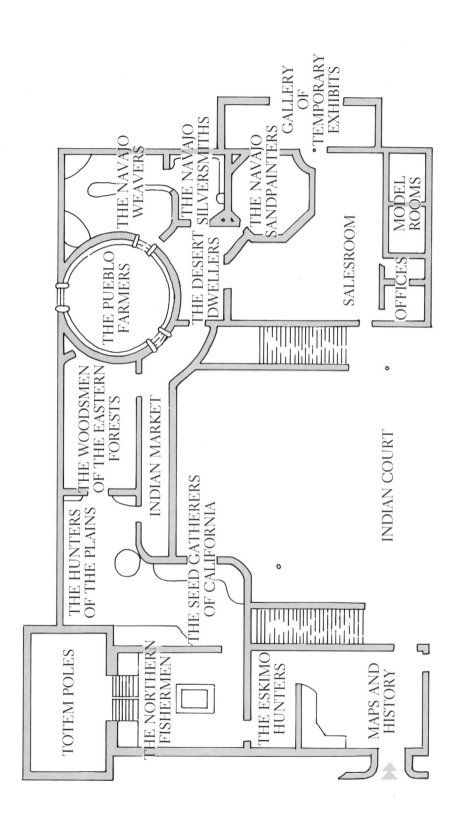

TOTEM POLES

THE HUNTERS OF THE PLAINS

THE WOODSMEN OF THE EASTERN FORESTS

THE PUEBLO FARMERS

THE NAVAJO WEAVERS

THE NAVAJO SILVERSMITHS

GALLERY OF TEMPORARY EXHIBITS

THE NORTHERN FISHERMEN

INDIAN MARKET

THE SEED GATHERERS OF CALIFORNIA

THE DESERT DWELLERS

THE NAVAJO SANDPAINTERS

SALESROOM

OFFICES

MODEL ROOMS

THE ESKIMO HUNTERS

INDIAN COURT

MAPS AND HISTORY

Indian cultures. To increase appreciation of the Indian exhibit, reading material was provided in the form of condensed information on Indian history and Indian civilization, as well as general narratives dealing with the aim and organization of the exhibit. Upon entering from the court, visitors first observed large maps of the United States and Alaska showing the great cultural divisions of Indian North America and establishing the geographic scope of the exhibit. Each of the cultural areas shown on these maps corresponded to a gallery in the building, so that a trip through the galleries virtually became a trip through Indian America. Below the map of the United States, a large wall label identified the various cultural areas presented in the exhibit.

The wall space not occupied by the maps displayed a pictorial history of the American Indians, designed and executed by Elizabeth Wilder, assistant director of educational activities. Thirty-six horizontal transparency panels became visible in sequence when the lights behind them flashed on. This general history of the Indians was divided into four large sections with six to twelve scenes in each: Indians coming from Asia, coming of the white people, Indians forced onto reservations, and the modern Indians. The last section dealt with the Indians' efforts, in cooperation with the government, to find their role in the contemporary world. On a shelf below these transparencies, additional maps, charts, and folders dealing with every aspect of Indian physical and cultural anthropology were available. This emphasis on the whole of Indian culture as related by archaeologists, ethnologists, physical anthropologists, cultural anthropologists, and linguists displayed the depth of understanding that d'Harnoncourt and the other planners of the Indian arts and crafts exhibit had for the cultural significance of Indian art.

The simple nature of "The Totem Pole Tower" enhanced the cultural symbolism found in Northwest Coast arts and crafts. Trunks of towering totem poles and monumental grave sculpture appeared in a diffused gray outdoor light. The room was fifty feet high and painted in horizontal bands of gray, becoming gradually lighter from bottom to top to emphasize the height of the room and to suggest the foggy atmosphere of the Northwest Coast. The tallest pole was thirty-five feet high, a specimen carved by the Tlinkit Indians.

In the warmly subdued light of a contrasting gallery, that of "The Woodsmen of the Eastern Forests," d'Harnoncourt fashioned the setting for woodland products by building wooden columns into the room to suggest the interior of a forest and supplemented the columns with stylized green canvas leaves hung from the ceiling. Both devices helped to create the impression of following a forest pathway. The room had been planned to include the work of all of the tribes east of a line extending from western Minnesota south to Texas. Displays were arranged in a corresponding geographical pattern. On the north wall was shown work from the Great Lakes area, from the Iroquois and Algonquin groups, and from the tribes in New England. The south wall was dedicated to the artifacts of the southern tribes while on the west wall, near the entrance door, was an exhibit of the art of those westernmost tribes of the region whose products showed great similarity to those of the Plains Indians. The gallery captions explained the complex patterns of tribal migrations over centuries in the eastern woodlands and detailed the ages of development behind the Indians' culture.

At the southeast corner of the gallery of "The Woodsmen of the Eastern Forests" began a short corridor that gradually curved leftward toward the entrance to the large high-ceilinged, circular gallery of "The Pueblo Farmers." In contrast with the eastern tribes, the old Indian culture still survived among the Pueblos almost without compromise. In the Pueblo Indian area of northern New Mexico and Arizona, corn remained the basis of existence, and d'Harnoncourt had designed the circular Pueblo room to show how the whole economic and spiritual life of the Pueblos revolved around the corn cycle. The room was fifty feet in diameter and twenty-five feet high. The ceiling was painted sky blue, the walls were white, and the display platform was an adobe color. The room was divided into four sections corresponding to the four main phases of the corn cycle. On the walls were four decorative paintings by Pueblo artists showing dances that took place during the four seasons. In the center of the room was a large four-sided column painted with representations of the four basic stages of corn in Pueblo life and situated to correspond to the four seasonal dances depicted in the paintings. Sowing the seed corn in spring was matched with the Kachina Dance recalling the kachinas who were the messengers of the gods, the growing green corn in summer was illustrated by the Corn Dance, the harvest of ripe corn in the fall was matched with the Crow Dance, and the storage of corn in the winter was represented with the Deer Dance. D'Harnoncourt's coordination of ceremonial and economic life was intended to show the systematic order of the Pueblo corn culture.

"The Navajo Weavers" gallery reflected the spatial characteristics of the Navajos' environment. Stark coloration provided a dramatic backdrop in a room that was fifty feet long, thirty-five feet wide, and divided from north to south by a high partition. The walls of the room were painted white, the partition turquoise blue, and the slanting platforms on which the blankets were displayed a deep orange to resemble the color of the sandstone cliffs in the Navajo country. The west side of the room where the visitors first entered was devoted to the old Navajo blankets and rugs, and the east side displayed modern Navajo weaving.

The emphasis of the weaving display always remained on the product. A skillfully conventionalized setting suggested rather than defined the blankets' environment. At first glance, the Navajo blankets displayed in front of the partition appeared only to be draped over upright poles placed at various levels on sandstone-colored platforms in front of the blue partition wall. After a moment, the realization came that this display was an abstraction depicting Navajos standing on cliffs gazing off into the sky. In this manner, attention focused intensely upon the textiles and the quality of the woven products in their natural setting. Elsewhere in the room, slanting display cases allowed observation of the full design of the woven products. Sometimes an individual display included a small piece of Indian-made furniture placed on the rug. In the portion of the Navajo gallery which was devoted to modern blankets and rugs, Navajo artists demonstrated the various processes in their weaving. The demonstrators worked on platforms so that visitors could gather on all sides to watch.

A much smaller, metal-lined room was devoted to "The Navajo Silversmiths." In this glittering display were many pieces of both old and modern Navajo silver. Here were necklaces, including those of beads shaped like conventionalized pomegranates often called "squash blossoms," rings, and bracelets, some set with turquoise. Bridles, belt buckles, and even several silver cups and tumblers were presented to delight the eyes and reflect the Navajos' skilled artistry.

The whole sequence of the Navajo arts and crafts display revealed the tribe's ability to change adopted forms until they became their own. The message presented was that in these, as in other fields, the Navajos had shown that, given the opportunity, they could combine their own ideas with those of non-Indians "to create a truly native civilization adapted to life in the modern world."[12]

Nowhere in the San Francisco presentation did d'Harnoncourt neglect the aesthetic. By limiting the number of objects to insure generous display space for each and by carefully selecting the objects, the aesthetic merit of Indian art was allowed to speak for itself. The display in "The Gallery of Temporary Exhibits" presented fine examples of Indian arts and crafts solely as works of art. Some of the work on display in this gallery was done by Indian artists during the time of the exposition.

Model rooms were designed to show the use of Indian-made articles in a contemporary setting and to overcome the widely held opinion that Indian products were gaudy and unrefined and, therefore, only appropriate for decorating hunting cabins or rustic cottages. D'Harnoncourt considered the model rooms an opportunity to show the decorative value and usefulness of Indian art in the modern home.[13] Articles like those displayed in the first model room were available for purchase on the Hopi, Zuni, and Rio Grande Valley Indian Reservations in New Mexico and Arizona. In contrast, the Indian products used in the second model room came from the Great Plains and the eastern woodlands regions. The furniture in both rooms was made in Indian schools and showed the Indians' craft skills, yet was not designed to appear Indian in style but contemporary.

The main sales area was a quality gift shop that stressed the artistic excellence of every piece rather than the product's romantic associations. One wall of this salesroom was devoted to Indian-made clothing accessories. D'Harnoncourt displayed some products to demonstrate their usefulness, for example, showing moccasins on leg models to show that they were not only decorative but also useful slippers of high quality. A fabric counter was set up in front of a concave wall to display the products of Indian home weaving industries, which were based on the high manual ability of Indian artisans that existed even in those regions where old craft traditions had been lost. Here high quality and tastefulness combined in merchandise that did not necessarily have Indian designs. No attention was paid in this shop to the tribal origins of the products, and the articles were arranged in such a manner as to make the individual pieces appear at their best.

Not only Indian arts and crafts but also the individual Indians were central to the presentation. Visible participation in all activities by representatives of various tribal groups was fostered at every opportunity. The same artists who acted as demonstrators also contributed to other activities. When Eleanor Roosevelt visited the exhibit on 20 March, she was greeted by a husband and wife of the Blackfoot tribe.[14] When the Maharajah of Kapurthala and his son visited the exhibit, Hastine Todokozie, a Navajo medicine man and sand painter, greeted them. Mabel Burnside, a Navajo weaver, was a demonstrator at the exhibit during the time of her commencement exercises at Wingate Vocational High School and received her diploma in a ceremony at the exposition.

A sincere effort was made to house the Indian participants comfortably and to avoid the carnival atmosphere of Indian camps at other fairgrounds. In San Francisco, the demonstrators and tribal representatives were housed privately in a building on adjacent Yerba Buena Island, where the United States Navy maintained a station. Even a grand piano was rented by the Indian Arts and Crafts Board for one month and used at what came to be called the Indian hotel. In all, sixty-four Indian participants and demonstrators of tribal arts and crafts work took part in the Indian exhibit. Sixty of the sixty-four were artists. They were painters, basket makers, bead workers, silversmiths, stone carvers, rug weavers, sand painters, potters, and totem pole carvers.[15] The Indians displayed themselves as worthy contributors to American culture. D'Harnoncourt and the Indian Arts and Crafts Board promoted the concept, but the Indians' artistic skills made the day.

Praise for the Indian exhibit at the 1939 Golden Gate International Exposition at San Francisco came from all quarters. "One of the most satisfying and educational exhibits that I have ever seen," wrote the undersecretary of the Department of Agriculture, Milburn L. Wilson. The chairman of the race relations department of Yale University, Charles T. Loram, called the Indian exhibit "far and away the most admirable demonstration of Indian culture that I have ever seen." Loram had come to San Francisco with twelve students representing several nations who were studying the force of the impact of Western civilization on minority groups. Their trip was made specifically to study the exhibit of Indian culture. Jay B. Nash, professor of education at New York University, told Collier that after spending considerable time at the Indian exhibit he believed it to be "one of the finest things I have ever seen assembled." The art critic for the *Los Angeles Times*, Arthur Miller, was more specific in his praise. "Among the acres of art exhibits on Treasure Island [site of the exposition], I got my keenest thrill from the arts and crafts of the American Indian. The explanation is simple—showmanship; it should give every museum official in the country something to ponder."[16]

Alfred Kroeber, the anthropologist from the University of California, Berkeley, told George Creel that he was proud to have been a member of the advisory committee which had a hand in selecting and supporting d'Harnoncourt in San Francisco. He called the exhibit "completely authentic" with "a superb aesthetic quality." Kroeber was "tremendously impressed" with what was "far and away the best display exhibit of Indian material or any other ethnological material which I have ever seen." Kroeber told Collier of his reactions to the Indian exhibit and added a few lines of praise for d'Harnoncourt. "The man has an incredible faculty of giving his arrangements the supreme aesthetic touch as well as complete originality," he said. "At the same time everything is completely authentic, and the tremendous diversity of our Indians is brought out fully without ever being preached or insisted upon." The superintendent of the Carson Indian Agency, Stewart, Nevada, felt the exhibit displayed "a thoughtful scheme and a feeling for advantageous display methods," which she credited to d'Harnoncourt. She thought the whole Indian exhibit appealed to the intellectual curiosity about Indians and Indian life that was "actually very keen in the general public but which has usually so inadequate a source for satisfaction." Eleanor Roosevelt seemed to sum up the reactions when she told a reporter for the *San Francisco Examiner*, "I am very enthusiastic about the Exposition in general, but I am simply mad about the Indian exhibit."[17]

D'Harnoncourt was aware of the excellent reactions to the Indian exhibit. After representatives of the American Library Association, the Museum Association, and the Museum Directors' Association had visited the exhibit during their respective conventions in San Francisco, six of the largest art museums in the East made tentative arrangements to cooperate with their local ethnological museums in arranging decorative Indian exhibits which would emphasize "the vitality and art value of Indian material instead of its ethnological significance." Charles Loram urged Collier to set up the exhibit permanently somewhere such as in the Interior Department building in Washington, D.C., where future students might profit from the splendid lessons it taught. Numerous inquiries made by commercial establishments for sources of Indian arts and crafts further underscored interest in the Indian exhibit. By September 1939, plans were being formulated with the Museum of Modern Art in New York City for an exhibit of Indian arts and crafts early in 1941.[18]

Despite the plan that many of the artifacts displayed at San Francisco would be shown in less than a year in a New York exhibit, all of the artifacts displayed in San Francisco were returned immediately to the private collectors and museums that owned them. The list of contributors was a lengthy one.[19] Accurate accounting and careful record keeping by the Indian Arts and Crafts Board's administrative clerk for the exposition, Godfrey Kibler, combined with his participation in the crating and shipping until the last piece was accounted for, contributed the final professional touch to a nearly flawless Indian Arts and Crafts Board effort.

To achieve this success, d'Harnoncourt had had to make some decisions that brought adverse reactions from certain quarters. Apparently he had discovered quite early that he could not obtain the type of cooperation from the Department of the Interior Office of Exhibits that he needed to construct the San Francisco exhibit. Early in the planning stages, George Dickens, the former general agent for the Alaskan Railroad whom Ickes had appointed chief of exhibitions for the Interior Department, was a party to the consultations over the design and construction of the Indian exhibit. Then d'Harnoncourt announced that he had secured architect Henry Klumb, whose salary and expenses came out of the meager Indian Arts and Crafts Board funds. Klumb's name appeared on all of the blueprints, and d'Harnoncourt acknowledged him as the official architect of the Indian exhibit. In order to placate some individuals in the Interior Department, Ickes on 27 March 1939 issued an order that said in part that the "Office of Exhibits, [within the] Office of the Secretary [of the Interior], was established for the purpose of designing and constructing displays and exhibits of various kinds, for expositions, conventions, fairs, and for educational purposes generally, for the Office of the Secretary, and for the several bureaus and divisions of the Department as well." With that background, Ickes came to the point: "The bureaus and divisions of the Department are accordingly instructed to confer with the Office of Exhibits whenever the construction of displays or exhibits is contemplated." He emphasized that "the further establishment of individual bureau exhibit units is prohibited and before contracting elsewhere for the design and construction of exhibits material, the bureau should first ascertain whether the Office of Exhibits is in a position to undertake the work proposed."[20]

Why Ickes waited until well after the Indian exhibit had opened to bring this up remained unclear unless Ickes was forced from within the Interior Department to take a public stand when no credit was given to Dickens for d'Harnoncourt's successful presentation. Ickes was always a strong supporter of the overall New Deal Indian effort although he and d'Harnoncourt had little official contact. Collier, Ickes, and the Indian Arts and Crafts Board gave d'Harnoncourt a free hand to do things in his own way. As far as architectural decisions were concerned, their trust was not misplaced. Others besides d'Harnoncourt were not satisfied with Dickens's work. *San Francisco Chronicle* art critic Alfred Frankenstein openly attacked the other exhibits in the San Francisco Exposition Federal Building that Dickens had completed. Frankenstein felt that "the ingenuity of those who arranged the materials ran away with itself, so that the accessories of the display dwarf the things shown." D'Harnoncourt and Klumb, Frankenstein continued, had "succeeded in keeping the emphasis always on the object, placing it in settings often subtly stylized to suggest rather than describe its environment."[21]

When George Creel announced regretfully on 2 October that the whole exposition would close on 29 October, the Indian exhibit had been seen by approximately 1,250,000 visitors.[22] Every possible effort had been made to give the visitors a representative picture of the Indian cultures of the United States and Alaska. By showing both past and present achievements of these cultures, the Indian exhibit had attempted to open new prospects for their future. All of the prefatory events and contributing personalities that made up the potential for success at San Francisco had combined with Indian Arts and Crafts Board resources to build a finely tuned display framework which was both scientifically sound and aesthetically appealing. The flexible role of an associative government agency had supported the effort perfectly.

All of the advantages garnered by the Indians from the 1939 San Francisco Exposition never could be measured fully. Certainly, the sales figures for Indian arts and crafts sold by the Covelo Indian Market did not provide a definite measuring stick. The Indian Arts and Crafts Board was optimistic that the San Francisco Indian exhibit had increased the public's interest in quality Indian products. Although the actual cash returns at San Francisco were not very impressive, still the market sold all of the high quality craft goods obtainable. The experience gained at San Francisco had shown beyond doubt that a large potential market existed for fine Indian arts and crafts. Navajo silver was the best example, for the Covelo Indian Market could be kept supplied with top quality silver only one-fifth of the time even though prices were 50 percent higher than those on or near the reservations. The salability of this type of ware, apparently due largely to the method of presentation, resulted in board plans to contact retailers to improve their display methods. The exhibit also presented an excellent opportunity to acquaint employees of the Indian Office interested in the futhering of Indian arts and crafts with the realities of a business enterprise and to convey to them a more complete picture of the various Indian cultures of the United States and Alaska.[23] For the Indian participants the experiences gained from travel beyond the reservations probably were considerable although also unmeasurable. The much-needed income for Indian demonstrators and employees totaled over $6,000, a sum that was provided not by the government but by the private contributions that d'Harnoncourt was so successful in arranging.[24]

The San Francisco Exposition served as a nationwide advertising medium for Indian arts and crafts and contributed to the creation of a better understanding of and a wider market for Indian products, yet the board's effort cost the federal government relatively little. The Indian exhibit served as a powerful stimulus for Indian arts and crafts production and presented a testing ground for the commercial value of various products from different parts of the country. In the process, it proved to be a stimulus, also, for the creation of cooperative Indian enterprises for the production of handcrafts. The Indian Arts and Crafts Board's financial statement for fiscal year 1939 showed a total expenditure of $42,015; less than a quarter of that amount was directly related to the Indian exhibit in the form of the salaries and expenses of d'Harnoncourt and Klumb. Simply functioning in an advisory capacity, the Indian Arts and Crafts Board had put on a $200,000 Indian exhibit at almost no expense to the United States government beyond the $50,000 allotted by the government exposition commission.[25]

Any attempt to repeat this same achievement at the 1940 San Francisco Exposition was financially impossible. The supreme effort had been made in 1939 to find every available source of money for a one-time exhibit. No plans were made for a 1940 repeat performance, and d'Harnoncourt did not entertain any thoughts in that direction. The fact that Congress appropriated only $200,000 for the United States government participation at San Francisco in 1940 certainly was no inducement, nor was the fact that this money was appropriated only on 14 May 1940, ten days before the exposition was scheduled to reopen. The Indian Arts and Crafts Board explained that it was unable in 1940 to continue its extensive participation in the San Francisco Exposition. The board limited its official activities to detailing an employee to supervise the administrative work, to supplying preliminary plans for the installation, and to rendering all advisory service possible. Since he could not be involved directly, d'Harnoncourt refrained from any personal participation.[26]

Difficulty plagued the 1940 exhibit from the start. Not knowing what funds would be available until the last moment, the government commissioner for the exposition, George Creel, waited until two weeks before a new Indian exhibit was scheduled to open to ask Samuel Alfred Barrett, former director of the Milwaukee Public Museum, to create an exhibit comprising about half of the space used for the Indian exhibit in 1939. D'Harnoncourt offered Barrett help "in terms of data and advice, within the limits of our available time."[27] The 1939 exhibit had been completely dismantled, and Barrett had to start from the beginning, a task made more difficult by the need for Mexican and South American material. The general theme of the 1940 display, which already had been decided upon before Barrett entered the picture, was "Indian Cultures of the Americas" and was oriented internationally toward the Pacific Ocean Indians. To help out, Tulane University and the University of California, Berkeley, agreed to allow Barrett to use the Mayan and Andean artifacts they had loaned for display in the Fine Arts Palace at the 1939 San Francisco Exposition. Probably because of such short notice, the Heye Foundation Museum of the American Indian in New York City refused to provide material for the Mexican, Central American, and South American displays. The same situation arose when Barrett tried to obtain material on display at the Milwaukee Public Museum. Barrett was reminded by the director that the rule prohibiting removal of material on display for loan to any sort of project also had been Barrett's policy when he was the director of the museum.[28]

Barrett's position was not enviable. Considering the handicaps, not the least of which was the obvious comparison to d'Harnoncourt's efforts the previous year, Barrett apparently deserved the qualified praise he received from one who had attended both expositions. "You have done a skillful and masterly job in making an entirely new exhibit this year, undoubtedly under severe handicaps," the former undersecretary of the Department of Agriculture and now the director of the Department of Agriculture's extension work, Milburn Wilson, told Barrett. Wilson added that he thought the presentation ranked "among the outstanding exhibits at the 1940 San Francisco Exposition."[29]

Some of d'Harnoncourt's San Francisco friends refused to go that far. Kroeber and others told d'Harnoncourt that the 1940 exhibit did not represent their specific point of view.[30] The main stress in 1939 had been upon aesthetic values and the secondary stress upon anthropology. In 1940 the emphasis was reversed, the very situation that d'Harnoncourt and the Indian Arts and Crafts Board were struggling to change in the interest of the living Indians. Also, the 1940 San Francisco Exposition had no Indian arts and crafts market. Nevertheless, d'Harnoncourt diplomatically remained uncritical and privately expressed his sympathy for the people in San Francisco who worked "under handicaps that made it impossible for them to produce a well-balanced show."[31]

10

FIELD WORK

To help the Indians help themselves, the Indian Arts and Crafts Board decided early to organize production and merchandising units. While primarily confined to the making of essential surveys during its first two years of existence, the board still managed to carry out some urgently needed organizational work. In a few areas such as western Oklahoma, some arts and crafts organization already existed, and the board had only to initiate projects and to stress quality production to achieve results. In other areas such as Nevada, government schools and energetic teachers provided the necessary nuclei of organizationl activity that required only the board's periodic encouragement and advice. In still other areas, like that of the Choctaws in eastern Oklahoma, the board had to develop a marketable craft and the necessary organization to keep production going. Because of this wide variation in the type and condition of tribal arts and crafts, any organization that would be of lasting value to its members had to be tailored and adjusted to local conditions. Only through full knowledge of each local situation could the board properly advise and correctly tailor each producing and merchandising unit.

Personal contact with the Indians and knowledge of conditions in the field contributed greatly to d'Harnoncourt's skill in deciding what had to be done and who could best accomplish the task. Reports of a need for arts and crafts encouragement among the Alaskan Indians and Eskimos came to d'Harnoncourt through the Indian Office Education Division. Virgil R. Farrell, government school teacher in Nome, provided such detailed reports based on his own activities and observations that the Indian Arts and Crafts Board, with the cooperation of the Education Division, created for him the position of arts and crafts supervisor for the Territory of Alaska. The position was under the Education

199

Division and not the Indian Arts and Crafts Board although Farrell worked under d'Harnoncourt's direction. Shortly after Farrell's appointment early in 1938, d'Harnoncourt planned an extensive trip to Alaska to assess conditions and to plan for the development of markets. A few days before he left, the opportunity to expand the board's work in the Territory of Alaska with the assistance of the Carnegie Corporation developed when d'Harnoncourt received a letter from Frederick Keppel asking him to look for new fields of activities in Alaska for the Carnegie Corporation. After six weeks in Alaska, d'Harnoncourt completed "a rich and indeed exciting account of the wealth and virility of the surviving crafts in the Territory."[1]

He found that most of the Indian arts and crafts work in Alaska was being produced for the tourist trade, with a few exceptions like Chilkat blankets, dug-out canoes, and occasional articles of clothing and moccasins. As on most reservations in the United States, the articles made for home consumption, d'Harnoncourt noted, were of the finest quality and in no way inferior to the work produced by former generations, and the more isolated the village, the higher the percentage of quality work. Visiting relatively isolated Klukwan, d'Harnoncourt observed two men constructing canoes and learned that the majority of canoes used still were made locally. He found three weavers working on Chilkat blankets and two blankets that had been finished during the last few weeks. Of the five blankets, two were to be given to local Indian residents and the others were for sale although they were not made for specific traders and might eventually remain in the village. D'Harnoncourt saw several pieces of beadwork that were in progress or that had been finished recently. The artists produced this beadwork mainly for the tourist trade, yet some of the best pieces were strictly for Indian use, such as the dance bags, which did not seem to have much attraction for the tourists. D'Harnoncourt also discovered some carved dishes and spoons and learned that at least one man carried on the silverwork tradition.[2]

Pride in the old arts was still alive in the small village of Klukwan. D'Harnoncourt visited six homes, four of which contained the carved house posts that had been saved by their owners from their original homes. Two of the houses contained the painted partition walls of the owners' former homes. The importance of quality work along traditional lines was evident in Klukwan not only in the careful preservation of the old pieces and in the high standards of present production but also in the conversations d'Harnoncourt had with different villagers. He reported that "almost everybody spoken to emphasized the importance of doing work the 'right way,' and the fear of people that the old arts may deteriorate or disappear was heard everywhere." The local teacher's wife was the only non-Indian person living in the small community.

A slightly different situation was found in the somewhat less isolated village of Hydaburg. Very few white people lived in Hydaburg. Surrounded by canneries and nearer to the main-traveled road, the Indians of Hydaburg practiced no art for local consumption except the making of dug-out canoes. The inhabitants, members of the Haida tribe, had come to the area from several nearby, now-deserted villages. D'Harnoncourt reasoned that this would explain why he saw no house posts or painted partition walls preserved in Hydaburg. Most of the monumental carvings, totem poles, grave poles, and large paintings had been left in the deserted villages, although the people of Hydaburg still talked of them as their personal possessions.

Interest and pride in the old arts were just as alive in Hydaburg as they were in Klukwan, d'Harnoncourt observed, since each home he visited had a number of fine old pieces of Haida art to show. One of the older men, John Wallace, had participated in carving monumental poles in the earlier villages and impressed d'Harnoncourt with his interest in carrying on the old-style work. After returning to the United States, d'Harnoncourt invited Wallace and his son to participate in totem pole carving demonstrations at the San Francisco Exposition. Wallace had carved a forty-five-foot pole for the Waterfall Cannery the previous year. Although his sharp eye discerned that Wallace had adopted an indiscriminate method of painting his work, d'Harnoncourt considered this to be mainly a concession to the taste of the white client or trader. Beadwork in Hydaburg, d'Harnoncourt reported, was made for sale but was still fine quality. Their basketry, however, was "not too good."

Contrasts also existed between the larger communities that were mainly tourist centers or had predominantly white populations. Sitka and Ketchikan both were visited by d'Harnoncourt and exemplified this contrast. Sitka's fewer visitors were from more expensive tours than those that stopped at Ketchikan, a fact that d'Harnoncourt felt helped to explain why the few shops in Sitka dealing in Indian goods were more aware of the merit of quality. Sitka was more conscious of its historic appeal, he observed, and it boasted about a park that had as its main attraction a collection of totem poles. D'Harnoncourt considered this historic awareness to be a vital aspect of the people's attitude. Even the school, he found, had engaged a young native carver of considerable ability to conduct an optional, yet well-attended, course in totem pole carving after school hours. The attitude of the older people in Sitka was similar to that found in Hydaburg, and the number of old pieces of artwork kept in the homes was also considerable. Here in Sitka, d'Harnoncourt with his artistic senses, skill, and knowledge detected traces of a new aesthetic attitude among the younger people, an attitude that replaced the purely traditional values of Indian arts and crafts with artistic ones. In contrast, the replacement of traditional values in Ketchikan "leaned more to the purely commercial side." As the second largest community in southeastern Alaska and with several large stores, Ketchikan was a natural stopping point for all boats coming from Seattle. D'Harnoncourt's observations added to his firm conviction that his role should be to encourage high standards in order to gain acceptance in the more affluent segment of the market, a market which ultimately would produce greater economic rewards from higher prices and a wider and more stable market than that of the inexpensive souvenir trade.

Compared with that of the Alaskan Indians, the potential of the Alaskan Eskimo artists remained undeveloped. While d'Harnoncourt did not visit any of the isolated Eskimo communities, he was confident that Farrell's reports were an accurate analysis of the arts and crafts situation.[3] Farrell and his wife had used their own time and efforts to organize some production and sale of Eskimo arts and crafts, but because most goods were produced in relatively isolated communities, the Farrells had limited results. The main production consisted of fur goods and ivory with most of the fur goods used by the Eskimos themselves. Farrell succeeded in adapting the old traditional garments for the non-Eskimo while still retaining their native characteristics. D'Harnoncourt also attributed a successful widening of the market for ivory goods to the Farrells' work. Their contribution was an outstanding exception in a deteriorating Alaskan arts and crafts situation.

Alaska presented a challenge to d'Harnoncourt and the Indian Arts and Crafts Board. Very few dealers in Indian goods in Alaska showed any appreciation of good craftwork, d'Harnoncourt reported, and those who were discriminating were interested in the old pieces. With little encouragement from the traders, the contemporary artists were experiencing a situation similar to that of the Indian artisans in the United States, competition from machine- or factory-made products, which along with the gradual native adaptation to white products threatened to destroy the beauty and skills found in their rich cultural heritage.

Competition for the Alaskan Indian and Eskimo artists came mainly from the Indian-style products made in Seattle with labor-saving devices and from those products imported from Japan. Indian-style products from Japan seemed to be declining as a damaging competitive force felt by the Alaskan Indians and Eskimos. An increasingly negative public opinion about Japan was cited by d'Harnoncourt as contributing to a considerable fall in the sales of the higher-priced Japanese imitations. While the danger of Japanese imports to the Alaskan production currently was overrated, he believed, the traders still carried on profitable sales in Japanese goods in the very low-priced class, the fifteen- and twenty-five-cent items. D'Harnoncourt felt that the Alaskan Indians could not compete profitably with the Japanese goods. Surprisingly, he found that most merchants made no effort to represent Japanese goods as Alaskan Indian-made, and apparently most tourists purchasing them knew their origin but seemed to hope that the gift recipients "would not know the difference." Even so, many of the pieces were plainly stamped "Made in Japan." Certain that handmade products could not compete with them, d'Harnoncourt considered four measures that might help in restricting their sales: educating the public through propaganda, taking additional steps to enforce the labeling of Japanese goods, and, if possible, segregating them to one specific space in the store, prohibiting their importation and sale, if possible, and creating a government label for Alaskan Indian-made goods.[4]

The objects made in Seattle and labeled "Indian-made" presented a much more serious situation, primarily because Indians from the United States participated in their production and the style of work more closely copied the Alaskan style. Such work easily misled the tourists searching for the genuine articles, d'Harnoncourt observed. Although the discriminating person readily recognized the character that only could be produced in an all-handmade piece, many people were misled and Alaskan carving was underrated by people seeing an inferior product. D'Harnoncourt again saw the only protective measures to be education of the public and creation of a label for handmade Alaskan Indian and Eskimo products. Even further, if every retail shop that was carrying machine-made imitations also would show some of the finest carved work made by the Indians and Eskimos, a reputation could be established for Indian-made products that would make it desirable even for the souvenir hunters to own a handmade product. D'Harnoncourt believed that by this means the production of fine pieces of high quality would benefit not only the quality market but also favorably influence sales in the low-priced fields.[5]

D'Harnoncourt's lengthy and important report made specific observations about the arts and crafts situation in Alaska and proposals for the Indian Arts and Crafts Board to meet Alaskan needs. The apparent needs were two-fold: first, stimulation, guidance, and protection of work done currently by Alaskan Indians and Eskimos that satisfied the needs of the local tourist market, and second, stimulation of a supplementary production of quality merchandise for the discriminating buyer in order to establish a reputation for fine craft techniques for Alaskan goods and to give the best artists an opportunity to exploit their abilities. To meet these needs d'Harnoncourt proposed creating a government trademark to distinguish the handmade Alaskan articles from imitations and a separate local arts and crafts committee label for quality work. The first was not to be a quality mark, but simply a certificate that the product was made by an Alaskan Indian or Eskimo, was handmade under conditions not resembling a workshop or factory system, and was made of materials obtained locally with specific exceptions. This trademark was to consist of a rubber stamp to be applied directly to the object, or in the case of basketry, fabrics, and furs, of a label attached to the object by a wire caught in a lead seal. Small articles such as ivory figures would be stamped "U.S. Eskimo" or "U.S. Alaskan Indian." The stamping of the products was made easier because the Alaskan Indians and Eskimos lived in towns and villages and the Indian Arts and Crafts Board could create in each community a local arts and crafts committee of three headed by a local government representative such as a teacher. In the case of the quality label, the committee was to select only the finest work for labeling and to sign each label with its signature or mark after providing a detailed description of the product.

D'Harnoncourt did not want to expand government bureaucracy and control. Instead, he proposed to assist the Alaskan Indians and Eskimos through an associative relationship involving government support of local or individual initiative. "The aim of this project," he explained, "is to make the village carry the responsibility of the selection of goods to be eligible for the certificate of quality, by endorsing the local club rather than the individual object." Any misuse of the board's endorsement would result in the withdrawal of the board's sponsorship. The labels were to belong to the board and any unused labels had to be returned to the board by the local committee or club if the board withdrew its sponsorship.

D'Harnoncourt stressed the need for the individual communities to feel that the projects were completely their own and that the initiative was also theirs. To this end, each project had to be designed to fit local circumstances. The plan d'Harnoncourt outlined for Klukwan, the village he believed best qualified at that moment to start the project, involved the use of a research worker from the University of Washington to instigate the arts and crafts movement in an unofficial capacity. The research worker was to work in cooperation with the local government teacher, who, when the project was ready for realization, would become a member of the local arts and crafts club and act as its financial advisor and probably as treasurer.

D'Harnoncourt justified this approach as advisable in Klukwan because the research worker currently in the village was familiar with the community and its production and also had the confidence of the older people. In order to make the project appear spontaneous and locally initiated, the research worker would not appear at any time as an official representative of the board or of the Indian Office. Although the board's procedure in organizing similar production and merchandising units elsewhere in Alaska and in the United States was adjusted individually to local conditions, the basic concept of relying on the local community to initiate and to carry on the project was followed conscientiously even though an initial, discreet nudge in the proposed direction came from the board.

Seven months later, the secretary of the interior approved d'Harnoncourt's recommendation for a government mark of genuineness for Alaskan Indian and Eskimo handmade products. Separate regulations were established for Eskimo and Indian products because of their differences. The same criminal penalties for deception provided in the Indian Arts and Crafts Board Act applied. The government stamp was to be applied to the articles with a rubber stamp provided by the Indian Arts and Crafts Board. Each stamp was to bear a distinctive letter and could be used only by the person to whom it was issued. After the distinctive letter the stamp would read:

( )
HAND-MADE
ALASKAN INDIAN   [or]   HAND-MADE
U S   ALASKAN ESKIMO
INDIAN ARTS & CRAFTS BOARD   U S
I D   INDIAN ARTS & CRAFTS BOARD
                                              I D

or, in the cases of articles too small to carry that stamp:

( )   ( )
U S I D   [or]   U S I D
ALASKAN INDIAN   ALASKAN ESKIMO.

On baskets and fabrics which offered no surface for the application of such a rubber stamp, the stamp was to be placed on a paper tag and attached by a wire caught in a lead seal disc furnished by the Indian Arts and Crafts Board.[6]

The attention the board gave to Alaskan Indian and Eskimo products paid huge future dividends not only for the artists but also for the survival of the Indian Arts and Crafts Board itself when it faced skeptical congressional appropriations subcommittees.

Virgil Farrell proved to be the driving force behind the successful Alaskan arts and crafts organization. In December 1938, he reported having contacted over the previous year fifty-eight stations during eight months in the field. In the process he reached fifty-seven Alaskan dealers of Indian and Eskimo trading merchandise in an effort to gain greater outlets for native arts and crafts. In his report on his activities for calendar year 1938, Farrell showed that the combined work of the Education Division and the Indian Arts and Crafts Board had contributed to the sale of more than $98,000 worth of craft products. He reported that of that amount approximately $78,000 worth of Alaskan Indian and Eskimo goods were sold that would not have been sold otherwise. About 60 percent of that amount represented brand new income to the artists, and about 40 percent represented improved income which they received because of higher prices for better quality goods. These figures impressed d'Harnoncourt, who sincerely believed that Farrell had made "an outstanding record."[7]

Because Farrell was an employee of the Indian Office Education Division of the Interior Department and not of the Indian Arts and Crafts Board, he had more funds available and could engage in business activities that the board was prohibited from carrying out. As a result, organized marketing developed more rapidly in Alaska than in the United States. The Indian Arts and Crafts Board, true to its mandate, provided advice and technical assistance not only to Farrell but also to the Alaskan Indians and Eskimos whenever possible, and as a result could rightfully take some credit for the commercial development of arts and crafts in Alaska.

The formula was simple but effective. In order to help the artists to market their goods, a central clearing house for the temporary storage of the craft items was established at the Interior Department's Juneau office. The policy was to sell only on a wholesale basis to dealers. A catalogue was printed and sent out to the dealers listing and pricing the craft articles. In this manner orders were solicited at a minimum of expense and immediate shipment was possible. The Juneau office at first filled all of the orders, but as the system developed many orders were shipped directly from the field station to the dealers. The field stations usually were the local Interior Department schools where the cooperation and work of the teachers played an important role.[8] The Indian Arts and Crafts Board encouraged Alaskan Indian and Eskimo initiative and also sought out and supported the work of other agencies in the bureaucracy to realize the board's goals. Again, the coordinating, associative role of the Indian Arts and Crafts Board and New Deal Indian policy encouraged other federal offices to contribute to Indian arts and crafts development where otherwise no notable success might have been achieved.

Where tribes began to feel a new confidence in their tribal future and in the future of their arts and crafts, they used the cooperative as a vehicle for voluntary economic organization. In Nevada, Washoes, Paiutes, and Shoshones organized in late 1935 the Wa-Pai-Shone Craftsmen, a cooperative trading post that was established permanently under Nevada law in 1936. Active membership was limited to qualified Indians living in the area, yet inactive membership was available to anyone in the country willing to pay a three-dollar initiation fee and annual dues. The objectives of the cooperative were "to revive and perpetuate interest in the traditional handiwork of the Indians of the Great Basin; to protect their design and the standards of their work, to increase production, and to facilitate marketing." Capital was provided by unidentified friends who made non-interest-bearing loans to the cooperative. Primarily offering Washoe and Death Valley baskets, the group achieved sales the first year totaling $786 of which the Indians received $629. These figures evidently represented a successful year, for branches were planned for McDermott, Nixon, Schurz, and Dresslerville, Nevada.[9]

Collier was convinced of the advantages of the cooperative system for the Indians and, indeed, for all society. In fact, he devoted an entire issue of *Indians at Work* to the subject of cooperation, and his editorial reviewed the experiment carried out by forty-three spinners ninety years earlier at Rochdale, England. According to Collier, the Rochdale Cooperative "brought more gain to human society than the efficient or inefficient administration of all the governments, all the businesses of Europe in the same years." Cooperation, Collier wrote, was a new social, political, economic, and human-relations institution that was worldwide in availability and all-embracing in possible effects. The Rochdale spinners had changed the direction of history; they had achieved "a method of human advancement into a domain never entered before." These views of Collier's were not idle thoughts, for cooperatives were destined to play an ever increasing role in the preservation of Indian arts and crafts.[10]

In the summer of 1937, staff members of the board made a preliminary survey among the Choctaw Indians in southeastern Oklahoma where an entirely different arts and crafts situation existed. For them the traditional craft products either had little market appeal or had dis-

208

appeared entirely. Under such circumstances, the board's policy was to afford the group the opportunity to learn new industries. As a consequence, the Indian Arts and Crafts Board decided to promote the making of homespun yarn as a home industry, a craft which would provide the workers with an opportunity to develop a skill and at the same time achieve a style of their own. The tradition of spinning, introduced by white settlers many years earlier, had not died out entirely in McCurtain County, where the project was to be developed with the cooperation of the Five Civilized Tribes Agency. Only four spinning wheels were still in occasional use to manufacture yarn to be knitted into sweaters and caps for home consumption. The limited output was negligible and the quality was not up to commercial standards. The wool used came from a small number of local sheep in the possession of members of the tribe. The yarn made from this wool was very crude and had a market value of only ninety cents a pound, a price that would not produce any return for the spinner.[11]

After the initial survey of the arts and crafts situation among the Choctaws, the board's next step was to conduct technical or market research. Such research determined that most of the homespun yarn used in America was imported from Scotland and Scandinavia and was very costly. To provide the fullest technical advice and assistance designed to improve and to enlarge production and to make it commercially valuable for the Choctaws, the board asked the Education Division of the Indian Office to lend the services of Mabel Morrow, a spinning teacher, to assist in the project. Morrow began work in Idabel, the center of McCurtain County, on 15 October 1937. Six additional spinning wheels were added to the four already in use. A Choctaw man made three of the six spinning wheels from his own design, and the remainder were loaned to the project by the supervisor of Indian schools for eastern Oklahoma. The board obtained twenty-five pounds of wool through donations like that of the Sequoyah Orphan Training School (Oklahoma).[12]

The results of the technical assistance stage of the Choctaw project were encouraging. During the first two months approximately fifty persons expressed interest at demonstration sessions and twenty of them actually participated in the production of yarn. Ten of these spinners improved their technique to such an extent that they produced yarn of commercial quality. About eight pounds of beginners' yarn was used by the spinners to knit garments for home consumption and four pounds either was sold or retained by the board to make up samples for future orders. By the end of three months the Choctaw spinners had improved their spinning to such an extent that the board was able to market some of their yarn at $3.50 per pound.[13]

D'Harnoncourt was justifiably optimistic that the results to date warranted a plan for future activities. He first retained the services of the spinning instructor for three additional months and then acquired two additional spinning wheels and six wool cards. Next, he sought to insure an adequate supply of wool. After consultation with the superintendent of the Five Civilized Tribes, the decision was made to ask the Indian Office farm agent at Idabel to assist in the acquisition of the nucleus of a flock of sheep that would grow with the local needs. A government loan was needed to purchase the sheep, and Mabel Morrow helped to organize a cooperative or credit association of spinners to obtain the loan and to advance the project.[14]

Continuing to offer management assistance, d'Harnoncourt determined that over the first year of the project the number of spinners producing commercially marketable yarn could be increased to twenty-five, which would result in a total production of between 600 to 700 pounds of yarn. Assuming the same progress over a second year, the project would become self-supporting. A minimum production of 1,200 pounds a year salable at $3.50 per pound was required to produce $4,200 for the group. Of the sale price of $3.50 per pound, $2.50 would go to the spinner for time and material. The one dollar difference would go to the project's managing and marketing expenses.[15] The fact that seventy-five spinners were members of the Choctaw Spinners Association by 1939 testified to the popularity of the Indian Arts and Crafts Board project. Yet, d'Harnoncourt still was not satisfied with what he called a minimum production capable of sound commercial results. He aimed for further developments of far greater scope because of the lack of competition in the homespun yarn market. The board, he stated, would assist, eventually, with the introduction of vegetable dyes and the manufacture of articles from the yarn.[16]

Optimism was high for the future of the Choctaw spinning project during its first year and a half of operation although the results did not live up to expectations. For 1939, the first full year of operation, the Indian Arts and Crafts Board reported the production of 284 pounds of handspun yarn and a total sales of $735. D'Harnoncourt was not satisfied and determined to improve the situation. Organizational difficulties within the project had appeared, and production had lagged to such an extent that outside commercial orders could not be accepted. In his advisory capacity, d'Harnoncourt suggested an organizational plan that provided for a more efficiently functioning unit. Aware that the Education Division under Willard Beatty was planning to develop a large spinning and weaving project throughout the area of the Five Civilized Tribes, d'Harnoncourt's plan reorganized the Choctaw spinning project to fit as a local unit into the larger project. The supervisor of Indian education for Oklahoma would be in charge and at the same time be responsible to the superintendent of the Five Civilized Tribes. With the approval of the superintendent, the supervisor of education would appoint a regional supervisor of weaving, to whom the local supervisors of spinning would be responsible since the quality of the work under their direction determined the quality of the yarn. Such a hierarchy of interest, d'Harnoncourt hoped, would contribute to a more efficient project.[17]

After the organizational plans were approved and carried out, d'Harnoncourt attacked the production problems that also contributed to the failure of the project to become self-supporting. The small margin of profit under the existing methods of production had to be increased. To produce one pound of yarn, a spinner spent thirty hours or a week's work which included scouring and carding. At $2.50 per pound, the spinners were earning $1.30 for a week's work after fifty cents was used to buy the raw wool and seventy cents was deducted for management costs. D'Harnoncourt found that commercially cleaned and carded wool was easier to spin and could increase the weekly output to four or five pounds. To maintain the product's integrity and marketability as homespun yarn, the Indian Arts and Crafts Board required that three considerations be met before the commercial scouring and carding aspect was adopted: the scouring and carding could not be done in a penitentiary or other institution whose relationship with the product might make the sale of the yarn on the open market difficult or impossible, care had to be taken to maintain the character of homespun yarn in order

not to endanger sales by producing material which in its perfection re-
sembled the machine-made product, and a tag had to be devised and
approved by the Indian Office attorneys to indicate that only the spinning and not the carding or scouring was done by hand. After the implementation of d'Harnoncourt's suggestions, the Choctaw Spinners
Association reported a total sales of $1,018 for 1941.[18]

The Indian Arts and Crafts Board also developed a weaving project
at the Sequoyah Orphan Training School. Using the Choctaw spinners'
yarn, the students successfully produced a quality handwoven fabric.
During 1939, the first year of operation, eighteen student weavers at
the school produced 138 yards of handspun, handwoven material for a
total of $1,294 in sales. A market was found for all salable material
produced. In 1942 sales jumped to $2,248. As with the Choctaw
spinners, the Indian Arts and Crafts Board helped to organize a cooperative at the Sequoyah school as a production and marketing unit. The
Sequoyah Weavers Association joined the growing list of cooperative
Indian arts and crafts associations initiated and encouraged by the board.
A mark of the Sequoyah Weavers Association's success was seen in the
real concern expressed by Congressman Charles Henry Leavy, Democrat from Washington, at the House Subcommittee on Appropriations
hearings in 1940 after Collier had finished describing the activities and
progress made at the Sequoyah school. "The volume of these fabrics is
not sufficient to become a factor in the textile industry[?]" asked the
congressman, showing his priorities. Collier told Leavy that such a situation could not occur for years, and even then the unique quality of
Indian weaving would establish its own market segment. "They [the
Indian weavers] will not hurt the textile industry at all," he stated. Willard Beatty assured Leavy that the situation of the Indian weavers would
be similar to that of the Southern mountaineer weavers who found their
own bottomless market in the exclusive tailoring and dressmaking
establishments.[19]

The congressman's concern may not have been entirely misplaced.
Beatty was so proud of the work of the Choctaw Spinners Association
and the Sequoyah Weavers Association that he wore a business suit
that was tailored from their materials to the House appropriations subcommittee hearings in 1942. He told the subcommittee that "the goods

cost me $38.75 for two pants, coat, and vest. . . . It cost me $60 to have it tailored. My associate, Mr. Fickinger, had one that cost him $37 to have made up." Beatty also informed the congressmen that his friend Charles Laughton, a movie actor, had purchased forty yards of drapery material from the Sequoyah Weavers Association at $14 a yard and considered the price to be a bargain.[20]

In developing each individual Indian arts and crafts project, the board sought to begin in such a way that the project eventually would become self-supporting and independent of the government. The board's objective in every instance was to interest local agencies in cooperating with the board with the view of having all of the board's projects eventually absorbed by local enterprise.[21]

The resolutions of the council of the 6,181 member Papago tribe in Arizona provided an example of an early arts and crafts project initiated by the Indian Arts and Crafts Board and carried out by the active participation of tribal government. With the advice of the Indian Arts and Crafts Board, the Papago Council on 6 November 1937 formally requested Collier to obtain legislation authorizing the use of $3,000 on deposit in the United States Treasury to the credit of the Papagos. The money had been entered in the Treasury records under "Proceeds of Labor, Papago Indians of Sells Agency, Arizona." The money, said the council, would be used for the purchase of Papago baskets and other Papago handcrafts, and the payment of travel expenses, wages, salaries, and incidental expenses necessary for the preparation and showing of a Papago exhibit at the 1939 San Francisco Exposition. The council also requested authorization to sell all baskets and handcrafts purchased with this same fund and the right to deposit all proceeds with the superintendent of the Sells Agency in a special fund to be used only at the direction of the Papagos.[22]

Out of these plans to display and to sell their tribal crafts at the San Francisco Exposition came the unanimous decision by the Papago Council in September 1938 to create a tribal board known as the Papago Arts and Crafts Board. The board was composed of three commissioners whose function was to promote the economic welfare of the Papagos through the development of Papago arts and crafts and the expansion of the market for these products. The chairman of the Papago Council was also chairman of the arts and crafts board during his term of office.[23]

The powers of the Papago Arts and Crafts Board were markedly similar to those of the Indian Arts and Crafts Board. The Papago Council exhibited confidence in the intent of the Indian Arts and Crafts Board when it directed the Papago board "to cooperative with and assist the Indian Arts and Crafts Board . . . in its work on the reservations under the jurisdiction of the Papago Tribe." The Papago board's independent action was limited, nevertheless, to ward status by the brief clause in the resolution requiring the board to advise and consult with the superintendent of the Sells Agency over any disbursement of money.[24]

Experience and knowledge attained over a two-and-one-half-year period in handling their own arts and crafts promotion was apparent in the Papago Council resolution of 28 March 1941 and its amended form of 14 June 1941, which replaced the expired 1938 resolution creating the Papago Arts and Crafts Board. The Papago Council had determined that over the previous two years the Papago board had benefited the tribe, and it made the board a permanent part of tribal government. The board's organization was made more independent of the superintendent's control by combining the work of the treasurer with the new position of general manager, a salaried post appointed by the Papago Arts and Crafts Board with the consent of the council. This 1941 Papago tribal resolution provided evidence of success on the part of the Indian Arts and Crafts Board in its effort to foster initiative and self-help among the Papagos. Additional evidence was provided when first year sales of $1,685 in 1939 jumped to $4,700 by 1941.[25]

Experience brought direction and success to the Papago board. The new tribal council resolution contained specific directives for the board such as to encourage and to teach the best methods of producing the arts and crafts of the Papagos, to conduct a wholesale and retail business in their products, to advertise the products, and to represent the Papagos at fairs, rodeos, and other similar exhibitions. The success enjoyed by the Papago Arts and Crafts Board in carrying out these functions was established late in 1940 when the Papago community began construction of an arts and crafts center. D'Harnoncourt recognized the outstanding work done by the Papago board and Indian Arts and

Crafts Board specialist Gwyneth Harrington when he told the Papago Council that its progress constituted a fine example for arts and crafts work all over the country.[26]

In another situation, the individual approach by d'Harnoncourt and the Indian Arts and Crafts Board helped the Coeur d'Alenes to return to their ancient craft techniques and at the same time adapt them to modern needs. Again a community school was the starting point for activities that would benefit the whole tribe. In 1937, a new member of the staff of instructors at the Convent of Mary Immaculate in DeSmet, Idaho, on her own initiative formed an arts and crafts club. Sister Providencia of the Order of the Sisters of Charity of Providence, later to be known to many admiring Indians as "Sister Buckskin," corresponded with d'Harnoncourt and later sent him samples of buckskin articles made by the Coeur d'Alenes. Sister Providencia, the daughter of Congressman John H. Tolan, Democrat from California, attributed the craft revival on the reservation to d'Harnoncourt's suggestion in 1937 that the Coeur d'Alenes have an exhibit at the 1939 San Francisco Exposition. The board's criticisms and suggestions when further samples of Coeur d'Alene crafts were sent to Washington in 1938 assisted the Indians in establishing standards, in improving and adapting buckskin articles to modern tastes, and in seeking a craft specialty.[27]

No board survey was needed in Idaho; all d'Harnoncourt had to do was to advise Sister Providencia and to guide her exceptional organizational powers. A personal visit by d'Harnoncourt to the Coeur d'Alene Reservation provided additional incentive and suggestions for improving the work. The commercial success of Sister Providencia's Kateri Club, named for Kateri (Catherine) Tekakwitha, a Mohawk heroine, was determined at the San Francisco Golden Gate Exposition. Their products included buckskin pouches, gloves, belts, purses, moccasins, jackets, tiny dolls for zipper pulls, moccasins with "trailers" to mislead the evil spirits, and dolls similar to those played with seventy-five years earlier by Indian girls of the Rocky Mountain tribes. Sister Providencia credited the Kateri Club's success at the Golden Gate Exposition to the board's suggestion that they abandon heavily beaded articles and concentrate on well-cut, handsewn, practical articles, such as gloves and

215

jackets. The praise for the Coeur d'Alene wares at the San Francisco Exposition created a new pride in their craftwork, and their newly established reputation provided a wide market. The Coeur d'Alenes responded with efforts to stabilize production by setting up a tanning project at DeSmet and by establishing a separate glove-making unit managed by the Indians.[28]

Sister Providencia, like d'Harnoncourt, did not rest on her laurels. Through her personal efforts she obtained a contract with a large department store in Spokane, Washington, to market all of the gloves the Coeur d'Alenes could make. Because of the war, glove making in Europe was at a standstill and buyers were looking eagerly at the domestic market to meet the demand for these high quality articles.[29] The wide recognition given the Idaho Indians not only added to their own pride and self-respect, claimed Sister Providencia, but also brought new respect from non-Indians. Increased employment and educational opportunities were made available to Kateri Club members. On 30 January 1941, Eleanor Roosevelt, Jane Ickes, Helen Douglas (wife of actor Melvyn Douglas), many congressmen, and other prominent persons visited the House Indian Affairs Committee room to see an exhibit of handcrafts produced by the Indians of the Northwest. The exhibit was sponsored by the House Indian Affairs Committee and was arranged by Sister Providencia.[30]

By early 1941 d'Harnoncourt's advice to and encouragement of Sister Providencia and the Coeur d'Alenes in Idaho had affected the lives and well-being of countless Indians in the Northwest. The movement spread to Washington, Montana, Wyoming, and Oregon, and the Kateri Club's membership included not only the Coeur d'Alenes but also the Kootenai, Yakima, Spokane, Kalispel, Nez Perce, Colville, Flathead, and Arapahoe Indians. The Indians received 80 percent of the income from sales, and the remaining 20 percent went for expenses. The movement now developed into three divisions: the Kateri Club, pledged to the cause of Indian leadership and to the revival and modernization of Indian crafts, was an educational, social, and cultural organization for Indians; the Kateri Cooperative, all-Indian in membership and government, had no tribal, religious, or monetary restrictions and was entirely Indian-supported; and the Kateri craft school, for Indian girls of high school age, gave social and craft instruction for extended participation in the club program. Sister Providencia remained the only non-Indian directly connected with the movement.[31] By helping to elevate the Coeur d'Alenes' craftwork to a level much higher than that of the mere souvenir for tourists, the Indian Arts and Crafts Board contributed to the economic and cultural well-being of the Indians. With each individual project, the board was achieving its goal of eventual acceptance of Indian arts and crafts as a part of both Indian and non-Indian life in the twentieth century.

No two projects began in the same manner or developed at the same pace. Small arts and crafts clubs were promoted with the cooperation of the Indian Arts and Crafts Board among the Sioux on the Pine Ridge, Rosebud, and Cheyenne River Reservations in South Dakota and the Standing Rock Reservation in North Dakota. These activities resulted in a definite improvement in the quality and an increase in the quantity of arts and crafts produced in the area. Indian groups in nearby Montana also cooperated with the board to produce readily marketable articles. The board assisted many of these groups to obtain some of the needed raw materials. The board also assisted in providing markets for the products of these small groups.[32]

As the board received demands from all parts of the country for field workers to supervise craft programs, its resources were inadequate to meet the needs. The board adjusted by keeping the field workers as mobile as possible. After determining that a satisfactory program had been developed in a specialist's assigned area, the board shifted the employee to a new area for intensive development work. At the same time, the specialist was required to maintain occasional contacts in an advisory capacity with the established area. Through this mobility, a limited number of trained Indian Arts and Crafts Board workers gradually extended the arts and crafts development program on a permanent basis to nearly all Indian groups.[33]

The publicity and advertising leading up to and surrounding the Indian arts and crafts display at the San Francisco Golden Gate Exposition in 1939 and presentations in other American cities acted as an impetus to further growth of Indian handcraft marketing organizations under the guidance of the Indian Arts and Crafts Board. Various museums, such as those in Worcester, Buffalo, and Chicago, had asked for a traveling exhibit and were willing to finance such a project. D'Harnoncourt suggested that these exhibits would provide an opportunity to organize Indian arts and crafts for sale in all of the cities where the exhibit was to be shown. To take advantage of the opportunity presented by these prestigious public displays and market their own products, the Indians needed tribal organizations to represent them, organize their production, and handle both wholesale and retail sales. Where museums might have been reticent to cooperate with purely commercial institutions, d'Harnoncourt believed that they would not hesitate to give full cooperation to Indian cooperatives or tribal organizations. The opportunity to establish financially successful operations in conjunction with the museums was viewed, in turn, as having the potential to stimulate interest in Indian arts and crafts in stores that previously never had considered them desirable merchandise.[34]

Acting in part with this reasoning, d'Harnoncourt proposed that the Indian Arts and Crafts Board help establish larger and thus more costly organizations for the Pueblo and Navajo arts and crafts production. The Pueblo Handicrafts Market was suggested as a project for the Tesuque Pueblo under the United Pueblos Agency. Initial funding of the Pueblo cooperative was to come from funds on deposit with the United Pueblos Agency in the amount of $1,215 under account "T-2 Tesuque Pueblo Indian Rehabilitation Trust Fund" and approximately $2,000 expected from the Indian Market as proceeds from the sale of Indian arts and crafts at the San Francisco Exposition.[35] The aim of the Pueblo Handicrafts Market was to organize, to improve, and to increase the production and sale of all the handcrafts of all Indian groups and communities under the supervision of the United Pueblos Agency. To meet this goal, the Pueblo Handicrafts Market would endeavor to find new markets, to experiment with the improvement of production and merchandising methods, and to engage actively in the buying and selling of these products. Any profits from the market's transactions were to be used either for enlarging arts and crafts facilities or for distribution among the participating artists. The Indian Arts and Crafts Board stressed that the market should not handle any products of inferior quality. Wherever the use of specified raw materials or specific production methods could be established, written standards were to be adopted. Where quality was the result of skill or taste only, the supervisor of the market or his designated appointee had to determine the eligibility of the product for purchase by the market. Like the standards, the criteria employed in the subjective judgment were to be in written form and available for public use. A trademark for all the merchandise to be handled by the market was to be submitted by the Tesuque Pueblo to the Indian Arts and Crafts Board and registered with the United States Patent Office.[36]

The Indian Arts and Crafts Board plan for the Pueblo Handicrafts Market specifically outlined the relationship and degree of governmental support as the enterprise grew. Under this plan, the market would become, in time, a self-supporting business. Having learned from the organizational and financial problems experienced earlier by the Choctaw Spinners Association, the board emphasized that the Pueblo Handicrafts Market must provide a sufficient markup in all its commercial transactions to cover its full cost of management and operation and to allow for expansion of its activities. Until the available volume of marketable quality products was sufficient to produce an entirely self-supporting business without increasing the markup beyond its practical limits, government agencies were to lend personnel services and facilities. The Indian Arts and Crafts Board considered such government assistance at the beginning of the project as part of the program of economic rehabilitation, to be curtailed in proportion to the growth of the market and finally discontinued as soon as the volume of sales reached a point where complete economic independence was possible. A four-step plan with a series of sample budgets that would lead the market from semidependence with projected sales of $7,200 to complete independence with projected sales of $33,000 was provided for the Tesuque Pueblo with the understanding that local conditions would determine some modifications.[37]

The Indian Arts and Crafts Board detailed management techniques to meet the local conditions. Where in Florida, the initial arts and crafts situation of the ninety-two-member Seminole tribal group at Brighton required only a government teacher to serve as part-time manager of their Seminole Crafts Guild,[38] the larger Pueblo Handicrafts Market was to receive a full-time supervisor loaned by the United Pueblos Agency until the market could afford to employ its own personnel. A storehouse with adequate wholesale market facilities, an office for the supervisor and bookkeeper, and a display room also were to be contributed on the same basis by the United Pueblos Agency. An up-to-the-minute bookkeeping system showing all aid received by the market from outside sources was an important element in the Indian Arts and Crafts Board plan. Since payment to the individual artists under the usual government routine involved vouchers, checks, and accompanying delays, the plan called for a cash reserve fund to enable the craft buyer to make on-the-spot payments.[39]

The plan submitted by the Indian Arts and Crafts Board for the Pueblo Handicrafts Market reflected specific local conditions, exhibited sound business principles, and displayed knowledgeable perception. The board's plan provided a vision of things to come toward which the Indians could work and stepping stones which would lead them from vision to reality. The board was helping the Indians to help themselves on an increasing scale. These plans were not relief measures requiring periodic renewal.

Accordingly, in 1940, a trust indenture agreement was concluded by and between the Tesuque Pueblo, the council of the pueblo of Tesuque, the Indian Arts and Crafts Board, and three trustees from the Tesuque Pueblo, creating what was now to be called the Pueblo Indian Arts and Crafts Market. The board's role under the agreement was pivotal. While the trustees' duties were very similar to those of the five-member Indian Arts and Crafts Board, the trustees held their positions only with the permission of the board, which could add to or remove any or all of the trustees at any time. Even their initial appointment had to meet with board approval. The board for its part agreed to supply at cost to the trustees the management, personnel, and supervision necessary for the operation of the market. The general manager of the Indian Arts and Crafts Board under the terms of the agreement was empowered to act on behalf of the trustees, to hire employees, and to do any or all things directly or indirectly connected with the operation of the market.[40]

The Tesuque Pueblo's trust in d'Harnoncourt seemed boundless. The extension of these powers to the board was not duplicated with any other Indian group, and d'Harnoncourt appeared not to have exercised any of these powers. Certainly, the Indian Arts and Crafts Board Act forbade such involvement, and nowhere in the board's suggested plan of operation for the Pueblo market was even the suggestion of such power hinted. Only the confidence that the Tesuque Pueblo had in d'Harnoncourt and Collier could explain the powers of management handed to them in the agreement. Reliance on and trust in the advice of the board was not misplaced, for the Pueblo Arts and Crafts Market sold $4,600 worth of merchandise in 1941, its first full year of operation.[41]

Tribal loans were often the foundation of successful arts and crafts enterprises. These loans were provided under the Indian Reorganization Act and the Oklahoma Indian Welfare Act, both of 1934, in which Congress authorized the secretary of the interior to make loans from specifically appropriated funds to Indian tribes or to groups of Indians chartered as corporations. The tribes or corporations could invest the money borrowed either in corporate enterprises or in loans to members of the tribes or corporations. Under conditions where the number of craftworkers in a group was small or when a tribe was not chartered, initial production work could be started with the aid of a government subsidy. Such subsidies were not made as formal loans, but rather were funds supplied to the crafts group for the purpose of starting a self-sustaining revolving fund. When the revolving fund reached an adequate point, the subsidies were reduced or withdrawn. Provision was made in the initial agreement with the crafts group for repaying subsidies from the increasing revolving funds.[42] In this manner the Indian Arts and Crafts Board remained within its charter and still was able to carry out its important organizational and marketing work.

The Navajos carried out a major Indian Arts and Crafts Board venture by building on earlier efforts funded under the tribal rehabilitation funds provided by the Indian Reorganization Act. This project began in 1938 to prepare crafts for display at the San Francisco Exposition. The Navajo Arts and Crafts Guild grew out of further Indian Arts and Crafts Board effort in 1940 to create a more permanent institution of benefit to the Navajo artists and the Navajo tribe.

The plan of operation submitted by the Indian Arts and Crafts Board and approved by the Navajo Tribal Council was similar to the Pueblo Arts and Crafts Market. Rather than start up slowly, this project called for a loan of $10,000 to get things started the first year and another $10,000 loan the second year to increase operating capital. All mention of the possible contribution of the Indian Arts and Crafts Board and even the board's name was absent from the Navajo agreement nor was the Indian Arts and Crafts Board a signing party to the agreement.[43] Nevertheless, the Navajo Arts and Crafts Guild was reported by the board as a production and merchandising unit "supervised by or collaborating with the Indian Arts and Crafts Board" in 1942. The sales figures for the Navajo guild that year were a phenomenal $16,000, second only to those reported for Alaska.[44]

Not all Indian Arts and Crafts Board surveys eventually culminated in projects or associative enterprises. Early in 1940, arts and crafts specialist Alice Marriott's survey of the Indian arts and crafts of Wisconsin and Michigan was optimistic about future developments although very little of the crafts from the region had been marketed outside the locale and a significant market was not yet in existence. The fact that local museums, women's clubs, and chambers of commerce were eager to sponsor exhibitions and sales of arts and crafts work convinced Marriott that the area was ready for a great expansion in the local marketing of crafts. The twelve reservations in Michigan and Wisconsin were populated variously by Chippewa, Potawatomi, Winnebago, Menominee, Ottawa, and Oneida Indians. Marriott pointed out the advantage of working in this large area where non-Indian people were conscious of their Indian neighbors' cultural attributes.[45]

Although Marriott recommended the employment of a full-time arts and crafts field worker for the Great Lakes area, the Indian Arts and Crafts Board took no step to provide this service. The lack of a product with a sufficiently established appeal and market, the greater demands of other areas such as Alaska and the Southwest, the limits imposed by appropriations and available personnel, and the possibility that other agencies could be coordinated to achieve the same progress in the area with only the occasional advice and participation of the board were all part of the board's position. When balancing all of the factors, the Great Lakes area appeared to the board to be able to profit for the time being just as well under only an advisory and coordinating role by the Indian Arts and Crafts Board.

Apart from the all-important cultural implications for the Indians, the question of a viable market was most important in d'Harnoncourt's considerations. Stimulating the production and display of high quality arts and crafts by means of producing and merchandising organizations would have had limited rewards and become self-defeating without a market to appreciate and to absorb that production. Sound management was a major attribute of the board under d'Harnoncourt's leadership.

11

THE MUSEUM OF
MODERN ART—1941

WHILE THE SAN FRANCISCO EXPOSITION was still in progress, d'Harnoncourt started making arrangements with Alfred H. Barr, Jr., director of the Museum of Modern Art, for an exhibit of Indian arts and crafts at the museum in New York City. The board authorized him to contribute the necessary field work, to handle the assembly of display materials, to arrange with the museum's staff the planning of the installation, and to design and provide small movable installation materials. By 30 September 1939 he had the blessings of both the Indian Arts and Crafts Board and the Board of Trustees of the Museum of Modern Art. The scope of the exhibit agreed upon was far beyond any expectations that d'Harnoncourt had had. "The museum is willing to turn over to us not only one floor as I had hoped, but the entire building and its large court," he exclaimed.[1] D'Harnoncourt prepared a tentative content outline the same day.

Research and promotion provided the framework upon which d'Harnoncourt constructed a completely new display. Never lacking imagination or vision, he knew exactly what would be appropriate to accomplish the goals for which the Indian Arts and Crafts Board had been created. Just as all concerned had accepted his plans in San Francisco, no hesitation, debate, or controversy developed over any of his plans in New York. They seemed perfectly conceived and worthy of everyone's cooperation. He wanted the exhibition to create a new interest in Indian arts and crafts, to help develop the marketing of Indian products, to disprove the mistaken idea that America had no native art, to demonstrate that Indian arts and crafts could have a place in modern fashions and decoration, and to prove that the products of contemporary Indian artists were both useful and beautiful. The exhibition would be another step in the New Deal Indian policy of assisting the Indians toward self-support and toward cultural as well as economic freedom.[2]

The expression of New Deal Indian policy in the Indian arts and crafts exhibition at the Museum of Modern Art fit into the role upon which the New York museum based its existence. "As the Museum of Modern Art is a living museum, not a collection of curious and interesting objects," proclaimed President Roosevelt in a telephone address at the dedication of the museum's new building on 10 May 1939, "it can, therefore, become an integral part of our domestic institutions—it can be woven into the very warp and woof of our democracy. Because it has been conceived as a national institution," Roosevelt continued, "the Museum can enrich and invigorate our cultural life by bringing the best of modern art to all of the American people."[3] Even the operational philosophy of the Museum of Modern Art provided a vehicle for Indian Arts and Crafts Board policy.

The pressure of war increased daily and heightened the national introspection that attempted to analyze and to measure the strengths and weaknesses of the United States. D'Harnoncourt helped to focus some of this interest on Indian contributions to American culture at a time when the nation wanted to display proudly its banners to a world believed to be rapidly disintegrating into a chaotic struggle with totalitarianism. Collier could not have asked for a better expression of public support not only for the major tenets of the Indian Arts and Crafts Board and New Deal Indian policy but also for his personal philosophy of cultural pluralism than when Roosevelt declared, "We know that only where men are free can the arts flourish and the civilization of national culture reach full flower." The New Deal movement in Indian art was based on these principles. Indian art could not come from non-Indian art any more than Indian culture could be dictated by non-Indian culture. Only the Indians could decide what adaptations best suited their needs as their future unfolded. Just as totalitarianism was wrong for non-Indian culture so also was it wrong for Indian culture. Politically sensitive and artistically perceptive, Roosevelt's speech confirmed this New Deal belief. "The arts cannot thrive except where men are free to be themselves and to be in charge of the discipline of their own energies and ardors. The conditions for democracy and for art are one and the same. . . . In encouraging the creation and enjoyment of beautiful things," he concluded, "we are furthering democracy itself."[4]

Upon d'Harnoncourt fell the ultimate responsibility for the Museum of Modern Art presentation. To carry on this work of the Indian Arts and Crafts Board was important but to do so at such little cost to the government seemed even more important at the time. Collier told the 1940 House Subcommittee on Appropriations that the new exhibit would not cost the board anything. D'Harnoncourt planned once again to obtain funds from the various foundations that had supported the board's work in San Francisco. He carried on preliminary discussions with these foundations and found their reactions so enthusiastic and encouraging that he told Alfred Barr that he had little doubt left that "we can obtain what we need."[5]

D'Harnoncourt's preliminary plan called for three major divisions of the available indoor space: prehistoric Indian art, living Indian cultures, and contributions of Indian art to the contemporary American scene. Objects in the prehistoric gallery would be shown for their aesthetic value only and would include Mound Builder stone and clay work, Bering Strait carvings and engravings, eastern Alaska carvings, Florida gold and clay work, and prehistoric Pueblo basketry, pottery, and weaving. The last section would be followed by historic and contemporary Pueblo art which would lead into the second division composed of the eight areas presented in the San Francisco exhibit. The division on the contributions of Indian art to the contemporary American scene was to be subdivided under three headings: the first, Indian art as a means to understanding the function of art in a community where it is part of all economic, social, and ceremonial life; the second, Indian art as a means to understanding the relationship between production, raw material, function, and form; and the third, the uses of Indian art in the modern world, as in a home, in personal adornment, and as fine art. In addition to this indoor exhibit, an outdoor exhibit would show Indian architecture, its techniques, forms, and materials. Thirteen major sponsoring institutions were listed as potential contributors in 1939, a list that changed as further preparations took place.[6]

Indian Art of the United States, the New York exhibition catalogue, was the product of the difficulty d'Harnoncourt had producing a catalogue for the San Francisco exhibit. He never seemed satisfied with nor gave his full approval to the Vaillant book, *Indian Arts in North America,* a book which also disappointed him because it only reached the market after the San Francisco Exposition had closed. Vaillant's work did not provide the needed catalogue of the materials on display at San Francisco nor did it sufficiently stress the aesthetic aspect of Indian art, tending instead to emphasize anthropological and ethnological interpretations. Small pamphlets had been prepared by d'Harnoncourt and Douglas and were used in San Francisco to fill the gap created by the lack of an overall display catalogue. These pamphlets doubtlessly were designed to be the basis for the still-hoped-for exhibit catalogue that the two men were struggling to complete before the San Francisco Exposition closed. When George Creel announced that the exposition would close 29 October, a month earlier than previously expected, d'Harnoncourt already was committed to the Museum of Modern Art exhibit, so he "stopped the presses" on the San Francisco book. With few changes and little added expense, he reasoned, the book would be ready in plenty of time for New York. Under this arrangement, catalogue costs for the new exhibit were kept to a minimum.[7] The plan worked smoothly and the Museum of Modern Art issued the book simultaneously with the opening of the New York exhibit on 22 January 1941. *Indian Art of the United States* by Douglas and d'Harnoncourt contained 204 pages, sixteen color plates, and 200 halftone prints, followed the arrangement of the exhibit, and provided both a comprehensive presentation of Indian art and a guide to the exhibition. *Art Digest* called the book "a compact, vital, and absorbing record of America's indigenous civilization" and praised the "clear, authoritative text."[8]

The biggest challenge d'Harnoncourt faced in his preparations for New York stemmed from his plans for the prehistoric exhibit. Part of the exhibit was to consist of five large reproductions in color of specific rock paintings, three panels showing pictograph design styles from all parts of the country to give an idea of the wealth of designs typical for this art form, and finally, several explanatory labels and a map showing the location of the most important pictographs. As nearly as possible, he wanted life-size reproductions on canvas screens of the original pictographs. The largest one of the five reproductions, showing the pictographs of the Basket Makers in Barrier Canyon, Utah, would be sixty feet long by fourteen feet high. The other four sections, showing pictographs from California, Texas, New Mexico, and Idaho would be each approximately eight feet wide by fourteen feet high. The largest of the three panels of design styles would measure fifty feet by fourteen feet, and the two smaller ones would be twenty feet and ten feet wide by

fourteen feet high respectively. D'Harnoncourt had obtained preliminary drawings of the pictographs through the cooperation of Holger Cahill, director of the Works Progress Administration Federal Art Project.[9]
The startling presentation of the Utah pictographs reproduced in life-
size proved to be a difficult and daring accomplishment, one that nearly
did not open on time. Barrier Canyon lay about forty miles south of
Green River City, Utah, and what was known as Pictograph Gallery
began about one mile upstream from the junction of Barrier Canyon
and Green River. A full-fledged expedition with supplies had to be organized in order to do the needed photographic work. Cahill contacted
the deputy director of the Works Progress Administration art program,
Thomas G. Parker, who, in turn, contacted several local guides in Utah
to see if they could arrange for the expedition. The local Utah Works
Progress Administration art project administrators delayed and procras-
tinated, first to avoid the summer heat, then to obtain payment to cover
costs before the project began. D'Harnoncourt could not get institution and foundation money for this project before October when these
organizations normally made up their fall and winter budgets.[10]

D'Harnoncourt rapidly was running out of time. The financial arrangements remained tangled. In his Washington Works Progress
Administration office, Parker wanted the question of the sponsor's contribution fully settled before the expedition got under way. When the
immediate money situation appeared to be resolved, the expedition
still did not get under way until after the settlement of disagreements
between the guides and the Works Progress Administration. Once the
expedition started everything went according to plan. Many of the photographic techniques used had to be invented on the spot to fit the difficult location of the pictographs. Following the expedition, the delays
began again, first over materials the Works Progress Administration
wanted, then over the size of the murals, until finally on 4 January
1941, seventeen days before the opening in New York City, the Works
Progress Administration refused to deliver the murals without first receiving a purchase order for a special camera and accessories. The murals were finished and ready to be shipped. Obviously, the camera was
not needed for the pictograph project. In the end, the pictograph reproductions were shipped on 13 January and the camera contract awarded
on 17 January.[11]

A worried Ethel Petty, the board's administrative clerk, added to d'Harnoncourt's problems at this time by advising him that the board's financial picture for the remainder of the 1941 fiscal year was "not too clear." The board's expenditures and obligations for the first six months amounted to $28,106, she related, which left $20,294 to take care of expenses for the remaining six months. The salaries of permanent employees would require $15,240 to the end of the fiscal year, which would leave only $5,054 for travel and other expenses. The other expenses included payment for the now mandatory services of the Interior Department Office of Exhibits for its recent work on the model and display stands, payment to the New York Works Progress Administration for its work in connection with the Museum of Modern Art exhibit, and payment for crating and transportation of all the exhibits. "Do you think we can make it?" Petty asked. No wonder that Collier became concerned for d'Harnoncourt's health. A month later Collier reported to his son, Donald, in Chicago, that d'Harnoncourt was "gaining strength daily."[12]

Elsewhere cooperation marked the board's efforts. No problems like those in Utah occurred with the New York City Works Progress Administration art project. That agency quickly provided the large five-foot by five and one-half-foot maps and fourteen-foot by eighteen-foot map panels plus various other large panel constructions. The Peabody Museum also was helpful. Director Donald Scott and his staff helped to make scale drawings from the 1938 excavations of Hopi murals that had been painted around 1500. Scott also recalled that ten years earlier someone had sent him some photographs of fragments of rocks with pictographs. These fragments were traced to Holbrook, Arizona, and from them the Peabody Museum painstakingly reconstructed additional mural replicas. The Museum of Modern Art, already deeply involved in the board's efforts, contributed $2,500 for salary and round trip travel expenses to bring Frederic Douglas to New York from Denver, to participate officially in the exhibit.[13]

Even a Swiss clothing designer had an important role in the Museum of Modern Art exhibit. After some preliminary conversations, d'Harnoncourt sent the designer, Fred A. Picard of New York City, a collection of Indian-made articles to be incorporated as accents in Picard's modern women's apparel which would be shown at the Museum of Modern Art exhibit. D'Harnoncourt assured Picard that only his fashion designs would be used in the exhibition. D'Harnoncourt agreed to furnish any materials needed to manufacture the clothing in addition to the Indian-made articles.[14]

D'Harnoncourt continued to remain in touch with Eleanor Roosevelt and to keep her informed about the progress of the Museum of Modern Art exhibit. He went so far as to tell her that he believed that the Museum of Modern Art exhibit would be "far more interesting than that at the San Francisco Fair." He spoke about newly secured prehistoric Indian paintings and sculpture that were entirely unknown to the public and that undoubtedly would create "a new conception of Indian artistic ability." He also referred to the board's considerable progress in developing contemporary production that would "prove that Indian art deserves its place in modern life." Like the San Francisco exhibit, the Museum of Modern Art project had been undertaken by the board, he explained, "as a means of creating a new interest and understanding of the Indian and his work among the general public." D'Harnoncourt said that the interest already shown in the exhibit by both the press and the public made the board hopeful that the exhibit would "play a prominent part in creating a new public attitude toward the Indian," and, in turn, "become an important aid in his economic and cultural rehabilitation."[15]

D'Harnoncourt persuaded Eleanor Roosevelt to sign the foreword for the exhibition catalogue, *Indian Art of the United States*. The foreword summarized the important message that he and the Indian Arts and Crafts Board were struggling to present. "At this time, when America is reviewing its cultural resources, this book and the exhibit on which it is based open up to us age-old sources of ideas and forms that have never been fully appreciated. In appraising the Indian's past and present achievements, we realize not only that his heritage constitutes part of the artistic and spiritual wealth of this country, but also that the Indian people of today have a contribution to make toward the America of the future." The sources of Indian art reached far beyond America's borders to the north and to the south, the foreword pointed out, a fact which emphasized that hemispheric interchange of ideas was as old as humanity on this continent. The foreword concluded by acknowledging "a cultural debt not only to the Indians of the United States but to the Indians of both Americas."[16]

"I earnestly believe that this exposition and its interpretation through our industries will mark a real epoch," the publisher of *Women's Wear Daily*, Morris De Camp Crawford, proclaimed. "Once again, the long-neglected arts of our . . . peoples will come to the aid of this machine age of ours," he predicted. "Once again craftsmen and craftsmanship, and the traditions of art, which grow up in craftsmanship, will furnish inspiration for our productive mechanical devices." Such public support by a representative of American industry long had been sought by the Indian Arts and Crafts Board and reflected a high degree of success for d'Harnoncourt's promotional and educational program. "In the plethora of our productive facilities, we should never lose sight of the fact that inspiration in design, in texture, in color, and in technology comes from the craft ages of the past," Crawford continued. "It might be well to remember that our own Indians . . . are among the greatest craftsmen the world has ever known." Crawford told how, during the First World War, *Women's Wear Daily* had suggested the use of examples from "the craft ages of the past" and many ideas from the arts of the American Indians were represented in American merchandise. He also referred to the 1919 exhibit at the American Museum of Natural History, which had demonstrated the influence of their great collections on the costume and fabric industries of New York. Finally, Crawford set his seal of approval on an exhibit he had yet to see. "I look with confidence to a much wider and more discriminating use of this material," he prophesied, "as it will be presented in the Museum of Modern Art under René d'Harnoncourt's sympathetic magic."[17]

In an interview with Mabel Greene from the *New York Sun*, d'Harnoncourt also characterized Indian art as a truly native art that was alive and useful in the modern day. The Museum of Modern Art exhibit was being held, he said, to show a very strong and live art existing in America that belonged solely to this country. "Too many people think that America has no folk arts or handicrafts such as those which are such an integral part of older European countries," he declared. "The modern Indian can produce artistic things whose beauty and utility are keyed to modern life. They have been doing it for generations." Then, almost as if he were issuing a call for patriotic support, d'Harnoncourt concluded that Indian arts and crafts were "the oldest and most American of any we have in this country."[18]

230

As the opening day approached, Secretary Ickes issued a press release announcing "the largest and most comprehensive exhibition of
Indian art ever assembled." He stressed that the Museum of Modern
Art Indian Exhibit was an important part of New Deal Indian policy,
one which was designed to assist the Indians toward self-support and
toward both cultural and economic freedom. The exhibit was intended
to provide a comprehensive picture of Indian arts themselves, Ickes
explained, rather than to show the forms of dress and design they may
inspire although he pointed out the presence of the small collection of
women's fashions which showed Indian materials and products as they
fit into modern apparel. Ickes's press release praised the work of the
Indian Arts and Crafts Board in effecting substantial increases in the
sales of Indian art products and thereby giving economic self-reliance
and an improved standard of living to many Indians. The exhibit at the
Museum of Modern Art, he concluded, would be "a picture of the
ancient Indian moving out into modern American and world life while
holding fast to his ancient genius and devotions."[19]

To accommodate d'Harnoncourt's display, the Museum of Modern
Art practically rebuilt three floors of its building. All the interior walls
were removed and new arrangements of walls and floor spaces made
under d'Harnoncourt's direction with the assistance of his collaborator,
Douglas, and his consulting architect and designer, Klumb. The whole
exhibition was installed in a setting of temporary walls, partitions, and
screens, with bases, counters, and other equipment made for the purpose.
Artificial lighting was arranged to provide brilliantly colored backgrounds,
emphasis of objects, light at unusual angles, and dramatic shadow
effects.[20]

As visitors approached the Museum of Modern Art from a distance,
they easily spotted the first dramatic evidence of the Indian arts and
crafts exhibit. Placed in front of the museum was a thirty-foot totem
pole carved and painted in likenesses of a raven, a killer whale, a devil-
fish, a sea lion, and a shark. Although the exhibit could have been
viewed with profit starting at any point, the usual procedure involved
beginning at the top, or third floor, with the section on "Prehistoric
Art," working down to the historic and contemporary Indian art or the
"Living Traditions" section on the second floor, and concluding with
the display of contemporary work particularly suited for the twentieth

century in the section called "Indian Art for Modern Living" found on the main floor.

Because current knowledge of the material or the aim of its display varied greatly from one section to another, different display methods were used. In the case of prehistoric Indian work, d'Harnoncourt admitted, archaeology had not been able yet to give a clear picture of the backgrounds that produced the different developments, except in the Southwest. Although the general divisions into which the work fell provided the basis for the grouping of the objects in this prehistoric section, the main difficulty was to bring out the inherent character of the objects themselves. D'Harnoncourt accomplished this with most of the items by the selection of very simple display materials of appropriate color, texture, and proportion. Specialized treatment was needed with particular pieces like the pipe sculpture from the Adena Mound in southern Ohio, known as the "Adena Man." Only eight-inches tall and reminiscent of Mexican carvings, this Ohio sandstone pipe easily could be recognized as representative of the artist's conception of monumental scultpure. D'Harnoncourt stressed this quality by displaying the small carving in front of a huge photomural of itself.[21]

When the physical conditions under which the prehistoric artists expected their work to be seen were known, the installation suggested that atmosphere. In the case of the Hopi mural reconstructions supplied by the Peabody Museum, eight mural replicas were painted by Hopi descendants under the direction of Hopi artist Fred Kabotie and exhibited in a setting patterned after the original. The murals were painted on layers of adobe backed by thin sheets of wood which formed the walls of a series of small, low, ceremonial chambers or kivas lighted only by a hole in the center of each ceiling just as their prototypes were lighted hundreds of years earlier in the Southwest.

Organization to make the exhibit more enjoyable and meaningful again characterized d'Harnoncourt's presentation. Facing the third floor entrance was a twenty-five-foot wide and twelve-foot high map made by the New York City Works Progress Administration art project showing the areas where the engravers of the Arctic, the stone carvers of the Northwest Coast and the Far West, the painters of the Southwest, and the sculptors of the East lived during the prehistoric period. Then the replicas of the dark, confined, ceremonial chambers, encircled with a continuous band of mural paintings, were followed by a wide, bright space suggestive of the vast outdoor setting of the rock paintings. Here was the twelve and one-half-foot by sixty-foot full-size reproduction on canvas of the pictograph of the tall figures painted many centuries earlier on the sandstone walls of Barrier Canyon. The reproduction was so long that no single wall in the museum was large enough to hold it, so it was hung in a gradual curve from wall to wall which nearly duplicated the original setting. The pictograph was in the only room on the third floor where actual daylight was used to any extent.

D'Harnoncourt wanted the main impression of the prehistoric section to come from a collection of sculpture and ceramics which was displayed with classic simplicity in rather severe white-walled rooms.[22] Sophistication and craft skill marked this early art. The pottery jars, sculpture, pipes, and other objects from the middle and eastern states provided, according to d'Harnoncourt, the finest examples of both naturalistic and conventionalized sculpture in an indigenous art including the African. Outstanding in this display area was a pottery effigy jar in the shape of a frog.

D'Harnoncourt provided a potential source of surprise in the prehistoric display by showing the number of regions where material had been found. Hardly a state in the country was not represented. He highlighted the prehistoric display with the designs on the large food bowls found in New Mexico in 1925. In Pueblo pottery the painted decoration was not necessarily subordinate to the form of the bowl. Instead, the decoration often was the most important feature. These deep food bowls produced by the Mimbres culture were nine inches to eleven inches in diameter and were decorated with highly conventionalized living creatures ranging from insects and animals through human beings to strange and pleasing monsters of unknown identity. While all artists of the ancient Southwest, like the Mimbres people, were masters of geometric designs arranged in complex patterns, the Mimbres culture's interest in organic forms was unique for that region. The highly imaginative lobster design on a Mimbres bowl seemed so foreign to traditional Pueblo culture as to suggest the influence of an exceptionally gifted individual. This style of painting on twelfth-century Mimbres black and white pottery succeeded in giving living subjects a strange animation and in bringing out their most essential characteristics.[23] Despite this singularity, a technically skillful execution of traditional geometric form elements still remained the basis for these unusual Mimbres designs and thereby maintained the ancient Southwest design tradition.

The simplicity of the prehistoric setting was designed to allow concentration on the individual aesthetic achievement each article represented. A limitation on the use of captions and labels helped in this effort. The unity of design, which had remained continuous over the centuries, served to emphasize the living tradition that Indian art represented.[24]

On the second floor, another very large map, this time indicating the various historic Indian cultures, introduced the "Living Traditions." The nine divisions were the same as those used in the San Francisco exhibition with the exception of the addition of the "Apache Mountain People" group as a distinct entity separate from the "Desert Dwellers of the Southwest." In contrast to the prehistoric section, the objects on the second floor were presented as expressions of the widely varied Indian cultures which produced them. The presentation was quite similar in style to that at San Francisco. Each of the nine rooms on the floor represented one of the main Indian cultural areas. The proportions and color schemes of each room and its display material had been planned by d'Harnoncourt to suggest the essence of the physical surroundings in which the culture developed or of the created setting in which the objects were seen and used. D'Harnoncourt usually grouped together in a manner intended to suggest their original usage objects that were made essentially for part of a costume or tribal activity. Other objects having a strong aesthetic value independent of their setting were singled out and shown one by one, as highlights of the styles of the different areas. In the California room, for example, the classic basketwork was shown on plain stands whose size and shape were determined by the form of the various baskets. On the other hand, material used in the White Deer ceremony in the forest country of northern California was arranged as a tableau in order to convey the exotic quality of the ceremony. An albino deerskin, embroidered with red woodpecker feathers and placed high on a pole, looked half like an animal, half like a strange banner, while at its feet shimmered a pile of white shell necklaces, huge abalone shells, and carved obsidian blades. The background was dark and dome-shaped suggesting the depths of the forest at night.

Elsewhere, on a wall in the Plains room, hunting and ceremonial equipment was arranged to suggest those activities.[25] Just as in the prehistoric display, captions and labels were few in number, small in size,
and brief in wording, usually limited to basic identification and the
name of the contributor.

Four cases along one wall in the Plains room contained some particularly fine stone pipes shown as pieces of sculpture. Here were pipe
bowls carved out of stone by mobility-minded Indians who valued light-
ness and portability. Usually they made plain L- or T-shaped bowls,
yet here d'Harnoncourt showed the work of an unknown artist who had
used imagination and independence to create a true piece of sculpture
in the form of a horse's head.[26]

A forest of grave posts rose out of dim light just before the Northwest
Coast room. This installation had presented a special problem for
d'Harnoncourt because of the region's tremendous scope. The range of
work stretched from exquisite spoons and bowls of mountain sheep horn,
carved to translucent thinness by the Haida and Tlinkit Indians, to the
fierce wooden figures carved by the Salish people for use in ceremonies
or as grave posts. As in San Francisco, the proportions and lighting of
the main part of this gallery suggested the interior of a huge wooden
house of the region, with its central firelight and deep shadows. Off in
one corner of the room, lighting effects were used to emphasize the
quality of the horn spoons and bowls. In the darkness each piece was
individually lighted from beneath to bring out its delicacy and translu-
cence. Massive objects like wooden bowls and big food storage boxes
appeared behind footlights on a long platform and in lighted recesses
in the other walls.[27]

At this point the reaction to the exhibition might have been one of
picturesque and romantic connotations. Art critic Jean Charlot recognized this momentarily while visiting the exhibit yet observed with further reflection how the Indian artists had managed to assert individual
greatness within an accepted framework of tribal norms. Unlike Euro-
pean-oriented artists, Charlot noted, the Indian pipe carvers, basket
weavers, or sand painters did not seem to suffer the problem of having
to strengthen their artistic individualities in proportion to the weakness
of the thread between their work and their tradition. The spiritual content of Indian work, the manual perfection heightened by the chal-

lenge of technical impediments, and the balance obtained between objective conventions and the personal quota of individual genius, all displayed for Charlot the attitude of the Indian artist as one of classical integrity. The success of the Museum of Modern Art exhibit in relation to its purposes and goals was reflected in this response by an informed art critic. For Charlot the show existed on a plane other than "a shop window revival of feather work and leather tooling."[28]

Art Digest also saw the rich tradition in Indian art that d'Harnoncourt wanted to impress upon the visitors to the Museum of Modern Art exhibit in order to erase the misconception of the modern Indian as a producer of cheap curios and souvenirs. Illusive as it was, the reviewer commented, beneath the manifold art of these traditional tribes and their contemporary descendants remained a unity. This unity was not in any symbols, either abstract or naturalistic, not in any content, nor even in any style, but in the manner of approach. This critic concluded that the Indian was as "direct in his art as he was in his life, confident and self-reliant, scornful of 'effects.' "[29]

So far, d'Harnoncourt had presented only Indian objects free from non-Indian associations. In the first floor section devoted to "Indian Art for Modern Living," he showed that contemporary Indian work had a place in and filled a need in the twentieth century. The installation was purposely similar to that used to display the finest modern jewelry, clothing accessories, and articles for the home. Here silverwork, quill and animal-skin work, pottery, baskets, rugs, and many other types of contemporary pieces had an opportunity to show their natural affinity for the simple forms of a thoroughly modern setting.

The extensive exhibition catalogue that d'Harnoncourt had provided expressed the reasoning behind this modern display. In the catalogue d'Harnoncourt referred to the popular misconception that the Indians were on the decline because no place existed for them in the twentieth century. He readily admitted that the Indian artists, under the pressure of non-Indian demand, had produced many things merely for their souvenir value. He also admitted that some of the Indians' traditional crafts were so specialized that they could be used only in their original environment. At the same time, d'Harnoncourt pointed out the basic soundness and vigor of Indian art, which constantly produced articles that reflected the strength of Indian traditions and that fit perfectly into the contemporary scene. As a matter of fact, d'Harnoncourt concluded in no uncertain terms, Indian art filled a concrete need in the contemporary United States. Indian art's inseparable relationship to America, to the land, and to its unexplored wealth of forms, contributed to modern American art and life. [30]

D'Harnoncourt described what he considered to be good Indian artistry. Such work, he noted, was done without the interference of non-Indians, included restrained as well as bright colors, and usually leaned to economy rather than to complexity of design. Good Indian artwork showed a careful balance of design and color and, as a result, was neither restless nor confused. D'Harnoncourt identified this subtle control of elements and the close relationship between function and form to be what aligned Indian work with the aims of most other contemporary designers and made it blend with any surroundings that were truly of the twentieth century. [31]

Even more important was d'Harnoncourt's emphasis on the need to recognize good Indian art as a growing and changing expression of cultural life which at the same time maintained its essential identity. The Museum of Modern Art exhibit showed how this identity had persisted in every new form created by every new impulse of Indian life, a process that would continue as long as Indian people existed. Interesting examples of such developments could be seen in the growing production of handwoven materials prepared by the bolt and other handloomed articles. New products were emerging in wood, silver, animal skin, pottery, and other media. Although the Indian Arts and Crafts Board was not involved, d'Harnoncourt recognized the recent developments among various tribes of several new art forms which were closer to the non-Indian concept of art and sought to replace all functional value with aesthetic value. These, too, were considered by d'Harnoncourt as part of the cultural change in Indian life. Prominent examples were the murals and watercolors executed by Indian painters in New Mexico, Oklahoma, and the Dakotas. In d'Harnoncourt's view, these paintings retained much of the style and the feeling for proportion which were displayed in traditional Indian art and well might be the beginning of a new phase of Indian art. [32]

D'Harnoncourt's message at the Museum of Modern Art Indian Exhibit was clear. Although the full development of the potential market

for Indian work and the organizing of the production to meet the requirements of modern merchandising promised to be a slow and delicate process, the moral and economic benefits the effort would yield to
the Indian producers and the enrichment provided for all of society
made the task a major responsibility of America.[33]

"Every kind of congratulation, dear friend. It was a superb achievement," telegrammed Frank Crowninshield, author, editor, and one of
the founders of the Museum of Modern Art, on the opening day. *New
York Times* art critic Edward Alden Jewell called the Museum of Modern Art Indian Exhibit "an event of the very highest importance." Despite its size, d'Harnoncourt's exhibit was one of the least fatiguing shows
he had ever seen, and wandering through the adventurous maze was
"sheer delight." The installation was "infinitely painstaking, though never
in the least labored; intricate, and often—if you choose to consider it
so—'theatrical'; yet always marshaled in its imaginative flights, always
creating an appropriate effect, establishing a helpful atmosphere." The
effort represented "a high water mark in museum technique." Jewell
applauded d'Harnoncourt's selection of objects shown and observed that
despite the approximately one thousand items involved the visitor never
had a sense of mere numbers, "never a sense of dense, unsifted bulk."[34]

The praise continued to come in. Max Weber, a pioneer American
modernist painter, told Alfred Barr how much he enjoyed "this magnifi-
cent Indian exhibition" and said he now believed "we have the *real*
sur-realists [sic] right here in America." The *Washington Star* also picked
up this similarity between Indian creations and the best of the modern
tradition. D'Harnoncourt was quoted as interpreting this relationship
as one not to be explained by actual contacts. Instead, he believed humanity must concede the existence of universal human concepts that
find expression in specific art forms. These art forms never had been
discarded by the Indian artists and had been rediscovered by modern
art. Evidence of these specific forms were the use of double profiles by
both Indian and modern artists, the surrealism in Indian masks, the
similarity between modern murals like Picasso's and the prehistoric murals from Hopi pueblo ruins, and the resemblance of Indian housepost
sculpture to works of Alexander Calder. In both Indian art and modern
art the forms were simple, as seen in the streamline motion and a feeling for mass and simplicity expressed in Eskimo carvings and modern

sculpture. The writer for the *Washington Star* seemed to be part of what *Art Digest* called "an unsuspecting public" to which was revealed "an important accomplishment that must be now ranked with the main artistic achievements of the world." *Antiques* magazine saw a quickened interest in Americana: the arts and crafts of the American Indians were being rediscovered and reappraised as a source of ideas, forms, and designs, as well as for their intrinsic merit.[35]

"Epoch-making,"[36] "fundamental and of such quality,"[37] "touching, grandiose, intimate, awesome,"[38] "one of the most comprehensive ever presented, and certainly most intelligently staged,"[39] were phrases used to describe the culmination of d'Harnoncourt's efforts in the Museum of Modern Art. Eleanor Roosevelt came as promised, and saw the exhibit with d'Harnoncourt as her personal guide. "I think it is one of the most exciting and thrilling exhibitions I have been to in a long while," she reported in her newspaper column "My Day." She commented about the beauty of the silverwork of Ambrose Roan Horse, a Navajo silversmith from Cornfields, Arizona, and a teacher at one of the Indian schools, who was present to explain his art. Also on hand to welcome her and to answer her questions were Fred Kabotie, the Hopi painter, and Nellie Buffalo Chief of Rosebud, South Dakota, and Elsie Bonser of Pine Ridge, South Dakota, both Sioux artists skilled in porcupine quillwork and fine beadwork. D'Harnoncourt had requested that the Interior Department use its funds to provide for these Indian guests throughout most of the exhibit. In summary, Mrs. Roosevelt concluded she never before had "the sense of centuries of development which lie back of the arts of our Indian people."[40]

The Museum of Modern Art exhibit seemed to be riding, if not leading, the surge of public interest in things truly American. Critic Jean Charlot distinctly saw the phenomenon. "The show . . . at the Museum of Modern Art finds Americans stranded on their own continent in recoil from a beset world," he declared. "The patriotic angle may well weigh the scales in favor of these hundred-per-centers of American art, beside whom even Thomas Craven's roster of Americans acquires an immigrant flavor." Necessity contributed some of the attention the Museum of Modern Art generated. With foreign imports cut off by the war, fashion designers turned homeward for inspiration in 1941. In looking around for things completely American, they joined the thousands who rediscovered the American Indians. From the first day of the exhibit, fashion artists were observed on all three floors of the museum sketching Indian designs or trying to capture in paint the Seminoles' amazing sense of color which made inexpensive cottons look like exquisite color fabrics. An average of 1,350 people a day paid admission to explore the Museum of Modern Art exhibit.[41]

Early in March the moment seemed ideal to focus further attention on New Deal Indian policy by inviting scientists, administrators, Indians, and the public to participate in a four-day institute at the Museum of Modern Art on the future of the American Indians. Officially, the conference was held "for the purpose of attracting and informing the general public and to bring together specialists from whose discussions new understandings and policies will arise."[42] The attention of the participants was called to the fact that the Indian population was growing much more rapidly than that of the general population and that some population experts predicted that its 1940 figure of 361,000 would be doubled by 1980. Furthermore, America had no geographical frontiers left. As with any expanding minority, the Indian situation would give rise to new social and economic problems which called for planned action. The idea for an institute to be held with the cooperation of the Indian Office, the Indian Arts and Crafts Board, and the Museum of Modern Art originated from earlier discussions with Oliver LaFarge, president of the American Association on Indian Affairs, formerly called the National Association on Indian Affairs. In February, Collier issued travel orders for twenty top administrators in the Indian Office to attend from 4 to 7 March.[43]

The time had come to look ahead, La Farge had decided. He and Collier were principal speakers at the opening meeting, after which group discussions raised questions about the future. Consideration of the place of Indian religion in the modern world touched upon the values that Indian religion with its dynamic philosophy of love of the land and of natural resources might have for non-Indians. William Duncan Strong and Ruth Bunzel of Columbia University, and Alice Corbin Henderson, who had spent most of her life in the Pueblo country, read papers on Indian religion.[44]

The choice of the museum setting and d'Harnoncourt's exhibit for this group discussion was perfect. No one among these leaders could doubt the brightness of the future of Indian arts and crafts. Describing for them the Indian arts and crafts picture, d'Harnoncourt expressed his belief that the American Indians were the outstanding, if not the only, producing group in the country that still had a feeling for tools, for materials, and for traditional design.[45]

In the midst of the positive approach and accomplishments of the Indian Arts and Crafts Board at the 1939 San Francisco Exposition and the 1941 Museum of Modern Art exhibit, d'Harnoncourt added a reflective touch that few recognized, or if they did hesitated to comment upon. On the cover of the Museum of Modern Art Indian Exhibit catalogue was a shield design of a bear charging fearlessly into the thick of a salvo of bullets. For those who recognized this symbolic reference to the years of private and official efforts to stamp out Indian culture and to substitute non-Indian ways, the Museum of Modern Art exhibit provided reassurance that that tragic mistake had not been fatal.[46]

12

OPPOSITION

Disruptive and threatening obstacles often blocked the road to the realization of Collier's dream of public acceptance of Indian arts and crafts as a part of the American cultural heritage, acceptance which he also hoped would produce additional economic support for the Indians. The necessary foundation of the Indian Arts and Crafts Board program was a relatively small appropriation. Yet, when Collier requested $45,000 to establish and to operate the board from July 1936 to June 1937, suspicious and doubtful congressmen on the appropriations subcommittees authorized only $42,500. Their objection was the salary of $10,000 for the general manager, the most important employee of the board. An adjustment had to be made in the general manager's salary to fit the congressional mandate. Increased travel requirements and field commitments necessitated by the board's realization that its work required close contact with the individual reservations brought the fiscal year 1938 appropriation request to $50,000, yet Congress again granted only $42,500. Almost as if the board had become resigned to the size of the appropriation allowed for the previous two years, it did not request any increase for its third year of operation. Still, the House cut the request for $42,500 by $1,500, although the Senate later restored that reduction. Again it was the salary of the general manager, now $7,500, that irritated the House appropriations subcommittee.

While the salary of the general manager was the excuse for reducing the appropriation for 1939, in reality, the congressmen objected to government employment of a foreign-born person. The job scarcity produced by economic depression no doubt accounted for their desire to provide support for native-born Americans before all others. The fact that d'Harnoncourt's Germanic accent permeated his almost flawless English did not help the situation when he presented the Indian Arts and Crafts Board appropriation request to the House subcommittee. The hearings on the 1939 appropriation displayed an expertise and knowledge only d'Harnoncourt could have provided, yet the outcome was a disaster both for d'Harnoncourt and for the board because he never appeared before a congressional subcommittee again, and his knowledge of Indian arts and crafts was lost at the board's most crucial moments.

European political developments influenced congressional judgment. To some of the provincial and increasingly xenophobic congressmen it seemed incomprehensible that a foreigner, a European at that, was being paid with public money to make policy for and to advise the American Indians. After the House reduced d'Harnoncourt's salary from $7,500 to $6,000, the chairman of the Senate subcommittee, Senator Carl Hayden, explained to Collier that the "objection that was apparently raised in the House was that he [d'Harnoncourt] had only recently applied for citizenship in this country." Aware of an anti-fascist attitude in Congress, Collier explained that d'Harnoncourt was about to get his final citizenship papers and that he was an Austrian by birth.[1]

National politics also contributed to growing opposition to New Deal Indian policy early in the so-called second New Deal period not only in committee hearings but also in Congress generally. Indian Office relations with congressional committees during this New Deal period exhibited stiffening congressional opposition. Important 1935 Indian Claims Commission bills, for example, failed to get full consideration in the House. Then from 1937 on, fueled partially by the New Deal fight with Congress over Roosevelt's court reorganization plan, bitter attacks on the policy, organization, and leadership of the Indian Office and the Indian Arts and Crafts Board marked the relations between Congress and the Indian Office, primarily at the pivotal appropriations subcommittee hearings.[2]

Collier supported the Roosevelt court reorganization proposal through loyalty to an administration which had supported his Indian policy and from his fear of the dangers to Indian welfare from an overburdened court system, a situation which Roosevelt for political reasons blamed on aged or infirm judges. Collier knew that a sympathetic federal court system was vital in the battle to protect Indian artists from the producers of machine-made Indian products. Another important factor to Collier from both personal and political standpoints was the need to protect his relationship with the Denman family. In March 1936, United States Circuit Court Judge William Denman had developed a federal court reorganization plan that in part was incorporated in Roosevelt's 1937 court plan.[3]

During the hearings conducted by the 1937 Senate Committee on Indian Affairs for the current "Survey of Conditions of Indians in the United States," Senator Burton Wheeler and Senator Dennis Chavez, Democrat from New Mexico, encouraged testimony attacking New Deal Indian policy in general and the Indian Arts and Crafts Board in particular. The witness, Alice Lee Jemison, identified herself as the Washington representative of Joseph Bruner, the president of the American Indian Federation. She was a mixed-blood Seneca and, like Bruner, advocated immediate and complete Indian autonomy. In testimony before the House Indian Affairs Committee in 1935, both Jemison and Bruner had attacked Collier's ideas and the Indian Reorganization Act as communist-oriented. The Indian arts and crafts program got similar attention when Jemison complained to the 1937 Senate Indian Affairs Committee that Collier was educating Indian children to do nothing but arts and crafts work and telling them that "now we are fitting you for life on the reservation . . . and arbitrarily making them supply arts and crafts for government controlled cooperatives." The Indian Arts and Crafts Board, she said, had absolutely arbitrary control of all Indian arts and crafts. Since Collier was both the commissioner of Indian affairs and the chairman of the Indian Arts and Crafts Board, Jemison charged that federal statutes governing trading with the Indians made the production of Indian arts and crafts and the marketing of such products "solely and absolutely a government-controlled and directed industry."[4]

Vaguely citing what she called "plenty of evidence," Jemison asserted that in the past trading posts established on reservations had operated to the detriment of the Indians. With that background, Jemison reasoned:

> the production of Indian arts and crafts and the sale of them as a "cooperative enterprise" will result in nothing more or less than Indians being forced to turn out mass production of standardized articles, for which they will receive little or nothing in comparison with sale prices; that they will be forced to trade at the "cooperatives," and otherwise coerced into

conformity with the program; and . . . that under the present Bureau system of governing the Indians and the Wheeler-Howard and the Thomas-Rogers Acts, such "enforced" cooperation and such "enforced" production is nothing more or less than communism as practiced in Soviet Russia.[5]

Expressing the long-held rapid assimilationist concept in Indian affairs, Jemison believed that the Indians had a golden opportunity knocking at their door and left alone would develop that opportunity through individual initiative and effort in the American way. Regrettably, Collier was not present for the 21 April 1937 hearings, for his response, if allowed, would have been very illuminating.

Both Wheeler and Chavez quickly picked up on Jemison's unsubstantiated, two-year old charges that some of Collier's family had been connected with an architectural firm in New York that had received contracts for designing Indian schools. Assistant Commissioner William Zimmerman, Collier's representative at the hearings, protested such testimony in Collier's absence, but Senator Wheeler only responded that Collier could have been present had he wanted to be at the hearing. Wheeler demanded that Zimmerman immediately answer the charges for Collier.[6] This situation exemplified the change in atmosphere within the Democratic party that developed in 1935 and surfaced during the Roosevelt court plan confrontation as former New Deal supporters moved publicly to embarrass and to discredit New Deal administrators. Once again political considerations began to play their overriding role in Indian welfare.

Reacting to this threat to the progress of New Deal Indian policy, some of the independent welfare groups united behind Collier's efforts. The American Indian Defense Association, for example, floundering without Collier's crusading leadership, now reorganized and consolidated with Oliver LaFarge's National Association on Indian Affairs. The resulting American Association on Indian Affairs, according to its officers, Haven Emerson and LaFarge, was completed in 1937 "just in time to make possible a strong defense of the achievements of the past years."[7]

Opposition also came from James Graves Scrugham, Democrat from Nevada, on the House Subcommittee on Appropriations. He attacked the Indian Arts and Crafts Board despite the success of the Wa-Pai-Shone Craftsmen cooperative in his own state. Scrugham declared that the Indian Arts and Crafts Board had not been efficient in the performance of its functions. He said this lack of satisfactory results was "probably due to unfamiliarity with the problems of the Indians, rather than an absence of earnest endeavor on the part of the Board." Such an accusation was incomprehensible in view of the combined experience in Indian matters found on the board. Scrugham blamed Indian Arts and Crafts Board rules and regulations for causing an increase in the price of some of the Indian commodities, particularly silverwork, which, he said, lessened the sales of these articles and increased the sales of machine-made products. He pointed to the increase in machine-made jewelry factories as proof of his allegation. The board, he stated, had too stringent production and merchandising restrictions for its approval of Indian goods and apparently catered to wealthy purchasers. He praised the commercial organization of the factory system and saw the success of this system as due principally to an effective plan of distribution and a profitable and harmonious relationship with retailers. Inconsistently and incongruously, he concluded that "today there is an over-production in Indian merchandise and the real Indian craftsmen are in need of better leadership in the science of quantity distribution and sales." His thinking was representative of business-oriented people who felt that only the mass-marketing of a product could result in profit and success. They believed that Indian arts and crafts would flourish only if placed in the market on a quantity basis that would meet and stifle the undesirable competition.[8]

According to Scrugham, the Indian Arts and Crafts Board had failed in its duties. Appending a note to his letters to Collier and Ickes, he stated that he was sending a copy to Congressman Edward T. Taylor, Democrat from Colorado, chairman of the House Subcommittee on Appropriations, because Taylor was "primarily responsible for the appropriations granted to the Arts and Crafts Board of the Indian Service."[9]

With the existence of the Indian Arts and Crafts Board as well as his own employment at stake, d'Harnoncourt presented Collier with a concise rebuttal of Congressman Scrugham's accusations. D'Harnoncourt pointed out that the criticism could apply only to the board's regulations for the production of Navajo, Pueblo, and Hopi silverwork because this was the only set of standards stressing high quality that the board had issued. The regulations for all-wool Navajo woven fabrics and the regulations for Alaskan Indian and Eskimo products called solely for the minimum requirements of being Indian-made and made of the material claimed in the name of the product. He explained that the silver standards of the board dealt just with one type of silver without condemning any other types as not genuine. The only government regulations on the sale of Indian silver concerned with genuineness alone were those issued by the secretary of the interior in a letter to the National Park Service, regulations which had not been modified or superseded by the regulations issued by the board.[10]

In criticizing the board's insistence on the use of slug silver, Scrugham also was criticizing the regulations for the National Park Service which were based on this criterion for genuineness. All traders connected with the Navajo Reservation had supported this regulation, said d'Harnoncourt, because they claimed it was the Navajo artists' sole protection against the bench work product. Dropping the slug clause would endorse most of the products of the workshops in Albuquerque and Santa Fe that were using laborsaving devices. Dropping the slug clause would not hinder the flow of entirely factory-made products that came from the East and from California since they were able to undersell any Indian handmade products. D'Harnoncourt was convinced that such factory-made products could be fought only by enforcing strict truthfulness in advertising and by educating the buying public.[11]

D'Harnoncourt questioned the factual basis for Scrugham's attack. Regarding Scrugham's reference to the apparent success of machine-made and manufactured Indian jewelry, d'Harnoncourt pointed out that the increase of both bench work enterprises and factories began before the publication of the board's regulations. No mention was made by Scrugham of all of the other board activities such as the spinning project in Oklahoma and organizations for production in the Dakotas and southern Arizona. Finally, d'Harnoncourt stated that the economic philosophy of the board was not prejudiced against mass production of low-priced Indian goods in principle, but endorsed only such production that brought the Indians reasonable recompense for their work.[12]

Congressman Scrugham's accusations required an answer, yet the situation had not progressed to the point where a direct rebuttal would serve the best interests of the board. Instead, the relative neutrality of board member Ebert Burlew, whose Interior Department position provided some strength of authority, seemed the most diplomatic method of defusing this threat to the existence of the board. Burlew briefly pointed out that personnel and funds available for carrying on the work of the board were insufficient for undertaking all phases of the Indian arts and crafts program simultaneously. It, therefore, was necessary, he said, to concentrate on certain specific problems. Burlew's aim was conciliation rather than confrontation as he told Scrugham that while the board's procedure "may seem slow in obtaining desired results, and may even seem, as you suggest, to be defeating its own purpose, it is believed that a little more time should be allowed in which to judge the vision of the present policies."[13] The tactic succeeded, for Scrugham sent no more letters of complaint.

Collier was politically realistic, nevertheless, and was aware of the administrative pitfall of promising more than could be delivered. In his annual report for fiscal year 1938, he cautioned that the Indian Arts and Crafts Board did not wish "to delude the public, the Indians, or itself" into assuming that the increased arts and crafts production was the answer to all of the Indians' economic problems. The number of Indians interested in, and capable of, superior arts and crafts work could not be expanded indefinitely, and the market could absorb only a limited amount of goods.[14]

Collier's caution was necessary, too, because of murmurings of discontent from the traders over the silver standards established a year earlier by the Indian Arts and Crafts Board. The competition from factory-made silver jewelry, the fears aroused over the strictness of the government silver standards, and the delays in making the government mark available created a situation that compelled d'Harnoncourt to warn Collier that silver production in the Southwest would constitute "a major problem for the Board in the coming year [1939]." The problem, he believed, involved not only financial but also very important social and cultural questions. As an example, d'Harnoncourt cited the increase in bench work on or near the Navajo Reservation, and he pointed out that this competition could force the Navajo silversmiths to rearrange their entire form of life because bench work called for living in communities.[15]

At the same time that d'Harnoncourt saw the important social consequences of the factory system for the Navajo, Pueblo, and Hopi sil-versmiths, the traders in the field were concerned with the more immediate economic needs which the government standards were sup-posed to improve. Unfulfilled expectations exacerbated by the brief, but acute, 1937–38 recession in the business recovery, played a major role in their complaints. The United Indian Traders Association at a meeting on 28 May 1938 discussed the desirability of either changing the silver standards or creating a whole new set of standards. Instead of the anticipated market growth from higher quality products, the "eco-nomic factor of price" had ruled out 90 percent of the buying public, the traders complained, because the public would not or could not pur-chase silver made under the new standards and the resulting higher prices. The traders also complained about the threat from factory-made jewelry dealers who were underpricing the licensed dealers, the accom-panying threat that the Indian silversmiths ultimately would be thrown out of work, the impossibility of distinguishing between the skilled workers' hand-cut sets or stones and the machine-cut stones, and the difficulty of telling the difference between some manufactured jewelry and the genuine article.[16] The traders did not discuss the problem cre-ated by some silversmiths who made things more difficult for them-selves when under price competition from the machine-made and factory systems they began to take shortcuts in the production of their silver-work and thus could not obtain certification by the board.

Two independent silversmiths, who also marketed their own products, publicly depicted the Indian Arts and Crafts Board as an organization established to protect Indian arts but which now, in effect, worked against them. "Regulations imposed by the Board are so strict that the average independent Indian craftsman cannot live up to them in commercial production and make any money," charged John Boyd, a Domingo, and Diego Abeita, an Isleta who was the manager of The Tewa, an Indian arts and crafts shop in Isleta, New Mexico. Abeita also charged that the traders could get products stamped by the board that the origi-nal artists could not. Pointing to a sore spot, Abeita attacked the board for not having an Indian artist represented among its members. Abeita was not against the board itself but wanted the board to cooperate and rescind the regulations.[17]

Complaints from individual traders about the Indian silver situation continued in 1939, yet figures of the Indian Arts and Crafts Board showed a considerable increase in overall interest in better quality silverwork despite the adverse economic situation. The board claimed that 2,322 pieces had been stamped during fiscal year 1938 (July 1937 through June 1938) while only approximately 500 pieces of equal quality could have been found a year earlier. Since the stamping device only became available in April 1938, this immediate and heavy usage appeared to attest to its acceptance. On the other hand, C. G. Wallace, a trader from Zuni, New Mexico, wrote a year later to the manager of the Indian arts and crafts shop in the Interior Department building in Washington, D.C., that he found it "humanly impossible to stay in the arts and crafts business." Only one other store in Zuni, Wallace complained, had attempted to stay with the new arts and crafts jewelry while all the others had dropped it a year earlier. Wallace was not unsympathetic to the standards and appeared simply to be expressing his frustration over the conditions which produced the situation, specifically, the machine and factory competition and the immediate financial needs of the Indians. Wallace said he had to buy a lot of jewelry from the Indians every day, but that it was not of a quality to take a government stamp.[18] Plainly the effects of the 1937–38 recession had not provided the best circumstances for evaluating the new silver standards, for increased spending produced by better economic conditions in the country would have provided an additional incentive for the Indians to make higher quality silverwork. Adverse economic conditions often forced the Indians to produce more quickly and usually with less quality in the hope of avoiding increased destitution. The work of lower quality which resulted was difficult to sell while high quality work maintained a relatively stable market. The Indians innocently made their own circumstances more desperate.

Fortunately, the 1937–38 recession was comparatively short and the economic pressure on the Indians and the traders began to subside slowly in 1939 as increased tourist travel and defense industry employment brought badly needed income to the Indians in the Southwest. The United Indian Traders Association in December 1939 requested that the Indian Arts and Crafts Board change the silver regulations to allow the use of acetylene or other mechanical blowtorches, to require dies be handmade by Indians, and to allow power buffing of the silver by either the Indians, traders, or dealers, yet no action was taken.[19] The silver standards remained unchanged despite the criticism they aroused and the disadvantages experienced by some of the Indians.

In the fall of 1939, d'Harnoncourt had admitted that the standards of genuineness and quality for Navajo, Pueblo, and Hopi silver had not solved the fundamental problems of silver production in the Southwest. Applying only to a small part of the general output, the standards had a limited influence on the market. An extensive merchandising and public education campaign was necessary, d'Harnoncourt believed, in order for the silver standards and the board's work to benefit a greater number of Indian silversmiths. D'Harnoncourt pointed to the experience gained at the 1939 San Francisco Exposition as proof that a large potential market existed for quality handmade silver products.[20]

Without giving up on the silver standards, d'Harnoncourt suggested a plan of action for the board's approval. To solve the most important problem, which was the production of low-priced goods, d'Harnoncourt felt that the first necessary step was to collect data on the earnings of the various silversmiths who were producing low-priced jewelry with the help of labor-saving devices and data on the earnings of those silversmiths who were making their jewelry entirely by hand. The Indian Arts and Crafts Board regulations did not touch the low-priced producers although the National Park Service had established regulations requiring the use of slug silver in all objects sold in the national parks as genuine Indian silverwork. In d'Harnoncourt's view, the park service regulations were not the answer. Since the working of slug silver involved more labor and increased costs, and since a mark of distinction was given to all work done with slug silver regardless of quality, the slug-silver worker had no incentive to produce a high quality product and resorted to hasty and slipshod work in order to compete with sheet-silver competition. Any decision by the board on the silver situation was considered important by d'Harnoncourt for the far-reaching economic consequences that would affect a large group of Indians and many traders. Because no reliable data existed on production costs, wages, and quantity output, d'Harnoncourt suggested that the board send a researcher to the Navajo country to compile the needed data.[21]

Accordingly, a survey of the tools, costs, and volume involved in the Southwestern silver production was carried on from 22 June to 21 December 1940 in an effort to evolve standards which would cover the whole field of Southwestern silver. A twenty-seven-year-old research worker, John Adair, who had made a special study in 1938 of the technology and history of Navajo silversmithing, was employed by the board on a temporary basis for the purpose of making the survey.[22] The survey report was concise and factual. Collier called the information "somewhat shocking." In particular, Collier was aroused by the statement that of all the Indian-style silver that was sold, only 23 percent was produced on the reservations and was wholly Indian-made; the balance was made partly by machine, and much of that by machinery run by white people.[23]

Along with all the statistical information Adair gathered in his survey, he also made some very penetrating observations. His findings dismissed the controversy over rolled versus slug silver. The popular belief that rolled silver was more brittle and more easily bent out of shape than hammered silver was untrue. According to Adair, the difference in strength depended solely on the gauge of the silver. The naked eye, he maintained, could not tell the difference between a silver bracelet made of rolled silver and a bracelet made of slugs hammered out by hand if the hand-hammered one were expertly finished. Although Kenneth Chapman of the Laboratory of Anthropology had developed a precision instrument to detect a bracelet made with rolled silver by measuring small differences in gauge over its surface, no rolled silver product finished by hand hammering, Adair revealed, could be detected by this instrument. Since Chapman had the only measuring device other than a microscope that was believed to be able to test for the use of slug silver, and because anyone interested in having his silver receive the Indian Arts and Crafts Board stamp had to contact Chapman, the early difficulty the silversmiths and traders experienced in obtaining the trademark was understandable.[24]

Adair pointed out that traders objected to sending their silver to Chapman in Santa Fe for stamping because they lost valuable time in which to offer that silver for sale. To make the silver standards effective, a staff of people to inspect and to pass on the silver would have been necessary, and the board had no funds for additional employees. The traders were either unwilling to accept the time-consuming responsibility for applying the trademark or, because of the lack of a viable rolled silver detection device, those that were willing were not given the stamps with which to do the job. After the trademark had been in limited use for over a year, some traders and retail dealers refused to stock stamped silver because they felt it acted as a detriment to total sales. Buyers had begun to ask why some silver pieces and not others were stamped and had become suspicious of the majority of the dealers' stock.[25]

Adair's recommendations based on his findings called for a completely different approach to government standards for Navajo, Pueblo, and Hopi silver and the regulations for the use of the government trademark. Because a definitive test to distinguish rolled silver from hammered silver was impossible except by a metalurgist observing the difference in the molecular structure, regulations against the use of sheet silver or rollers could not be enforced among the traders. In order to be effective, Adair insisted, the Indian Arts and Crafts Board regulations had to be changed to specify only minimum requirements as to whether the piece was "handmade, well-finished, of substantial weight, with good design and good turquoise." Rather than to specify how the silver jewelry should be made, the Indian Arts and Crafts Board regulations should concentrate on the quality of the finished piece.[26]

Adair's report was ignored. Collier continued to be hopeful that the board would be able to evolve standards which would cover the whole field of Southwestern silver. This did not happen. The immediate imperative to solve the silver problem faded with the new flow of money into the area from increased defense industry spending in the Southwest and a general confusion accompanying the wartime government.[27]

Even so, the silver problem was too complex ever to be solved satisfactorily by government regulation. John M. Cooper, president of the American Anthropological Association in 1940, saw the problem when he pointed out that immediate short-range policies to solve the Indians' problems had to reckon with the rapidity with which changes were being wrought by Indian-white cultural contact. According to Cooper, long-range policies had to deal with the inevitability of these changes, for no way existed to slow or to stop them. The practical problem, he stated, was to guide the adjustment along channels that would do the most good and the least harm to both Indians and non-Indians. To develop such a program in guiding toward adjustment for the common good, the elements of unselfish goodwill and the fullest knowledge must be present. Of the two, goodwill was the most important in Cooper's view although knowledge was also imperative if all were to adjust intelligently and to escape the blunders made by earlier generations.[28] Without a doubt, the Indian Arts and Crafts Board was an unprecedented tool in the program to develop cultural and economic adjustment for the common good. Under d'Harnoncourt's guidance, the board demonstrated both unselfish goodwill and a search for the fullest knowledge. To d'Harnoncourt's credit the Adair survey was planned and carried out despite the shadow it might cast on the overall effectiveness of the silver standards. The fact that the silver standards never succeeded fully or ever were changed was not an abject defeat for the board. The silver standards should be viewed instead as a qualified success: a specialized government attempt to help individual Indians to help themselves, an effort that was an example of unselfish goodwill.

Difficulties with Congress became more heated early in 1939. Assuming Roosevelt's support, feeling encouraged by his efforts at administrative reorganization which eventually would bring the Budget Bureau under the President's direct control, and needing additional personnel in the field, the Indian Arts and Crafts Board requested an appropriation increase of $7,500. The Bureau of the Budget approved the request.[29] Roosevelt supported Ickes's and Collier's Indian program, and Mrs. Roosevelt long had admired d'Harnoncourt's work and had taken a personal interest in his efforts. Fully aware of this support and personal interest, congressmen who apparently had become disillusioned and disenchanted with Roosevelt could not pass up an opportunity to strike directly at the White House by attacking and attempting to curtail the work of the Indian Arts and Crafts Board. Strengthened by this politically motivated support from fellow Democrats on the House Interior Department Appropriations Subcommittee, Congressman Jed Johnson, Democrat from Oklahoma, increased his attacks to the point where he became totally unreasonable. Supporting criticism came from other subcommittee members, particularly Congressman James M. Fitzpatrick, Democrat from New York, present at the 1939 Indian Arts and Crafts Board appropriation hearings.[30]

The atmosphere at the hearings was discouraging to the representatives of the board. Johnson attacked the board ostensibly over his disappointment at the lack of progress made on the Kiowa Reservation. He accused Collier of reneging on a personal promise to build an arts and crafts center in the Kiowa area of western Oklahoma. In Collier's presence Johnson told Kenneth Disher, the Indian Arts and Crafts Board assistant manager, that "if there had been any great progress made [in Oklahoma] in the last four or five years, I have not heard of it." Disher explained that the Indian Arts and Crafts Board was handicapped in this area of Oklahoma because the Kiowa jurisdiction and tribes did not have the funds with which to work. Johnson only protested further that this was a tiresome complaint without substance because he had voted "for practically all you have asked for this purpose." Congressman Fitzpatrick then jumped in to ask the unanswerable question: "Can you tell the Committee how many Indians [in] the last three or four years have become self-supporting as a result of this work?" Without waiting for an answer, Johnson testily added, "Tell us of one Indian in the entire United States who has become self-supporting because of your arts and crafts division." Again without pause, Fitzpatrick qualified the future existence of the Indian Arts and Crafts Board. "If they [the Indians] are not made self-supporting," he warned, "we should not provide money simply to make positions. The object is to make the Indians self-supporting, and if that is not happening," threatened Fitzpatrick, "we should do away with the whole thing."[31]

In refusing to be sufficiently patient about assessing the work of the board over a long span of time, Fitzpatrick and Johnson primarily were intent on embarrassing and discrediting New Deal administrators and programs. The House subcommittee cut the appropriation request for 1940 back to the 1939 level of $42,500, but then a more patient and sympathetic Senate subcommittee restored the cut. Agreement finally was reached, and $46,250 was appropriated with the provision that $1,000 was to be used to employ an urgently needed second stenographer to handle the increasing load of correspondence which the board was required to carry on.

"This [the Indian Arts and Crafts Board] is one of the most productive things that is being done in the entire Indian Service," Commissioner Collier told the Senate Subcommittee on Appropriations in 1940.[32] Riding on a crest of success generated by the 1939 Indian exhibit at San Francisco, the board confidently sought $48,500 for fiscal year 1941, an increase of $2,250 from the 1940 appropriation, the highest appropriation received to date. Of this new amount, $2,150 was requested to handle the expansion of the board's activities in production and merchandising work and included an Indian arts and crafts specialist for the Arizona-New Mexico area. The remaining $100 was for administrative promotions. Increasing the scope of the board's activi-ties also had necessitated additional personnel in the Washington office to handle an increased volume of work. To meet this additional load of work, the board's appropriation request sought an increase from $16,000 to $18,000 in the amount of the appropriation that could be expended for personnel services in the District of Columbia.[33]

The 1940 House hearings ended on an often-repeated note, a reference to d'Harnoncourt's position as general manager. Congressman Fitzpatrick asked Collier if the board still had the same general manager as it had last year, and after Collier's simple "yes," Jed Johnson asked Collier whether he still thought d'Harnoncourt was doing a good job. Collier's answer left no room for doubt. "We think he is doing a better and better job. D'Harnoncourt has shown extraordinary business ability," he responded. Despite such acclaim, both the House and the Senate refused the $2,000 increase for personnel in the Washington office and the $100 promotional increase in salaries. On the other hand, they allowed the rest of the appropriation requested for fiscal year 1941 for a total of $48,400. While this appropriation was the highest received by the board to date, the amount was still less than what had been suggested by the 1934 Young committee as necessary for the board's projected tasks. Yet Collier apparently had no plans to increase the board's budget beyond its immediate needs. He assured the Senate subcommittee that the Indian Arts and Crafts Board was operating on a very modest budget. "It is a research and promotional agency," he stated. "We are deliberately holding down their budget."[34]

Collier's patience in the face of opposition, an asset that contributed heavily to his skill both as a politician and a diplomat, seemed boundless. Occasionally his reflective nature displayed the sensitivity he attempted to control and to hide throughout most of his commissionership. One such occasion occurred in June 1938 as he wrote an editorial for *Indians at Work* while enroute to Guatemala for a brief vacation. "What is there," he asked, "—is there anything—that makes the Indians' effort (in the United States), and our governmental effort with the Indians worthwhile?" Pondering his own question, Collier displayed the historical awareness that guided and motivated New Deal Indian policy generally and the work of the Indian Arts and Crafts Board specifically. The work, he observed, first of all, involved the importance of faithfully executing a public trust. The origin and the continuing motive of this trust were significant in the Indians' case. The origin blended conquest, public convenience, and conscience, yet he considered the continuing motive to be something other than mere inertia and the entanglements of contract and of white advantage.[35]

Collier saw his answer in a deep-seated public morality. "The great public looks upon and supports the government Indian work as an effort to do historical justice, to protect the weak, and to keep alive values which are deep in the white man's own consciousness. No other country," Collier reflected, "has brought, in the absence of necessity political or economic, so much of what may be called idealism, conscientiousness, or romanticism to its work for its Indians: perhaps, not for any minority or dependent group anywhere in the world." Collier was speaking not only for his time but across many years and without regard to the question of whether it had done harm or good.[36] Collier believed he had an historic mission, a mission sanctioned by the knowledgeable American public, one that was demanded for the continued growth of American cultural integrity. Indian arts and crafts played an important part, in Collier's view, not only in America's cultural past but also in America's cultural future as an example of and source for cultural achievement. The effort was not only worthwhile, it was also necessary. No other reasoning could explain Collier's tenacity in the development of government assistance to Indian arts and crafts.

13

PINNACLES AND PITFALLS

AT THE SAME TIME that America was searching for a strengthened national heritage in the face of fascist threats to democracy, many Americans finally came to recognize their responsibility to maintain the artistic inheritance that Indian culture and, indeed, all of American culture provided. In a 1941 address dedicating the National Art Gallery in Washington, D.C., President Roosevelt articulated a changed public attitude toward art generally. Until quite recently Americans had considered art to be something foreign, something imported that existed only in museums, he stated. Now awakened to American art, they have discovered that they had a part in its development. This changed general attitude toward art derived from an awareness that art was not something just to be owned but something to be made, an emphasis on the knowledge that the act of making, and not the act of owning, was art. From this awareness also came the knowledge that art was not simply a treasure from the past or an importation from another country, but "part of the present life of all the living and creating peoples—all who make and build." In an even larger current context, Roosevelt labeled works of art "the symbols of the human spirit, and of the world the freedom of the human spirit made."[1]

Within this receptive official frame of mind, the work of the Indian Arts and Crafts Board and the skillful efforts of d'Harnoncourt reached their apogee. Collier appeared ecstatic before the 1941 House Subcommittee on Appropriations. The Museum of Modern Art exhibit, he exclaimed proudly, showed Indian art as a fine art to be ranked with any fine art. Furthermore, he told subcommittee members, the exhibit had been "an enormous success." The publicity had been very productive No exhibit held at the Museum of Modern Art had attracted more attention. The exhibit was "running up the demand for Indian quality

258

goods until the demand is running away from the supply, and our problem now is to supply the demand." Two months later he told the Senate Subcommittee on Appropriations the same thing. "At San Francisco they did conduct a market, but at the Modern Art Museum it was purely a matter of showing what the Indians could do and creating a demand," he commented. "As a matter of fact, we have created much more demand than we have been able to supply."[2]

Collier unhesitatingly credited the aggressive efforts of the Indian Arts and Crafts Board for the increase in popularity being experienced by Indian arts and crafts. He believed that the board had achieved this situation by carrying on an extensive program of public education in Indian arts and crafts by means of the Indian exhibit at the 1939 San Francisco Exposition and the 1941 Museum of Modern Art Indian Exhibit. The board of trustees of the Museum of Modern Art, in the same vein, thanked the Indian Arts and Crafts Board for "its cooperation and invaluable services in connection with the preparation and installation of the exhibition," and for the enthusiastic services of d'Harnoncourt and Klumb, "whose expert knowledge and skill together with that of their assistants, were responsible for the exhibition's influence and success."[3]

Everything was moving forward according to d'Harnoncourt's plans. The successful exhibits in San Francisco and New York drew popular attention to Indian arts and crafts. Other private and public organizations and museums without direct stimulus from the board now stepped in and carried on the promotional function of presenting Indian arts and crafts to the public as valuable and desirable contemporary products. This arrangement seemed to make it possible for the board to concentrate on the production and merchandising phases of its program.[4]

Such hopes almost fell by the wayside, however, as the possibility of involvement in government museum administration threatened the board's limited resources. The United States government had decided to join the promotional ranks by establishing a museum devoted solely to presenting the culture of the Plains Indians. Working through a Public Works Administration project for the National Park Service, the federal government had set aside $150,000 for a building to be erected at Two Medicine Lake in Glacier National Park in Montana. Before construction could begin, Ickes determined that the project belonged more properly to the Indian Office than to the National Park Service and turned the funds over to Collier, who naturally began to involve the Indian Arts and Crafts Board.[5]

Probably fearing a lack of sufficient funds to carry on the board's assigned tasks let alone to administer a museum properly, d'Harnoncourt refrained from any personal participation. The role of museum administrator was given to John C. Ewers of the Museum Division of the National Park Service, who was detailed to the Indian Office to plan and to arrange the exhibits. The plans included dioramas, mural maps, and artifacts that illustrated the characteristics of the culture of the Plains Indians. Some of the display methods developed at San Francisco and New York were employed, and a salesroom for Indian arts and crafts was included. Although the museum was located on the Blackfoot Reservation west of Browning, Montana, all of the Indians of the Plains were to be included in its scope.[6]

When the modern, two-story, brick structure, located on grounds covering almost two city blocks, opened on 29 June 1941, it represented the largest government project yet undertaken to aid Indian groups in reviving their crafts and to furnish them with an outlet for the marketing and sale of their goods. At the opening, the building was dedicated by Willard Beatty and John Ewers without direct Indian Arts and Crafts Board participation.

The concept of the Museum of the Plains Indian fit the board's philosophy perfectly. For years the Blackfeet and neighboring Plains tribes had set up an annual three-month summer encampment on the highway just outside Glacier National Park at St. Mary, Montana. Here the craftworkers pitched their tepees alongside an old log cabin, dressed themselves in buckskin garments, and worked at their crafts, creating a nostalgic scene reminiscent of pioneer days. In 1936, the Blackfeet were the first group in the Plains area to organize an association and to occupy a building for summer sales, and they earned about one thousand dollars that year.[7] Although their sales jumped to an estimated eight thousand dollars by 1940 as the number of tribes participating increased, such trading establishments along the highways in Indian country were viewed by the board to be of little help in the development of the Indian arts and crafts business. Their sales were mainly souvenirs, which in many cases did not produce sufficient returns for the Indians to make it worth their while to continue as artists. Previously, the board had

assisted in the establishment of a permanent crafts building at the Rosebud Indian Agency, South Dakota, and another at the Oglala Boarding School on the Pine Ridge Reservation, South Dakota. Several rooms
at the Flandreau Indian School, Flandreau, South Dakota, and at the
Sioux Indian Museum in Rapid City, South Dakota, were established
as craft shops. The Gros Ventre and Assiniboin tribes on the Fort Belknap
Reservation, Montana, had taken over and decorated the old agency
headquarters near Harlem, Montana, where part of the building was
used as a meeting place for the tribal council and the balance for crafts
rooms. The Kootenai and Salish tribes of the Flathead Reservation in
western Montana recently had voted to donate tribal funds for the organization of a crafts association and similar efforts were beginning on
the Fort Peck Indian Agency in Poplar, Montana. Now goods from all
these smaller shops could find their way to the Museum of the Plains
Indian with its many rooms for museum exhibits, for Indian craft technique demonstrations, and for sales, assembly, and shipping.[8]

The Indian Arts and Crafts Board under d'Harnoncourt maintained
only an advisory role in its relations with the government's museum
enterprises both at Browning and at Rapid City, South Dakota, where
the much smaller Sioux Indian Museum had been established jointly
in 1939 with the local city government. This stance was necessary if
the board was to continue as a low-budget organization designed to operate through existing agencies and devoted to the more comprehensive goals of opening wider markets and improving and increasing
production on the many reservations.

No doubt remained in 1941 that an improvement in the quality of
Indian-made articles had occurred under the supervision of the board
or that the reception of these articles by the public had established definitely the existence of opportunities for Indian arts and crafts to build
up quality markets all over the United States. No longer could anyone
question the Indian artists' ability to produce articles that were both
decorative and useful, nor could anyone doubt that the public was willing to purchase such articles if they could be procured. The obstacles
to be overcome now became the small volume of production and the
difficulties in distribution.[9] For several years the board had been encouraging the Indians to create cooperative producing and merchandising enterprises that would enable them to deal directly with their new

markets. The demands of these new markets by 1941 had forced the board to concentrate its efforts almost exclusively in this direction. The market had exploded, according to Collier, who estimated the total gross income from Indian crafts to run above a million dollars a year.[10]

Specific new steps were taken to promote and to protect the work of these Indian producing and merchandising enterprises. The board long had looked to the establishment of trademarks and had instituted them for Navajo silver and woven products and Alaskan native products although the great number of tribes and the wide variety of their products made the use of a single trademark system almost impossible. Realizing that it was unrealistic to expect the public to remember a large number of different trademarks and, at the same time, believing that each tribe should use one of its own symbols as a trademark, the board proposed to establish certain sizes and proportions for all trademarks of these Indian organizations. Such an arrangement would make them readily recognizable as part of an Indian trademark system, yet the system would allow individuality in detail. Discussions with the United States Patent Office followed, and the system was prepared for the use of the Indian enterprises on a voluntary basis.[11]

Along these same lines, the board began to develop a file of Indian production and marketing organizations. Registry with the board for placement in this file would give the trademark owner the right to use its trademark on a tag with an inscription reading: "Registered with the Indian Arts and Crafts Board as an Indian organization for trading in fine Indian handicrafts." By the end of fiscal year 1943, cooperative production and marketing associations were operating among the Navajo, Pueblo, Seminole, Papago, Alaskan, and southern Plains Indian tribes and within many other tribal groups. In November 1942 the southern Plains Indians opened an arts and crafts center at the Fort Sill Indian School, Lawton, Oklahoma. An Indian Arts and Crafts Board specialist advised on the development of the crafts center and at the same time temporarily was assigned as acting curator of a fledgling Southern Plains Indian Museum.[12]

To develop these and other related activities in the fields of production and marketing research, Indian Arts and Crafts Board work during fiscal year 1942 had to be intensified greatly, and necessity dictated the need for temporary employment of specialists in the various crafts. In order to meet these increased costs, the board requested and received an appropriation of $50,000 for fiscal year 1942, a minor increase of $1,600 from the 1941 appropriation. No doubt influenced by the Museum of Modern Art exhibition's success, the House Appropriation Subcommittee's hearings went more smoothly than others to date. Nevertheless, the House predictably made its usual cut in the amount of money requested for personnel services in the District of Columbia, which, while it did not affect the total appropriation, would seriously limit the productive capacity of the board's central office. The hearings in the Senate, therefore, centered on a fight to restore the House cut.

The sum of $16,000 for operating the board's Washington office had been allowed by the Bureau of the Budget and was available for 1942 if the congressional subcommittees approved, yet the House subcommittee had drastically reduced that amount to $12,000.[13] The $16,000 limitation had provided for the employment in the Washington office of only five persons including the general manager. Under the production and marketing phase of the board's work, consultations and correspondence with other federal agencies such as the Patent Office, the Bureau of Standards, the Federal Trade Commission, and the Department of Commerce, as well as with nationwide business organizations and trade papers were required. Also, additional personnel were needed to furnish the Indian production groups with information relating to style trends, market conditions, and customers' credit. Since the board's Washington staff had been barely adequate during the promotional stage of its work, the greater volume of work required by this changed emphasis seemed to demand a revision upward rather than downward in the necessary funding. As the board became more involved each year in the organized arts and crafts activities carried on by the Indian Office field representatives and many outside agencies, its volume of work increased proportionately. About one hundred and fifty employees of the Indian Office relied on the board for advice, criticism, and instructions. The reduction proposed by the House subcommittee would have compelled a reduction in the Washington office to three employees, a situation which would have affected the ability of the board to function in the manner and to the extent prescribed by the act of Congress that created it. Perhaps the most convincing argument came when Collier told the senators that without the $16,000 District of Columbia limitation the 1941 Museum of Modern Art exhibit could not have been done at all.[14] Fortunately, in the end the Senate subcommittee was receptive to the board's dire need to retain its minimum Washington staff.

To win the Senate subcommittee's approval, Collier again had to reassure the senators that the definite policy of the board was not to increase its expenditures. He cited the nearly static budget requested year after year as proof that the Department of the Interior was not attempting to create another large agency nor did any such idea ever exist. "The Board is a research, planning, and promotional agency, working through other agencies," Collier insisted.[15]

The elements for a collision between the board on the one hand and the congressional appropriations subcommittees and the Bureau of the Budget on the other hand were apparent before the next round of appropriation hearings began in 1942. Fear of a growing bureaucracy, the desire to embarrass and to discredit New Deal programs and officials, an obvious rejection of d'Harnoncourt's qualifications to serve the American Indians, and personal campaigns by some congressmen to win favored attention for their Indian constituents all had emerged to stand in the path of Indian Arts and Crafts Board activities from the day the Indian Arts and Crafts Board Act was passed in 1935. The direct involvement of the United States in a world war provided the open invitation to carry out a campaign of obliteration against the Indian Arts and Crafts Board and other aspects of Collier's New Deal Indian policy.

Less than one month after Pearl Harbor, the Bureau of the Budget recommended that for purposes of wartime efficiency, economy, and decentralization, the Indian Office be transferred from Washington to Chicago. Collier told the heads of the various Indian Office divisions that the Bureau of the Budget's recommendation did not arise suddenly. Rather, it was more than a year old. "The decision was reached," Collier asserted, "not by Budget men in contact with our work . . . , but by another group who are not in contact with our work at all." He characterized that other budget group as one "seeking dictatorship minus a goal." That group planned to use the war emergency to accomplish a dictatorship over other administrative offices including

Congress and the president himself, in order to control subsequent peace-time functions of the government. Four days later, Collier privately blasted the Bureau of the Budget for having edged its way to vast and irresponsible power. It had obtained a series of executive orders and had construed these orders to increase the maximum authority vested in the director of the Bureau of the Budget, he charged. Hinting at conspiracy, Collier expressed his belief that these operations had been carried out so quietly that their significance had not been realized by the public and perhaps not even by most members of Congress. He was convinced that the Bureau of the Budget had made itself into a legislative body.[16]

This threat posed by the Bureau of the Budget and the move to Chicago had deep implications for the Indian Office and for the Indian Arts and Crafts Board. Collier was fully conscious of the serious administrative difficulties which would accrue from a separation of the Indian Office from the other branches of government administration. The Indian Arts and Crafts Board, for example, would suffer critical impairment away from the other government agencies, particularly the Department of the Interior, with which coordination was so often necessary.

More encouraging was the surprising refusal of the Bureau of the Budget to cut Collier's request for the Indian Arts and Crafts Board for 1943 despite the bureau's policy of widespread, war-induced budget cuts. The relatively small Indian Arts and Crafts Board appropriation was available, the Bureau of the Budget decided, and now all Congress had to do was to approve the appropriation. This did not happen.

Collier was crestfallen by the drastic cuts administered by the congressional appropriations subcommittees to the 1943 budget request for the Indian Office. When the House hearings began, Chairman Johnson sarcastically asked Collier if he recognized the fact that America was in the throes of a death struggle and if he was cooperating to the fullest in the war effort. After Collier answered affirmatively to both questions, Johnson wanted to know if his cooperation included severe cuts in his appropriation request. Collier then pointed out that the Bureau of the Budget had imposed a huge cut in Indian Office funds before Pearl Harbor and after that date again had asked him to give up more but this time had allowed him to suggest what he would give up.

"Now," Collier continued, "we are endeavoring to keep the essential things not only alive but operating efficiently."[17]

In view of these circumstances, the budget proposed for the Indian Arts and Crafts Board for 1943 appeared to substantiate all the praise that Collier had been claiming for the board. His refusal to cut the board's budget when he voluntarily had curtailed severely other Indian Office divisions provided further proof of Collier's enthusiastic support for the work of the board and gave credence to his earlier public statement about Indian Arts and Crafts Board work: specifically, "nothing which we are doing . . . represents as big [a] return to the Indians for the amount we are putting into it." Not only did Collier ask for a $50,000 appropriation again in 1943 including an increase of $7,500 in the District of Columbia limitation but he also asked for an additional $550 to make in-grade promotions allowed under the 1941 Ramspeck Act.[18]

After a lengthy arts and crafts presentation by Willard Beatty, who was representing the board in Collier's absence, a not unfriendly House subcommittee unceremoniously cut the 1943 appropriation by one-fifth to $40,350 with $16,000 to be spent in Washington, D.C.

In the more than two months between the House and Senate hearings in 1942, unrest among the Pueblos in the Southwest surfaced. Just as in the conflict over the silver standards in 1938, a participant in this new controversy was Diego Abeita, the Isleta Pueblo silversmith. According to Abeita's undated "Petition from the Pueblo of Isleta in New Mexico: A Declaration of Grievances by the Pueblo Indians of Isleta Pueblo," which was filed with the Senate Committee on Indian Affairs, Abeita considered himself to be the secretary and spokesman of the Isleta Pueblo Council, and his co-petitioner, Elias Jiron, claimed to be the governor of the pueblo of Isleta. These claims to office were disputed, however, not only within the Isleta Pueblo Council but also within the All-Pueblo Council. Abeita's petition pointed an accusing finger at the Indian Office and charged it with constant meddling in the internal affairs of his pueblo, a situation, he complained, which "created a turmoil, diversity, and disorganization" that now threatened a complete collapse of community government. The immediate events which brought about Abeita's petition centered around the decision of Sophie D. Aberle, superintendent of the United Pueblo Agency, to recognize officially another person, Frank Marrujo, as governor of the pueblo because he had submitted evidence supporting his claim of election and Abeita had not complied with her request that he do so, also. Such a decision, if allowed to stand, would set up "a despotism among the Indians like that which has not been known," Abeita charged.[19] Contrary to the Pueblo custom of full official discussion and approval with the All-Pueblo Council, Abeita and Jiron instituted civil proceedings in a local New Mexico court even though the New Mexico Indians had been under the sole jurisdiction of the secretary of the interior since a 1913 federal district court decision. Their attorney was Stanley Miller, the son-in-law of none other than Dennis Chavez, the Democratic senator from New Mexico.[20]

Rumbles of discord had developed earlier at the meeting of the All-Pueblo Council of 30 August 1941, which Collier had attended. Abeita related in his petition that after Collier had closed this meeting to the press, he, Abeita, had recommended reorganization of the Indian Arts and Crafts Board, full accreditation for the Albuquerque and Santa Fe boarding schools as high schools, and modification of the stock reduction program. Now in April 1942, Abeita called the Indian Arts and Crafts Board "a sad failure" and not beneficial in any way to the Indians' cause. He called the board's rules and regulations archaic, complained that no artists or Indians were members of the board, and that the board had not improved the economic possibilities for Indian arts and crafts. "All they have done has been to put on a couple of exhibits of work done at the Santa Fe and Albuquerque Indian schools by children for the purpose of aggrandizing Mr. Collier and Mr. d'Harnoncourt in the eyes of the American public," Abeita claimed, "and in so doing they thereby promoted the products of child labor in competition with native craftsmen." Therefore, Abeita concluded, "we now recommend that the appropriation for the Arts and Crafts Board be forthwith eliminated." Between his 30 August 1941 recommendation to reorganize the Indian Arts and Crafts Board and this April 1942 petition, Abeita had become unalterably opposed to the whole concept of the board. He now wanted "these high-sounding, nonessential positions and programs, designed solely to accommodate the friends of John Collier and Sophie D. Aberle, eliminated." Abeita admitted in his petition that he had been in close personal contact with Senator Chavez when he,

Abeita, revealed that the senator had informed him in February 1942 of exactly when Collier planned to be in the Pueblo area so that Abeita could press his demands personally.[21]

On 4 May 1942 Collier responded to Abeita's petition to the Senate Committee on Indian Affairs by writing directly to Elmer Thomas, the chairman, who also happened to be a member of the Senate Interior Department Appropriations Subcommittee. His letter included eleven other letters that he had received from Pueblo Indians, all of whom were elected officials in their pueblos, repudiating the Abeita petition. Collier pointed out in his letter that while the petition had been signed by four of the nineteen pueblo governors, the Zuni and Cochiti governors had withdrawn their signatures, and the Sandia and Taos governors had no evidence that they had gone through the customary procedure of calling a meeting of their councils and principal people and submitting the matter to them. Collier also included statements from the president and the secretary of the council of all of the New Mexico pueblos repudiating the petition circulated by the unofficial group at the Isleta Pueblo. All of this evidence, Collier claimed, showed that the complaints referred to in the petition were in part trivial, in part false, and almost entirely in bad faith. "I do not exhaust the documentary evidence but only furnish enough to establish the fatuousness of the campaign," Collier added, "that is being carried forward by an individual Isleta Indian, Diego Abeita, under the influence and advice of white persons." After reaffirming his belief that the Indian Arts and Crafts Board had been, when one considered the very small appropriation upon which it operated, probably the most productive single activity of the Indian Office, Collier cited the triviality of the other Abeita complaints, all of which centered around Superintendent Aberle and were without foundation. He ended his letter by referring to Abeita as "an excitable, aggrieved, injudicious, individual Indian" who had placed himself in a position of leadership with a minority faction of one pueblo and was in consultation with white people, including an attorney retained by this faction.[22]

Twelve days after Collier sent his letter to Thomas, the Senate Subcommittee on Appropriations hearings started. The subcommittee began by announcing a witness who was appearing in support of an amendment proposed by Senator Chavez to the 1943 Interior Department appropriation bill. Chavez's amendment called for the elimination of the Indian Arts and Crafts Board.[23]

The witness, West L. Robertson, or Ish-ti-opi, attacked everything the board had done. Only after repeated questioning did Robertson reveal his atypical Indian background. Born in 1902 in Oklahoma, Indian Territory, among the Choctaw Nation, he went to school in Oklahoma and California and received a degree from the University of Oklahoma in 1924. Subsequently, as a resident of New York City, his activities were "singing and lecturing and putting in time on research." Robertson began his testimony by reading a prepared statement in which he claimed that after a thorough investigation by "interested authorities," whom he did not identify, and casual observation by "slightly interested citizens," the consensus of opinion was that the Indian Arts and Crafts Board had not functioned "in the manner that was intended by the forces which backed its inception, nor according to the instructions for the bill."[24]

The rest of Robertson's testimony was even more startling. He called the Museum of Modern Art Indian Exhibit a "pitiful display." He referred to d'Harnoncourt as "an Austrian by birth and not long in this land," and mistakenly claimed that d'Harnoncourt retained an assistant with the title of "Director of Indian Murals" who was a "full-blooded Swede" who only recently had received his United States citizenship. Then Robertson called d'Harnoncourt's public education policy a miserable failure and pointed as an example to *Indian Art of the United States* which he said contained gross, flagrant misinformation on every other page. In conclusion, Robertson asked that the Indian Arts and Crafts Board and its expense be struck from the budget and that after the war Congress take steps to establish a commission of Indian cultural relations.[25]

Every sentence Robertson uttered could not help but have astounded anyone or any group familiar with the work of the Indian Arts and Crafts Board. Certainly the senators themselves should have been ranked at the forefront of such a group, yet Senator Chavez claimed he had invited Robertson to testify only after many conversations with him, and not a single senator interrupted during his lengthy testimony. Concluding his staged presentation, Chavez asked Robertson if it was correct to say that "as far as helping the Indian is concerned in the way of giving

him a little better economic situation the Arts and Crafts Board . . .
has not helped the Indian whatever." Predictably, Robertson agreed.
Chavez then asked Senator Elmer Thomas if he had any questions.
Thomas replied, "No. I have talked with Mr. Robertson on many
occasions, and I share his viewpoint with respect to the matter he has
been discussing."[26]

Two days later at the same hearings, Senator Chavez disclaimed any
motive or responsibility for this flagrantly irresponsible testimony. He
asserted that his interest in the subject developed only when the matter
was called to his attention by several parties who were interested in it.
Nevertheless, members of the Senate subcommittee now had testimony
upon which they could base their attack on the Indian Arts and Crafts
Board. Whether the testimony was truthful or not did not seem to matter to the senators. They ignored any attempt to correct the record and
proceeded to direct their immediate attack at d'Harnoncourt with the
ultimate goal of completely destroying the board.[27] Within a year's time,
the Indian Arts and Crafts Board had been pushed from its pinnacle of
success into a battle for its survival.

Someone had to defend the board. Collier was on a long-planned
trip to the Indian country, and d'Harnoncourt was left to prepare the
presentation for the Indian Arts and Crafts Board. After his one experience with an appropriation hearing, d'Harnoncourt never had appeared
again before a congressional committee, and 1942 was to be no exception.
Collier usually was present at the appropriation hearings both in his
capacity as commissioner and as chairman of the Indian Arts and Crafts
Board and had handled a major share of the presentations although
personal antagonisms with subcommitee members had begun to limit
his effectiveness, and after the heavy cut by the House subcommittee,
he may have refrained from appearing before the Senate group. Willard Beatty's genial temperament and smooth presentations had served
the board's cause many times, yet he never seemed capable of dealing
with troublesome situations when such situations arose, and he had
not been an official member of the Indian Arts and Crafts Board for
over four years although his Indian Office Education Division worked
closely with the board. Left to represent the board during the Senate
Appropriations Subcommittee hearings was Indian Office Finance Offi-

cer William B. Greenwood, who had replaced Samuel Dodd in 1938. Assistant Indian Commissioner William Zimmerman also was present to provide additional testimony. While Greenwood previously had worked closely with the board's fiscal matters, he had little working knowledge of the board's field activities, and Zimmerman had even less. D'Harnoncourt's tactic under these conditions was to have an extensive mimeographed report of the Indian Arts and Crafts Board's activities since its organization in 1936 ready to be given to each Senate subcommittee member at the proper moment and to be read into the record.[28]

Two days after the Robertson episode, the Senate subcommittee allowed Greenwood to respond to some of the charges. Then, Senator Carl Hayden asked the traditional and most difficult question of all: as the result of the work of the board, had an actual increase in sales of Indian handwork taken place? While the answer unquestionably was "yes," Greenwood had to explain the obvious impossibility of the board's field staff of only four people trying to maintain records of sales made by all Indian arts and crafts organizations and individual Indian artists.

He cited the example of the small Papago Arts and Crafts Board which had a first year income in 1939 of $1,685 and then two years later reported an income of $4,700. In another example, Alaskan Indian arts and crafts had produced an income of $98,257 in 1938, and in 1941 its income totaled $180,908. Greenwood stressed to the subcommittee that while the board did not attempt to take credit for all increases in sales everywhere, no one could question that the board's efforts had resulted in a new interest on the part of the general public and a new interest on the part of the Indians themselves in their arts and crafts.[29]

Nevertheless, the Senate subcommittee attacked d'Harnoncourt personally. Senator Kenneth Douglas McKellar, Democrat from Tennessee, opened by citing the House subcommittee's authorization of $40,350 of which $16,000, or two-fifths, was to be spent for personnel in Washington, D.C., and objected to spending so much of the appropriation in Washington where no Indians lived. "Who gets that money?" he demanded. Chavez interrupted to add that Indians had contacted him asking the same question in their belief that the money was not helping the Indians but rather was helping someone in the Washington office. Greenwood explained that the Washington staff currently was composed of four people including the general manager. He failed to add that two of the four people were Indians. McKellar now had his target. "How much does he get?" he asked, referring to the general manager. Greenwood responded, "He gets $7,500 a year." Was he a citizen of the United States? Where was he from? What were his qualifications? Do they have Indians in Austria? Does an education in Austria form a good background for the management, treatment, and control of Indians in America? How did he happen to be selected? Greenwood was completely at a disadvantage under this barrage from the senators.[30]

The intent of the senators on the subcommittee was to destroy d'Harnoncourt because of his native origins and, thereby, to satisfy their personal xenophobia and partisan motivations. More single-minded in this respect than most of the other senators, Chavez carried with him the memory of the controversy surrounding his appointment to the Senate in 1935. After challenging the 1934 reelection of Bronson Cutting, Republican from New Mexico and a staunch supporter of Collier as Indian commissioner, Chavez lost and petitioned the Senate charging fraud in the New Mexico election. When Cutting was killed in an airplane accident in May 1935 before the Senate could respond to the petition, Chavez was appointed by the governor of New Mexico to fill the vacant seat. At the moment Chavez was sworn in, five Progressive-bloc senators vented their political objections by walking out of the Senate chamber. Conservative and isolationist, Chavez consistently voted against liberal measures and publicly upheld the use of patronage by his own example and voting record. In 1937 Chavez had led the Navajo protest against Collier's stock reduction program and even then had sought to oust Collier for what he called Collier's extravagance and coercion.[31]

For most of the other senators involved, their attack on the Indian Arts and Crafts Board provided what appeared to be a final target for a long-simmering conservative and isolationist response to the most recent and liberal Roosevelt New Deal programs and for their rejection of a growing internationalism brought on by the war. On the other hand, Elmer Thomas seemed rudderless and swayed with anything that came his way. His unexplainable attitude continued in 1943 and became an even greater hindrance to Collier's Indian policy.

Under this two-day attack in the Senate subcommittee hearings, the board had nowhere to turn for immediate help. The war effort held Roosevelt's attention, and he could not be expected to assist. His cabinet, including Secretary Ickes, shared the same wartime burden and was generally unavailable for purely domestic problems. The removal of Japanese-Americans to Arizona was absorbing a great deal of Collier's time since almost all of the personnel for this enormous resettlement project were recruited from the Indian Office and were largely under Indian Office supervision.

Attempting to answer the question from Senator Joseph O'Mahoney, Democrat from Wyoming, regarding how d'Harnoncourt came to be the general manager of the board, Zimmerman explained d'Harnoncourt's role in reviving the sale of Mexican arts and crafts in the United States and how this had led to his selection. Senator Rufus Cecil Holman, Republican from Oregon, burrowed deeper and asked what d'Harnoncourt's sales record was in Mexico. Of course, Zimmerman could not answer. Thereupon, Senator McKellar wanted to know if d'Harnoncourt ever had made a report on what he did as general manager of the board. This was the opening d'Harnoncourt had hoped for and for which he had supplied Zimmerman with mimeographed copies of just such a report. The board now took the offensive as a long list of accomplishments was read to listeners, who had asked for it yet really did not want to listen to it.[32]

Anticipating the subcommittee's request for sales figures, d'Harnoncourt's report carefully pointed out that the activities of the board stimulated sales of Indian products not only in affiliated agencies but also in many independent businesses, which made it impossible to give exact figures for the total increase in sales due to the board's work. With that background, d'Harnoncourt provided the senators with sales figures for all Indian organizations connected with the board whose figures were available. Total comparative figures for the eleven organizations' first year after contact with the Indian Arts and Crafts Board and for 1941 showed an impressive almost 100 percent increase. During the San Francisco exhibition, many dealers reported increases as high as 30 percent in their sales volume, d'Harnoncourt continued, and they credited these increases both to the exhibit and to the improvement in quality that had been stimulated by the board. Just what credit the board should

273

claim for increases in 1940 and 1941 was difficult to say because the increased travel within the United States due to European conditions was considered an important sales stimulant. Even when sales figures from Indian producing and merchandising organizations associated with the board took into consideration that some of the artists currently selling to these Indian organizations previously had sold to other business enterprises or directly to the consumer, no doubt existed that income had been augmented. By eliminating the middlemen and conducting a more efficient operation, Indian organizations were able to pay higher prices to the producers. Also, by specializing in merchandise that was less popular with existing sales agencies, the Indian organizations were able to charge higher prices for their exclusive line of products.[33] D'Harnoncourt told the senators that exhibits of Indian arts and crafts had created a demand for quality products on the national market that was beyond the present capacity of production. To meet this demand, fifteen Indian production and marketing organizations, twelve of which were created with the assistance of the board, were now in operation and many others were to be established in the near future. These enterprises, in essence, were cooperatives that would, in time, become completely self-supporting. Furthermore, they were financed either by contributions from the tribe or by government loans. At the same time, the board's efforts to protect Indian artists against unfair competition from imitations or through misrepresentations in advertising were apparent in the presentation of twelve cases to the Federal Trade Commission for action. None of the cases had been carried into the courts because the persons charged had ceased their infringement or the use of language indicating that their products were Indian-made goods when they were not Indian products.[34]

Then in an humanitarian appeal, d'Harnoncourt broadly outlined the job of the Indian Arts and Crafts Board. Speaking in the most general terms, he referred to the board's assignment as that of bringing together the market of the twentieth century and the Indian artists, whose production philosophy and production habits corresponded to those of the European Middle Ages. With that aim, he continued, the board now had established the indisputable fact that the Indian artists could produce merchandise that answered the demands of the modern market. In the board's producing and merchandising organizations, the board also had created the tools with which the gap between the medieval production habits and the methods of the modern market could be bridged. D'Harnoncourt urged the senators to realize that "it takes time to span such a wide gap." The early Indian production approach of creating a basket, a pot, or a piece of weaving on the basis of necessity or for an occasional family gift had to be replaced. To learn to produce as a professional was something entirely new to most Indian artists, and "to stimulate the creation of this new professional attitude is the educational task of our Board."[35]

Impressed or not, the senators returned once more to their attack on d'Harnoncourt. Referring to the section in the Indian Arts and Crafts Board Act which allowed the board to charge a fee for the use of government trademarks of genuineness and quality, Senator McKellar asked how much had been collected. When Greenwood informed him that $960 had been received for about twenty licenses, McKellar exploded. He was assuming incorrectly, even after all of the previous explanations of the overall nature of the board's work, that d'Harnoncourt's $7,500 salary had produced only such a small return. Then Senator Chavez took over momentarily to ask about the personal background of d'Harnoncourt's assistant, Kenneth Disher, who was stationed in the field and not included in the Washington staff. Chavez's only interest was whether or not Disher was an American citizen.[36]

Cloaking his motives in patriotism, Chavez issued his call for an end to the board. He compared the board with the Reclamation Bureau which had been wiped out by the Budget Bureau even though it had assisted in essential wartime food production. If such an important matter as reclamation was sidetracked, Chavez concluded, the efforts of the Indian Arts and Crafts Board very well could be ended, also. Greenwood was equal to the moment and advised the senators that the Indians would need all the assistance they could get in improving their economic conditions despite the war. Many of them, particularly the very young and the older, were not benefiting from wartime employment opportunities. Greenwood predicted that the tourist trade would inevitably fall off to practically nothing, and, as a result, arts and crafts production income would drop drastically. Without the stimulus and the assistance of the board, Greenwood warned, the Indians would suffer a very severe loss. He struck a responsive note in Senator Hayden.[37]

Chavez was given the last word by the subcommittee, and he made the most of it. Previously having claimed that the matter had been called to his attention by representatives of several of the Pueblo Indians in his state, Chavez now revealed that he also had received information personally from Albert Grorud, special assistant and attorney for the Senate Committee on Indian Affairs. Grorud had been involved directly in the 1938 Senate Indian Affairs Committee hearings which had allowed American Indian Federation members to denounce without rebuttal both Collier and the Indian Office. Now, Grorud had told Chavez that he had found general Indian dissatisfaction with the board's management. Grorud was deemed an authority by Chavez because he was supposed to have visited practically all of the reservations in the last few years on behalf of the Senate Indian Affairs Committee in order to learn firsthand information regarding Indian matters.[38]

The attack once more settled on d'Harnoncourt. According to Grorud, the main reasons for the complaints were that the Indians were not receiving any benefits from the activity, that they got a meager price for their products, as they always had, and that, if in the retailing of these same commodities, the prices were two or three times as much as the Indians got, that money accrued to the benefit of the retailer or the management of the Indian Arts and Crafts Board. Chavez attempted to substantiate these serious charges by claiming he had information that d'Harnoncourt had his Interior Department Building office full of Indian goods and that he raised the prices 15 to 50 percent above what he had paid to the traders. Chavez did not explain whether or not he was referring to the Indian arts and crafts shop, which had been established in the Interior Department Building under the sponsorship of the federal employees' Welfare and Recreation Association with no connection to the Indian Arts and Crafts Board.[39]

Continuing on this same track, Chavez charged that most of the money appropriated went for salaries and travel expenses "not to the Indian country to inquire about the welfare of the Indian, himself, but for visits to museums, galleries, and other places of congregation of the white man and not the Indian." Then, Chavez used the confidential-source-who-could-not-be-identified technique to disclose that the activity of the board was not in the good graces of other agencies of the Indian Office and added that "of course, they are handicapped, and many of them do not dare to express their real feeling." In the end, Chavez invoked wartime patriotism and implied that the board was un-American because it did not have an Indian as a board member.[40]

The Senate subcommittee cut approximately 20 percent from the amount approved by the House subcommittee so that the board received only $32,750 for fiscal year 1943, the lowest amount ever appropriated for its work. D'Harnoncourt, nevertheless, remained optimistic and continued to plan for future board activities. He believed that the board had been fortunate to have had an opportunity to present its case "to some of the members of the subcommittee" and to persuade them to look at reports and figures "before it was too late."[41] As a result of his efforts, the Indian Arts and Crafts Board was allowed to continue.

14

THE WAR AND
FORCED DISINTEGRATION

DESPITE D'HARNONCOURT'S ENDEAVORS and brave optimism, the activities of the Indian Arts and Crafts Board had to be cut drastically after the middle of 1942, and an inescapable downhill slide began. His ambitious plans for the 1943 fiscal year included development of organized production in existing arts and crafts units, development of wartime and permanent markets, and protection of the Indian artists from emergency measures that created disproportionate hardships. He hoped to get grants from outside sources to carry on some of this work.[1] In a further effort to maintain as many services and as much personnel as possible, d'Harnoncourt voluntarily accepted a $1,000 pay cut so that he now received $6,500 a year for his work. Even before the 1942 appropriation hearings, he had received offers of employment elsewhere. Nelson Rockefeller asked Commissioner Collier for d'Harnoncourt's services in the Office of the Coordinator of Inter-American Affairs on a half-time basis, an arrangement that quietly took place in the ensuing months.[2] In addition, rumors circulated that d'Harnoncourt was considering an offer to teach at Harvard. Although he emphatically denied the Harvard story, he did admit to some offers from other universities. D'Harnoncourt rejected these offers because, he said, the present emergency offered "so much to do that can be of help." While his scope of interest always had included the international Indian situation, now he had the backing of Rockefeller and, with that, the authority to begin to achieve "some concrete results" on several planned projects in Latin America.[3] The war and individual congressmen gradually were dismantling the Indian Arts and Crafts Board and slowing its momentum.

Most of the projects the board had helped initiate continued on their own to grow and to become stronger during fiscal year 1943, a tribute to the sound advice the board had provided. A 38 percent increase totaling

$79,115 occurred in the sale of Indian crafts through the activities directly or indirectly sponsored by the Indian Arts and Crafts Board during the 1942 calendar year.[4] Actually, except for Alaska, the volume of output had dropped while the immense improvement in the quality of output had been maintained. The higher prices received for these quality items accounted for the increased total income.[5]

By 1943, the overall effect of the war on Indian arts and crafts varied considerably. In some places an almost complete cessation of craftwork resulted. On the Papago Reservation in Arizona, for example, the making of baskets, previously a substantial business, practically ceased. The majority of the Papagos went to California to work in shipbuilding yards, airplane factories, and wherever else they could find employment, so that barely enough Papagos remained on the reservation to take care of the Indian-owned cattle and the Indian agriculture. Ironically, the hand skills which many of the younger Indians had refined at their crafts under the encouragement of the board in the battle against industrialization of their arts helped them to get many of the better jobs in the war industries where manual skills were particularly in demand.[6]

While the diminution on the Navajo Reservation was not equal to that on the Papago Reservation, a serious decrease in Navajo arts and crafts production occurred and created an even greater shortage of rugs which, in turn, drove up prices. The English-speaking Navajos had left to enter the Army or wage employment in war industries. The Fort Wingate Ordnance Depot, near Gallup, attracted nearly two thousand young Navajos, not more than a dozen of whom spoke English, and the employer used the English-speaking Navajos to give the others instructions. This relatively high-paying work involved loading and unloading trains of explosives. Another depot near Flagstaff, Arizona, also hired many Indians. The effect of the war industries seemed quite general throughout the Southwest.[7]

To the rest of the Indian population, the war brought about the greatest exodus of Indians from reservations that ever had taken place. Out of a total of approximately 65,000 able-bodied men between eighteen and fifty years of age, 30 percent joined the armed forces and about 25 percent were engaged in war industries and other war services. In addition, more than 10,000 men, women, and children left the reservations for varying time periods to work on farms and ranches. Therefore, at least half of the able-bodied men and about one-fifth of the other employable persons were drained from the reservations. In 1943, 8,683 fewer Indian families resided at home than in 1941.[8]

Variations from the pattern were common. In most of Montana and portions of the Dakotas, for example, little diminution in craftwork occurred. The group of Indians who had been doing the major portion of the craftwork in those areas was beyond the age wanted in war industries, so they continued their craft activities. The Northern Plains Indian Crafts Association, the outlet for producer cooperatives among the Indians of Montana and Wyoming, increased its business from $6,907 in 1943 to $11,135 in 1944. In Oklahoma, where the younger people went either into the armed services or into war work, the Indian Arts and Crafts Board began to train the older group for certain types of craftwork. Where beadwork had been traditional, the board began to stress other crafts to compensate for the loss of income caused when Czechoslovakian beads no longer were available.[9]

The war had created the curious situation of taking away Indian artists and, at the same time, eliminating foreign sources of handcrafts for the large retail stores. Imported handcrafts from China, India, South America, and southern Europe no longer could be obtained, so the interest in American Indian handcrafts increased to the point where a burgeoning of the market was possible if sufficient craftworkers only were available.[10]

Many new problems developed with the war, threatening any gains and forcing the board to seek solutions while operating under severely strained resources. The impact of the war economy on the production and merchandising of Indian arts and crafts required the board's intervention to keep up production among those groups that were unable to participate in work which was directly connected with the war. This effort was particularly important since many of the war jobs available to Indian labor, such as construction work on factories located near the reservations, were only of a temporary nature. General regulations governing production and commerce during the war emergency were formulated primarily to fit industrialized production and, as a result, created excessive hardship among Indian artists. The War Production Board regulation prohibiting the use of wool in the manufacture of drapes and floor coverings, for example, threatened to bar thousands of Navajo weavers from earning a cash income. Inasmuch as these Indian weavers were not in a position to change their technique or to use other raw materials and since the total wool consumption by Indian weavers was relatively small, the board presented their case to the War Production Board, and an exemption was secured for textiles that were both handspun and handwoven.[11]

The restriction on the use of silver for purposes non-essential to the conduct of the war presented a similar yet more difficult problem. Silver was considered an essential war metal, replacing both tin and copper for a variety of uses in solder, engine bearings, and non-corrosive machinery parts.[12] The War Production Board crackdown came on 1 October 1942 and limited the availability of silver to a priority rating. Months of extensive negotiations by the board in an effort to relax the restrictions on the comparatively small amount of silver used by Indian smiths were to no avail. Finally, on 25 February 1943, the War Production Board issued an amendment to the silver conservation order which exempted all manufacturers who used hand tools exclusively.[13] The board next had to intervene on the question of establishing price ceilings and the posting of price lists based on the price levels of Indian products as of certain dates in the past. Because many Indian products were not made in accordance with accepted standards and varied from piece to piece, arrangements had to be made to allow for an evaluation of those products for which no precedent had been established.[14]

Increasingly stringent wartime transportation regulations forced the board to organize new temporary retail outlets in areas not affected by travel limitations. Experimental sales outlets were set up near some of the largest army camps as, for example, at Fort Sill, Oklahoma, where some 5,000 officers and 50,000 service people were stationed. D'Harnoncourt considered this location, which happened to be situated among Congressman Jed Johnson's constituents, to be so important that he directed a board field worker to expand a small school shop which was located near the camp and sold the products of the Indian school children. The expanded shop was to include the products of surrounding tribes for display and sale.[15]

Catering to the service people was most productive in Alaska where they were buying native crafts as rapidly as the items could be produced. Alaskan arts and crafts sales rose from $242,100 in 1943 to $420,201 in

1944. According to Beatty, who was in Alaska late in 1942, the demand was for native craft products not just souvenirs. The service people wanted something made completely by the native artisans. The largest single item in Alaskan sales was sewn animal-skin products. These products were crafted by the Eskimos located around Nome and down the coast as far as Hooper Bay. Mukluks, which were waterproof boots that reached up to the knee and had a sole of walrus or seal skin, and parkas, which were made with a zipper up the front and a hood, had been purchased in large quantities not only by individual service personnel but also by the earlier Byrd expedition and more recently by the Army Air Corps.[16]

Concerned over the social impact that the sudden addition of $200,000 cash, $40,000 from the Byrd expedition and the remainder from the Army Air Corps, would have on an Eskimo community, Beatty carried out a rather hastily constructed study of the Nome Eskimo community late in 1941. According to Beatty, the group was about as poor and downtrodden as any community in the world could be and one that had been practically on relief for most of the last ten years. Beatty was surprised to find that the sudden riches generally had been spent to insulate houses, to buy stoves, radios, warm clothing, electric lights, new furniture, rugs, and children's school books. Alcoholic consumption was down among the Nome Eskimos, whose population varied with the seasons from a low of 800 in the winter to a high of 3,500 in the summer when the Seward Peninsula gold mines were in full operation.[17] Whether or not the study was technically sound and valid by modern standards, it did reflect a sense of interest and responsibility that the Indian Office maintained in the overall effect arts and crafts had on the population.

Before representatives of the board went to Alaska, the craftworkers were defrauded by the traders who were working with the sale of Alaskan products. The artists brought their products to centers like Nome and were able to stay in town only for limited periods of time because they had to return to their homes before bad weather set in. The traders refused to do business until it was almost time for the craftworkers to leave and then bought up the crafts at a fraction of the asking price. The artists of King Island, for example, who now sold $10,000 to $15,000 worth of ivory craftwork each year, previously had to let the same production go at a half or a third of what the market ordinarily would have brought them. Until the start of the war, the Indian Arts and Crafts Board had coordinated its efforts with the representatives of the Indian Office in Juneau who used the *North Star*, a Department of the Interior boat, the steamers of the Alaskan service, or a Coast Guard cutter to handle the purchase of craft products from the artists and then turned around and sold these same products in Juneau to the various wholesalers and retailers in that city at a 2 percent markup to cover handling costs. While the actual source of the funds used for these purchases never was revealed publicly, the money apparently came from the Credit Division of the Indian Office Education Division. This same source continued to provide the necessary funds to finance new Alaskan arts and crafts marketing methods as conditions required. Under the Indian Office purchasing procedure the profits of some of the Nome traders dropped while, at the same time, the better prices increased the flow of Alaskan crafts. The general feeling among most of the Alaskan traders was favorable over the years.[18]

When the Navy took over the *North Star* and the Coast Guard cutters were on wartime patrols, the board taught the artists to send their craftwork through the postal service and to receive a check by mail for their work. The whole operation worked efficiently because the post office in Alaska operated almost entirely by airplane yet charged only the regular postal rates. Even more importantly, remotely located Indian- and Eskimo-owned stores, which had been organized through the efforts of the same credit division of the Indian Office Education Division under Beatty, received credit to purchase craft products from the artists. The system provided that after the storekeeper shipped the arts and crafts to the government station in Juneau, the credit division credited the storekeeper's account.[19]

The cost of the Alaska arts and crafts program was shared by the Indian Arts and Crafts Board and the education division of the Indian Office. The board supported a supervisor of animal-skin sewing in Nome at $2,000 and a clerk in the Juneau office at $1,800. Beatty's education division paid $6,000 for teachers of native crafts in a number of the Alaska day and boarding schools, and it also paid the salary of one supervisor of native arts and crafts in Alaska at $3,500. In addition, the Indian Office had a teacher in each village in Alaska who was assigned the duty of keeping track of the sales to traders and to the Indian Office.[20]

One such Indian Office teacher, Lillian V. Russell, described in 1944

283

the wartime work of the thirty to forty Eskimo women animal-skin sewers in the small village of Shishmaref near Hoonah, northeast of the Bering Strait. Since late 1941 this small group had manufactured 562 pairs of standard, army-regulation mukluks. The teacher's records showed that after the animal skins had been dried and scraped, the preparation of the boot soles, the making of the sinew thread, and the sewing of one pair of these army mukluks required an average of seven to nine days. By early 1944, the Shishmaref Eskimo sewers had spent 23,603 hours at this work, using 4,496 legskins, and making 20,232 yards of sinew thread. These same women also made the mukluks, parkas, and fur pants for the 250 inhabitants of their village. Rarely, the teacher observed, did the Eskimo women extinguish their lanterns before one o'clock in the morning.[21]

Despite the significant role arts and crafts played and would continue to play in Indian life, the Indian Arts and Crafts Board, probably because of wartime considerations, reduced its usually small budget request to $32,750 in 1943, only to have the House Appropriations Subcommittee cut the request to $25,000 even though the Bureau of the Budget had approved the larger amount. Beatty's informed and sometimes inspired presentation provoked little discussion. To make matters even more difficult, the House imposed a $9,000 limit on expenditures for personnel in Washington, D.C. The board could not continue to operate under those conditions. Two months after the House hearings, the board made a last plaintive request to the Senate subcommittee for adequate funding. The situation was one of life or death for the board and all it had worked to achieve.

Asking only for the same amount allowed for 1943 and a $13,000 limit for personnel in Washington, the board easily justified the request and warned the Senate Appropriations Subcommittee that the amount included in the bill by the House would be insufficient to permit even the restricted activities that the board had carried on during the past year. The House amount would not pay the salaries of an already overtaxed field force of five persons that kept in touch with the established development work which still required advice and encouragement for continued growth. Indian arts and crafts sales outlets alone now numbered about 800, of which 55 were in Alaska, 262 in Arizona, and the remainder spread around the rest of the United States, all of which stood to gain from Indian Arts and Crafts Board activity. The danger existed that everything that had been accomplished would be lost and that the entire program would end in complete failure. A limitation of $9,000 placed on salaries in the District of Columbia would not be sufficient to allow payment of a general manager's salary at $6,500 and an administrative clerk's salary at $2,700. To carry on the work at headquarters, which involved the planning and the direction of board activities and the administrative control of personnel matters, the general manager required a minimum staff of three clerks. In addition, temporary help was needed from time to time when the burden of work was unusually heavy.[22]

Finance Officer William Greenwood then began what turned out to be the shortest Indian Arts and Crafts Board appropriation hearing to date. Citing the essential nature of the program and the substantial advances that the board had made in reviving and stimulating the production of Indian arts and crafts, he called the senators' attention to the tremendous public interest involved, as evidenced by a demand for Indian arts and crafts far in excess of the ability of the Indians to supply at the present time. Commissioner Collier next took his turn at pleading with the subcommittee. He repeated once more what he had told them when the appropriation was first set up and money was easier to obtain, namely, that the board would never ask for more than its first request, $50,000, and that it intended to operate through existing agencies and not build up to be a large independent unit. He reminded the subcommittee that the board never had needed any more than that initial amount and even when the appropriation was cut from $50,000 to $32,750 the board still had been able to do its job. He concluded by warning the subcommittee that if the appropriation went down below that figure, "I don't know how we can keep the Indian going." To emphasize his point, Collier reiterated his long-held belief that he knew of no other small expenditure "so beneficial in the way of productive economy to the Indian as this little sum."[23]

Collier might as well have addressed an empty room for all the good it did. The congressional subcommittees established the appropriation for fiscal year 1944 at $25,000 and set the District of Columbia limitation at $9,000. A complete reorganization of the board now was necessary.

Impossible as it seemed, matters became even worse. Within a week after the Senate Appropriations Subcommittee hearings in June 1943, the Senate Committee on Indian Affairs published Partial Report 310, "Survey of Conditions Among the Indians of the United States; Analysis of the Statement of the Commissioner of Indian Affairs in Justification of Appropriations for 1944, and the Liquidation of the Indian Bureau." First, the report attacked the accuracy and motives of a mimeographed statement prepared by Collier which he had presented to the House Appropriations Subcommittee on 31 March to provide data on the functioning of the Indian Office and to justify the 1944 appropriation request. Then, it recommended closing all Indian day and boarding schools, stopping all payments of tuition for Indian pupils in local public schools, turning over all Indian hospitals to the United States Public Health Service, turning over management of all Indian forests to the Department of Agriculture, liquidating the Indian Office, abolishing the Indian Arts and Crafts Board, distributing all tribal funds on a per capita basis, and withdrawing federal protection from all Indian property.[24] The Indian Office was not given a chance to be heard relative to the report's contents, and only Senators Elmer Thomas, Burton Wheeler, Dennis Chavez, and Henrik Shipstead, Farmer-Laborite from Minnesota, had signed the document. This misleadingly titled Senate report received widespread publicity in all parts of the country. Two weeks later Collier revealed that no press association or newspaper had questioned Secretary Ickes or himself about the report.[25]

Both Collier and Ickes were shocked. The report's implications still were unknown. Collier told Thomas, the committee chairman, that he believed that the Senate committee's report did not represent the senator's own sentiments or purposes. He based his belief on personal conversations with the senator, his public statements, and his actions. Collier also cited Thomas's hard work, even after the report was issued, to secure more adequate appropriations for the upcoming fiscal year. Collier may have been doing his diplomatic best to salvage as much as he could from the immeasurable damage done to continued acceptance of his Indian policy before anything more disastrous could happen, for he also told Thomas that he was satisfied that the report did not reflect the views of the rest of the senators either and that none of them had prepared the document. Although Collier refused to name the actual framers of the report, he had no one left in a position of power to blame other than Albert Grorud, the special assistant and attorney for the Senate Indian Affairs Committee who long had antagonized Collier and the Indian Office. Five days after Collier's letter to Thomas, Ickes also wrote the senator. Ickes told Thomas that his share in the substantial progress that had been made in the current administration of Indian affairs was so large that it came as "a great shock" to find his name attached to a document which contained so many false charges. "Most, if not all, of the report's recommendations strike at the heart of policies which you have hitherto championed and sponsored," Ickes continued, "I can only surmise that in signing the document in question you placed confidence in the accuracy of an investigator who did not merit such confidence."[26]

The report was replete with misleading statements, none of which referred directly to the Indian Arts and Crafts Board except to call for its outright elimination for an "annual savings in excess of $20,000." According to Collier, the report was motivated by hatred. The unnamed persons who framed the report made no effort to conceal a hatred for Indians and not merely for the Indian Office, Collier observed. "They hate all those qualities in the Indian which keep him proudly an Indian. They hate any protection, any advantage which he may possess." The framers of the report in Collier's view hated particularly all those who have "deep, authentic knowledge of Indians and deep caring for Indians." They hated science, research, and knowledge, Collier pointed out, for they specifically wanted to "eliminate research and studies . . . eliminate all specialists, including anthropologists, various specialists in education, sociologists, social workers, and program planners." Collier labeled their brand of hatred a local brand, yet "not temperamentally distinguishable from the overseas varieties."[27]

Letters were the best Collier and Ickes could do to attempt to correct the damage resulting from the publicity given to the report. Collier characterized the whole report as "entirely nihilistic." Thomas used the newspapers to assure his Oklahoma constituents that the report applied only to the Five Civilized Tribes and not to the other Indians of that state when in reality that was not the case. Collier was upset that no newspaper was investigative enough to question him about the matter, and he was not attuned to the planned press conference procedures that were more common in later years. Instead he went directly to Thomas for "a friendly but insistent talk." Thomas thereupon denied that he meant the recommendations and admitted that he had signed the report without examining it. At the same time, Thomas made no effort to recall it or to correct it, Collier disclosed, nor did he take any steps to rid himself of the "poisoner" who had misled him into signing the document by misrepresenting its contents. Far from satisfied, Collier called on Chavez personally and found he also had signed the report without reading it "because Thomas had read it closely." Chavez proposed an indefinite future conference between himself, Collier, and Thomas. Collier observed that Chavez's actions had no personal importance for the senator. Assistance from the President, Collier further noted, was impossible during this war period.[28] Collier did not know where to turn for help to keep his Indian policy and programs going.

After 1942, Indian Office morale slumped seriously. The reasons for this were diverse. Reduced appropriations practically suspended capital investment in Indian country. Land acquisition, expanded irrigation, new roads, and construction all had stopped and the cutback in Indian employment weakened the basis for Indian self-support and future tribal strength. The Indian Division of the Civilian Conservation Corps ended abruptly. Indian Office personnel and Indian leaders departed. The Indian Office's move to Chicago in August 1942 made face-to-face communication with Congress and other administrative agencies in Washington difficult and often impossible. The Indian Arts and Crafts Board encountered these same wartime hardships even though its small staff remained in Washington. The board's close working relationships had suffered a serious blow. Fully aware of these grave problems, Collier warned his Indian Office employees that no handicap could defeat them except the loss of morale.[29]

By July 1943, the Indian Arts and Crafts Board needed more than morale. The lack of funds forced the termination of most of the field representatives. Before the end of the year d'Harnoncourt's field assistant, Kenneth Disher, resigned to become executive secretary of the Allegheny State Park Commission in New York. D'Harnoncourt, for his part, was far from defeated. His earlier collaboration with the Museum of Modern Art and his friendship with Nelson Rockefeller, who had become president of the museum in 1939, led to his further involvement in the field of art. While Rockefeller was coordinator of inter-American affairs, d'Harnoncourt arranged a series of art exchanges between the United States and Latin America.[30] Then in January 1944, d'Harnoncourt resigned as Indian Arts and Crafts Board general manager to become vice-president in charge of foreign activities and director of the Department of Manual Industries at the Museum of Modern Art. His career with the Indian Arts and Crafts Board was not over, for Collier took this opportunity to appoint d'Harnoncourt first as a member of the board and then in May as chairman of the board replacing Collier himself, the position Collier had sought to fill since 1935. In this position, d'Harnoncourt continued to give his time and ability although he received no salary.[31]

The membership of the Indian Arts and Crafts Board by the second half of 1944 included d'Harnoncourt as chairman, John Collier, Alfred Kidder, James Young, who had replaced Louis West in 1940, and Willard Beatty, who had replaced Ebert Burlew when Burlew was promoted within the Department of the Interior in 1943. The only other changes in the five-member board had occurred in 1942 with the death early in the year of Lorenzo Hubbell, and with the appointment late in the year of Jones Narcho, Jr., a Papago Council officer from Sells, Arizona, to fill the vacancy created.

When d'Harnoncourt left the position of general manager, the board's plan was to abolish that position and to substitute a business manager, a production supervisor, and a merchandising supervisor. The board's field employees, who were in direct contact with the Indian artists, stimulated their production of traditional crafts, advised them in regard to changes in style or execution to more nearly meet the demands of the non-Indian market, and guided the introduction of homecrafts into areas where the native crafts had died out, were eliminated by May 1944. Emphasis on commercial supervision now replaced research and specialization as the board's priority in order to take advantage of the possibilities of commercialization of the traditional crafts and homecrafts which representatives of the board had developed during the previous eight years.[32]

Under the circumstances, the board's plan was both wise and ambitious, yet implementation appeared to be almost impossible. Designed to fit existing situations, the personnel arrangement would have allowed the board to move ahead despite the less than favorable conditions under which it now operated if only efficient, practical people with business experience could be found. To provide some administrative responsibility after d'Harnoncourt joined the Museum of Modern Art on a full-time basis, the Indian Office temporarily loaned a former superintendent of Haskell Institute in Lawrence, Kansas, G. Warren Spaulding, to the Indian Arts and Crafts Board to serve as acting business manager. After several months, the Indian Office Education Division loaned Randolph McCurtain, a Choctaw from Oklahoma, to replace Spaulding as business manager.[33] No other changes were made. The board fully recognized the impossibility of obtaining a production supervisor and a merchandising supervisor at the same salaries paid to the former field workers, so in order to carry out the reorganization plan during fiscal 1945, it once more found it necessary to ask Congress for additional funds.[34]

Again the Bureau of the Budget approved the Indian Arts and Crafts Board's full request and all that remained was for the House and Senate Appropriations Subcommittees to approve the use of money already considered available. Citing the attrition in personnel and services which the 1944 allocation had caused, the board warned that a continued carrying on of board activity on such a reduced scale would impair the effectiveness of the program. On that basis, it requested a total of $45,000 for the 1945 fiscal year. Justification was based on the need to reestablish a field organization plus the need to cover other expenses such as implementing the introduction of trademarks and other necessary steps in a general promotional scheme for the various Indian organizations just being established. The need to provide a credit-rating service for the different Indian enterprises, to purchase certain business publications and obtain subscriptions to others, and to resume the purchase of samples of Indian craftwork essential for carrying on intensified business activities also were presented to further justify the appropriation increase. Under the board's reorganization plan adequate funds for travel expenses were essential. The production supervisor could be effective only if able to constantly confer with the managers of the numerous Indian organizations, and the merchandising supervisor would have to keep in contact with the retailers and also make several buying trips each year to arrange for the procurement of raw materials. During the first year, at least, the business manager would have to become acquainted with most of the organizations in the field in order to be able to act intelligently as a liaison officer between the divisions in the Indian Office in Chicago concerned with Indian arts and crafts.[35] The board knew from experience exactly what its needs would be.

Now the House subcommittee had to be convinced that the work of the Indian Arts and Crafts Board was essential. Citing the recent efforts of the decimated board staff to look out for the Indians in connection with the rulings of the War Production Board and the Office of Price Administration, Willard Beatty tried to show the House subcommittee how the board actually was contributing to the war effort. He explained that by helping the groups of the very young and those of the older Indians who could not shift to other skills, who could not be provided with equivalent work, and whose craft was a unique art contribution which also helped to keep them off the relief roles, the board was contributing to the survival of people who otherwise might require extensive federal relief expenditures. Such expenditures, he informed the apparently cost-conscious subcommittee, would involve putting $300,000 to $400,000 a year in the way of relief into the Navajo Reservation alone. When Jed Johnson asked Beatty how the board would spend the increase if it were granted, Beatty replied with what was by now considered to be the correct Pavlovian response: the money would be spent for salaries of people out in the field. Just to be sure, Johnson rephrased his question and asked: "This money would not be spent in the Washington Office?" After Beatty's reassuring negative answer, Johnson still persisted. "Or in Chicago?" he asked. "Nor in Chicago either, Mr. Chairman," Beatty added submissively. Without even being prompted, Beatty assured Johnson that d'Harnoncourt had retired as general manager of the board. In conclusion, Beatty pointed to the coming day when war industries would close down, Indians would return to the reservations, and everyone involved would realize the importance of having preserved this vital and permanent source of Indian income.[36]

Beatty's appeal before the House Appropriations Subcommittee for additional funds was almost fruitless. The only gains were in overtime pay and in the limitation on expenditures for personnel in the District of Columbia, which, now that d'Harnoncourt was off the payroll, was raised from $9,000 to $12,500. The subcommittee officially concluded that an increase in the current appropriation for "a non-war activity

291

should not receive consideration until after the war period." When the Senate subcommittee hearings began almost two months later, the board's efforts were very brief and to the point. Calling the 1944 reduction a most unfortunate cut, the board informed the subcommittee that at no time during the life of the Indian Arts and Crafts Board had the non-Indian demand for Indian arts and crafts equaled that of the last twelve months. During that time Indian artists had been dispersed as never before, and, lacking field employees, the board was not able to bring the buyers and the artists together to take advantage of the current interest, a step which might have resulted in long-term advantage to the Indians. The board stressed that if it failed at this time to secure for the Indians the markets which now were opening to them, it well may have lost for them a permanent economic opportunity that might be difficult to re-gain when cheap imported handcrafts again became abundantly avail-able. To assist the Indians to gain and to hold these markets would be of incalculable value, the board asserted. When Collier's turn came, he predicted that "after the war, arts and crafts are going to be a major factor in [the] Indian economy. The Board has achieved this result, and it is needed to sustain it." He revealed that all the board could do under the 1944 appropriation was to keep contact with the wholesale and retail outlets, clothing designers, and interior designers, and try to maintain contact with the field. Thus ended the shortest appropria-tion hearing in the almost eight years of the board's existence. Senator Hayden closed the hearing by remarking: "I think the committee un-derstands the situation."[37] No change was made in the House sub-committee report.

Individually motivated congressmen in the final analysis were imme-diately responsible for the disintegration and the near demise of the Indian Arts and Crafts Board. The failure to approve the use of the Bureau of the Budget designated funds for a relatively inexpensive yet vitally important organization rested on them alone. Drawing on the conflict over rapid and forced assimilation of the Indians into white society versus New Deal support for cultural pluralism and a liberal approach to national, racial, and ethnic backgrounds, the conservative, xenophobic, and isolationist congressmen used what unrest existed over federal participation in Indian affairs to mask their fear of a threat to what they considered to be traditional American ways. If we have to help the Indians, they believed, we should do so, not with a planned program, but by the long-tried and simple direct dole, a method, they seemed to forget, that actually exacerbated the Indian problem. Fear of foreign influence, emphasis on financial gains rather than on cultural preservation, rejection of specialized knowledge, and a selfish, parochial attitude toward the broad, liberal approaches to Indian cultural existence supported by New Deal Indian policy, all contained racist overtones. Desiring to let the Indians join the individualized American system of profit and loss, of sink or swim, and the sooner the better, the congressmen echoed the assimilationist views of the supporters of the American Indian Federation. In addition, their fear that outside influence and world turmoil could destroy America's cultural attainments created an attitude that blocked out any vision of a cultural democracy.

The difference in viewpoint between Collier and the chairman of the House Appropriations Subcommittee became open animosity in 1944. In a letter to the assistant commissioner of Indian affairs, William Zimmerman, Jed Johnson referred to Collier's and Ickes's "personal appeal and pernicious political activity" against him recently in Washington despite which he had won reelection. Johnson now darkly hinted at prosecution of Collier under the Hatch Act of 1939, which forbade political campaigning by federal officeholders below the policy-making echelon in the executive branch of the government. Collier told Zimmerman that Johnson was in error. While Johnson was an "unworthy member of Congress" and, through ignorance and selfishness, rather than active malice, was "an enemy of Indian welfare," Collier claimed he had engaged in no political activity related to Johnson. "Had I the power to relieve Congress, the Indians, and the country of the unhappy load imposed upon them by Mr. Johnson," Collier stated, "I would use the power. I do not have the power and have not tried to use it."[38]

Equally frustrated by the actions of the Senate Appropriations Subcommittee, Collier sought further understanding of its behavior. Suspicious over some of the activities of Albert Grorud, Senator Wheeler, and possibly Subcommittee Chairman Thomas, Collier consulted Ickes on the matter late in November and told him about a possible conspiracy to buy Indian lands in California and to resell them at a great profit to themselves. Although Collier assigned an Indian Office employee to investigate, nothing developed to warrant Collier's further attention.[39]

No doubt feeling as though he had been flailing at windmills, on 4 December 1944 Collier prepared a long letter to Ickes detailing his view of the current situation and his reasons for deciding to resign as commissioner. He began by defining New Deal Indian policy as a program directed toward "setting free the native genius of the Indian, enabling and helping the establishment of profound democracy among the Indians, transforming the economic situation of the Indians, and turning their life-tide from the direction of death to that of life." That policy, Collier observed, was understood and supported in Congress for a very few years. Then the practical success of those policies was sabotaged from within Congress.[40]

Collier placed the blame for this change squarely on the House Interior Department Appropriations Subcommittee. Specifically, he saw the problem stemming from the first year of the New Deal when the Senate directed the preparation of a modernized budget and appropriations system. According to Collier, this new arrangement would have eliminated the archaic system of hundreds of special appropriations and limitations and would have freed the Indian Office to use the appropriated funds in a flexible manner where they were needed. Instead, this modernized appropriations approach was blocked by the House Appropriations Subcommittee. Year by year, Collier continued, the funds that Congress intended in the Indian Reorganization Act of 1934 and the funds that the president, through the Bureau of the Budget, intended in his whole policy, were cut down and down by the House subcommittee. As an example among many, Collier pointed to "the extremely productive work of the Indian Arts and Crafts Board," which had been "starved nearly to death" in recent years. This sabotage by the subcommittee had become congressional policy, Collier believed, through perfunctory approval rather than responsible thinking, while even the director of the Bureau of the Budget considered these same actions "coercive upon the Budget."[41]

Collier expressed amazement that, even as the situation grew worse each year under the grinding action of an omnipotent subcommittee that "scorned and even hated the program of Indian regeneration," the

Indian Office had been able to increase its results year by year. He explained this phenomenon by citing the power and the genius of the policy itself. While he believed that the development of liberty and democracy for the Indians would move ahead in the long run, Collier was concerned that the potentialities of New Deal Indian policy and the productiveness of the Indian Office were diminished grievously and critically by the destructive control of the subcommittee whose actions Congress did not seem willing to correct. Also of primary consequence in Collier's considerations was the action of the Bureau of the Budget, which he believed was pursuing a long-range policy when it used the need for war agency space in Washington to compel the Indian Office to move to Chicago, a move that increased incalculably the handicaps and strains which already existed. Altogether, Collier concluded, the situation not only had stripped the Indian Office of funds but also of the authorities required if the policy of Indian self-regeneration was to go forward. He saw no hope that the House Committee on Appropriations as a whole would discipline its subcommittee, no hope that the House would discipline its appropriations committee, and no hope for an overthrow of the seniority system, the courtesy system, or the absolutism of the appropriations committee. Nothing except the "determined, sustained intervention of the President himself would avail," Collier believed, and he felt that at this time in the war the president could not make that effort and should not be asked to do so. Collier had determined that he personally was given wholly to the pursuit of aims which instinctively were viewed as alien or hostile by the very people in Congress whose approval was needed if the effort was to succeed.[42]

Ickes fully agreed with Collier's views and thought that his letter showed his real qualities. While Ickes attempted to dissuade Collier from retiring from the Indian Office, he privately expressed the belief that nothing would keep Collier from resigning, a step that he could not blame Collier for taking. Ickes openly admitted that the administration of Indian affairs had been taken over by the chairman of the House Appropriations Subcommittee in whose district were a number of Indians in whom the chairman was personally and politically interested. While Ickes did not name these Indians specifically, the direct inference was to former members of the now defunct anti-Collier, assimilationist organization, the American Indian Federation.[43]

Citing the same basic reasons he had presented to Ickes, Collier submitted his resignation to Roosevelt on 19 January 1945, effective with the appointment of a successor, in order to work toward ethnic democracy for the Indians of all nations in the Western Hemisphere. With his departure from the board on 30 April 1945, the first and most significant period in the history of the Indian Arts and Crafts Board came to an end.[44]

EPILOGUE

THE WORK OF THE Indian Arts and Crafts Board after 1945 varied with the amount of money available, yet the policy of helping the Indians to help themselves remained strong. René d'Harnoncourt and John Collier had provided a firm foundation for the future of Indian arts and crafts by emphasizing respect for Indian culture, a respect which time and changing conditions only strengthened. The board's responsibility never wavered or became tainted with special interests. Few government bodies could boast of such a record.

The years immediately following the war years were the most difficult. Earlier warnings that the work of the board had to be maintained in order to prepare for postwar Indian needs proved to be accurate. Wages from war work vanished. Dependency allotments from active service personnel dwindled and disappeared with the dismantling of the armed forces. The predicted downward trend in family income, which never had been adequate, took place, and the board lacked the experienced leadership and sufficient resources to provide the level of assistance needed. Ironically, the board did not use all of the funds that were appropriated and instead returned the balance to the Treasury Department. As late as 1948, the board's work still centered around attempts to rehabilitate and reestablish those producing groups that had ceased to operate during the war years and whose markets had been lost because the Indians were unable to supply the demand. Even under these hardships, arts and crafts sales by Indian cooperative enterprises generally increased except in Alaska where the departing service personnel had left a vacuum in the market.

With the appointment in 1951 of a full-time general manager, the board began once more to apply itself with determination and purpose. At the same time, appropriations increased. By 1954, near the peak of the government's efforts to terminate federal responsibility for the administration of Indian affairs, the Indian Arts and Crafts Board was ignoring administration policy and successfully carrying out its assigned tasks and even a few extra activities including museum administration.

Momentum continued to increase in the sixties as opposition to government termination policies developed. In 1960 and 1961, the board successfully pushed for the establishment of the Institute of American Indian Arts in Santa Fe for the purpose of providing innovative, heritage-centered instruction for young Indian artists from all parts of the country. Expansion of the board's staff took place along with increased emphasis on technical assistance in production and marketing. Public recognition of the importance of Indian arts and crafts and the work of the board was apparent as six states passed additional Indian arts and crafts protective legislation between 1955 and 1965. Federal recognition of that importance came in a display of both historic and contemporary Indian arts and crafts under the auspices of the Indian Arts and Crafts Board in the United States Federal Pavilion at Expo '67 in Montreal.

Congressional attitudes came to exhibit greater understanding of the purposes for the board, and the appropriations subcommittees fully supported the board's rapidly expanding activities. Increasing sales of Indian arts and crafts gave evidence that the faith that d'Harnoncourt had had in their future was not misplaced. Why the concept was so difficult for certain congressmen to accept earlier may be explained by the nature and force of their individualism. Time proved their error.

D'Harnoncourt, Collier, and all associated with the formative years of the board would be proud to see that the product of their vision continued to provide the assistance they unselfishly began under New Deal Indian policy.

APPENDIX

THE INDIAN ARTS AND CRAFTS BOARD ACT
27 AUGUST 1935

An Act To promote the development of Indian arts and crafts and to create a board to assist therein, and for other purposes.

Be it enacted by the Senate and House of Representatives of the United States of America in Congress assembled, That a board is hereby created in the Department of the Interior to be known as "Indian Arts and Crafts Board," and hereinafter referred to as the Board. The Board shall be composed of five commissioners, who shall be appointed by the Secretary of the Interior as soon as possible after the passage of this Act and shall continue in office, two for a term of two years, one for a term of three years, and two for a term of four years from the date of their appointment, the term of each to be designated by the Secretary of the Interior, but their successors shall be appointed for a term of four years except that any person chosen to fill a vacancy shall be appointed for the unexpired term of the commissioner whom he succeeds. Both public officers and private citizens shall be eligible for membership on the Board. The Board shall elect one of the commissioners as chairman. One or two vacancies on the Board shall not impair the right of the remaining commissioners to exercise all the powers of the Board.

The commissioners shall serve without compensation: Provided, That each Commissioner shall be reimbursed for all actual expenses, including travel expenses, subsistence and office overhead, which the Board shall certify to have been incurred as properly incidental to the performance of his duties as a member of the Board.

SEC. 2. It shall be the function and the duty of the Board to promote the economic welfare of the Indian tribes and the Indian wards of the Government through the development of Indian arts and crafts and the expansion of the market for the products of Indian art and craftsmanship. In the execution of this function the Board shall have the

299

following powers: (a) To undertake market research to determine the best opportunity for the sale of various products; (b) to engage in technical research and give technical advice and assistance; (c) to engage in experimentation directly or through selected agencies; (d) to correlate and encourage the activities of the various governmental and private agencies in the field; (e) to offer assistance in the management of operating groups for the furtherance of specific projects; (f) to make recommendations to appropriate agencies for loans in furtherance of the production and sale of Indian products; (g) to create Government trade marks of genuineness and quality for Indian products and the products of particular Indian tribes or groups; to establish standards and regulations for the use of such trade marks; to license corporations, associations, or individuals to use them; and to charge a fee for their use; to register them in the United States Patent Office without charge; (h) to employ executive officers, including a general manager, and such other permanent and temporary personnel as may be found necessary, and prescribe the authorities, duties, responsibilities, and tenure and fix the compensation of such officers and other employees: *Provided*, That the Classification Act of 1923 as amended, shall be applicable to all permanent employees except executive officers, and that all employees other than executive officers shall be appointed in accordance with the civil-service laws from lists of eligibles to be supplied by the Civil Service Commission; (i) as a Government agency to negotiate and execute in its own name contracts with operating groups to supply management, personnel, and supervision at cost, and to negotiate and execute in its own name such other contracts and to carry on such other business as may be necessary for the accomplishment of the duties and purposes of the Board: *Provided*, That nothing in the foregoing enumeration of powers shall be construed to authorize the Board to borrow or lend money or to deal in Indian goods.

SEC. 3. The Board shall prescribe from time to time rules and regulations governing the conduct of its business and containing such provisions as it may deem appropriate for the effective execution and administration of the powers conferred upon it by this Act: *Provided*, That before prescribing any procedure for the disbursement of money the Board shall advise and consult with the General Accounting Office:

Provided further, That all rules and regulations proposed by the Board shall be submitted to the Secretary of the Interior and shall become effective upon his approval.

SEC. 4. There is hereby authorized to be appropriated out of any sums in the Treasury not otherwise appropriated such sums as may be necessary to defray the expenses of the Board and carry out the purposes and provisions of this Act. All income derived by the Board from any source shall be covered into the Treasury of the United States and shall constitute a special fund which is hereby appropriated and made available until expended for carrying out the purposes and provisions of this Act. Out of the funds available to it at any time the Board may authorize such expenditures, consistent with the provisions of this Act, as it may determine to be necessary for the accomplishment of the purposes and objective of this Act.

SEC. 5. Any person who shall counterfeit or colorably imitate any Government trade mark used or devised by the Board as provided in section 2 of this Act, or shall, except as authorized by the Board, affix any such Government trade mark, or shall knowingly, willfully, and corruptly affix any reproduction, counterfeit, copy, or colorable imitation thereof upon any products, Indian or otherwise, or to any labels, signs, prints, packages, wrappers, or receptacles intended to be used upon or in connection with the sale of such products, or any person who shall knowingly make any false statement for the purpose of obtaining the use of any such Government trade mark, shall be guilty of a misdemeanor, and upon conviction thereof shall be enjoined from further carrying on the act or acts complained of and shall be subject to a fine not exceeding $2,000, or imprisonment not exceeding six months, or both such fine and imprisonment.

SEC. 6. Any person who shall willfully offer or display for sale any goods, with or without any Government trade mark, as Indian products or Indian products of a particular Indian tribe or group, resident within the United States or the Territory of Alaska, when such person knows such goods are not Indian products or are not Indian products of the particular Indian tribe or group, shall be guilty of a misdemeanor and be subject to a fine not exceeding $2,000 or imprisonment not exceeding six months, or both such fine and imprisonment.

It shall be the duty of each district attorney, to whom the Board shall report in writing any violation of the provisions of this section which has occurred within his jurisdiction, to cause appropriate proceedings to be commenced and prosecuted in the proper courts of the United States for the enforcement of the penalties herein provided.

SOURCE: *U.S. Statutes at Large*, 49:891–93.

ABBREVIATIONS
USED IN THE NOTES

AAIA   Association on American Indian Affairs, Princeton University

BCIM   Bureau of Catholic Indian Missions Records, Marquette University

BIA   Records of the Bureau of Indian Affairs, Central Classified Files, National Archives, Record Group 75

BIC *Report*   *Report of the Board of Indian Commissioners*

CIA *Report*   *Report of the Commissioner of Indian Affairs*

DC   District of Columbia

HLI   Harold L. Ickes Papers, Library of Congress

IACB   Records of the Indian Arts and Crafts Board, National Archives, Record Group 435

IRA   Indian Rights Association Papers, Microfilm

JC   John Collier Papers, Yale University

LM   *Proceedings of the Lake Mohonk Conference of Friends of the Indian*

NA   National Archives

OCIA   Records of the Office of the Commissioner of Indian Affairs, Office File of Commissioner John Collier, National Archives, Record Group 75

OSI   Records of the Office of the Secretary of the Interior, Central Classified Files, National Archives, Record Group 48

RA   Rockefeller Archives, Upper Tarrytown, New York

RD   *Reports and Documents Concerning the Activities of the Indian Arts and Crafts Board*, Library of Congress

RDOH   René d'Harnoncourt, Oral History, Columbia University

RG   Record Group

SI *Report*   *Report of the Secretary of the Interior*

NOTES

Chapter 1: Harbingers

1. CIA *Report*, 1863, pp. 105–6; CIA *Report*, 1885, p. 155; CIA *Report*, 1887, pp. lxix, 172.
2. LM, 1890, p. 20.
3. Ibid., p. 21.
4. Ibid., p. 47.
5. LM, 1894, pp. 71, 74.
6. LM, 1897, p. 62; LM, 1899, p. 80.
7. CIA *Report*, 1900, p. 515; LM, 1901, p. 27.
8. LM, 1901, pp. vi, 29–30.
9. Ibid., p. 28.
10. CIA *Report*, 1903, p. 11.
11. CIA *Report*, 1904, p. 405; "Letter to the Editor on the Subject of American Indian Basket-work," *International Studio* 20 (August 1903):144–46.
12. CIA *Report*, 1905, p. 12.
13. Ibid., pp. 12, 271.
14. LM, 1908, p. 16.
15. Robert G. Valentine to Mrs. A. W. Trenholm, 3 June 1912, BIA, box 1211, file 913.1; CIA *Report*, 1912, p. 36; Charles L. Davis to the Commissioner of Indian Affairs, 21 December 1912, BIA, box 1212, file 915.
16. Davis to the Commissioner of Indian Affairs, 21 December 1912, BIA, box 1212, file 915.
17. Davis to the Superintendents in the Navajo Country, 25 October 1912; Davis to the Commissioner of Indian Affairs, 21 December 1912, BIA, box 1212, file 915.
18. Davis to the Commissioner of Indian Affairs, 21 December 1912.
19. Edgar B. Meritt to George Southerland, 13 February 1914, BIA, box 1212, file 915.
20. Meritt to Walter Runke, 17 February 1915, BIA, box1212, file 915; CIA *Report*, 1914, pp. 36–37; CIA *Report*, 1915, p. 54.
21. CIA *Report*, 1917, p. 39.

22. Clipping from the *Albuquerque Journal*, 6 March 1917, BIA, box 1212, file 915.

23. CIA *Report*, 1916, p. 32; clipping from the *Albuquerque Journal*, 6 March 1917, BIA, box 1212, file 915.

24. CIA *Report*, 1916, p. 32; CIA *Report*, 1917, p. 39; unsigned, "Memorandum for the Commissioner of Indian Affairs, [1917]," BIA, box 1212, file 915.

25. The CIA *Report*, 1917, p. 116, listed the 1913 Indian income from native industries as $1,316,298 and the 1917 Indian income from native industries as $1,315,112. Unsigned, "Memorandum for the Commissioner of Indian Affairs, [1917]," BIA, box 1212, file 915; CIA *Report*, 1918, p. 60; CIA *Report*, 1920, p. 113.

26. *Annual Report of the Indian Industries League, 1915*, BIA, box 1212, file 915. Colonel John S. Lockwood of Boston was president and Daniel Smiley, the younger half-brother of the late Lake Mohonk Conference founder Albert K. Smiley, Matthew K. Sniffen, Herbert Welsh, Warren K. Moorehead, Francis LaFlesche, and Charles A. Eastmen were among the thirteen vice-presidents of the 1915 Indian Industries League.

27. Roy T. Bishop to Senator George E. Chamberlain, 9 May 1915; Leo Crane to the Commissioner of Indian Affairs, 11 June 1915; Meritt to Chamberlain, 12 October 1915, BIA, box 1212, file 915.

28. CIA *Report*, 1920, p. 113.

29. Natalie Curtis, "Our Native Craftsmen," *The Southern Workman* 48 (August 1919):389, 396. Natalie Curtis was the daughter of Edward Curtis, the premier photographer of American Indians.

30. Ernest L. Blumenschein and Bert G. Phillips, "Appreciation of Indian Art," *El Palacio* 6 (No. 12, 1919):178–79.

31. Curtis, "Our Native Craftsmen," p. 389.

32. Mary Austin to Franklin K. Lane, 16 January 1919, OSI, box 1423, file 5–3.

33. Edgar L. Hewett, "Native American Artists," a paper read at the Ann Arbor, Michigan, meeting of the Archaeological Institute of America, 29 December 1921, *Art and Archaeology: The Arts throughout the Ages* 13 (March 1922):105.

34. Ibid., pp. 103, 109.

35. Edgar Holger Cahill, "America Has Its 'Primitives,' " *International Studio* 75 (March 1922):80–81, 83.

36. CIA *Report*, 1922, p. 47; "Indian Shop in New York," *El Palacio* 13 (No. 12, 1922):160; "First Annual Exhibition of Indian Arts and Crafts under the Auspices of the Museum of New Mexico, September 1922," *El Palacio* 12 (No. 9, 1922):123–24.

37. Melville Clyde Kelly, "Free the Indians and Serve America," *Congressional Record* booklet of the House speech on 4 August 1921 (Government Printing Office, 1921), pp. 9–10. For a full discussion of the conflict in Indian

Notes

affairs between reformists and the United States government from 1920 to 1933 see Kenneth R. Philp, *John Collier's Crusade for Indian Reform, 1920–1954* (Tucson: University of Arizona Press, 1977). Lawrence C. Kelly's *The Navajo Indians and Federal Indian Policy, 1900–1935* (Tucson: University of Arizona Press, 1968) presents the major controversies concerning government Indian policy as it related to the Navajos.

38. CIA *Report*, 1923, pp. 17–18, 20–21.

39. CIA *Report*, 1924, pp. 13–14.

40. National Association on Indian Affairs, "Booklet Number Two, [1923]," Microfilm No. 39280, Library of Congress, Washington, DC; "Announcement of Purposes of the American Indian Defense Association, Incorporated," 21 May 1923, JC, part I, series IV, box 23, folder 007. The October 1927 *American Indian Life*, a newsletter published by the American Indian Defense Association, stated that that organization had offices operating in eight cities across the country: New York City; San Francisco, Santa Barbara, Los Angeles, and Pasadena, California; Salt Lake City, Utah; and Oshkosh and Wauwatosa, Wisconsin. Until this time, the most important reform organization was the missionary-oriented Indian Rights Association, which was founded in 1882 in Philadelphia by Henry S. Pancoast and Herbert Welsh.

41. John Collier, "The American Congo," *The Survey* 50 (1 August 1923): 467. For a personal recollection of the Indian reform movement see John Collier, *From Every Zenith: A Memoir* (Denver: Sage Books, 1963).

42. Hubert Work, "Indian Policies: Comments on the Resolutions of the Advisory Council on Indian Affairs, June 1924," booklet (Washington, DC: Government Printing Office, 1924), pp. iv–v, BCIM.

43. Ibid., pp. 1–16.

44. Ibid., p. iv.

45. U.S., Congress, House, Committee on Appropriations, *Hearings before a subcommittee of the House Committee on Appropriations on H.R. 9136,* 70th Cong., 1st sess., 1927, pp. 188–90. The director of the Industrial Section was Harry W. Shipe.

46. Popularly known as the "Cowboy Professor," Edward Everett Dale was in the cattle industry prior to the advent of the homesteaders. He wrote his doctoral dissertation under Frederick Jackson Turner at Harvard on the topic of the cattle industry in the Southwest. Lewis Meriam to William F. Willoughby, 2 November 1926; Meriam to Willoughby, 2 May 1927, Private File of Lewis Meriam, Institute for Government Research, Brookings Institution, Washington, DC. For biographical information about Dale, some of his published articles, and an excerpt from his unpublished autobiography, see Arrell M. Gibson, ed., *Frontier Historian: The Life and Work of Edward Everett Dale* (Norman: University of Oklahoma Press, 1975). Lewis Meriam et al., *The Problem of Indian Administration*, Institute for Government Research, Studies in Administration (Baltimore: Johns Hopkins Press, 1928), pp. 372, 648, 651.

Later, the Institute for Government Research also was known as the Brookings Institution, Washington, DC.

47. Ibid., pp. 651–52.
48. Ibid., pp. 646, 412.
49. Ibid., pp. 652, 617, 616.
50. Ibid., p. 652.
51. Ibid., pp. 533, 125, 652, 651.
52. Ibid., pp. 439, 448, 5, 510. The Meriam Report tabulations were based on the latest figures available at the Indian Office.

Chapter 2: Controversy

1. Collier, "Hammering at the Prison Door," *The Survey* 60 (July 1928):389.
2. SI *Report*, 1928, pp. 20–21; "Income of Indians from Native Industries by States for the Fiscal Year Ended 30 June 1928," OSI, box 1423.
3. Ebert K. Burlew to Hans Paul Caemmerer, 10 October 1928; Caemmerer to Burlew, 29 October 1928, OSI, box 1423, file 53; "Department of the Interior Press Release, 28 February 1929"; Caemmerer to Burlew, 7 June 1929, IACB, box 2, file 910.
4. William A. Kinnan to Burlew, 18 June 1929, IACB, box 2, file 910.
5. Kinnan to Burlew, [June 1929], OSI, box 1423, file 53.
6. Herbert Hoover, "Address before the Gridiron Club, Willard Hotel, Washington, DC, 14 December 1929," vol. 1, pp. 472–73; "Address before the Conference of Business Leaders, Chamber of Commerce of the United States, 5 December 1929," vol. 1, pp. 453–56; "Address before the Fifty-sixth Annual Convention of the American Bankers' Association, Cleveland, Ohio, 2 October 1930," vol. 2, pp. 399–400; "Radio Address from the White House on Lincoln's Birthday, 12 February 1931," vol. 3, pp. 71–76; "Address at the Dinner of the Indiana Republican Editorial Association, Indianapolis, 15 June 1931," vol. 3, pp. 306–7, *Public Papers of the Presidents of the United States: Herbert Hoover: Containing the Public Messages, Speeches, and Statements of the President* (Washington, DC:Government Printing Office, 1977). For a full discussion of the Hoover philosophy of governemnt see Ellis W. Hawley, "Herbert Hoover, the Commerce Secretariat, and the Vision of an 'Associative State,' 1921–1928," *Journal of American History* 61 (June 1974):116–40, and Ellis W. Hawley et al., *Herbert Hoover and the Crisis of American Capitalism* (Cambridge, Mass.: Schenkman, 1973).
7. Chester E. Faris to the Commissioner of Indian Affairs, 12 July 1929, IACB, box 2, file 910. Accordingly, the seed was planted. A year later, Indian trader H. Creasy Master of Zuni, New Mexico, wrote the special commissioner to the Navajos, Herbert J. Hagerman, suggesting "an association formed of Indian traders and dealers together with any [one] interested in the advancement of Indian crafts." The superintendent of the Zuni Indian Agency echoed Master's suggestion. Hagerman responded encouragingly and identified the

purposes in formulating an Indian trader association to be to raise the standard of Indian goods, to educate the public, and to protect the public from factory-made goods as opposed to the genuine Indian handcrafts. Yet not until August 1931 did the traders officially organize after Hagerman saw how their work and that of the privately supported Indian Arts Fund of Santa Fe might be joined if both adopted the same minimum standards for Indian arts and crafts. The new United Indian Traders Association saw its principal object to be combating the competition of machine-manufactured Indian jewelry which was adding to the financial problems the traders faced as part of the national economic crisis in 1931. H. Creasy Master to Herbert J. Hagerman, 17 April 1931; G. A. Trotter to Hagerman, 4 August 1931; Hagerman to Trotter, 19 August 1931, IACB, box 3; M. R. Tillotson to the Director, National Park Service, 4 November 1931, IACB, box 1, file 910.

8. Collier to William Atherton Du Puy, 20 July 1929, BIA, box 1203, file 900; "Minutes of the American Indian Defense Association Meeting in New York on 19 May 1925," JC, part I, series IV, box 25, folder 22; Collier to Charles J. Rhoads, 21 July 1929, BIA, box 1203, file 900.

9. Collier to James W. Young, 8 January 1926; Betty Young to Collier, 11 February 1927, JC, part I, series I, box 11, folder 219.

10. Collier to Charles Fahy, 23 January 1928, part I, series I, box 3, folder 54; Collier to Young, 1 February 1928, part I, series I, box 11, folder 219; Charles deYoung Elkus to Collier, 6 February 1928, JC, part I, series I, box 2, folder 36.

11. Young to Rhoads, 1 September 1929, BIA, box 1203, file 900.

12. Ibid.

13. Ibid.

14. Young to Collier, 22 September 1929, JC, part I, series I, box 11, folder 219; Young to Rhoads, 30 September 1929, BIA, box 1203, file 900.

15. Rhoads to Young, 10 October 1929, JC, part I, series I, box 11, folder 219.

16. J. Lloyd Ambrose to Rhoads, 28 October 1929; Rhoads to Ambrose, 6 November 1929; Rhoads to Young, 6 November 1929, BIA, box 1203, file 900.

17. SI *Report*, 1929, pp. 14–15, 35.

18. Collier to Rhoads, 6 December 1929; C. L. Walker to Rhoads, 26 November 1929; Rhoads to Young, [November 1929]; Walker to Rhoads, 26 November 1929, BIA, box 1203, file 900.

19. Collier to Young, 25 January 1930; Young to Collier, 29 January 1930, JC, part I, series I, box 11, folder 220; Collier to Ray Lyman Wilbur, 20 February 1930, OSI, part I, box 1423; Meriam to Guy Moffett, 25 January 1932, RA, Spellman Fund, series 4, box 2, folder 196; Collier, "Confidential Bulletin," American Indian Defense Association, 4 December 1929, JC, part I, series IV, box 23, folder 9.

20. Collier, "The Immediate Tasks of the American Indian Defense As-

sociation, Inc.," 10 December 1929, p. 4, JC, part I, series IV, box 24, folder 16.

21. "Outline of Proposed Indian Cooperative Marketing Board," BIA, box 1203, file 900.

22. Hagerman to Rhoads, 10 January 1930, BIA, box 1203, file 900. Rhoads gave Young a personal letter of introduction in which he stated that Young was making a study for Rhoads of the marketing of Indian arts and crafts and requested all of the information and help possible. Rhoads to Young, 5 December 1929, BIA, box 1203, file 900.

23. Faris to Rhoads, 14 January 1930; Ambrose to Rhoads, 20 February 1930; Collier to Rhoads, 10 January 1930, BIA, box 1203, file 900.

24. "A New National Enterprise in Indian Arts and Crafts," American Indian Life 15 (January 1930):6.

25. Collier telegram to Young, 31 January 1930, JC, part I, series I, box 11, folder 220.

26. Collier, "Very Confidential Bulletin," American Indian Defense Association, 5 February 1930, JC, part I, series IV, box 23, folder 9; Young to Collier, 29 January 1930, JC, part I, series I, box 11, folder 220.

27. H.R. 9719 and S. 3520, 71st Cong., 2d sess., (1930).

28. Ulric J. Mengert to Matthew K. Sniffen, 12 December 1929, BIA, box 1203, file 900.

29. Collier to Sniffen, 14 December 1929, BIA, box 1203, file 900. Collier cited examples of the government operating lumber mills, flour mills, and tribal herds, licensing Indian traders, and conducting schools and hospitals, all exclusively for Indian use. Complicated banking operations and the sale and rental of Indian property provided additional examples of such Indian-centered activity. All the government now would be doing, Collier explained, would be licensing a corporation and giving it the monopoly control of a certificate.

30. Meriam to Moffett, 25 January 1932, RA, Spellman Fund, series 4, box 2, folder 196.

31. Collier, "Confidential Bulletin of the American Indian Defense Association, 11 February 1930," JC, part I, series IV, box 23, folder 9. Collier's description of Rhoads's muddled outlook rang true, for Rhoads privately admitted his confusion in a conversation with Edward Everett Dale, formerly of the Meriam survey staff, after some months of effort to carry out the mandate of the Meriam Report. "The appointment as Commissioner of an experienced business executive with little knowledge of Indian affairs, and in consequence, no preconceived ideas might be excellent in theory but not so good in practice," Rhoads reportedly told Dale. He declared that he was appalled by the intricate nature of the Indian situation and the mass of detailed information necessary to arrive at even a reasonable understanding of all its complexities. Edward Everett Dale, The Indians of the Southwest: A Century of Development under the United States (Norman: University of Oklahoma Press, 1949), p. 155.

32. Collier to Young, 14 February 1930, JC, part I, series I, box 11, folder 220.

33. Collier, "Suggestions for the Interior Department Report on the Frazier-Leavitt Bill, 14 February 1930," JC, part I, series I, box 11, folder 220.

34. Percy Jackson to Lynn J. Frazier, 17 February 1930; Benjamin V. Cohen to Collier, 19 February 1930; Collier to Frazier, 19 February 1930, BIA, box 1203, file 900.

35. Other founding members of the Indian Arts Fund of Santa Fe included the following: Frank G. Applegate, artist, Santa Fe; Kenneth M. Chapman, curator of the State Museum, Santa Fe; Andrew Dasburg, artist, Santa Fe; Samuel J. Guernsey, curator of archaeology, Peabody Museum, Harvard University; Meredith Hare, Huntington, Long Island; Irene Lewisohn, New York; James H. MacMilan, Spanish and Indian Trading Company, Santa Fe; Margaret McKittrick, chairman, New Mexico Association on Indian Affairs; Harry P. Mera, co-founder of the Indian Arts Fund; Sylvanus G. Morley, archaeologist, Carnegie Institution, Washington, DC; B. J. O. Nordfelt, artist, Santa Fe; Mrs. Richard Pfaffle, Santa Fe; Marie Robinson, Santa Fe; James L. Seligman, Old Santa Fe Trading Post; Mrs. Joseph Lindon Smith, New York; Charles Springer, Cimarron, New Mexico; Nathan B. Stern, New York; and Mrs. Maurice Wertheim, New York. Amon Carter Museum of Western Art, *Quiet Triumph: Forty Years With the Indian Arts Fund, Santa Fe* (Santa Fe: Indian Arts Fund, 1966), p. iv. Austin to Collier, 18–20 February 1930, JC, part I, series I, box 1, folder 8; Young to Collier, 25 February 1930, JC, part I, series I, box 11, folder 220.

36. Young to Collier, 25 February 1930; Collier to Young, 27 February 1930, JC, part I, series I, box 11, folder 220; Trotter to Rhoads, 6 March 1930, BIA, box 1203, file 900.

37. The problem was evident in places other than just the Southwest. Rose Wheelock of the Catawba Indian Reservation, Catawba, South Carolina, told a 1930 Senate investigating subcommittee of the Committee on Indian Affairs that if the Indian artists had a market somewhere they could do better. The limited tourist demand for pottery in South Carolina evaporated in the winter when times were hard and the Indians' needs were greater. When the pottery was taken to the merchants, it had to be sold "for nearly nothing in order to sell it at all." Concerned superintendents and Indian traders reflected the general feeling of anxiety over the worsening plight of the Indian craftsmen. The proprietor of the Leupp, Arizona, trading post, Stanton K. Borum, pleaded with the Western Navajo Indian Agency superintendent to join everyone together to do something about the imitation Indian jewelry that was floooding the market at the expense of the authentic Indian product. U.S., Congress, Senate, Committee on Indian Affairs, *Hearings before a subcommittee of the Senate Committee on Indian Affairs on S. 263, a bill to investigate Indian affairs*, 71st Cong., 1st sess., 1930, pt. 16, pp. 7563–64; Stanton K. Borum to Walker, 16 March 1930, BIA, box 1203, file 900.

38. Burlew to the Director, Bureau of the Budget, 5 March 1930; J. Clawson Roop to Wilbur, 21 March 1930, BIA, box 1203, file 900.

39. Collier to Elkus, 31 March 1930, JC, part I, series I, box 2, folder 38; Collier telegram to Young, 3 April 1930, JC, part I, series I, box 11, folder 220.

40. Collier to Elkus, 14 April 1930, part I, series I, box 2, folder 38; Meriam to Moffett, 25 January 1932, RA, Spellman Fund, series 4, box 2, folder 196; Collier to Elkus, 15 April 1930, JC, part I, series I, box 2, folder 38.

41. Austin to Collier, 6 May 1930, JC, part I, series I, box 1, folder 8; Robert T. Lansdale to Rhoads, 9 April 1930, BIA, box 1203, file 900.

42. Austin to Collier, 13 April 1930; Austin to Collier, 6 May 1930, JC, part I, series I, box 1, folder 8.

43. Unsigned letters from traders in Amelia E. White to Rhoads, 10 April 1930; White to Scott Leavitt, 10 April 1930, BIA, box 1203, file 900.

44. Rhoads, "Memorandum for the Secretary, 1 March 1930," BIA, box 1203, file 900; Collier to Young, 18 March 1930, JC, part I, series I, box 11, folder 220; Elkus to Rhoads, 12 April 1930; Rhoads to Elkus, 19 April 1930, JC, part I, series I, box 2, folder 38.

45. Collier to Austin, 18 April 1930, JC, part I, series I, box 1, folder 8.

46. Austin to Wilbur, 19 April 1930, OSI, box 1423.

47. Ibid.; Austin to Rhoads, 26 April 1930, BIA, box 1203, file 900.

48. Austin to Collier, 22 April 1930, JC, part I, series I, box 1, folder 8. Collier reproached Austin for "invidious" language and then three weeks later surprisingly sent five dollars to Austin to enroll the American Indian Defense Association in the Indian Arts Fund and diplomatically asked for any further "relevant remarks." Collier to Austin, 25 April 1930, BIA, box 1203, file 900; Collier to Austin, 12 May 1930, JC, part I, series I, box 1, folder 8.

49. S. J. Res. 173, 71st Cong., 2d sess., (1930).

50. Indian Rights Association, "New Opportunities For Indians," pamphlet, IRA, Historical Society of Pennsylvania (Glen Rock, N. J.: Microfilming Corporation of America, 1975), reel 103, plate C27, p. 13.

51. Young to Rhoads, 28 April 1930, BIA, box 1203, file 900.

52. Young to Collier, 3 May 1930; Collier to Young, 8 May 1930, JC, part I, series I, box 11, folder 220.

53. Immediate problems included the following: preventing the starvation of Indian children, furnishing them with reasonably adequate clothing, putting into effect elementary social service measures, curbing brutal treatment such as the flogging of children, establishing the right of tribal groups reasonably to assert themselves in matters affecting their tribes, and the less immediate yet more far-reaching matters of placing the reclamation of Indian lands on a reorganized basis and lifting from Indian shoulders the more than $3,000,000 of crushing debt that the American Indian Defense Association believed had been unjustly placed upon them by the government. Haven Emerson and the Board of Directors of the American Indian Defense Association

to Wilbur, 6 May 1930, in "The Association's National Board Addresses Secretary Wilbur"; Wilbur to Emerson, 7 May 1930, in "Secretary Wilbur Replies to the Board"; Emerson to Wilbur, 9 May 1930, in "Dr. Emerson Replies to Secretary Wilbur"; American Indian Defense Association Board of Directors to Wilbur, 27 May 1930, in "The National Board Replies to Secretary Wilbur," *American Indian Life* 16 (July 1930):20, 22–25.

54. Collier to Young, 12 May 1930, JC, part I, series I, box 11, folder 220.

55. American Indian Defense Association, "The Emergency in Indian Arts and Crafts," 10 November 1930 (mimeographed), BIA, box 1203, file 900. Reports from traders expressed this same concern for the Navajos. The Navajo rugs were cheaper than they had been for many years. The low market price for wool had forced the Navajos to weave their wool and thereby had contributed to an oversupply of rugs. One trader's concern drove him to write Scattergood requesting clean, discarded clothing "which may still be of service to some poor Navajo and his family." The trader, Lloyd Ambrose of the Crownpoint Trading Company, promised to see that "some worthy Navajo gets your package on Chrisitmas Day." The superintendent of the Eastern Navajo Agency, Samuel F. Stacher, also stressed the bleak outlook facing the Navajos when he suggested to Rhoads that he ask all civic organizations, such as the Boy Scouts, Red Cross, 4-H Clubs, Campfire Girls, and the Federated Women's Clubs, to purchase at least one or more Navajo blankets simply "as something special." If each branch brought one blanket, thousands would be sold, Stacher reasoned, and this would give the blanket industry an impetus, for at the present time few were being made "as no one wants to buy." In the depth of winter, when Chester Faris, the Southwest district superintendent, asked Rhoads to do something to find a wider market for Indian arts and crafts, Rhoads replied that he believed "the new traders' organization might find it practicable to do something of this kind. [It was] not practicable for [the] Indian Service to do it." Ambrose to J. Henry Scattergood, 15 November 1930, BIA, box 1203, file 900; Samuel F. Stacher to Rhoads, 1 November 1930; Rhoads to Faris, 6 February 1931, IACB, box 1.

56. "Indian Trading Posts in Eastern Cities," *The School Arts Magazine* 30 (March 1931):480; "Indian Trading Post, Inc.," prospectus, [1930].

57. Fred Leighton to Rhoads, 26 November 1930; Rhoads to Leighton, 15 December 1930, IACB, box 1.

58. Young to Collier, 4 November 1930; Young to Collier, 20 November 1930, JC, part I, series I, box 11, folder 220; Leighton to Collier, 15 September 1933, JC, part II, series I, box 8, folder 010-0205.

59. Rhoads, "Memorandum for Mr. Scott, 29 December 1930," BIA, box 1203, file 900.

60. White to Rhoads, 23 June 1930, BIA, box 1203, file 900; Oliver LaFarge to Rhoads, 7 December 1931, IACB, box 1; White to J. Carson Ryan, 16 February 1931; C. H. Danforth to Wilbur, 3 March 1931; Lansdale, "Memoran-

dum for Rhoads and Scattergood, 19 March 1931"; Scattergood to Lansdale, 20 March 1931; Margaret McKittrick to Ryan, 6 November 1931, BIA, box 1203, file 900. For a detailed biography of LaFarge see D'Arcy McNickle, *Indian Man: A Life of Oliver LaFarge* (Bloomington: Indiana Unviersity Press, 1971).
  61. SI *Report*, 1930, p. 60.

Chapter 3: Essays

1. Faris to McKittrick, 17 June 1930, BIA, box 1203, file 900; U.S., Congress, Senate, Committee on Indian Affairs, *Hearings before a subcommittee of the Senate Committee on Indian Affairs on S. 416, Survey of the Conditions of the Indians of the United States*, 71st Cong., 3d sess., 1931, part 18, p. 9718.
  2. Senate, *Hearings on S. 416*, 71st Cong., 3d sess., 1931, part 18, p. 9686.
  3. Ibid., p. 9135.
  4. Ibid., pp. 10216–25.
  5. Ibid., pp. 8969–70.
  6. Ibid., p. 9721.
  7. Ibid., pp. 10211, 9555, 8993–94, 9722.
  8. Collier to Young, 29 May 1931; Young to Collier, 2 September 1931, JC, part I, series I, box 11, folder 221.
  9. Collier to Young, 18 January 1932, JC, part I, series I, box 11, folder 221; S. 3511, 72d Cong., 1st sess. (1932); Young to Collier, 13 January 1932; Young to Collier, 21 January 1932, JC, part I, series I, box 11, folder 221.
  10. Rhoads, "Memorandum for the Secretary, [1932]"; Scattergood, "Memorandum for the Secretary, [1932]," BIA, box 1203, file 900.
  11. Joseph M. Dixon to Frazier, 14 February 1933, BIA, box 1203, file 900.
  12. Scattergood to American Arts Exposition Corporation, 22 October 1930, IACB, box 1, file 047; "Amelia Elizabeth White Donates Her Collection of Indian Art to the People," *Art Digest (Arts Magazine)* 12 (15 February 1938):12; Rhoads to White, 3 November 1930; White to Rhoads, 19 February 1931, IACB, box 1, file 047.
  13. White to Rhoads, 23 January 1931; Rhoads to White, 27 January 1931, IACB, box 1, file 047.
  14. Blueprints by John Mead Howells; "Official Guide of the Third International Antiques Exposition at Grand Central Palace, New York City, 27 February to 7 March 1931"; White to Rhoads, 11 February 1931, IACB, box 1, file 047.
  15. Rhoads to White, 4 April 1931; George W. Harper to the Indian Office, 10 March 1932; Rhoads to Harper, 15 May 1932, IACB, box 1, file 047.
  16. "Editorial," *New York Times*, 1 December 1931, p. 28; Frederick Webb Hodge, Herbert J. Spinden, and Oliver LaFarge, eds., *Introduction to Ameri-*

can Indian Art: To Accompany the First Exposition of American Indian Art Selected Entirely with Consideration of Esthetic Value (New York: Exposition of Indian Tribal Arts, Inc., 1931; reprint ed., Glorieta, New Mexico: Rio Grande Press, 1970), p. 9.

17. Wilbur to White, 20 November 1931, OSI, box 1423, file 5–3; Hodge et al., *Introducton to American Indian Art*, pp. 65, 61.

18. Walter Pach, "The Indian Tribal Arts," *New York Times*, 22 November 1931, sec. 8, p. 13. See also Eunice Fuller Barnhard, "Indian Art Comes into Its Own," *New York Times*, 29 November 1931, sec. 5, pp. 12–13, and "Native American Art: An Editorial," *New York Times*, 1 December 1931, p. 28.

19. Ralph Flint, "Tribal Arts of the Indian Now on Exhibition," *Art News* 30 (5 December 1931):5. See also Edward Alden Jewell, "A Tradition Lives On," *New York Times*, 6 December 1931, sec. 9, p. 18, and "Indian Tribal Arts Exhibition Starts on Long Tour of Nation," *Art Digest* 6 (15 December 1931):32.

20. John Sloan to Rhoads, 23 July 1932; Rhoads to Sloan, 25 July 1932, IACB, box 1.

21. Raymond H. Bitney to Commissioner of Indian Affairs, 5 May 1932, IACB, box 1; James L. Rush, "Weekly Report to the Director of Extension and Industry," 6 May 1933, IACB, box 3; Henrietta Kolshorn Burton, *The Reestablishment of the Indians in Their Pueblo Life through the Revival of Their Traditional Crafts: A Study in Home Extension Education* (New York: Columbia University Bureau of Publications, 1936), pp. 5–8; CIA *Report*, 1935, p. 124; Carl T. Hayden to Rhoads, 13 July 1932; Hayden to Rhoads, 2 August 1932; Scattergood to Hayden, [1932], IACB, box 1.

22. *Congressional Record*, 75:9541, 11369, 11523-24, 11651; *United States Statutes at Large*, 47:269.

23. SI *Report*, 1932, p. 74.

24. Trotter to Rhoads, 24 October 1929, IACB, box 2, file 910; clipping from Gallup newspaper [1930], IACB, box 3; Mary-Russell F. Colton, "Wanted—A Market for Indian Art," *Southern California Business*, October 1930, IACB, box 1, file 047; Tillotson to Director of the National Park Service, 4 November 1931, IACB, box 1, file 910; Senate, *Hearings on S. 416*, 71st Cong., 3d sess., 1931, p. 9720; Tillotson to Director of the National Park System, 4 November 1931, IACB, box 1, file 910; Rhoads to Godfrey G. Goodwin, 4 March 1932, IACB, box 6.

25. Federal Trade Commission, *Jeffrey Jewelry Company*, Docket 2004, 21 September 1932, IACB, box 2; Federal Trade Commission, *Beacon Manufacturing Company*, Docket 1873, 28 June 1932, IACB, box 7.

26. Sam G. Bratton to Rhoads, 8 August 1932; Rhoads to Bratton, 15 August 1932; Arthur E. Demaray to Rhoads, 17 August 1932, IACB, box 1; E. B. Dale to Harold L. Ickes, 13 June 1933, IACB, box 4.

27. *United States Statutes at Large*, 38:719–21.

28. *Transcript of Record* for *Federal Trade Commission* v. *Maisel Trading Post, Inc.* (United States Circuit Court of Appeals, Tenth Circuit, no. 976), 17 May 1932–21 August 1933, pp. 1–2, IACB, box 7.

29. Ibid., pp. 2–3.

30. Ibid., pp. 3–7, 141–68.

31. Ibid., pp. 227–30.

32. Ibid., pp. 230–31.

33. Ibid., p. 232.

34. Ibid.

35. Ibid., pp. 233–34.

36. Clipping from the *Gallup Independent*, 24 October 1933, OSI, box 5.

37. Hugh B. Cox, "Memorandum for John Dickinson, 6 October 1936," pp. 1–4, IACB, box 7.

38. Ibid.; *Interpretation of Final Order, Federal Trade Commission* v. *Maisel Trading Post, Inc.*, in *United States Circuit Court of Appeals, Tenth Circuit, April Term, 1936*, no. 976, 21 July 1936; Cox, "Memorandum for Dickinson, 6 October 1936," p. 5, IACB, box 7.

Chapter 4: New Deal, New Effort

1. William Zimmerman, Jr., "The Role of the Bureau of Indian Affairs since 1933," *The Annals of the American Academy of Political and Social Science* 311 (May 1957):31; Ickes, "Memorandum for the Press, 5 April 1933," IRA, reel 120, frame 91. An in-depth account of how John Collier became Indian commissioner can be found in Lawrence C. Kelly, "Choosing the New Deal Indian Commissioner: Ickes vs. Collier," *New Mexico Historical Review* 49 (October 1974):269–88.

2. Collier, "Statement at Swearing into Office, 21 April 1933," *American Indian Life* 22 (July 1933); 2–3.

3. CIA *Report*, 1933, p. 71.

4. Ibid., p. 106.

5. Ickes to Elkus, 19 April 1933, HLI, Indians, folder 1.

6. Collier to Leslie Van Ness Denman, 27 April 1933, JC, part II, series I, box 4, folder 004–0066; Ickes to Charles E. Merriam, 31 July 1933, HLI, Indians, folder 1. Wick Miller, a New Mexico Indian trader who was hired to provide fifty-five Navajo and Pueblo Indians and to conduct the trading post, claimed to have lost most of his five thousand dollar investment. Wick Miller to Anna Wilarth Ickes, 23 July 1933, HLI, Indians, folder 1.

7. "A Permanent Exhibition of Indian Art at the Indian Office," *Indians at Work* 2 (15 February 1935):40; Harry W. Shipe, "Memorandum for Collier, 3 November 1934," IACB, box 2.

8. Collier, "To the Aid of Indian Artists," *Indians at Work* 1 (1 January

1934):32–33; Mrs. Charles (Nina Perera) Collier and Caroline Thompson, "Public Works of Art Project and Indians," *Indians at Work* 1 (15 January 1934):19–20; "Oklahoma Indian Artists under Public Works of Art Projects," *Indians at Work* 1 (15 February 1934):38–39.

9. Nina Collier, "News from Indian Artists under the Public Works of Art Projects," *Indians at Work* 1 (1 April 1934):37–38.

10. Nina Collier, "Memorandum for Harry L. Hopkins, 30 April 1934," BIA, box 1211, file 913; Nina Collier, "Survey of Indian Arts and Crafts, April 1934," State Historical Society, Madison, Wisconsin; Collier to Ickes, "Weekly Report No. 18, 5 May 1934," JC, part II, series II, box 36, folder 036-0013; Nina Collier, "Memorandum for Cahill, 12 March 1936," IACB, box 1.

11. Nina Collier, "Memorandum for Cahill, 26 March 1936," IACB, box 1. Another meeting with Indian Office officials produced an estimated annual cost for her program of $316,000 for three hundred individual Indian artists.

12. Ickes to Hopkins, 28 April 1936; Hopkins to Ickes, 19 May 1936, IACB, box 1.

13. Nina Collier to Young, 29 June 1934, BIA, box 1211, file 913.

14. Young to LaFarge, 7 September 1934, AAIA, box 6.

15. Nina Collier, "A New Step in Merchandising Indian Arts and Crafts," *Indians at Work* 2 (15 December 1934):19.

16. Ibid., pp. 20–21; Collier to Elkus, 23 November 1934, OCIA, box 5.

17. U.S., Congress, House, Indian Affairs, *Hearings before a subcommittee of the House Committee on Indian Affairs on H.R. 7781, Indian Conditions and Affairs*, 74th Cong., 1st sess., 1935, pp. 334–47, 357. Donald Parman in "J. C. Morgan: Navajo Apostle of Assimilation," *Prologue: The Journal of the National Archives* 4 (Summer 1972):83–98, attempts to explain Morgan's anti-government stand by stressing his early indoctrination and success in assimilating into white society. Laurence M. Hauptman in "Native American Reformers of the 1930s and 1940s: A Reinterpretation," a paper presented at the 74th annual meeting of the Organization of American Historians, Detroit, Mich., 2 April 1981, pp. 22–23, 1, stated that over 80 percent of the members of the American Indian Federation came from the individualized Five Civilized Tribes of eastern Oklahoma. Their objectives were to repeal the Indian Reorganization Act of 1934, to remove Collier, and to abolish the Indian Office. Other works dealing with the American Indian Federation and forces opposed to Collier include John L. Freeman, "The New Deal for the Indians: A Study of Bureau-Committee Relationships in American Government" (Ph.D. dissertation, Princeton University, 1952) and Graham D. Taylor, *The New Deal and American Indian Tribalism: The Administration of the Indian Reorganization Act, 1934–45* (Lincoln: University of Nebraska, 1980).

18. Ibid., pp. 345–47.

19. Ibid., pp. 335, 882, 21. For a biographical sketch of Bruner, see Philp, *John Collier's Crusade for Indian Reform*, pp. 171–72.

20. Usher L. Burdick, "Report on the Macy Contract," IACB, box 1.

21. Collier to Zimmerman, 9 May 1935, IACB, box 1. For a somewhat one-sided account of the political life of Jemison, see Laurence M. Hauptman,, "Alice Jemison: Seneca Political Activist, 1901–1964," *The Indian Historian* 12 (Summer 1979):15–22.

22. Zimmerman to Burdick, 9 May 1935, IACB, box 1.

23. Nina Collier, "The Success of the Macy Sale of Indian Arts and Crafts," *Indians at Work* 2 (1 February 1935):31–32.

24. Ickes, "Memorandum for Collier, 21 June 1933," IACB, box 4.

25. Collier telegram to the Principal of the United States Indian School, Santa Fe, New Mexico, 17 May 1935; Collier telegram to LaFarge, 17 May 1935; Hillory A. Tolson to Collier, 22 July 1935; Ickes, "Memorandum for Demaray, 31 May 1935."

26. Collier, "Memorandum for Ickes, 20 May 1935"; Shipe, "Report of Interview with H. Reed Newport, 20 May 1935"; John J. Dempsey to Ickes, 23 May 1935; Theodore A. Walters to Dempsey, 31 May 1935, IACB, box 1.

27. Demaray, "Memorandum for All Park Superintendents, 4 June 1935"; Ickes, "Memorandum for Arno B. Cammerer, 8 June 1935"; Cammerer, "Memorandum for All Park Superintendents and Custodians, 8 July 1935."

28. Director, Office of Investigations for the Department of the Interior to Ickes, 2 July 1935; Julius Gans to Ickes, 21 October 1935; Ickes to P. J. McGough, 7 July 1935, IACB, box 1.

29. Gans to Collier, 3 December 1935; Gans to the Chairman of the Indian Arts and Crafts Board, 3 December 1935, IACB, box 1. As of this date no actual board existed.

30. Charles West to William J. Barker, 13 February 1936; Young to Collier, 30 August 1935; Collier to Dempsey, 24 February 1936, IACB, box 1.

31. National Recovery Administration, *Codes of Fair Competition*, Approved Code 175, "Medium and Low-Priced Jewelry," 23 December 1933, IACB, box 2.

32. "Minutes of Conference on Codes of Fair Competition," 26 April 1935, AAIA, box 6.

33. "Memorandum on Conference Concerning Indian Arts and Crafts and the National Recovery Administration Codes, 26 April 1935," IACB, box 1, file 4921.

Chapter 5: The Committee on Indian Arts and Crafts

1. Elkus to Ickes, 17 July 1933, HLI, Indians, folder 1; Young to the President of the University of Chicago, [n.d.], JC, part I, series I, box 11, folder 220; Ickes to Henry [Dear Harry] F. Dickenson, 29 April 1933, Indians, folder

1; Ickes, "Diaries," 7 December 1940, p. 2, HLI, Library of Congress microfilm, reel 4, plate 5048; Collier to Young, 19 July 1933, BIA, box 1211, file 913.

2. Collier to Young, 19 July 1933, BIA, box 1211, file 913.

3. Collier, "Editorial," *Indians at Work* 1 (15 September 1933):3.

4. "Editorial," *Indians at Work* 2 (1 May 1935):1.

5. Collier, "Editorial," *Indians at Work* 1 (1 December 1933):1–3. An analysis of the vanishing Indian concept and its part in Collier's collectivist philosophy can be found in Tom Holm, "Indians and Progressives: From the Vanishing Policy to the Indian New Deal" (Ph.D. dissertation, University of Oklahoma, 1978).

6. Young to Collier, 7 May 1932, JC, part I, series I, box 11, folder 221; Collier telegram to Young, 11 November 1933, BIA, box 1211, file 913.

7. Ickes to Young, 22 Novmber 1933; Young to Ickes, 1 December 1933, BIA, box 1211, file 913.

8. Collier to Young, 13 December 1933, BIA, box 1211, file 913.

9. Collier to Young, 26 December 1933, BIA, box 1211, file 913.

10. Ickes, "Department of the Interior Press Release, 11 January 1934," IACB, box 4.

11. Austin to Young, 27 January 1934; Young to Collier, 1 February 1934, BIA, box 1211, file 913; Collier, "Editorial," *Indians at Work* 2 (15 August 1934):7.

12. Allan G. Harper to Collier, 28 January 1934, BIA, box 1211, file 913; *American Indian Life* 23 (January 1934):1, 13.

13. Collier to Young, 30 January 1934; Young to Collier, 1 February 1934, BIA, box 1211, file 913; Young to LaFarge, 1 March 1934, AAIA, box 6.

14. Young, "Memorandum for Members of the Indian Arts and Crafts Committee, [1 March 1934]," AAIA, box 6.

15. Ibid.

16. LaFarge to Elkus, 18 April 1934, AAIA, box 6.

17. Collier telegram to Young, 11 August 1934; Young to Collier, 13 August 1934; Collier to Young, 15 August 1934, BIA, box 1211, file 913; Collier, "American Indian Defense Association Bulletin, 22 November 1932," JC, part I, series IV, box 23, folder 10. The Wheeler-Howard Act was signed by President Roosevelt on 18 June 1934. This legislation also was known as the Indian Reorganization Act.

18. Young to Collier, 5 September 1934, BIA, box 1211, file 913; LaFarge, "Confidential" note attached to a copy of the "Report of the Committee on Indian Arts and Crafts," September 1934, AAIA, box 6; Elkus to Collier, 11 September 1934, JC, part II, series I, box 4, folder 004-0080; Elkus to Ickes, 11 September 1934, IACB, box 4.

19. The following material comes from the "Report of the Committee on Indian Arts and Crafts," September 1934, pp. 1–13, AAIA, box 6. LaFarge

personally annotated a copy of the committee report with the names of the committee members who were primarily responsible for the individual passages.

20. Harper to Stella Atwood, 13 May 1935, AAIA, box 1.

21. Collier to Elkus, 4 October 1934, BIA, box 1211, file 913.

22. Collier to Ickes, 8 October 1934, IACB, box 4.

23. Ibid.; LaFarge to Young, 1 November 1934; Young to LaFarge, 6 November 1934, AAIA, box 6.

24. Elkus to Collier, 15 November 1934, IACB, box 4.

25. Collier to Young, 27 December 1934; Collier to Ickes, 8 October 1934, IACB, box 4.

26. Ickes to LaFarge, 18 January 1935, AAIA, box 6.

27. Young to LaFarge, 24 January 1935, AAIA, box 6; Walter V. Woehlke to John Reeves, 31 January 1935, AAIA, box 1.

28. William H. Hastie to Collier, 31 January 1935, BIA, box 1211, file 913.

Chapter 6: The Indian Arts and Crafts Board

1. Collier to Young, 19 February 1935, BIA, box 1211, file 913; Young to Collier, 27 February 1935, IACB, box 4.

2. Collier, "Memorandum for Ickes, 1 March 1935"; Ickes to Collier, 5 March 1935, IACB, box 4.

3. H.R. 6468, 74th Cong., 1st sess. (1935); S. 2203, 74th Cong., 1st sess. (1935).

4. Ickes to Will Rogers, 18 May 1935, *House Report* no. 973, 74th Cong., 1st sess., ser. 9887.

5. Ibid.

6. Ibid.

7. Harper to LaFarge, 27 May 1935, AAIA, box 1.

8. Department of the Interior, "Memorandum for the Press for Release in the P.M. of Monday, 27 May 1935," AAIA, box 1; Collier to Carl Atwood Hatch, 27 May 1935, IACB, box 1.

9. LaFarge to M. L. Woodard, 28 May 1935, AAIA, box 6.

10. LaFarge to Harper, 28 May 1935, AAIA, box 1.

11. LaFarge to Thomas, 28 May 1935; LaFarge to Hatch, 28 May 1935, AAIA, box 1.

12. *Congressional Record,* 79:9402.

13. Ibid.

14. *Senate Report* no. 900, 74th Cong., 1st sess., ser. 9879; *Congressional Record,* 79:9508; Ickes to Berton I. Staples, 21 June 1935, IACB, box 4; *Congressional Record,* 79:10061.

15. *Congressonal Record,* 79:11961–62.

16. Collier, "Memorandum for Ickes, Bi-weekly Report No. 11, 2 August 1935," JC, part II, series II, box 36, folder 036-0014.

17. *New York Times*, 10 August 1935, p. 13; *Congressional Record*, 79:14030, 14078, 14572; *United States Statutes at Large*, 49:891–93. See the Appendix for a complete copy of the Indian Arts and Crafts Board Act.

18. Collier, "Memorandum for Ickes, 29 August 1935," JC, part II, series II, box 36, folder 036-0014.

19. Ibid. Despite Collier's fears, the Federal Trade Commission continued to investigate complaints upon request and frequently prosecuted cases similar to that involving the Maisel Trading Post Company. Subsequent cases involved such then familiar names as Woolworth, Weber and Heibroner of New York City, *Boys Life Magazine*, The Denver Dry Goods Company, the Louisville Pottery Company, the Wigwam of Colorado Springs, and the Altman Neckwear Corporation. None of these had to be carried to the lengths required in the Maisel case. Louis C. West to Barker, 1 March 1937; West, "Memorandum for Ickes, 29 December 1936"; West to Boy Scouts of America, 2 April 1937; West to Denver Dry Goods Company, 6 April 1937; West to Louisville Pottery Company, 29 June 1937; Federal Trade Commission, *Louisville Pottery Company*, Docket 3296, [1938]; René d'Harnoncourt to The Wigwam, 6 August 1938; Oscar L. Chapman to the Federal Trade Commission, 19 August 1939, IACB, box 6.

20. Elkus to Ickes, 17 September 1935, OSI, box 5.

21. Ickes to Elkus, 25 September 1935, OSI, box 1423, file 5–3.

22. Collier to Young, 19 September 1935, BIA, box 1211, file 913; Young to Collier, 12 October 1935, IACB, box 4.

23. Collier to Young, 31 October 1935; Collier telegram to Young, 14 December 1935; Young telegram to Collier, 15 December 1935, BIA, box 1211, file 913.

24. Young telegram to Collier, 15 December 1935, BIA, box 1211, file 913; Collier telegram to Young, 17 December 1935; Collier to Young, 17 December 1935, IACB, box 4.

25. Collier, "Memorandum for Burlew, 3 January 1936," IACB, box 4.

26. Collier to Russell Garth, 26 December 1935; A. E. Bates to Collier, 15 January 1936, IACB, box 4.

27. Collier, "Memorandum for Ickes, 18 January 1936," IACB, box 4.

28. Ibid. For a short biography and selected writings of Kidder see Richard B. Woodbury, *Alfred V. Kidder* (New York: Columbia University Press, 1973).

29. Morris De Camp Crawford to Nina Collier, 23 January 1936, JC, part II, series III, box 46, folder 87; Crawford to Ickes, 5 February 1936; Ickes to Crawford, 21 February 1936, IACB, box 4; Crawford to Ickes, 9 March 1936; Collier to Ickes, 10 March 1936, BIA, box 1211, file 913.

30. Ickes to Lorenzo Hubbell, 17 February 1936; Robert B. Harshe to Ickes,

25 February 1936; Ickes to Samuel W. Rayburn, 24 March 1936, IACB, box 4; Collier, "Memorandum for Ickes, 28 April 1936"; Collier telegram to Rayburn, 5 May 1936; Rayburn telegram to Collier, 5 May 1936, BIA, box 1211, file 913.

31. Collier to Edward A. Filene, 6 May 1936, BIA, box 1211, file 913.

32. Collier, "Memorandum for Ickes, 28 April 1936," BIA, box 1211, file 913.

33. Delos Walker to Collier, 12 May 1936; Filene to Collier, 15 May 1936; Nina Collier telegram to John Collier, 25 June 1936; Collier to Elkus, 28 October 1936, BIA, box 1211, file 913; Collier, "Memorandum for Ickes, 15 January 1937," JC, part II, series II, box 36, folder 036-0015.

34. U.S., Congress, House, Committee on Appropriations, *Hearings before a subcommittee of the House Committee on Appropriations on H.R. 10630*, 74th Cong., 2d sess., 1935, p. 651.

35. Collier, "Editorial," *Indians at Work* 3 (15 July 1936):2.

36. House, *Hearings on H.R. 10630*, 74th Cong., 2d sess., 1935, pp. 651, 657.

37. Ibid., p. 832.

38. Collier, "Memorandum for Ickes, 29 August 1935," JC, part II, series II, box 36, folder 036-0014; Collier to Young, 30 August 1935, BIA, box 1211, file 913; also see *Indians at Work* 3 (15 September 1935):41; Denman to Collier, 31 March 1936, JC, part II, series I, box 4, folder 004-0067.

39. House, *Hearings on H.R. 10630*, 74th Cong., 2d sess., 1935, pp. 830–31.

40. Ibid., pp. 832–33.

41. *United States Statutes at Large*, 49:891–93; House, *Hearings on H.R. 10630*, 74th Cong., 2d sess., 1935, pp. 829–30.

42. Ibid., p. 830.

43. Ibid., pp. 832–33.

44. Collier to Alfred V. Kidder, 2 July 1936, IACB, box 1; Ickes to Collier, 7 July 1936, IACB, box 4.

45. Collier to Elkus, 8 July 1936, BIA, box 1211, file 913.

46. Collier to Young, 9 July 1936, BIA, box 1211, file 913.

47. Collier to Elkus, 28 October 1936, BIA, box 1211, file 913; Collier, "Memorandum for Ickes, 15 January 1937," IACB, box 9.

48. Collier to Denman, 10 January 1936, IACB, box 1.

49. Willard W. Beatty, "Greatest of Indian Resources," *Indians at Work* 3 (1 May 1936):27. An excellent account of New Deal Indian education policy under Beatty is found in Margaret Szasz, *Education and the American Indian: The Road to Self-Determination since 1928*, 2d ed. (Albuquerque: University of New Mexico Press, 1977), pp. 37–122.

50. "Department of the Interior Press Release, 4 February 1936," IRA microfilm reel 120, frame 91.

51. Ibid. After the departure of W. Carson Ryan, Jr., on leave a year earlier to engage in research work for the Spellman Foundation, Collier was hardpressed to find a new director of Indian education of the same stature. Collier called the enlisting of Beatty's services "almost too good to be hoped for." Collier, "Editorial," *Indians at Work* 3 (15 February 1936):3.

52. Beatty, "Planning Indian Education in Terms of Pupil and Community Needs," *Indians at Work* 4 (1 September 1936):6.

53. *Congressional Directory*, 71st Cong., 3d sess., 1930, p. 307; SI *Report*, 1936, pp. 45–46.

54. *Indians at Work* 3 (15 April 1936):32.

55. H. Warren Shepard, "Report on the Project for the Technical Improvement of Pueblo Pottery," January 1936, BIA, box 1211, file 913.

56. New Mexico Association on Indian Affairs, "Old Art in New Forms," reprinted in *Indians at Work* 4 (1 December 1936):13.

Chapter 7: René d'Harnoncourt and the First Years of the Board

1. Monroe Wheeler, contributor, *René d'Harnoncourt: A Tribute, 8 October 1968*, Memorial Service, Sculpture Garden, Museum of Modern Art (n.p. [1968]).

2. Elizabeth Cutter Morrow and René d'Harnoncourt, *Painted Pig* (New York: Alfred A. Knopf, 1930); Morrow and d'Harnoncourt, *Bird, Beast, and Fish: An Animal Alphabet* (New York: Alfred A. Knopf, 1933); d'Harnoncourt, *Mexicana: A Book of Pictures* (New York: Alfred A. Knopf, 1931).

3. Interview with Mrs. Sarah d'Harnoncourt, New York City, 23 April 1979; Michael Scully, "Pan America's Crossroads Store," *The Pan American* (January 1942):11; d'Harnoncourt, RDOH, pp. 1–2.

4. d'Harnoncourt, RDOH, pp. 2–5. Dr. Atl was the pseudonym for Geraldo Murillo. He used no first name.

5. Ibid., pp. 3, 8–9.

6. Ibid., pp. 10–14, 20.

7. Ibid., pp. 20–22.

8. Ibid., pp. 33–34.

9. Ibid., pp. 42–43.

10. Constance Warren to Collier, 31 July 1936, BIA, box 1211, file 913.

11. d'Harnoncourt, "Introduction," RD, p. 7.

12. For a lengthy discussion of the role of specialists in the New Deal Indian Office see Graham D. Taylor, "Anthropologists, Reformers, and the Indian New Deal," *Prologue: The Journal of the National Archives* 7 (Fall, 1975):151–62.

13. U.S., Congress, House, Committee on Appropriations, *Hearings be-*

fore a subcommittee of the House Committee on Appropriations on H.R. 6958, 75th Cong., 1st sess., 1937, pp. 1011–12.

14. "Minutes of the Regular Meeting of the Indian Arts and Crafts Board, 24 October 1936"; Collier to Elkus, 28 October 1936, BIA, box 1211, file 913.

15. West to all Indian agencies (form letter), 24 October 1936; H. A. Andrews to West, 29 October 1936; T. B. Hall to West, 31 October 1936, IACB, box 5.

16. House, *Hearings on H.R. 6598,* 75th Cong., 1st sess., 1937, p. 1006; West, "Standards for Indian Jewelry," *Indians at Work* 4 (1 November 1936): 15–16.

17. Collier, "Memorandum for Ickes, 22 October 1936"; Collier, "Memorandum for Ickes, 6 November 1936," JC, part II, series II, box 36, folder 036-0014; "Indian Silver Work Standards Announced by the Indian Arts and Crafts Board," *Indians at Work* 4 (15 March 1937):45.

18. U.S., Department of the Interior, Indian Arts and Crafts Board, "Statement Announcing Standards for Navajo, Pueblo, and Hopi Silver, 9 March 1937." A copy is in the Milwaukee Public Library, Milwaukee, Wisconsin.

19. U.S., Department of the Interior, Indian Arts and Crafts Board, "Standards for Navajo, Pueblo, and Hopi Silver and Turquoise Products, 9 March 1937," OSI, box 3516, file 5–3. A copy is in the Milwaukee Public Library.

20. U.S., Department of the Interior, Indian Arts and Crafts Board, "Regulations for the Use of Government Mark on Navajo, Pueblo, and Hopi Silver, 2 April 1937," OSI, box 3516, file 5–3. A copy is in the Milwaukee Public Library.

21. U.S., Department of the Interior, Indian Arts and Crafts Board, "Regulations for the Use of Government Certificate of Genuineness for Navajo All-Wool Woven Fabrics, 20 October 1937," OSI, box 3516, file 5–3.

22. Ibid.

23. Ibid.

24. Fred Harvey to the Indian Arts and Crafts Board, 19 November 1938; J. M. Drolet to the Indian Arts and Crafts Board, 21 November 1938, IACB, box 13.

25. d'Harnoncourt to Ethel Petty, 7 December 1938, IACB, box 13.

26. Petty, "Memorandum, 25 November 1938"; Harvey to the Indian Arts and Crafts Board, 19 November 1938; Woodard to d'Harnoncourt, 22 December 1938, IACB, box 13; U.S., Congress, House, Committee on Appropriations, *Hearings before a subcommittee of the House Committee on Appropriations on H.R. 4852,* 76th Cong., 1st sess., 1939, p. 177.

27. Collier, "Memorandum for Ickes, 6 May 1937," JC, part II, series I, box 36, folder 036-0015.

28. West form letter and questionnaire to each reservation superintendent or agent, 29 April 1937, IACB, box 6.

29. Collier, "Memorandum for Ickes, 6 May 1937," JC, part II, series I, box 36, folder 036-0015.

30. Collier to West, 15 June 1937, BIA, box 1211, file 913.

31. d'Harnoncourt, "Memorandum for Collier, 13 June 1938," IACB, box 9; Collier, "Memorandum for Ickes, 26 June 1938"; Collier, "Memorandum for Ickes, 15 July 1938"; Ickes to Collier, 30 June 1938, BIA, box 1211, file 913.

32. d'Harnoncourt, "Memorandum, 5 December 1938," IACB, box 4.

33. d'Harnoncourt to West, 26 February 1938; d'Harnoncourt to West, 21 March 1938, IACB, box 9.

34. d'Harnoncourt to Burlew, 28 June 1938, IACB, box 12; " 'The Last of the Mohicans' Works for Her People," *Indians at Work* 2 (15 September 1934):24.

35. "Department of the Interior Press Release, [1938]"; d'Harnoncourt, "Memorandum, 5 December 1938," IACB, box 4.

36. Civil Service Form No. 375, 19 October 1938, IACB, box 5; d'Harnoncourt to Burlew, 28 June 1938, IACB, box 12.

37. U.S., Department of the Interior, Classification Sheet, Form I-356, IACB, box 5.

38. Gwyneth B. Harrington to Petty, November 1938; clipping from the *Albuquerque Journal*, 20 September 1942, IACB, box 5.

39. U.S., Congress, House, Committee on Appropriations, *Hearings before a subcommittee of the House Committee on Appropriations on H.R. 9621*, 75th Cong., 3d sess., 1938, p. 217.

40. This summary of d'Harnoncourt's philosophy is based on d'Harnoncourt's "Indian Arts and Crafts and Their Place in the Modern World," a paper he presented at the Inter-American Conference on Indian Life, Patzcuaro, Michoacan, Mexico, 14–24 April 1940, RD, pp. 155–60.

Chapter 8: Planning, Promoting, and Financing the San Francisco Exhibit

1. d'Harnoncourt, "North American Indian Arts," *Magazine of Art* 32 (March 1939):164.

2. House, *Hearings on H.R. 4852*, 76th Cong., 1st sess., 1939, pp. 165, 170; CIA *Report*, 1938, p. 234.

3. House, *Hearings on H.R. 4852*, 76th Cong., 1st sess., 1939, p. 165; U.S., Congress, House, Committee on Appropriations, *Hearings before a subcommittee of the House Committee on Appropriations on H.R. 8745*, 76th Cong., 3d sess., 1940, p. 199.

4. Denman to James Andrew Meeks, 8 July 1935, JC, part II, series I, box 4, folder 004-0066; Collier to Denman, 18 May 1936, JC, part II, series I, box 4, folder 004-0067; Denman to West, 5 July 1936; Leland W. Cutler to Denman, 24 July 1936, IACB, box 9.

5. Denman, "A Presentation of Indian Cultures and Their Arts: Suggested

for the Golden Gate International Exposition," *Women's City Club Magazine* 10 (July 1936):31, 14. The complete July issue is in IACB, box 20.

6. CIA *Report*, 1936, p. 159.

7. House, *Hearings on H.R. 4852*, 76th Cong., 1st sess., 1939, p. 166; U.S., Congress, House, Committee on Appropriations, *Hearings before a subcommittee of the House Committee on Appropriations on H.R. 9621*, 75th Cong., 3d sess., 1938, pp. 220–21.

8. RDOH, p. 47.

9. Denman, "Notes and Suggestions for a Plan for an Indian Presentation at the San Francisco Bay Bridge Exposition of 1939, 27 October 1936," IACB, box 9.

10. West, "Memorandum for Collier, 3 November 1936," IACB, box 9.

11. Elkus to Collier, 26 December 1936; d'Harnoncourt to Collier, 26 December 1936; Cutler to d'Harnoncourt, 30 December 1936, IACB, box 9.

12. d'Harnoncourt to Elkus, 13 January 1937; Elkus to Collier, 31 December 1936, IACB, box 9.

13. Collier, "Memorandum for Ickes, 15 January 1937"; Collier, "Memorandum for Ickes, 28 January 1937," JC, part II, series II, box 36, folder 036-0015.

14. d'Harnoncourt to Collier, 30 January 1937, IACB, box 20.

15. Collier to George Creel, 1 February 1937, IACB, box 9.

16. S.J. Resolution 88, 75th Cong., 1st sess., pp. 19, 1 (1937), *Senate Joint Resolutions*, vol. 31, NA.

17. Collier to Creel, 1 February 1937, IACB, box 9; S.J. Resolution 88, 75th Cong., 1st sess., pp. 23–25 (1937), *Senate Joint Resolutions*, vol. 31, NA.

18. Collier to d'Harnoncourt, 3 March 1937, IACB, box 9.

19. Clipping from the *San Francisco Examiner*, 7 April 1937, p. 3, IACB, box 20.

20. Collier to Denman, 21 April 1937, IACB, box 20; Denman telegram to d'Harnoncourt, 4 June 1937, IACB, box 9.

21. d'Harnoncourt to Denman, 10 July 1937; d'Harnoncourt telegram to Denman, 15 July 1937; Department of the Interior, Order No. 1210, 2 September 1937, IACB, box 9; d'Harnoncourt to Charles Amsden, 6 October 1937, IACB, box 4; d'Harnoncourt telegram to Amsden, 11 October 1937; Denman to d'Harnoncourt, 6 January 1938, IACB, box 9.

22. d'Harnoncourt to Creel, [November 1937], IACB, box 9.

23. d'Harnoncourt to Mrs. J. M. Helm, 29 January 1938; d'Harnoncourt to Denman, 31 January 1938; d'Harnoncourt to Creel, 1 February 1938; Eleanor Roosevelt, "My Day," clipping from the *Washington Daily News*, 31 January 1938; Eleanor Roosevelt, "My Day," clipping from the *Washington Daily News*, 28 February 1938, IACB, box 9.

24. d'Harnoncourt, "Memorandum for Collier, 17 March 1938," IACB, box 9.

25. Clippings from the *Pueblo* (Colorado) *Star Journal*, 8 June 1938; the

Breckenridge (Texas) *Sun*, 10 June 1938; the *Paducah* (Kentucky) *Sun Democrat*, 17 June 1938; and the *San Francisco* (California) *News*, 2 July 1938, IACB, box 21.

26. d'Harnoncourt to Frederic H. Douglas, [1938], IACB, box 13; d'Harnoncourt to Elkus, 13 January 1937, IACB, box 9; House, *Hearings on H.R. 6958*, 75th Cong., lst sess., 1937, pp. 1010–11.

27. d'Harnoncourt to David H. Stevens, 23 June 1937; Rockefeller Foundation, General Education Board, "Grants-in-aid, 28 June 1937," RA, RG1.1, series 200, box 209, folder 2495.

28. Stevens, "Report of Interview with René d'Harnoncourt, 6 January 1938," RA, RG1.1, series 200, box 209, folder 2495; Philippa Whiting to d'Harnoncourt, 30 January 1938, IACB, box 20; d'Harnoncourt to Stevens, 14 February 1938, RA, RG1.1, series 200, box 209, folder 2495.

29. Norma S. Thompson to Roy Chapman Andrews, 24 March 1938; Petty to Whiting, 21 March 1938; Whiting to d'Harnoncourt, 28 March 1938; George C. Vaillant to d'Harnoncourt, 1 April 1938; d'Harnoncourt to Vaillant, 28 April 1938; Vaillant to d'Harnoncourt, 3 May 1938, IACB, box 20; George C. Vaillant, *Indian Arts in North America* (New York: Harper and Brothers, 1939), p. xiii.

30. Vaillant to Stevens, 29 May 1939, RA, RG1.1, series 200, box 209, folder 2495; "Review of *Indian Arts in North America*," *Antiques* 39 (March 1941):114.

31. Clipping from the *San Francisco Chronicle*, 16 October 1938, IACB, box 20.

32. d'Harnoncourt to Martin A. Roberts, 8 September 1939, IACB, box 16; d'Harnoncourt to Cahill, 7 December 1938, IACB, box 14.

33. George C. Dickens to Collier, 22 December 1936, IACB, box 9.

34. Dickens, "Memorandum for Collier, 22 December 1936"; d'Harnoncourt to Elkus, 5 January 1937; "Budget Proposed by California Group, [1937]"; "Possible Reduction of Items II, III, V, and VI in the Budget Proposed by the California Group, [1937]," IACB, box 9.

35. d'Harnoncourt to Collier, 3 August 1937, IACB, box 5; d'Harnoncourt to Collier, 16 August 1937, IACB, box 4; S.J. Resolution 88, 75th Cong., lst sess., pp. 14–15 (1937), *Senate Joint Resolutions*, vol. 31, NA.

36. "Expenses Connected with the Indian Representation, 1 October 1937"; Burlew to Creel, 13 October 1937; Creel to Burlew, 14 October 1937, IACB, box 9.

37. d'Harnoncourt to Denman, 6 October 1937; d'Harnoncourt to Denman, 13 October 1937, IACB, box 9.

38. Creel to Burlew, 14 October 1937, IACB, box 9.

39. Creel to d'Harnoncourt, 27 October 1937; Collier to Elkus, 13 November 1937, IACB, box 9; Nathan R. Margold to Ickes, 10 November 1937, IACB, box 20.

40. d'Harnoncourt to Denman, 31 January 1938, IACB, box 9; Collier,

"Memorandum for Ickes, 16 February 1938," JC, part II, series II, box 36, folder 036-0015.

41. d'Harnoncourt to Denman, 16 February 1938; Creel to Ickes, 25 February 1938, IACB, box 9.

42. Creel to Ickes, 25 February 1938, IACB, box 9.

43. d'Harnoncourt to Denman, 16 February 1938, IACB, box 9.

44. E. G. Ryder, "Memorandum for Erich Nielson, 21 September 1938," IACB, box 9; Collier, "Memorandum for Ickes, 12 August 1938," JC, part II, series II, box 36, folder 036-0015; Frederick P. Keppel to Grace McCann Morley, 4 November 1938, IACB, box 13.

45. d'Harnoncourt, "Memorandum for Collier and Burlew, 6 November 1938," IACB, box 9.

46. d'Harnoncourt to Robert Lister, 16 November 1938, IACB, box 13.

47. Stevens, "Report on Interview with d'Harnoncourt, 9 June 1938"; d'Harnoncourt to Stevens, 24 June 1938, RA, RG1.1, series 200, box 209, folder 2495; d'Harnoncourt to Warren, 15 April 1938; Warren to d'Harnoncourt, 23 April 1938, IACB, box 21; House, *Hearings on H.R. 4852*, 76th Cong., lst sess., 1939, p. 177.

48. d'Harnoncourt to Owen M. Boggess, 13 January 1939, IACB, box 13; Clyde Hall, "Incorporated Indians of Round Valley, California, Manage Unique Market Place for Handicrafts of Many Tribes at San Francisco," *Indians at Work* 6 (May 1939):5–7; Godfrey Lawrence Kibler to Clifford C. Anglim, 2 June 1939, IACB, box 12; d'Harnoncourt to Collier, 23 December 1938, IACB, box 9.

49. d'Harnoncourt to Collier, 30 December 1938, IACB, box 12.

50. d'Harnoncourt to Collier, 30 January 1939, IACB, box 5; Kibler to E. Raymond Armsby, 9 February 1939, IACB, box 14.

51. d'Harnoncourt to Collier, 30 December 1938, IACB, box 12. The Covelo Market arrangement brought an inquiry from the United States Treasury Internal Revenue Service about the government's role in the business, and the board through its administrative clerk assigned to the exposition, Godfrey Kibler, had to explain that employees of the United States government served the market in supervisory and advisory capacities only and that no government employees served in a selling capacity or handled the proceeds from sales at the Indian Market. Kibler to Anglim, 2 June 1939, IACB, box 12.

52. Collier, "Memorandum for Ickes, 14 January 1939," JC, part II, series II, box 36, folder 036-0015; "Agreement between the Covelo Indian Community of the Round Valley Reservation and the Indian Arts and Crafts Board, 4 January 1939," IACB, box 12; House, *Hearings on H.R. 4852*, 76th Cong., lst sess., 1939, p. 167.

53. House, *Hearings on H.R. 8745*, 76th Cong., 3d sess., 1940, p. 201.

54. d'Harnoncourt to Collier, 6 July 1939, IACB, box 9; Sister Providencia to d'Harnoncourt, 28 July 1939; d'Harnoncourt to Eleanor Roosevelt, 22 May

Notes

1939, IACB, box 16; House, *Hearings on H.R.* 8745, 76th Cong., 3d sess., 1940, p. 201.

Chapter 9: The 1939 San Francisco Exposition

1. d'Harnoncourt to Jean Rutherford, 2 December 1938, IACB, box 14.

2. U.S., Congress, House, Committee on Appropriations, *Hearings before a subcommittee of the House Committee on Appropriations on H.R.* 4590, 77th Cong., 1st sess., 1941, p. 183.

3. Ickes, "Secretary Ickes Views Indian Exhibit at Golden Gate International Exposition at San Francisco," *Indians at Work* 6 (April 1939): 21–22; clipping from the *Albuquerque Journal*, 20 February 1939, included in United Pueblo Agency, "Memorandum for Collier, 20 February 1939," IACB, box 9.

4. d'Harnoncourt, "North American Indian Arts," *Magazine of Art* 32 (March 1939):164.

5. d'Harnoncourt to Jewell, [1939], IACB, box 15.

6. d'Harnoncourt, "North American Indian Arts," p. 164.

7. d'Harnoncourt and Douglas, eds., *The Exhibition of Indian Arts and Crafts at the San Franciso Golden Gate International Exposition, 1939* (Ann Arbor, Michigan: University Microfilms, no publication order number, 1940), no plate numbers, IACB, box 20 (hereafter cited as d'Harnoncourt and Douglas, *San Francisco Exhibition, 1939*); d'Harnoncourt, "North American Indian Arts," p.165.

8. d'Harnoncourt to Jewell, [1939], IACB, box 15.

9. d'Harnoncourt, "North American Indian Arts," pp. 165, 167.

10. d'Harnoncourt to Jewell, [1939], IACB, box 15.

11. Unless otherwise noted, the sources used to provide a description of the Indian exhibit at the San Francisco Golden Gate International Exposition in 1939 were the following: d'Harnoncourt, "North American Indian Arts," pp. 164–67; d'Harnoncourt and Douglas, *San Francisco Exhibition, 1939*; d'Harnoncourt, "Indian Exhibit at San Francisco World's Fair Nears Completion," *Indians at Work* 6 (November 1938):10–13; d'Harnoncourt to Jewell, [1939], IACB, box 15; Kibler to Creel, 6 September 1940, IACB, box 15; d'Harnoncourt, preliminary draft for "North American Indian Arts," IACB, box 15; and Alfred Frankenstein, "Art on Treasure Island," *San Francisco Chronicle*, 22 October 1939, RD, pp. 137–40.

12. René d'Harnoncourt and Frederic H. Douglas, *Indian Art of the United States* (New York: Museum of Modern Art, 1941; reprint ed., New York: Arno Press, 1969), p. 118.

13. Cover page for model room plans and blueprints, 27 April 1938, IACB, box 31.

14. Kibler to Boggess, 22 March 1939, IACB, box 13.

15. Kibler to the Cline Piano Company, 3 October 1939, IACB, box 15.

The individual tribes represented among the sixty-four were the Navajo, Pomo,, Papago, Washoe, Blackfoot, Paiute, Sioux, Coeur d'Alene, Hopi, Tesuque Pueblo, Caddo, Cheyenne, Shoshone, Taos Pueblo, San Ildefonso Pueblo, Sia Pueblo, Cochiti Pueblo, Santa Clara Pueblo, and Haida.

16. Milburn L. Wilson to d'Harnoncourt, 15 August 1939, IACB, box 16; "Visitor at San Francisco Exposition to Urge That Indian Exhibit Be Made Permanent," *Indians at Work* 6 (May 1939):11; Jay B. Nash to Collier, 2 May 1939; Arthur Miller, *Los Angeles Times*, 23 April 1939, part III, p. 8, clipping in IACB, box 20.

17. Alfred L. Kroeber to Creel, 28 February 1939, IACB, box 16; Kroeber to Collier, 28 February 1939, IACB, box 9. For a biography of Kroeber see Theodora Kroeber, *Alfred Kroeber: A Personal Configuration* (Berkeley: University of California Press, 1970). Alida C. Bowler to d'Harnoncourt, 8 July 1939, IACB, box 16; clipping from the *San Francisco Examiner*, 21 March 1939, p. 8, IACB, box 20.

18. d'Harnoncourt to Collier, 6 July 1939, IACB, box 25; "Visitor at San Francisco Exposition to Urge That Indian Exhibit Be Made Permanent," *Indians at Work* 6 (May 1939):11; House, *Hearings on H.R. 8745*, 76th Cong., 3d sess., 1940, p. 199; d'Harnoncourt to Alfred H. Barr, Jr., 25 September 1939, IACB, box 36.

19. A selected listing of contributors to the Indian exhibit at the San Francisco Golden Gate International Exposition in 1939 included the following: Smithsonian Institution; Amelia White; New Mexico Museum of Art; Indian and Spanish Trading Post, Santa Fe; Rochester Museum of Arts and Sciences, Rochester, New York; Taylor Museum of the Colorado Springs Fine Arts Center, Colorado Springs, Colorado; United Pueblo Indian Agency, Albuquerque; Austin Ladd of the Crafts del Navajo, Coolidge, New Mexico; Milwaukee Public Museum; Phillips Academy Museum, Andover, Massachusetts; Fred Harvey Indian Department, Albuquerque; Museum of the American Indian, Heye Foundation, New York City; Denver Art Museum; Laboratory of Anthropology, Santa Fe; American Museum of Natural History, New York City; Brooklyn Museum, Brooklyn, New York; Indian Trading Post, Phoenix; Henry Moses, Sitka, Alaska; Harold Ickes; Washington State Museum; Haskell Institute, Lawrence, Kansas; Women's City Club of San Francisco; United States National Museum, Washington, DC; and Osage Tribal Museum,, Pawhuska, Oklahoma, IACB, boxes 19, 20.

20. Kibler to Kathryn M. Von Hinzman, 5 May 1939, IACB, box 13; "Financial Statement, Indian Arts and Crafts Board, Fiscal Year 1939," IACB, box 9; d'Harnoncourt and Douglas, *San Francisco Exhibition, 1939*; Ickes,, "Order Number 1365, 27 March 1939," IACB, box 18.

21. Frankenstein, "Art on Treasure Island," *San Francisco Chronicle*, 22 October 1939, RD, p. 137.

22. Creel, "Special Notice, 4 October 1939," IACB, box 15; d'Harnoncourt

to Horace Jayne, 21 November 1939, IACB, box 10. Both the San Francisco and New York expositions in 1939 closed five weeks earlier than had been planned because attendance figures had not reached their anticipated levels. San Francisco had expected twenty million visitors between 18 February and 2 December, yet only slightly more than half of that number was recorded when the exposition closed on 29 October. New York had planned for sixty million visitors and received only thirty-two million. *New York Times,* 8 October 1939, part IV, p. 2; *New York Times,* 29 October 1939, part IV, p. 8; *New York Times,* 30 October 1939, p. 12.

23. House, *Hearings on H.R. 8745,* 76th Cong., 3d sess., 1940, pp. 201, 197, 199.

24. House, *Hearings on H.R. 4590,* 77th Cong., 1st sess., 1941, p. 182.

25. House, *Hearings on H.R. 8745,* 76th Cong., 3d sess., 1940, pp. 199, 201; "Financial Statement, Indian Arts and Crafts Board, Fiscal Year 1939," IACB, box 9.

26. Public Resolution No. 71 (S.J. Resolution 200), 76th Cong., 3d sess. (1940); House, *Hearings on H.R. 4590,* 77th Cong., 1st sess., 1941, p. 182; d'Harnoncourt to Kenneth B. Disher, 17 June 1940, IACB, box 34.

27. d'Harnoncourt to Disher, 24 May 1940, IACB, box 34.

28. Samuel Alfred Barrett to George G. Heye, [May 1940]; Heye to Barrett, 15 May 1940, IACB, box 15; Ira Edwards to Barrett, 21 May 1940, IACB, box 17.

29. Kibler to Boggess, 18 June 1940, IACB, box 10; Wilson to Barrett, 8 September 1940, IACB, box 16.

30. d'Harnoncourt to Disher, 17 June 1940, IACB, box 34.

31. Frankenstein, "Art on Treasure Island: The Art of the Indian," *San Francisco Chronicle* [summer 1940], reprint ed., IACB, box 20; d'Harnoncourt to Disher, 17 June 1940, IACB, box 34.

Chapter 10: Field Work

1. House, *Hearings on H.R. 4852,* 76th Cong., 1st sess., 1939, p. 400; d'Harnoncourt to Collier, 27 April 1938, IACB, box 9; Collier, "Memorandum for Ickes, 16 June 1938," JC, part II, series II, box 36, folder 036-0015.

2. Unless otherwise noted, the source for d'Harnoncourt's observations on the arts and crafts situation in Alaska was d'Harnoncourt's "Report on Trip to Alaska, May 1938," IACB, box 20.

3. d'Harnoncourt to Claude M. Hirst, 19 December 1938, IACB, box 14.

4. "Modern Indian Artisans Turn Out Ancient Totems," clipping from *Seattle Sunday Times,* 27 February 1938, p. 12, IACB, box 20.

5. House, *Hearings on H.R. 9621,* 75th Cong., 3d sess., 1938, pp. 218–19.

6. U.S., Department of the Interior, Indian Arts and Crafts Board, "Regulations for Use of Government Marks of Genuineness for Alaskan Eskimo

Hand-Made Products," and "Regulations for Use of Government Marks of Genuineness for Alaskan Indian Hand-Made Products," 23 January 1939, OSI, box 3516, file 5–3.

7. House, *Hearings on H.R. 4852*, 76th Cong., 1st sess., 1939, pp. 400, 178–79; d'Harnoncourt to Hirst, 19 December 1938, IACB, box 14.

8. Virgil R. Farrell to Hirst, 21 November 1938, IACB, box 14.

9. "Indian Arts and Crafts Cooperative Completes Successful Year," *Indians at Work* 4 (1 April 1937):30–33.

10. Collier, "Editorial," *Indians at Work* 4 (1 April 1937):5–6.

11. House, *Hearings on H.R. 9621*, 75th Cong., 3d sess., 1938, p. 222.

12. d'Harnoncourt, "Memorandum on the Spinning Project Initiated by the Indian Arts and Crafts Board with the Cooperation of the Five Civilized Tribes Agency in McCurtain County, Oklahoma, 4 January 1938," RD, p. 97.

13. Ibid.; House, *Hearings on H.R. 9621*, 75th Cong., 3d sess., 1938, p. 222.

14. House, *Hearings on H.R. 4852*, 76th Cong., 1st sess., 1939, p. 165.

15. d'Harnoncourt, "Memorandum on the Spinning Project, 4 January 1938," RD, pp. 97–98.

16. House, *Hearings on H.R. 4852*, 76th Cong., 1st sess., 1939, p. 165; d'Harnoncourt, "Memorandum on the Spinning Project, 4 January 1938," RD, p. 98.

17. House, *Hearings on H.R. 8745*, 76th Cong., 3d sess., 1940, p. 198; d'Harnoncourt, "Memorandum on a Planned Reorganization of the Choctaw Spinning Project, [1939]," RD, p. 168.

18. d'Harnoncourt, "Memorandum on the Use of Commercial Carding and Scouring in the Spinning Projects in Eastern Oklahoma, [1939]," RD, pp. 169–70; U.S., Congress, Senate, Committee on Appropriations, *Hearings before a subcommittee of the Senate Committee on Appropriations on H.R. 6845*, 77th Cong., 2d sess., 1942, p. 698.

19. House, *Hearings on H.R. 8745*, 76th Cong., 3d sess., 1940, p. 198; U.S., Congress, House, Committee on Appropriations, *Hearings before a subcommittee of the House Committee on Appropriations on H.R. 2719*, 78th Cong., 1st sess., 1943, p. 101; House, *Hearings on H.R. 8745*, 76th Cong., 3d sess., 1940, p. 202.

20. U.S., Congress, House, Committee on Appropriations, *Hearings before a subcommittee of the House Committee on Appropriations on H.R. 6845*, 77th Cong., 2d sess., 1942, p. 196.

21. "Development of American Indian Arts and Crafts," *Monthly Labor Review* 46 (March 1938):657; House, *Hearings on H.R. 9621*, 75th Cong., 3d sess., 1938, p. 222.

22. "Resolution of the Papago Council, No. 16, 6 November 1937," RD, p. 128.

23. "Resolution of the Papago Council, No. 41, 3 September 1938," IACB, box 21.

24. Ibid.
25. "Resolution No. 145 [19 March 1941] as Amended by Resolution No. 150 [17 June 1941] by the Papago Council," RD, pp. 131–34; Senate, *Hearings on H.R. 6845*, 77th Cong., 2d sess., 1942, p. 698.
26. "Resolution No. 145 [19 March 1941] as Amended by Resolution No. 150 [17 June 1941] by the Papago Council," RD, pp. 131–34; d'Harnoncourt to Papago Tribal Council, 7 October 1940, IACB, box 31.
27. Sister Providencia to d'Harnoncourt, 3 February 1940, House, *Hearings on H.R. 8745*, 76th Cong., 3d sess., 1940, p. 207.
28. "Display of Northwest Indian Cooperative Craft Work Visited by Mrs. Roosevelt at the Capitol," *Indians at Work* 8 (March 1941):17–18 (hereafter cited as "Display"); Sister Providencia to d'Harnoncourt, 3 February 1940, House, *Hearings on H.R. 8745*, 76th Cong., 3d sess., 1940, p. 217.
29. "Display," *Indians at Work* 8 (March 1941):17–18.
30. Sister Providencia to d'Harnoncourt, 3 February 1940, House, *Hearings on H.R. 8745*, 76th Cong., 3d sess., 1940, p. 207; "Display," *Indians at Work* 8 (March 1941):17.
31. "Display," *Indians at Work* 8 (March 1941):17.
32. House, *Hearings on H.R. 8745*, 76th Cong., 3d sess., 1940, pp. 198–99.
33. Ibid., p. 200.
34. d'Harnoncourt, "Suggestions for Future Activities of the Indian Arts and Crafts Board: Submitted to the Members of the Board by the General Manager, 21 September 1939," RD, p. 167.
35. "Trust Indenture for Conduct of Pueblo Indian Arts and Crafts Market, 1940," RD, p. 109.
36. "Outline of a Plan of Operation for a Proposed Pueblo Handicrafts Marketing Organization to be Known as the Pueblo Handicrafts Market, n.d.," RD, p. 103.
37. Ibid., pp. 105–6.
38. d'Harnoncourt, "Memorandum on the Proposed Seminole Crafts Guild in Glades County, Florida, [1940]," RD, p. 100.
39. "Outline of a Plan of Operation for a Proposed Pueblo Handicrafts Marketing Organization to be Known as the Pueblo Handicrafts Market, n.d.," RD, pp. 107–8.
40. "Trust Indenture for Conduct of Pueblo Indian Arts and Crafts Market, 1940," RD, pp. 109–15.
41. Section 2 of the Indian Arts and Crafts Board Act specifically provided "that nothing . . . shall be construed to authorize the Board to borrow or lend money or to deal in Indian goods." Precedent for this restriction stemmed from earlier legislation. Section 14 of the Act of 30 June 1834 (*United States Statutes at Large*, 4:738) and section 10 of the Act of 22 June 1874 (*United States Statutes at Large*, 18:177) relating to the purchase of goods from Indians, now sections 68 and 87, title 25, *United States Code*, were modified by the Act of

19 June 1939 (*United States Statutes at Large*, 53:840–41) to allow employees of the United States government, including those in the Indian Office,
and under such rules and regulations as the secretary of the interior should
prescribe, "to purchase from any Indian or Indian organization any arts and
crafts . . . produced, rendered, owned, controlled, or furnished by any Indian
or Indian organization." This legislation was designed primarily to alleviate
the hardship of government employees of Indian blood who unjustly were kept
from patronizing businesses owned or operated by Indians such as grocery stores,
barbershops, or butchershops. Suggested by the Interior Department, this legislation was also an effort to allow government employees to patronize the very
cooperatives they were helping to foster throughout the Indian tribal areas.
The Indians had found difficulty in understanding the earlier restrictions because they appeared unjust and deprived the cooperatives of needed revenue.
Such a situation, the Interior Department believed in its report accompanying
the bill, retarded the development of Indian cooperatives. The Act of 19 June
1939 provided further "that no employee of the United States Government
shall be permitted to make any such purchases for the purposes of engaging
directly or indirectly in the commercial selling, reselling, trading, or bartering
of said purchases by the said employee." Senate, *Hearings on H.R. 6845*, 77th
Cong., 2d sess., 1942, p. 698.

    42. d'Harnoncourt, "Organization of Production and Merchandising Units,
n.d.," RD, p. 96.

    43. Navajo Tribal Council, "Plan of Operation for the Navajo Tribal Arts
and Crafts Project, [1940]," RD, pp. 117–20.

    44. House, *Hearings on H.R. 2719*, 78th Cong., 1st sess., 1943, p. 101.

    45. Alice L. Marriott, "Indian Arts and Crafts in the Great Lakes Area, 7
March 1940," RD, pp. 59, 64, 65.

Chapter 11: The Museum of Modern Art—1941

    1. d'Harnoncourt to Barr, 25 September 1939; d'Harnoncourt to Douglas,
30 September 1939, IACB, box 34.

    2. Department of the Interior, "Press Release, 13 January 1941," IRA, reel
120, plate 92.

    3. Franklin Roosevelt, "Radio Speech Attendant upon the Dedication of
the New Building of the Museum of Modern Art, New York City, 10 May
1939," *New York Times*, 11 May 1939, p. 29.

    4. Ibid.

    5. House, *Hearings on H.R. 8745*, 76th Cong., 3d sess., 1940, p. 201;
d'Harnoncourt to Barr, 20 October 1939, IACB, box 19.

    6. d'Harnoncourt, "Outline of Content of the Exhibition of Indian Art in
North America, 30 September 1939," IACB, box 34.

    7. d'Harnoncourt to Barr, 20 October 1939, IACB, box 19.

8. CIA *Report*, 1941, p. 436; Frank Caspers, "Review of *Indian Art of the United States,*" *Art Digest* 15 (1 March 1941):27.

9. d'Harnoncourt to Thomas C. Parker, 6 April 1940; Cahill to d'Harnoncourt, 2 November 1939, IACB, box 34.

10. Joe Brew telegram to Disher, 28 May 1940; Parker to d'Harnoncourt, 1 July 1940; d'Harnoncourt to Kibler, 25 September 1940, IACB, box 34.

11. d'Harnoncourt to Elzy J. Bird, 15 October 1940; Bird to d'Harnoncourt, 23 October 1940; Bird to d'Harnoncourt, 4 January 1941; Petty special delivery to d'Harnoncourt, 7 January 1941; Petty to d'Harnoncourt, 9 January 1941; Petty to d'Harnoncourt, 10 January 1941; Bird to d'Harnoncourt, 13 January 1941; Charles H. Eisenhart to Fommer Graflex Corporation, 17 January 1941, IACB, box 34.

12. Petty to d'Harnoncourt, 9 January 1941, IACB, box 34; Collier to Donald Collier, 19 February 1941, JC, part II, series I, box 3, folder 003-0050.

13. d'Harnoncourt to Jeoffrey Norman, 20 September 1940; Donald Scott to d'Harnoncourt, 4 April 1940; d'Harnoncourt to Douglas, 12 September 1940, IACB, box 34.

14. d'Harnoncourt to Fred A. Picard, 21 October 1940, IACB, box 34.

15. d'Harnoncourt to Eleanor Roosevelt, 7 September 1940; d'Harnoncourt to Eleanor Roosevelt, 19 December 1940; Eleanor Roosevelt to d'Harnoncourt, 23 December 1940, IACB, box 34.

16. d'Harnoncourt to Eleanor Roosevelt, 2 January 1941; d'Harnoncourt by special messenger to Eleanor Roosevelt, 2 January 1941, IACB, box 34; Eleanor Roosevelt, "Foreword," in d'Harnoncourt and Douglas, *Indian Art of the United States*, p. 8.

17. Crawford, "Exhibit of American Indian Art, Opening January 22 in New York, Expected to Mark Epoch in Style History," *Women's Wear Daily*, 10 January 1941, p. 10, IACB, box 37.

18. "All-American Art," *Art Digest* 15 (1 January 1941):17.

19. Ickes, "Department of the Interior Press Release, 13 January 1941," IRA, reel 120, plate 92.

20. "New York Museum Rebuilds Three Floors for Indian Exhibit," *Museum News* 18 (15 February 1941):1, 7; "Indian Art in the United States," *Design* 42 (March 1941):15. *Museum News*, published by the American Association of Museums, admired d'Harnoncourt's efforts. According to *Design* magazine, his methods of display were ingenious.

21. d'Harnoncourt, "Living Arts of the Indians," *Magazine of Art* 34 (February 1941):72.

22. Ibid., p. 76.

23. Jeanette Lowe, "Lo, the Rich Indian," *Art News* 39 (1 February 1941):7; d'Harnoncourt and Douglas, *Indian Art of the United States*, pp. 88–89.

24. Liston M. Oak, "Living Traditions in American Indian Art," *Antiques* 39 (March 1941):134.

25. d'Harnoncourt, "Living Arts of the Indians," pp. 76–77.

26. d'Harnoncourt and Douglas, *Indian Art of the United States*, p. 132. The interesting material used was called catlinite or pipestone and was found in many places on the Plains, ranging in color from cherry red to pale buff. When first quarried, pipestone was soft enough to be carved with a knife, yet the material hardened soon after exposure to the air. These pipes were used for many purposes such as tribal ceremonies, private rites, and pleasure. The outstanding horse's head pipe bowl had been collected near the Upper Missouri River by the War Department before 1868.

27. d'Harnoncourt, "Living Arts of the Indians," p. 77.

28. Jean Charlot, "All American," *The Nation* 152 (8 February 1941): 165–66.

29. "New York Views the Art of the Indian," *Art Digest* 15 (15 February 1941):22.

30. d'Harnoncourt and Douglas, *Indian Art of the United States*, p. 181.

31. Ibid., pp. 183–84.

32. Ibid., p. 184.

33. Ibid.

34. Frank Crowninshield to d'Harnoncourt, 22 January 1941, IACB, box 34; Jewell, "The Redman's Culture," *New York Times*, 26 January 1941, section 9, p. 9.

35. Max Weber to Barr, 1 February 1941, IACB, box 34; clipping from the *Washington Star*, 23 February 1941, IACB, box 32; "New York Views the Art of the Indian," *Art Digest* 15 (15 February 1941):11; Oak, "Living Traditions in American Indian Art," p. 134.

36. "New York Views the Art of the Indian," *Art Digest*, p. 11.

37. Allen Eaton to d'Harnoncourt, 16 April 1941, IACB, box 34.

38. Pach to Barr, 27 April 1941, IACB, box 36.

39. Oak, "Living Traditions in American Indian Art," p. 134.

40. Eleanor Roosevelt, "My Day," *New York Times*, 27 January 1941, RD, p. 144; E. Reeseman Fryer to Zimmerman, 13 March 1941, IACB, box 34.

41. Charlot, "All American," p. 165. Art critic Thomas Craven was the author of *Men of Art* (New York: Simon and Schuster, 1931) and *Modern Art: The Men, the Movements, the Meaning* (New York: Simon and Schuster, 1934). He also was the editor of *A Treasury of American Prints: A Selection of One Hundred Etchings and Lithographs by the Foremost Living American Artists* (New York: Simon and Schuster, 1939) wherein he discusses the emergence of American art to a position of world-wide prominence. Eleanor B. Williams, "Indian Arts and Crafts Make Fashion News as America Turns Attention to Native Resources," *Indians at Work* 8 (March 1941):13; *Indians at Work* 8 (March 1941):18; Senate, *Hearings on H.R. 6845*, 77th Cong., 2d sess., 1942, p. 704.

42. Collier, "Memorandum for Ickes, 24 February 1941," BIA, box 5.

43. Department of the Interior, "Press Release, 27 February 1941," IACB, box 37; Rosella Senders, "Indian History in the Making," *Indians at Work* 8 (April 1941):23.
44. Senders, "Indian History in the Making," pp. 23–25.
45. Ibid., p. 26.
46. Charlot, "All American," p. 165. Only Charlot observed and commented on d'Harnoncourt's symbolism.

Chapter 12: Opposition

1. U.S., Congress, Senate, Committee on Appropriations, *Hearings before a subcommittee of the Senate Committee on Appropriations on H.R. 9621,* 75th Cong., 3d sess., 1938, pp. 244–45.
2. Freeman, "The New Deal for Indians," pp. 467–68, 479; S. 2731 and H.R. 7837, 74th Cong., 1st sess., (1935); *Congressional Record*, 79:3492, 6688, 6746, 9740, 10463, 11975-76, 12240. For an in-depth study of the development of anti-administration forces over domestic issues, see James T. Patterson, *Congressional Conservatism and the New Deal: The Growth of the Conservative Coalition in Congress, 1933–1939* (Lexington: University of Kentucky Press, 1967).
3. *Who's Who in America*, s.v. "Denman, William." On the occasion of Justice Louis Brandeis's eightieth birthday in 1936 and three months before Roosevelt submitted his court plan to Congress, Collier had gone to great lengths in an editorial to praise the justice as "one of our great Americans." He even cited aspects of Brandeis's philosophy and method which were of particular interest to Indians. Collier was consistent only in his unwavering concern for Indian interests. Collier, "Editorial," *Indians at Work* 4 (1 December 1936):1–2.
4. U.S., Congress, Senate, Committee on Indian Affairs, *Hearings on S. 230, Survey of Conditions of the Indians in the United States*, 75th Cong., 1st sess., 1937, pp. 20715–16, 20766. Jemison cited sections 262, 263, and 265, title 25, *United States Code*.
5. Ibid., p. 20767.
6. Ibid., p. 20719.
7. Emerson and LaFarge, "An Appeal for Funds," enclosed in Emerson to LaFarge, 8 June 1937, AAIA, box 5. In 1946, the organization became the Association on American Indian Affairs.
8. James Graves Scrugham to Ickes, 12 December 1938, IACB, box 11.
9. Ibid.
10. d'Harnoncourt to Collier, 27 December 1938, IACB, box 11.
11. Ibid.
12. Scrugham to Collier, 12 December 1938; d'Harnoncourt to Collier, 27 December 1938, IACB, box 11.
13. Burlew to Scrugham, 29 December 1938, IACB, box 11.

14. CIA *Report*, 1938, pp. 234–35.
15. d'Harnoncourt to Collier, 27 December 1938, IACB, box 11.
16. Dean Kirk to d'Harnoncourt, 31 May 1938, IACB, box 14.
17. Diego Abeita to d'Harnoncourt, 30 May 1938, IACB, box 14; clipping from the *Albuquerque Tribune*, 10 May 1938, BIA, box 1211, file 913.
18. House, *Hearings on H.R. 4852*, 76th Cong., lst sess., 1939, p. 164; d'Harnoncourt, "Memorandum for Public Release, 6 April 1938," BIA, box 1211, file 913; C. G. Wallace to Josephine Glavis, 17 April 1939, IACB, box 14.
19. d'Harnoncourt to Hubbell, 9 April 1940, IACB, box 9.
20. d'Harnoncourt, "Suggestions for Future Activities of the Indian Arts and Crafts Board: Submitted to the Members of the Board by the General Manager, 21 September 1939," RD, pp. 165–66. The typewritten manuscript "Reports and Documents Concerning the Activities of the Indian Arts and Crafts Board" was compiled by the Indian Arts and Crafts Board, Washington, DC, in 1943. The document was microfilmed by the Library of Congress Photoduplication Service in 1974 and catalogued in the Microfilm Division under number 53332.
21. Ibid., p. 166.
22. CIA *Report*, 1941, p. 438; John Adair, "Report on the Silver Production of the Southwest, January 1941," p. 1, RA, general correspondence, 1954, box GC249, Indian Arts and Crafts Board (hereafter cited as Adair, "Silver Production").
23. House, *Hearings on H.R. 4590*, 77th Cong., lst sess., 1941, p. 184.
24. Adair, "Silver Production," pp. 16–17.
25. Ibid., p. 17.
26. Ibid.
27. CIA *Report*, 1941, p. 438; d'Harnoncourt to Young, 27 July 1942, IACB, box 9.
28. John M. Cooper, "Anthropology and the Indian Problems of the Americas," *Indians at Work* 7 (April 1940):10.
29. House, *Hearings on H.R. 4852*, 76th Cong., lst sess., 1939, p. 174.
30. The 1939 House Subcommittee on Interior Department Appropriations (76th Cong., lst sess.) was composed of the following members: Edward Thomas Taylor, Democrat from Colorado, chairman; Jed Joseph Johnson, Democrat from Oklahoma; James Graves Scrugham, Democrat from Nevada; James Martin Fitzpatrick, Democrat from New York; Charles Henry Leavy, Democrat from Washington; Robert Fleming Rich, Republican from Pennsylvania; Albert Edward Carter, Republican from California; and Dudley Allen White, Republican from Ohio. Congressmen Leavy, Carter, and White either were not present or did not contribute to the hearings on the Indian Arts and Crafts Board appropriation.
31. House, *Hearings on H.R. 4852*, 76th Cong., lst sess., 1939, pp. 174–75.

32. U.S., Congress, Senate, Committee on Appropriations, *Hearings before a subcommittee of the Senate Committee on Appropriations on H.R. 8745,* 76th Cong., 3d sess., 1940, p. 106.

33. House, *Hearings on H.R. 8745,* 76th Cong., 3d sess., 1940, p. 200.

34. Ibid., p. 208; Senate, *Hearings on H.R. 8745,* 76th Cong., 3d sess., 1940, p. 106.

35. Collier, "Editorial," *Indians at Work* 5 (July 1938):1–2.

36. Ibid., p. 2.

Chapter 13: Pinnacles and Pitfalls

1. Franklin Roosevelt, "Address at the Dedication of the National Art Gallery, Washington, DC, 17 March 1941," *New York Times,* 18 March 1941, p. 8.

2. House, *Hearings on H.R. 4590,* 77th Cong., lst sess., 1941, p. 185; U.S., Congress, Senate, Committee on Appropriations, *Hearings before a subcommittee of the Senate Committee on Appropriations on H.R. 4590,* 77th Cong., lst sess., 1941, p. 54.

3. CIA *Report,* 1941, p. 436; Francis Hawkins to Ickes, 20 May 1941, IACB, box 36.

4. d'Harnoncourt, "Suggestions for Future Activities of the Indian Arts and Crafts Board: Submitted to the Members of the Board by the General Manager, 21 September 1939," RD, p. 167; House, *Hearings on H.R. 6845,* 77th Cong., 2d sess., 1942, pp. 186–87.

5. Beatty to d'Harnoncourt, 10 January 1939, IACB, box 13.

6. "Plains Indian Museum to Open This Summer at Browning, Montana," *Museum News* 19 (15 May 1941):1.

7. "Now the Indians of the Plains Have a Museum of Their Own," *Indians at Work* 8 (July 1941):13.

8. House, *Hearings on H.R. 4590,* 77th Cong., lst sess., 1941, p. 182; "Now the Indians of the Plains Have a Museum of Their Own," pp. 13–14.

9. House, *Hearings on H.R. 4590,* 77th Cong., lst sess., 1941, p. 182.

10. Senate, *Hearings on H.R. 4590,* 77th Cong., lst sess., 1941, pp. 57, 54; Senate, *Hearings on H.R. 8745,* 76th Cong., 3d sess., 1940, p. 106. At the same time, Collier stressed that no one rightfully would attribute all of that income to the Indian Arts and Crafts Board. He pointed out the difficulty in determining how much the board had added to this income because the board did not buy or sell the Indians' products. The board was acting only "as a research and promotional agency, a consultant and contact agency," he emphasized. Senate, *Hearings on H.R. 4590,* 77th Cong., lst sess., 1941, p. 54.

11. House, *Hearings on H.R. 4590,* 79th Cong., lst sess., 1941, p. 182.

12. Ibid.; House, *Hearings on H.R. 2719,* 78th Cong., lst sess., 1943,

p. 101; Marriott, "Memorandum for d'Harnoncourt, 23 January 1943," RD, pp. 121–126. In this manner, Chairman Jed Johnson of the House Appropriations Subcommittee temporarily was placated. Not until 1947 was the permanent Southern Plains Indian Museum founded in Anadarko, Oklahoma, through the joint efforts of the federal and Oklahoma State governments. House, *Hearings on H.R. 2719,* 78th Cong., lst sess., 1943, p. 104.

13. Senate, *Hearings on H.R. 4590,* 77th Cong., lst sess., 1941, pp. 6, 52. In 1937 the authorization was $18,000; that figure was reduced in 1938 to $16,000, and the board had to wage a yearly battle in the subcommittee hearings to keep even that amount.

14. Ibid., pp. 6, 54.

15. Ibid., p. 56.

16. Collier, "Remarks of [the] Commissioner of Indian Affairs before a Meeting of [the] Heads of Divisions of the Office of Indian Affairs of the Department of the Interior, 9 January 1942"; Collier, "The Permanent Establishments Are Being Forced Out of Washington by the Budget Bureau Not to Meet War Requirements but for an Entirely Different Reason, 9 January 1942"; Collier, "Usurpation of Legislative Power by the Budget Bureau, 13 January 1942," JC, part II, series III, box 46, folder 118.

17. House, *Hearings on H.R. 6845,* 77th Cong., 2d sess., 1942, pp. 1–2.

18. House, *Hearings on H.R. 4590,* 77th Cong., 1st sess., 1941, p. 187; House, *Hearings on H.R. 6845,* 77th Cong., 2d sess., 1942, p. 186; *United States Statutes at Large,* 55:613–15.

19. Diego Abeita and Elias Jiron, "Petition from the Pueblo of Isleta in New Mexico: A Declaration of Grievances by the Pueblo Indians of Isleta Pueblo, Isleta, New Mexico, [March 1942]," in "Letter and Enclosures Filed by the Commissioner of Indian Affairs," Senate, *Hearings on H.R. 6845,* 77th Cong., 2d sess., 1942, pp. 712–16.

20. Patrick R. Olquin to Collier, 17 April 1942, Exhibit 2 in "Letter and Enclosures," Senate, *Hearings on H. R. 6845,* 77th Cong., 2d sess., 1942, p. 723.

21. Diego Abeita and Jiron, "Petition from the Pueblo of Isleta in New Mexico, [March 1942]," in "Letter and Enclosures," Senate, *Hearings on H.R. 6845,* 77th Cong., 2d sess., 1942, pp. 712–16.

22. Collier to Thomas, 4 May 1942, in "Letter and Enclosures," Senate, *Hearings on H.R. 6845,* 77th Cong., 2d sess., 1942, pp. 720–22.

23. Senate, *Hearings on H.R. 6845,* 77th Cong., 2d sess., 1942, pp. 691, 513–14.

24. Ibid., pp. 517, 514.

25. Ibid., pp. 513–16. Present at this 13 May 1942 Senate Interior Department Appropriations Subcommittee hearing were the following senators: Carl Trumbull Hayden, Democrat from Arizona, chairman; John William Elmer Thomas, Democrat from Oklahoma; Patrick Anthony McCarran, Democrat

from Nevada; Joseph Christopher O'Mahoney, Democrat from Wyoming; Dennis Chavez, Democrat from New Mexico; and Rufus Cecil Holman, Republican from Oregon.

26. Ibid., pp. 517–19.
27. Ibid., p. 689.
28. d'Harnoncourt, "Activities of the Indian Arts and Crafts Board since Its Organization in 1936," Senate, *Hearings on H.R. 6845*, 77th Cong., 2d sess., 1942, pp. 695–99.
29. Senate, *Hearings on H.R. 6845*, 77th Cong., 2d sess., 1942, pp. 690–91.
30. Ibid., pp. 691–93.
31. The five senators included Hiram Warren Johnson, Republican from California; Robert Marion LaFollette, Jr., Progressive from Wisconsin; George William Norris, Republican from Nebraska; Gerald Prentice Nye, Republican from North Dakota; and Henrik Shipstead, Farmer-Laborite from Minnesota. William Edgar Borah, Republican from Idaho, the organizer of the demonstration, was in the Supreme Court chamber when Chavez was called to the dais. "Progressives 'Cut' Chavez in Senate," *New York Times*, 21 May 1935, p. 13; *Current Biography*, s.v. "Chavez, Dennis."
32. Senate, *Hearings on H.R. 6845*, 77th Cong., 2d sess., 1942, p. 695.
33. Ibid., pp. 697–98.
34. Ibid., pp. 698–99, 691.
35. Ibid., p. 699.
36. Ibid., pp. 700–703. Kenneth Disher had attended Pomona College in California and Harvard University. Before coming to the Indian Arts and Crafts Board, he had been associated with the Museum of Northern Arizona and after that had served about four years with the National Park Service.
37. Ibid., p. 705.
38. Ibid., p. 711.
39. House, *Hearings on H.R. 2719*, 78th Cong., 1st sess., 1943, p. 105. As if to avoid just such a misconception in the future, the board began in 1943 to report to the congressional appropriations subcommittees the sales of the two government-employee-operated Indian arts and crafts shops in Washington, DC, the one in the Commerce Building and the other in the Interior Department Building.
40. Senate, *Hearings on H.R. 6845*, 77th Cong., 2d sess., 1942, p. 712.
41. d'Harnoncourt to Young, 27 July 1942, IACB, box 9.

Chapter 14: The War and Forced Disintegration

1. d'Harnoncourt to Young, 27 July 1942, IACB, box 9.
2. d'Harnoncourt to Disher, 2 January 1942, IACB, box 5.
3. d'Harnoncourt to Young, 27 July 1942, IACB, box 9.
4. House, *Hearings on H.R. 2719*, 78th Cong., 1st sess., 1943, p. 101..

5. U.S., Congress, Senate, Committee on Appropriations, *Hearings before a subcommittee of the Senate Committee on Appropriations on H.R. 2719*, 78th Cong., 1st sess., 1943, p. 434.

6. House, *Hearings on H.R. 2719*, 78th Cong., 1st sess., 1943, p. 105; U.S., Congress, House, Committee on Appropriations, *Hearings before a subcommittee of the House Committee on Appropriations on H.R. 4679*, 78th Cong., 2d sess., 1944, p. 81.

7. House, *Hearings on H.R. 2719*, 78th Cong., 1st sess., 1943, pp. 105–6.

8. CIA *Report*, 1944, p. 237.

9. U.S., Congress, House, Committee on Appropriations, *Hearings before a subcommittee of the House Committee on Appropriations on H.R. 6335*, 79th Cong., 2d sess., 1946, p. 995; House, *Hearings on H.R. 2719*, 78th Cong., 1st sess., 1943, pp. 106–8. For years, the only source for satisfactory beads had been Czechoslovakia, and when their importation ceased, Collier attempted to use Interior Department funds to purchase the remaining supply of these beads in the United States. Collier, "Memorandum for Ickes, 6 July 1940," OSI, box 3516, file 53.

10. House, *Hearings on H.R. 2719*, 78th Cong., 1st sess., 1943, p. 106.

11. CIA *Report*, 1942, pp. 252–53; James S. Knowlson, "Exemption to Order M-73, 17 July 1942," IACB, box 8.

12. Office of War Information, War Production Board, "Bulletin No. 1615, for release 29 July 1942," BIA, box 1415, file 817, serial no. 36052-41.

13. Clipping from the *Albuquerque Journal*, 6 December 1942; d'Harnoncourt telegram to Woodard, 25 February 1943, IACB, box 8.

14. CIA *Report*, 1942, p. 253.

15. House, *Hearings on H.R. 2719*, 78th Cong., 1st sess., 1943, p. 104; CIA *Report*, 1942, p. 253; d'Harnoncourt to Young, 27 July 1942, IACB, box 9.

16. House, *Hearings on H.R. 6335*, 79th Cong., 2d sess., 1946, p. 995; House, *Hearings on H. R. 2719*, 78th Cong., 1st sess., 1943, pp. 102–3.

17. Ibid., pp. 103–4.

18. Ibid., p. 102.

19. Ibid.

20. House, *Hearings on H.R. 6845*, 77th Cong., 2d sess., 1942, pp. 190–92.

21. Lillian V. Russell, "A Bit of Eskimo War Work," *Indians at Work* 11 (March–April 1944):5.

22. Senate, *Hearings on H.R. 2719*, 78th Cong., 1st sess., 1943, pp. 27–28; House, *Hearings on H.R. 2719*, 78th Cong., 1st sess., 1943, p. 107.

23. Senate, *Hearings on H.R. 2719*, 78th Cong., 1st sess., 1943, pp. 433–34.

24. *Senate Report* no. 310, 78th Cong., 1st sess., ser. 10756, pp. 18–22. Authority to make the Senate report was based on Senate Resolution 79, passed by the first session of the Seventieth Congress in 1928, and the continuing resolutions, passed for the same purpose by subsequent sessions of Congress.

Notes

For brief accounts of the report, see Philp, *John Collier's Crusade for Indian Reform, 1920–1954*, p. 208, and S. Lyman Tyler, *A History of Indian Policy* (Washington: Government Printing Office, 1973), pp. 139–41.

25. Collier, "Memorandum, 27 June 1943," JC, part II, series III, box 46, folder 112.

26. Collier to Thomas, 1 July 1943; Ickes to Thomas, 6 July 1943, JC, part II, series III, box 46, folder 112.

27. *Senate Report* no. 310, 78th Cong., 1st sess., ser. 10756, p. 22; Collier to Thomas, 1 July 1943, JC, part II, series III, box 46, folder 112; *Senate Report* no. 310, 78th Cong., 1st sess., ser. 10756, p. 19.

28. Collier, "Memorandum, 27 June 1943," JC, part II, series III, box 46, folder 112.

29. Collier, "Editorial," *Indians at Work* 10 (July, August, September 1942):1–2, 5.

30. U.S., Congress, Senate, Committee on Appropriations, *Hearings before a subcommittee of the Senate Committee on Appropriations on H.R. 4679*, 78th Cong., 2d sess., 1944, p. 15; Wheeler, contributor, *René d'Harnoncourt: A Tribute, 8 October 1968*, Memorial Service, Sculpture Garden, Museum of Modern Art (n.p.[1968]).

31. Senate, *Hearings on H.R. 4679*, 78th Cong., 2d sess., 1944, p. 255.

32. Ibid., pp. 254–55.

33. G. Warren Spaulding to d'Harnoncourt, 1 April 1944, BIA, box 1415, file 817. Chairman Johnson expressed his satisfaction over the appointment of McCurtain, a man whom he claimed he did not know yet a man he was certain would be efficient and would do a good job simply because he was a Choctaw Indian. U.S., Congress, House, Committee on Appropriations, *Hearings before a subcommittee of the House Committee on Appropriations on H.R. 3024*, 79th Cong., 1st sess., 1945, p. 105.

34. House, *Hearings on H.R. 4679*, 78th Cong., 2d sess., 1944, p. 78.

35. Ibid., pp. 78–79.

36. Ibid., pp. 81–83.

37. Senate, *Hearings on H.R. 4679*, 78th Cong., 2d sess., 1944, pp. 254–56.

38. Jed Johnson to Zimmerman, 14 July 1944; Collier to Zimmerman, 21 July 1944, JC, part II, series I, box 18, folder 018-0380.

39. Ickes, *Diaries*, 26 November 1944, HLI, reel 7, plate 9359.

40. Collier, "Memorandum for Ickes, 4 December 1944," JC, part II, series I, box 8, folder 008-0156.

41. Ibid.

42. Ibid.

43. Ickes, *Diaries*, 16 December 1944, HLI, reel 7, plate 9399. The American Indian Federation's unity ended in 1939 over a proposal under which the government would pay to each Indian or his Indian or non-Indian heirs $3,000

343

in final termination of federal responsibility. By 1941 unpatriotic extremism by some members destroyed what remained of the group's identity and formal organization ended. Hauptman, "Native American Reformers of the 1930s and 1940s: A Reinterpretation," pp. 22–23.

44. Collier to Franklin Roosevelt, 19 January 1945, JC, part II, series I, box 13, folder 013-0288; Ickes to Collier, 5 June 1945, JC, part II, series I, box 8, folder 008-0156.

BIBLIOGRAPHY

Records of the Federal Government
in the National Archives

Material from the following record groups was used in this study:

Record Group 48: Records of the Office of the Secretary of the Interior
  Central Classified File, 5-1, 5-3, and 5-4
Record Group 75: Records of the Bureau of Indian Affairs
  Central Classified File, 900 General Service
  Records of the Office of the Commissioner of Indian Affairs
Record Group 435: Records of the Indian Arts and Crafts Board

Other Archives and Personal Papers

Columbia University, New York, New York
  René d'Harnoncourt Oral History, Carnegie Corporation Project
Historical Society of Pennsylvania, Philadelphia, Pennsylvania
  Indian Rights Association Papers (available on microfilm, 136 reels)
Institute for Government Research, Brookings Institution, Washington, D.C.
  Private File of Lewis Meriam
Library of Congress, Washington, D.C.
  Harold L. Ickes Papers
Marquette University Library, Milwaukee, Wisconsin
  Bureau of Catholic Indian Missions Records
Princeton University Library, Princeton, New Jersey
  Association on American Indian Affairs Papers
Rockefeller Archives, North Tarrytown, New York
  General Correspondence
  General Education Board
  Rockefeller Fund Grants
  Spellman Fund of New York
Yale University Library, New Haven, Connecticut
  John Collier Papers

345

Printed Congressional Documents (in serial order)

"Indian Arts and Crafts," *Senate Report* no. 900, 74th Cong., 1st sess., ser. 9879. Report of the Senate Committee on Indian Affairs on the Indian Arts and Crafts bill (S. 2203).

"To Promote the Development of Indian Arts and Crafts and to Create a Board to Assist Therein, and for Other Purposes," *House Report* no. 973, 74th Cong., 1st sess., ser. 9887. Report of the House Committee on Indian Affairs on the Indian Arts and Crafts bill (H. R. 6468).

"Analysis of the Statement of the Commissioner of Indian Affairs in Justification of Appropriations for 1944, and the Liquidation of the Indian Bureau," *Senate Report* no. 310, 78th Cong., 1st sess., ser. 10756. Partial report of the Senate Committee on Indian Affairs pursuant to a survey of conditions among the Indians of the United States (S. R. 79).

Printed Materials for Legal Actions Involving Indian Arts and Crafts

All can be found in the Records of the Indian Arts and Crafts Board, National Archives, Record Group 435.

Transcript of Record, Federal Trade Commission v. Maisel Trading Post, Inc., in the United States Circuit Court of Appeals, Tenth Circuit, 17 May 1932, no. 976. (Box 7.)

Federal Trade Commission, *Order to Cease and Desist, Beacon Manufacturing Company, 28 June 1932, Docket 1873.* (Box 7.)

Federal Trade Commission, *Order to Cease and Desist, Jeffrey Jewelry Company, 21 September 1932, Docket 2004.* (Box 2.)

Interpretation of Final Order, Federal Trade Commission v. Maisel Trading Post, Inc., United States Circuit Court of Appeals, Tenth Circuit, April Term, 1936, no. 976. (Box 7.)

Federal Trade Commission, *Order to Cease and Desist, Louisville Pottery Company, [1938], Docket 3296.* (Box 6.)

Other Published Government Sources

Annual Report of the Board of Indian Commissioners
Annual Report of the Commissioner of Indian Affairs
Annual Report of the Secretary of the Interior
Congressional Directory
Congressional Record
Senate Joint Resolutions
United States Statutes at Large
Work, Hubert. "Indian Policies: Comments on the Resolutions of the Advi-

Bibliography

sory Council on Indian Affairs, June 1924." Booklet. Washington: Government Printing Office, 1924.

Public Papers of the Presidents of the United States: Herbert Hoover: Containing the Public Messages, Speeches, and Statements of the President. Washington: Government Printing Office, 1977.

Hearings before a subcommittee of the House Committee on Appropriations, Interior Department Appropriations.

Hearings before a subcommittee of the Senate Committee on Appropriations, Interior Department Appropriations.

U.S. Congress. Senate. Committee on Indian Affairs. *To Investigate Indian Affairs. Hearings before a subcommittee of the Senate Committee on Indian Affairs on S. 263, 71st Cong., lst sess., 1930.*

U.S. Congress. Senate. Committee on Indian Affairs. *Survey of the Conditions of the Indians of the United States. Hearings before a subcommittee of the Senate Committee on Indian Affairs on S. 416, 71st Cong., 3d sess., 1931.*

Indians at Work. A publication issued by the Indian Office from 1933 to 1945.

National Recovery Administration. *Codes of Fair Competition, Medium and Low-Priced Jewelry, Approved Code 175, 23 December 1933, no. 1215-1-01.*

U.S. Congress. House. Committee on Indian Affairs. *Indian Conditions and Affairs. Hearings before a subcommittee of the House Committee on Indian Affairs on H.R. 7781, 74th Cong., lst sess., 1935.*

U.S. Congress. Senate. Committee on Indian Affairs. *Survey of the Conditions of the Indians of the United States. Hearings before a subcommittee of the Senate Committee on Indian Affairs on S. 230, 75th Cong., lst sess., 1937.*

Statement Announcing Standards for Navajo, Pueblo, and Hopi Silver. Washington: Government Printing Office, 1937.

Standards for Navajo, Pueblo, and Hopi Silver and Turquoise Products. Washington: Government Printing Office, 1937.

Regulations for Use of Government Mark on Navajo, Pueblo, and Hopi Silver. Washington: Government Printing Office, 1937.

Regulations for Use of Government Certificate of Genuineness for Navajo All-Wool Woven Fabrics. Washington: Government Printing Office, 1937.

Amendment of Regulations Governing Navajo All-Wool Woven Fabrics: Use of Government Certificate of Genuineness. Washington: Government Printing Office, 1939.

Regulations for Use of Government Marks of Genuineness for Alaskan Indian Hand-Made Products. Washington: Government Printing Office, 1939.

Regulations for Use of Government Marks of Genuineness for Alaskan Eskimo Hand-Made Products. Washington: Government Printing Office, 1939.

Indian Arts and Crafts Board. "Reports and Documents Concerning the Activities of the Indian Arts and Crafts Board." 1943. (Typewritten.) Washington: Library of Congress Photoduplication Service, 53332, 1974.

Contemporary Publications

"All-American Art." *Art Digest* 15 (1 January 1941):17.

"Amelia Elizabeth White Donates Her Collection of Indian Art to the People." *Art Digest* 12 (15 February 1938):12.

American Indian Life. A bulletin published by the American Indian Defense Association from 1925 to 1936.

Blumenschein, Ernest L., and Phillips, Bert G. "Appreciation of Indian Art." *El Palacio* 6 (No. 12, 1919):178–79.

Burton, Henrietta Kolshorn. *The Re-establishment of the Indians in Their Pueblo Life through the Revival of Their Traditional Crafts: A Study in Home Extension Education.* New York: Columbia University Bureau of Publications, 1936.

Cahill, Edgar Holger. "America Has Its 'Primitives.' " *International Studio* 75 (March 1922):80–83.

Caspers, Frank. "Review of *Indian Art of the United States.*" *Art Digest* 15 (1 March 1941):27.

Collier, John. "The American Congo." *The Survey* 50 (1 August 1923):467–76.

———. "Hammering at the Prison Door." *The Survey* 60 (July 1928):389, 402–5.

Collier, Nina Perera. "Survey of Indian Arts and Crafts, April 1934." Washington, D.C., 1934. (Mimeographed.)

Colton, Mary-Russell F. "Wanted—A Market for Indian Art." *Southern California Business,* October 1930.

Curtis, Natalie. "Our Native Craftsmen." *The Southern Workman* 48 (August 1919):389–96.

d'Harnoncourt, René. "Living Arts of the Indians." *Magazine of Art* 34 (February 1941):72–77.

———. *Mexicana: A Book of Pictures.* New York: Alfred A. Knopf, 1931.

———. "North American Indian Arts." *Magazine of Art* 32 (March 1939): 164–67.

d'Harnoncourt, René, and Douglas, Frederic H., eds. *The Exhibition of Indian Arts and Crafts at the San Francisco Golden Gate Exposition.* Ann Arbor, Mich.: University Microfilms, no publication order number, 1940.

d'Harnoncourt, René, and Douglas, Frederic H. *Indian Art of the United States.* New York: Museum of Modern Art, 1941; reprint ed., New York: Arno Press, 1969.

Denman, Leslie Van Ness. "A Presentation of Indian Cultures and Their Arts: Suggested for the Golden Gate International Exposition." *Women's City Club Magazine* 10 (July 1936):14–15.

"Development of American Indian Arts and Crafts." *Monthly Labor Review* 46 (March 1938):655–58.

"First Annual Exhibition of Indian Arts and Crafts under the Auspices of the

Bibliography

Museum of New Mexico, September 1922." *El Palacio* 12 (No. 9, 1922):123–24.

Flint, Ralph. "Tribal Arts of the Indian Now on Exhibition." *Art News* 30 (5 December 1931):5.

Hewett, Edgar L. "Native American Artists." *Art and Archaeology: The Arts throughout the Ages.* 13 (March 1922):102–12.

Hodge, Frederick Webb; LaFarge, Oliver; and Spinden, Herbert J., eds. *Introduction to American Indian Art: To Accompany the First Exposition of American Indian Art Selected Entirely with Consideration of Esthetic Value.* New York: Exposition of Indian Tribal Arts, Inc., 1931; reprint ed., Glorieta, New Mexico: Rio Grande Press, 1970.

"Indian Art in the United States." *Design* 42 (March 1941):15–17.

"Indian Shop in New York." *El Palacio* 13 (No. 12, 1922):160.

"Indian Trading Posts in Eastern Cities." *The School Arts Magazine* 30 (March 1931):480.

"Indian Tribal Arts Exhibition Starts on Long Tour of Nation." *Art Digest* 6 (15 December 1931):32.

Lake Mohonk Conference. *Proceedings.* Published privately by the conference and also reprinted each year in the annual reports of the Board of Indian Commissioners.

"Letter to the Editor on the Subject of American Indian Basket-work." *International Studio* 20 (August 1903):144–46.

Lowe, Jeanette. "Lo, the Rich Indian." *Art News* 39 (1 February 1941):6–8.

Meriam, Lewis, Director; Brown, Ray A.; Cloud, Henry Roe; Dale, Edward Everett; Duke, Emma; Edwards, Herbert R.; McKenzie, Fayette Avery; Mark, Mary Louise; Ryan, W. Carson, Jr.; and Spillman, William J. *The Problem of Indian Adminstration.* Institute for Government Research, Studies in Administration. Baltimore: Johns Hopkins Press, 1928.

Morrow, Elizabeth Cutter, and d'Harnoncourt, René. *Bird, Beast, and Fish: An Animal Alphabet.* New York: Alfred A. Knopf, 1933.

Morrow, Elizabeth Cutter, and d'Harnoncourt, René. *Painted Pig.* New York: Alfred A. Knopf, 1930.

National Association on Indian Affairs. Booklet No. 2. No title and no date [1923]. In filmstrip No. 39280. Library of Congress, Washington, D.C.

"New York Museum Rebuilds Three Floors for Indian Exhibit." *Museum News* 18 (15 February 1941):1.

New York Times, 1925, 1926, 1931, 1935, 1939, 1941.

"New York Views the Art of the Indian." *Art Digest* 15 (15 February 1941): 10–11.

Oak, Liston M. "Living Traditions in American Indian Art." *Antiques* 39 (March 1941):134–36.

"Plains Indian Museum to Open This Summer at Browning, Montana." *Museum News* 19 (15 May 1941):1.

"Review of *Indian Arts in North America.*" *Antiques* 39 (March 1941):114.

Roosevelt, Eleanor. "Foreword." In d'Harnoncourt, René, and Douglas, Frederic H. *Indian Art of the United States.* New York: Museum of Modern Art, 1941; reprint ed., New York: Arno Press, 1969.

Scully, Michael. "Pan America's Crossroads Store." *The Pan American* (January 1942):8–11.

Vaillant, George C. *Indian Arts in North America.* New York: Harper and Brothers, 1939.

Books and Articles

Amon Carter Museum of Western Art. *Quiet Triumph: Forty Years with the Indian Arts Fund, Santa Fe.* Santa Fe: Indian Arts Fund, 1966.

Collier, John. *From Every Zenith.* Denver: Sage Books, 1963.

Dale, Edward Everett. *The Indians of the Southwest: A Century of Development under the United States.* Norman: University of Oklahoma Press, 1949.

Gibson, Arrell M., ed. *Frontier Historian: The Life and Work of Edward Everett Dale.* Norman: University of Oklahoma Press, 1975.

Hauptman, Laurence M. "Alice Jemison: Seneca Political Activist, 1901–1964." *The Indian Historian* 12 (Summer 1979):15–22.

Hawley, Ellis W. "Herbert Hoover, the Commerce Secretariat, and the Vision of an 'Associative State,' 1921–1928." *Journal of American History* 61 (June 1974):116–40.

Hawley, Ellis W.; Rothbard, Murray N.; Himmelberg, Robert F.; and Nash, Gerald D. *Herbert Hoover and the Crisis of American Capitalism.* Cambridge, Mass.: Schenkman, 1973.

Kelly, Lawrence C. "Choosing the New Deal Indian Commissioner: Ickes vs. Collier." *New Mexico Historical Review* 49 (October 1974):269–88.

———. *The Navajo Indians and Federal Indian Policy, 1900–1935.* Tucson: University of Arizona Press, 1968.

Kroeber, Theodora. *Alfred Kroeber: A Personal Configuration.* Berkeley: University of California Press, 1970.

McNickle, D'Arcy. *Indian Man: A Life of Oliver LaFarge.* Bloomington: Indiana University Press, 1971.

Parman, Donald. "J. C. Morgan: Navajo Apostle of Assimilation." *Prologue: The Journal of the National Archives* 4 (Summer 1972):83–98.

Patterson, James T. *Congressional Conservatism and the New Deal: The Growth of the Conservative Coalition in Congress, 1933–1939.* Lexington: University of Kentucky Press, 1967.

Philp, Kenneth R. *John Collier's Crusade for Indian Reform, 1920–1954.* Tucson: University of Arizona Press, 1977.

Rockefeller, Nelson A.; Wheeler, Monroe; Parkinson, Elizabeth Bliss; Barr, Alfred H., Jr.; Fortas, Abe; Moe, Henry Allen; Lippold, Richard; Lie-

Bibliography

berman, William S.; Goldwater, Robert; and Lowry, Bates, contributors. *René d'Harnoncourt: A Tribute, 8 October 1968.* Booklet for the Memorial Service in the Sculpture Garden of the Museum of Modern Art. N.p., [1968].

Szasz, Margaret. *Education and the American Indian: The Road to Self-Determination since 1928.* 2d ed. Albuquerque: University of New Mexico Press, 1977.

Taylor, Graham D. "Anthropologists, Reformers, and the Indian New Deal." *Prologue: The Journal of the National Archives* 7(Fall, 1975):151–62.

——. *The New Deal and American Indian Tribalism: The Administration of the Indian Reorganization Act, 1934–45.* Lincoln: University of Nebraska Press, 1980.

Tyler, S. Lyman. *A History of Indian Policy.* Washington: Government Printing Office, 1973.

Woodbury, Richard B. *Alfred V. Kidder.* New York: Columbia University Press, 1973.

Zimmerman, William, Jr. "The Role of the Bureau of Indian Affairs since 1933." *The Annals of the American Academy of Political and Social Science* 311 (May 1957):31–40.

Other Sources

d'Harnoncourt, Sarah. New York, New York. Interview, 23 April 1979.

Freeman, John L. "The New Deal for the Indians: A Study of Bureau-Committee Relationships in American Government." Ph.D. dissertation, Princeton University, 1952.

Hauptman, Laurence M. "Native American Reformers of the 1930s and 1940s: A Reinterpretation." Paper presented at the 74th annual meeting of the Organization of American Historians, Detroit, Mich., 2 April 1981.

Holm, Tom. "Indians and Progressives: From the Vanishing Policy to the Indian New Deal." Ph.D. dissertation, University of Oklahoma, 1978.

INDEX

Index

Staples, Berton I., 42, 56, 89, 92, 93, 101
Stevens, David H., 174, 181
St. Gaudens, Homer, 126
Stickley, Gustav, 3
Straus, Ralph, 82
Strong, William Duncan, 240
Subcommittee of the House Committee on Appropriations: (1930), and Louis Cramton, 33; (1939), membership, 338 n.30
Sunset Magazine, 103
Sunshine Society, 6
survey of the teaching of arts and crafts in Indian schools, 130
surveys, possible board activity 140, 142
sweating, 19, 132

Tahlequah State Teachers College, 80
Tamayo, Rufino, 125
Tantaquidgeon, Gladys, 140–41
Taos Lightning, 31
Taos Pueblo, 11, 45
Taos Society of Artists, 11
Taylor, Edward T., 119
Tesuque Pueblo, 45, 140, 218–21
Texas Centennial Exposition (1936), 123
Thomas, John William Elmer: joint resolution, 39; and Senate subcommittee hearings, 45–46; and Burton K. Wheeler, 105; and Indian arts and crafts bill (1935), 106; attitude toward West L. Robertson, 270; and Indian policy, 272; and Partial Report 310, 286–87
Tillotson, M. R., 51
Tlinkit Indians, 188
Todokozie, Hastine, 192
Tolan, John H., 215
trademarks, 23–24, 29–30, 40, 47 98, 219, 262; for Navajo, Pueblo,

and Hopi silver products, 132–34, 252–53; for Navajo wool products, 135–36; for Alaskan arts and crafts, 204–5, 206
traders, 7, 27, 28, 163, 308 n.7; and Cooperative Marketing Board bill (1930), 35; and second Indian arts and crafts bill (1932), 46–47; and report of the Young committee, 97–98; and Indian arts and crafts bill (1935), 109, 110
Travel Club of America Exposition, 14
tribal loans, 221
Trotter, G. A., 35
Truax, Charles Vilas, 110, 111
Tsa-to-ke, Munroe, 80

Union Pacific Railroad, 180
United Indian Traders Association, 47–48, 53, 89, 110, 137; and silver standards, 88, 249
United Pueblo Agency, 163
United States Golden Gate International Exposition Commission, 176, 177
United States Supreme Court, 57, 89
University of Denver, 114
University of Oklahoma, 115

Vaillant, George C., 174
Vigil, Martin, 93

Walker, Delos, 116
Wallace, C. G., 250
Wallace, John, 201
Wanamaker, John, 45
Wa-Pai-Shone Craftsmen, 208
war: effect on Indian and Alaskan populations and arts and crafts, 279–82
Warner, William, 113
War Production Board, 280–81
Washington, D.C., office staff, 263–64

363